God, in your Grace ...

But God, who is rich in mercy, out of the great love with which he loved us even when we were dead through our trespasses, made us alive together with Christ – by grace you have been saved – and raised us up with him and seated us with him in the heavenly places in Christ Jesus, so that in the ages to come he might show the immeasurable riches of his grace in kindness toward us in Christ Jesus. For by grace you have been saved through faith, and this is not your own doing; it is the gift of God – not the result of works, so that no one may boast. For we are what he has made us, created in Christ Jesus for good works, which God prepared beforehand to be our way of life.
(Eph. 2:4-10)

Let anyone who has an ear listen to what the Spirit is saying to the churches.
(Rev. 2:7)

God, in your Grace ...

*Official Report of the Ninth Assembly
of the World Council of Churches*

Edited by
Luis N. Rivera-Pagán

WCC Publications, Geneva

A report of the WCC's Ninth Assembly is also available in German from
Verlag Otto Lembeck (*www.Lembeck.de*).

The assembly reports and addresses contained here are also available in
French, German, Spanish and Portuguese on the assembly website at:
www.wcc-assembly.info

Cover design and layout: Marie Arnaud Snakkers
Photographs:
WCC/Paulino Menezes, Igor Sperotto, Aleksander Wasyluk, Peter Williams

ISBN 978-2-8254-1512-2

© 2007 WCC Publications, World Council of Churches,
150 route de Ferney, 1211 Geneva 2, Switzerland

Printed in France

CONTENTS

PREFACE

Samuel Kobia

As was true of the eight WCC assemblies before it, the 9th Assembly of the World Council of Churches, in Porto Alegre, Brazil from 14-23 February 2006, had its own special character.

The venue played a part: this was the first assembly to be held in Latin America, and the Latin American context was formative throughout the life of the assembly. The Latin American churches, the Latin American Council of Churches (CLAI) and the National Christian Council of Churches in Brazil (CONIC) were closely involved in the planning, preparation and running of the assembly. The administration of the Pontifical Catholic University of Rio Grande do Sul served as gracious hosts and partners. Both the local churches and individual Christians in their thousands, from Brazil and elsewhere in Latin America, took part in the assembly and joined enthusiastically in open discussion sessions.

Then there was the theme of the assembly, running through all the sermons, presentations and discussions, from the first day to the last: "God, in your grace, transform the world". Assembly participants obviously found the theme challenging. We know that, in the face of the many problems threatening humanity worldwide, things have to change. Yet many people are at a loss when it comes to practical steps for change. This sense of helplessness lay behind the idea of expressing the theme of the assembly in the form of a prayer. A similar prayer format was then also chosen for the Message from the assembly. The rich spiritual life of this assembly, and all that happened at this ecumenical gathering, were permeated by the concern to set the urgent problems of our times within the perspective of God's transforming grace, which is our hope.

The assembly was more than a business meeting, and participants were not limited to the official church delegations. The workshops in the Mutirão, which were open to the general public, saw thousands of people taking part, and the Ecumenical Conversations on 22 topics of pressing concern in church and society guaranteed that the assembly would not lose touch with the outside world. During our time in Porto Alegre, voices of youthful participants continually challenged us and called the World Council to keep up with the times as the ecumenical movement proceeds on our common journey into the future.

But what will participants at the Ninth Assembly retain of all this? How are the results to be judged and will these results lead to the renewal and strengthening of the ecumenical movement?

These questions can be answered only in reference to our increasingly globalized and conflict-torn world on the one hand, and the progressive fragmentation and individualization of social, church and personal life on the other. Our efforts must be directed at keeping the ecumenical flame burning by imaginatively and persistently urging all churches to be open to the path towards Christian unity and the renewal it can bring.

Formal actions of the assembly recommended four areas of programmatic priorities for the World Council of Churches in the period from the Ninth to the Tenth Assembly: (1) unity, spirituality and mission; (2) ecumenical formation, especially in the Christian education of our churches' youth; (3) global justice; and (4) providing a credible moral voice in the world. Additionally, the assembly directed that a youth advisory body be established and empowered to provide support and offer suggestions to WCC leadership in the years ahead.

Reviewing all that we experienced in Porto Alegre, we have begun the next stage of the ecumenical pilgrimage with a three-fold understanding of the place of the World Council within the web of relationships surrounding us. First, the WCC and its member churches are called to renew our commitment to **full and visible Christian unity** within the fellowship that is the Triune God's gift to us. Second, we are called to be **neighbours to all** amid the diversity of the human community, cooperating in resistance to common threats and engaging in dialogue for the sake of peace. Third, Christians today are ever more aware of the need to protect the earth, promote a culture of sustaining all life and demonstrating our **care for creation**. These dimensions of our life together in the twenty-first century are clearly reflected in the Message of the Ninth Assembly, and they provide essential guidance as we chart priorities and organize programmes for the coming years.

I extend my thanks, and the thanks of the World Council of Churches, to all who have worked and prayed that the Ninth Assembly and its practical consequences may faithfully proclaim the good news of God's love revealed to us in Jesus Christ.

Pentecost 2007

Rev. Dr Samuel Kobia
General Secretary
World Council of Churches

AN INVITATION TO PRAYER:
MESSAGE OF THE 9TH ASSEMBLY

Sisters and brothers, we greet you in Christ. As representatives of churches from all the world's regions, we gather in Porto Alegre, Brazil, meeting in the first decade of the third millennium, in the first assembly of the World Council of Churches held in Latin America. We have been invited here to join in *a festa da vida*, the feast of life. We are praying, reflecting on the scriptures, struggling and rejoicing together in our unity and diversity, and seeking to listen carefully to one another in the spirit of consensus.

Meeting in February 2006, we are made aware by Assembly participants of cries arising daily in their home countries and regions due to disasters, violent conflicts and conditions of oppression and suffering. Yet we are also empowered by God to bear witness to transformation in personal lives, churches, societies and the world as a whole.

Specific challenges and calls to action are being communicated to the churches and the world in the reports and decisions of the Assembly, such as: the quest for Christian unity; our mid-term call to recommitment to the Decade to Overcome Violence (2001-2010); discernment of prophetic and programmatic means to achieve global economic justice; engagement in inter-religious dialogue; full inter-generational participation of all women and men, and common statements addressing the churches and the world on public issues.

The theme of this Ninth Assembly is a prayer, "God, in your grace, transform the world". In prayer our hearts are transformed, and so we offer our message as prayer:

God of grace,

together we turn to you in prayer, for it is you who unite us:

you are the one God – Father, Son and Holy Spirit – in whom we believe,

you alone empower us for good,

you send us out across the earth in mission and service in the name of Christ.

We confess before you and all people:

We have been unworthy servants.

We have misused and abused the creation.

We have wounded one another by divisions everywhere.

We have often failed to take decisive action against environmental destruction,

poverty, racism, caste-ism, war and genocide.

We are not only victims but also perpetrators of violence.

In all this, we have fallen short as disciples of Jesus Christ

who in his incarnation came to save us and teach us how to love.

Forgive us, God, and teach us to forgive one another.

God, in your grace, transform the world.

God, hear the cries of all creation,

the cries of the waters, the air, the land and all living things;

the cries of all who are exploited, marginalized, abused and victimized,

all who are dispossessed and silenced, their humanity ignored,

all who suffer from any form of disease, from war

and from the crimes of the arrogant who hide from the truth,

distort memory and deny the possibility of reconciliation.

God, guide all in seats of authority towards decisions of moral integrity.

God, in your grace, transform the world.

We give thanks for your blessings and signs of hope that are already present
   in the world,

in people of all ages and in those who have gone before us in faith;

in movements to overcome violence in all its forms, not just for a decade but for
   always;

in the deep and open dialogues that have begun both within our own churches and
   with those of other faiths in the search for mutual understanding and respect;
in all those working together for justice and peace -
both in exceptional circumstances and every day.
We thank you for the good news of Jesus Christ, and the assurance of resurrection.

God, in your grace, transform the world.

By the power and guidance of your Holy Spirit, O God,
may our prayers never be empty words
but an urgent response to your living Word -
in non-violent direct action for positive change,
in bold, clear, specific acts of solidarity, liberation, healing and compassion,
readily sharing the good news of Jesus Christ.
Open our hearts to love and to see that all people are made in your image,
to care for creation and affirm life in all its wondrous diversity.

3

Transform us in the offering of ourselves so that we may be your partners in transformation
to strive for the full, visible unity of the one Church of Jesus Christ,
to become neighbours to all,
as we await with eager longing the full revelation of your rule
in the coming of a new heaven and a new earth.

*God, in your grace, transform the world. In the name of the Father, Son and Holy
   Spirit.*

Amen

PORTO ALEGRE 2006:
A POLYCENTRIC WORLD CHRISTIANITY

Luis N. Rivera-Pagán

INTRODUCTION

If by some sort of magical temporal transposition the founders of the World Council of Churches (WCC), who first met as an assembly in August of 1948 in Amsterdam, could have been present at the February 2006 inauguration of the ninth assembly in Porto Alegre, Brazil, they probably would have felt both perplexity and joy.

They would certainly have been amazed by the bewildering variety of peoples, cultures and churches present at the Porto Alegre assembly. No longer emanating primarily from Western Europe and North America, Protestants, Eastern and Oriental Orthodox, Anglicans, Pentecostals and Catholics, from all corners of the oikoumene, gathered February 14 to 23, 2006, at Porto Alegre, to deliberate the future of the ecumenical movement. It was a spectacular demonstration of the emerging polycentric character of Christianity as a world faith.

Churches from Africa, Asia, the Middle East, the Pacific and Latin America shared central stage with the powerful ecclesiastical institutions from the West and the North. Some 691 delegates representing 348 member churches from 120 countries, 2079 participants in the mutirãos, 154 accredited international journalists, hundreds of stewards and dozens of delegated representatives and observers filled up daily the attractive grounds of the Pontifícia Universidade Católica do Rio Grande do Sul, the site of the assembly. The entire event was a kaleidoscope of nations, cultures, races, languages and ecclesiastical traditions, a striking demonstration of the demographic shift from the West and the North to the South and the East taking place in world Christianity. At the onset of a new century and millennium, this demographic reconfiguration conferred new meaning and resonance to the catholicity of the church and the ecumenicity of the Christian faith.

The founders of the WCC would also have been delightfully surprised by the exuberance and vivacity of the Porto Alegre musical and artistic performances. The

A note of gratitude to Diane Kessler and Susan Richardson, who reviewed earlier drafts of this narrative, saved the author from many linguistic infelicities, and enabled him to write a more readable and elegant text.

1948 Amsterdam assembly was a serious, reflective affair. Those were sombre times, shadowed by the tragedies of world war, concentration camps and nuclear devastation. The gaping wounds of Auschwitz and Hiroshima were still too raw, too painful.

In contrast, the WCC's ninth assembly took place in Brazil, the land of the famous Carnival. (As the delegates were going home, millions of tourists were swarming into Brazil for this nation's annual paroxysm of sensual celebration.) No matter how august a body, the assembly could not escape the seductive musicality of the land and its people. From the initial proceedings of the inaugural plenary through the farewell to the assembly nine days later, in the splendidly dramatic Latin American plenary, and in the choir that enlivened the morning and evening common prayers, this was an event in which music, singing and dancing thrived gloriously. Even venerable archbishops, metropolitans and bishops found it extremely difficult not to move in a rhythmic manner. It was a joyful musical and artistic celebration of faith, life and hope in the midst of an acutely distressed world.

Perhaps most importantly, the founders of the WCC would have taken heart in the fact that, in these times of severe national, ethnic and religious antagonisms, hundreds of churches – approximately 350 of them from all over the world – were willing to gather together to praise God, study the Bible, share their stories, engage in theological dialogues, celebrate God's gift of reconciliation. The churches met in Porto Alegre to affirm, renew and deepen their commitment to Christ's prayer for unity: "I ask not only on behalf of these, but also on behalf of those who will believe in me through their word, that they may all be one. As you, Father, are in me and I am in you, may they also be in us, so that the world may believe..." (John 17:20f.)

Porto Alegre, 2006

Role and purpose of the assembly

The Constitution of the World Council of Churches defines it as "a fellowship of *See page 448* churches which confess the Lord Jesus Christ as God and Saviour according to the scriptures and therefore seek to fulfill together their common calling to the glory of the one God, Father, Son and Holy Spirit." The primary purpose of this council of churches is "to call one another to visible unity in one faith and in one eucharistic fellowship, expressed in worship and common life in Christ, through witness and service to the world, and to advance towards that unity in order that the world may believe."

The Constitution mandates the WCC to organize a general assembly, as its supreme legislative body, at approximately seven-year intervals. The purposes of the assembly are diverse. Some are basic to all complex organizations: to assess the work done since the previous assembly, to define the policy that will shape future endeavours, and to elect new officers. Others are specific to the nature of the WCC: to seek the visible oneness of the body of Christ in the communion of the proclamation of the Word and the celebration of the sacraments, and to overcome the gaping rifts and fissures that have disfigured the history of Christianity.

Ministering in the shadow of worldwide violence, devastation and suffering, WCC assemblies have also steadfastly engaged in the quest for justice and peace for all humanity. Exemplary of this prophetic dimension is the message of the 1948 Amsterdam assembly:

Amsterdam, 1948   *New Dehli, 1961*

> *We have to learn afresh together to speak boldly in Christ's name... to oppose terror, cruelty and race discrimination, to stand by the outcast, the prisoner and the refugee. We have to make of the Church in every place a voice for those who have no voice... We have to ask God to teach us together to say No and to say Yes in truth. No... to the defenders of injustice in the name of order, to those who sow the seeds of war or urge war as inevitable; Yes... to all who seek justice, to the peacemakers, to all who hope, fight and suffer for the cause of man...*

These words capture what became the constant guidelines for the WCC: the search, amid the disheartening fragmentation of churches, for unity in the communion of Word and sacraments, the prophetic denunciation of injustice and discrimination, the quest for peace among nations and peoples, and service to the destitute and downtrodden. Sometimes those actions have exacted the bitter price of intense outside animosity, as happened when the WCC developed its anti-racism and anti-apartheid programme, when it opposed the 2003 invasion of Iraq by the United States, when it has defended the rights of the Palestinian people to nationhood, when it invites the participation of all shades of Christian churches in the dialogue for unity.

Within these overarching guidelines, each assembly of the WCC has met under the banner of a general theme intended to discern and express succinctly the signs, hopes and challenges of its particular time:

Evanston, 1954   *Uppsala, 1968*   *Nairobi, 1975*

- Amsterdam, 1948: "Man's Disorder and God's Design."

- Evanston, 1954: "Christ – The Hope of the World."

- New Delhi, 1961: "Jesus Christ – The Light of the World."

- Uppsala, 1968: "Behold, I Make All Things New."

- Nairobi, 1975: "Jesus Christ Frees and Unites."

- Vancouver, 1983: "Jesus Christ – The Life of the World."

- Canberra, 1991: "Come, Holy Spirit – Renew the Whole Creation."

- Harare, 1998: "Turn to God – Rejoice in Hope."

- Porto Alegre, 2006: "God, in your Grace, Transform the World."

The Porto Alegre assembly shared the common tasks of its predecessors while also having several characteristics all its own. This was the first assembly of the twenty-first century, a sign of the renewed determination of the WCC member churches to persist in their common history of faith and witness. It was the first to take place in Latin America, a region of the world suffering acute social, ethnic, economic and political conflicts, at a historical moment when the peoples of that region had begun to look for alternatives to hegemonic, neo-liberal, financial globalization. It was held in Porto Alegre, a Brazilian city that since 2001 has been the site of the World Social Forum, a space of convergence for many social and political movements seeking more just and participatory options to the present global order.

The assembly took place at a moment in which powerful nations were once again clinging to war as a talisman to solve complex political difficulties, leaving in their wake immense human affliction. It faced the continuing pandemic of HIV and AIDS, with far too many churches still debating whether to see in that dreadful virus a divine scourge or a challenge to Christian compassion and solidarity. It occurred at a time in which, as in the darkest epochs of history, prayers had been converted into curses and maledictions, and religious identities and loyalties had become sources of acrimonious disputes; a time when a "clash of civilizations" was proclaimed and a renewed, crusading ethos and jihadist attitudes soured international relations and complicated inter-religious dialogue.

The Porto Alegre assembly also occurred in an environment of tense relations among traditional Christian confessional families (as witnessed by the Orthodox critiques of the WCC during the previous decade) and by turmoil inside many of them (as seen in the withdrawal of the North American Southern Baptist Convention from the Baptist World Alliance and in the turbulence within the Anglican Communion). Furthermore, the assembly coincided with the centennial anniversary of the events in Azusa, California, that gave birth to Pentecostal movements and churches that have changed dramatically the configuration of world Christianity.

Conversely, the assembly also occurred in the context of several decades of promising ecumenical advances and encounters, like the Leuenberg agreement between several European Lutheran, Reformed, United, Hussite, Waldensian and Czech Brethren churches; the doctrinal rapprochement between the Roman Catholic Church and the Lutheran World Federation that dramatically ended almost five centuries of intense theological disputation regarding the doctrine of justification; the 1982 Faith and Order consensus around the key matters of baptism, eucharist and ministry; as well as the gradual overcoming of several crucial Christological conflicts between Eastern and Oriental Orthodox churches. Hope, rather than distress, might be, for many experienced ecumenical leaders, the true sign of the times.

At a point in history when young people were expressing their profound disappointment with the world they were inheriting and claimed their right to shape the future, the WCC central committee had decided that Porto Alegre would be an assembly in which youth would play a prominent role. Young people, the committee decided, would be present on all assembly committees and participate in all plenary sessions and activities. This proved to be a daunting challenge, since many delegations were composed of ecclesiastical leaders – of whom few could be considered young.

Canberra logo

Harare cross

When arriving at the enticing Brazilian city of Porto Alegre, the question in the minds of delegates and observers was whether the World Council of Churches, a "venerable but vulnerable" institution in the poignant words of Diane Kessler, would be up to the challenges facing it. Few WCC assemblies have gathered in times so difficult and complex, times like those of which William Butler Yeats wrote in his poem "The Second Coming":

> *Things fall apart; the centre cannot hold…,*
> *The blood-dimmed tide is loosed, and everywhere*
> *The ceremony of innocence is drowned;*
> *The best lack all conviction, while the worst*
> *Are full of passionate intensity.*

The assembly theme

The immense logistical efforts required to move thousands of participants (delegates, observers, advisors, stewards, staff, journalists) from approximately 120 nations to Porto Alegre, and provide for their countless needs from visas to victuals, would far exceed the scope of this introduction. Yet the story would be incomplete without some mention of the essential theological and ecclesiological issues that the organizers of the assembly faced beforehand.

Primary among them was choosing a theme that would serve as the leitmotif of the assembly in its common prayers, Bible studies, theological conversations and policy deliberations. The theme selected was "**God, in your grace, transform the world.**" Intentionally in the form of a prayer, it acknowledges and underlines divine sover-

See pages 55-111

11

The hand of God   *Creation and the cross*   *The spirit of peace*   *The covenant rainbow*   *The transformed world*

eignty and initiative in history. But its petition is not ethereal or docetic, for it relates divine grace to the renewal of the world and entails a commitment on the part of the churches to participate in the divine process of transforming human history.

The theme reflected the robust theological influence that Orthodox churches had been exerting within the WCC in the reconciling process intended to overcome the tensions that shadowed the 1998 Harare assembly. There is a long and distinguished Orthodox theological tradition that interprets divine grace not only as the source of human justification (a typical Western outlook) but also as undergirding a process of radical ontological transformation (*theosis*) of God's spiritual and rational creatures. This Orthodox theological influence can be seen in the final report of the Special Commission on Orthodox Participation in the World Council of Churches, created by the Harare assembly, and in reflections by Orthodox theologians on the assembly theme, as embodied in the fine book *Grace in Abundance: Orthodox Reflections on the Way to Porto Alegre*, edited under the direction of Metropolitan Gennadios of Sassima (Geneva, 2005). The assembly worship committee, chaired by Metropolitan Gennadios, took special care to ensure that the common prayers would respect Orthodox liturgical sensibilities, and Archbishop Anastasios of Tirana and All Albania, an Orthodox primate, was invited to preach the homily on the assembly theme at the opening service of common prayer.

God, **in your grace,**
transform the world

A literary cascade

Weeks before the assembly began, the delegates received several written documents that would prepare them for the coming intense deliberations. The most significant were:

- A booklet, *Springs of Living Water: Bible Studies on Grace and Transformation*, edited by an international team of biblical theologians, to guide the daily Bible studies.

- The *Programme Book* containing specific matters related to the organization and procedures of the assembly; important documents to be discussed in the assembly, such as the final report of the Special Commission on Orthodox Participation in the World Council of Churches, the proposal on Alternative Globalization Addressing People and Earth (AGAPE), the ecclesiological proposal "Called to be the One Church", and suggested amendments to the Constitution and Rules of the WCC; documents useful as background information, including the reports on the proposed Global Christian Forum and of the Joint Consultative Group: WCC-Pentecostals; and information about the ecumenical conversations to take place among the participants as well as other events that would occur simultaneously.

- The *Eighth Report* of the Joint Working Group between the Roman Catholic Church and the World Council of Churches (Geneva-Rome, 2005).

Publications prepared for the assembly

- A beautifully illustrated report on the activities of the WCC since the past assembly, titled *From Harare to Porto Alegre, 1998-2006: An Illustrated Account of the Life of the World Council of Churches.*

Several online resources, including a report of a comprehensive pre-assembly evaluation of WCC programmes and strategies, were added to the suggested readings.

Other materials were distributed at the moment of registration in Porto Alegre, including:

- A *Handbook* with useful information: timetable, daily schedules, event locations, committee agendas and many other practical matters ranging from health assistance to pastoral care.

- A sizeable book of common prayer – *em tua graça: Resources for Praise and Prayer* – in five languages (Portuguese, English, Spanish, French and German) for use in the daily morning and evening devotions.

- A booklet – *Welcome to Brazil and Latin America* – with informative essays on the religious panorama of the host region, authored by six Latin American theologians.

During the assembly itself, delegates and participants received a daily cascade of reports, requests, manifestos, books and booklets of all sorts. Two especially significant

The Porto Alegre prayer book – em tua graça: Resources for praise and prayer

contributions included a book edited by several Brazilian theologians, *The Grace of the World Transforms God* (2006), a title that provocatively parodies the theme of the assembly, and an anthology of essays by several prominent Latin American theologians, *Grace, Cross and Hope in Latin America* (2006), published by the Latin American Council of Churches. The WCC featured a bookshop that distributed thousands of books, and other ecclesiastical organizations sold or gave away countless additional publications. One convenient source of information was the assembly newspaper, *Transforma o Mundo*, designed in an eye-catching, agile format, with synopses of events and attractive photographs, produced daily by a diligent assembly communication staff.

The inaugural session

The assembly formally opened on the afternoon of February 14 with the contagious rhythms of seductive Brazilian music and dance that were to become characteristic of all the plenary sessions. The moderator, His Holiness Aram I, Catholicos of the See of Cilicia of the Armenian Apostolic Church (Antelias, Lebanon), in opening the assembly, stressed its importance as the first WCC assembly of the twenty-first century and the first in Latin America, and he expressed the hope that the assembly might be a landmark in the history of the ecumenical movement.

The general secretary, the Rev. Dr Samuel Kobia, called the roll of delegates and presented the new member churches and associated national councils (most of which increased the presence of African, Latin American and Caribbean churches). To the applause of the assembly, Dr Kobia introduced three former WCC general secretaries: the Rev. Dr Philip Potter, the Rev. Dr Emilio Castro and the Rev. Dr

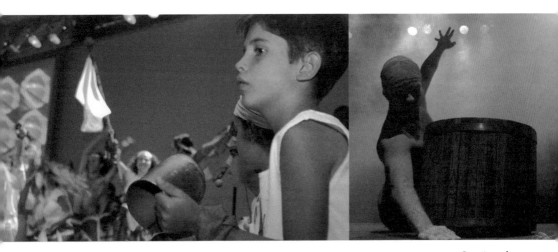

Opening plenary

Konrad Raiser. Philip Potter received a standing ovation for having attended all nine WCC assemblies beginning with the 1948 Amsterdam gathering. Messages of welcome were expressed by Bishop Adriel de Souza Maia, president of the National Council of Christian Churches of Brazil; Bishop Julio Holguín, president of the Latin American Council of Churches; Eliseu Santos, vice-mayor of Porto Alegre; and the Honourable Germano Rigotto, governor of the state of Rio Grande do Sul.

See page 328

Greetings were also read from three key ecclesiastical prelates, who emphasized the commitment of their churches to the ecumenical movement:

- His All Holiness Bartholomew I, Archbishop of Constantinople and Ecumenical Patriarch: "The Ecumenical Patriarchate is committed to the WCC and the ecumenical movement as a whole. It will continue to offer its witness and share the richness of its traditions in the search for unity among Christian churches, in all efforts towards reconciliation and peace and in the protection of creation which is a gift of God entrusted to humanity."

- The Most Reverend Dr Rowan Williams, Archbishop of Canterbury and spiritual leader of the Anglican World Communion, who would later address the assembly: "We keep in mind not just the world that is to be transformed, but the work of this assembly, the churches we each represent and indeed the future role of the WCC. In doing so, our underlying desire is surely for the combined witness of our churches to keep pace, in this fast-changing and often perplexing world, with what it means to be an effective sign of God's transforming grace."

Rev. Dr Samuel Kobia   *His Holiness Aram I*

- Pope Benedict XVI, Bishop of Rome and head of the Roman Catholic Church, through a letter read by Walter Cardinal Kasper, president of the Pontifical Council for Promoting Christian Unity: "Mindful of our shared baptismal faith in the Triune God, the Catholic Church and the World Council of Churches seek ways to cooperate ever more effectively in the task of witnessing to God's divine love. After forty years of fruitful collaboration, we look forward to continuing this journey of hope and promise, as we intensify our endeavours towards reaching that day when Christians are united in proclaiming the gospel message of salvation to all.... Reaffirming the Catholic Church's intention to continue a solid partnership with the World Council of Churches in its important contribution to the ecumenical movement, I invoke God's abundant blessings of peace and joy upon all of you."

Pope Benedict XVI's letter was apparently designed to clear away widely diffused misgivings produced by *Dominus Iesus*, the 2000 declaration of the Congregation for the Doctrine of the Faith (signed by Joseph Ratzinger, then Prefect of the Congregation), which had been perceived by many in the ecumenical movement as a regression to former exclusivist ecclesiological claims by the Roman Catholic Church. Cardinal Kasper, who headed a significant Roman Catholic delegation, reaffirmed in various public statements his church's adherence to the Second Vatican Council decree on ecumenism – *Unitatis redintegratio* – and its guiding principle that the "restoration of the unity of all Christians is one of [the Church's] main concerns".

Walter Cardinal Kasper   *Rev. Dr Philip Potter*

Finally, the assembly received greetings from Kofi Annan, secretary-general of the United Nations and also, following the norm that a young person should address all sessions, from Lourdes Saad Olivera, representing the World Young Women's Christian Association and the Young Men's Christian Association.

In the course of the assembly, additional greetings were sent by other prelates, among them His Beatitude Theodoros II, Pope and Patriarch of Alexandria and all Africa; His Beatitude Theophilos III, Patriarch of the Holy City of Jerusalem and all Palestine; His Holiness Moran Mor Ignatius Zakka I Iwas, Patriarch of Antioch and All the East and Supreme Head of the Universal Syriac Orthodox Church; His Holiness Abune Paulos, Patriarch and Catholicos of the Ethiopian Orthodox Church; and the Rev. Geoffrey Tunnicliffe, chief executive officer and international coordinator of the World Evangelical Alliance.

A praying assembly

The WCC central committee had decided that Porto Alegre would be a praying assembly – hence the decision to craft the assembly's theme as a prayer, "God, in your grace, transform the world". The central committee named a worship committee chaired by an Orthodox leader, Metropolitan Prof. Dr Gennadios of Sassima, of the Ecumenical Patriarchate of Constantinople, who edited the assembly prayer book *em tua graça: Resources for Praise and Prayer*. The preface of the book concisely describes the centrality of prayer for the whole gathering.

The assembly worship tent

Prayer is at the heart of Christianity... In prayer, human beings encounter their Creator and Redeemer, the Triune God... Prayer is central to the life of each assembly of the World Council of Churches... The assembly is primarily a place of... celebration and prayer to Almighty God...

Based on the experience of past assemblies, the worship committee took measures to prevent potential sources of conflict, including 1) carefully avoiding non-biblical, gender-inclusive language in reference to God; 2) impeding any attempt to force intercommunion or common eucharist among churches whose doctrinal differences hinder them from doing so; and 3) naming the times of collective devotion "prayer", or "common prayer", thus avoiding what for some churches is the unacceptable concept of "ecumenical worship". The graceful and serene chapel of the Pontifícia Universidade was available for those confessional families who wanted to celebrate the eucharist according to their own doctrinal and liturgical traditions.

The morning and evening prayers closely followed the assembly's leitmotif by dividing it into sub-themes for the daily devotions:

19

- God, in your grace, transform *the world* (February 14 & 15)

- God, in your grace, transform *the earth* (February 16)

- God, in your grace, transform *our societies* (February 17)

- God, in your grace, transform *our lives* (February 18 & 21)

Morning prayer

- God, in your grace, transform *our churches* (February 20)

- God, in your grace, transform *our witness* (February 22 & 23)

The prayer services were accompanied by daily symbols as a devotionally oriented means of exploring the life of faith.

- *Chains* (February 15) – The liberty of captives and release of prisoners (Isa. 61; Luke 4) as symbolized by broken chains.

- *Sunflowers* (February 16) – Symbols of resurrection (Isa. 65; Rev. 21) for some Latin American Indigenous peoples.

- *Incense* (February 17) – Symbol of prayers of confession of sin and pleas for mercy (Ps. 141:2).

- *Religious painting* (February 18) – The Risen Christ as the source of hope for the transformation of the world (I Pet. 3:18-20).

- *Chalice* (February 19) – An empty cup to symbolize the hope of the eucharistic celebration at which all may eat and drink together (Mark 10:38f.).

- *Water* (February 21) – Water as source of human life and Christian faith (Mark 1:10; John 4:14).

Evening prayer

- *Bread* (February 22) – The symbol of the basic human need for sustenance and of the Lord's table (Luke 11:3).

- *Seeds* (February 23) – The hope that the ninth assembly might be a seed of further achievements in the common Christian fellowship (Mark 4:27).

Most delegates and participants wholeheartedly embraced the prayer gatherings held under a huge tent at the entrance to the university and appreciated the efforts to ameliorate the tensions of past assemblies. Some, however, were displeased that almost a quarter of a century after the pivotal statement authorized by Faith and Order at Lima in 1982, *Baptism, Eucharist, Ministry*, and despite decades of ecumenical dialogue, the WCC was still unable to celebrate a common eucharist, the central Christian sacrament and act of worship. Perhaps some delegates remembered Emilio Castro's *cri de coeur* at the 1991 Canberra assembly: "How can we expect to overcome divisions of life and death in the world when we are not even able to offer together the sacrifice of the Lord…! [We] need to keep alive this nostalgia for the table of the Lord. This should be the last assembly with a divided eucharist!"

The ecumenical character of the assembly was dramatically symbolized in the opening prayer service by gifts brought to the altar from all regions of the world:

- Africa – a stone from the Turkana region of eastern Kenya, considered by anthropologists to be the cradle of humanity. It represents God's grace in creation and providence through the development of humankind.

Offering gifts

21

- Asia – a bell, symbolic of celebration and supplication in prayer and representative of the vital interchange between God and God's people, essential to the rich traditions of Asian spirituality.

- Caribbean – sugar cane, the source of numerous products fundamental to the islands, representing the strength, resilience and sweetness of the Caribbean people.

- Europe – a reindeer calfskin, a gift of the Sami herders, an Indigenous people in northern Europe, representing the Sami's grateful pride in their own cultural identity.

- Latin America – a Salvadoran cross, an emblem of suffering under violent regimes, yet a sign of hope for peace, reconciliation and justice.

- Middle East – a painting representing the only existing Coptic icon from the first millennium. The icon depicts the holy family's flight into Egypt as described in the second chapter of Matthew's gospel, a reminder of Christianity's origin in this region.

- North America – symbols of the earth's bounty: sweet grass presented by a representative of the First Nations, with corn and cultivated wheat.

- The Pacific – *Ie Toga* from Samoa/Polynesia, a woven mat used in ceremonies of forgiveness; a tanoa from Fiji/Melanesia, a ceremonial bowl that represents the gathering of peoples; and a stick chart from the Marshall Islands that maps the ocean's currents and symbolizes the environmental forces that surround us all.

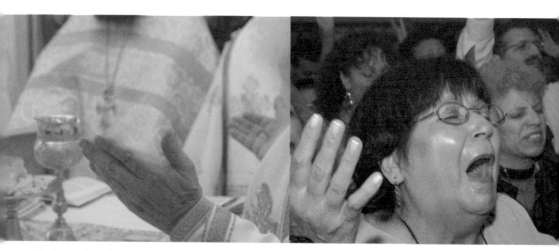

Worship with local congregations

The homily, devoted to the theme of the assembly, was preached by Archbishop *See page 55* Anastasios of Tirana and All Albania, who emphasized, among the many challenges facing the assembly, that:

> *Since our assembly is taking place in Latin America, the issue of poverty assumes absolute priority for all of us who worship and follow Him, who was born and died stressing the dignity of the poor and their inalienable value before God, who came "to bring good news to the poor" (Luke 4:18). In the face of all the poor – the hungry, estranged and refugees – we are obliged to discern the face of Jesus. Woe to us if, in the 21st century, we again relinquish the initiative for social justice to others, as we have done in past centuries, while we confine ourselves to our opulent rituals, to our usual alliance with the powerful.*

Finally, in a litany of commitment, all participants promised to "work for the heal-ing of our broken world", "treat all people with equal respect and dignity", "stand firm against all forms of discrimination", "cry out against exploitation", "listen to the voices of the humble", "seek peace" and "care for the earth".

A theological assembly

Bureaucratic matters frequently dominate assemblies of complex organizations, but that has yet to be the case with the World Council of Churches. The 1948 Amsterdam assembly was preceded by four books (*The Universal Church in God's Design, The Church's Witness to God's Design, The Church and the Disorder of Society* and *The Church and the International Disorder*) devoted to the theme of the gathering, "Man's

23

Disorder and God's Design", with essays by theologians of the stature of Karl Barth, Paul Tillich, Gustaf Aulén, George Florovsky, H. Richard Niebuhr, Edmund Schlink, Emil Brunner, Hendrik Kraemer, Lesslie Newbigin, Pierre Maury, Kathleen Bliss, Wilhelm Pauck, Reinhold Niebuhr, John C. Bennett, M. M. Thomas, Jacques Ellul and Joseph Hromadka, among others. Such a tradition is hard to follow!

The 2006 Porto Alegre assembly was a continuous theological conversation, or, to be more precise, a sequence of more or less conjoined and parallel theological dialogues. These dialogues went on in the forms of Bible studies, ecumenical conversations, bate-papos (Portuguese for informal chat), mutirão (a Brazilian word with Indigenous roots meaning a meeting place and an opportunity to converse and work together for a common purpose), an ecumenical theological seminar, a theological café and a series of thematic plenary sessions.

Following the daily morning prayers, all participants met for **Bible studies**. The delegates, observers, advisors and guests met in small home groups while the mutirão participants joined in English, Portuguese or Spanish speaking groups to study the same texts. Those experiences are too varied and expansive to evaluate here, but this author can, at the very least, bear witness to the theological profundity and pedagogical proficiency of the leaders of the Spanish-speaking mutirão group, the Latin American biblical scholars Néstor Míguez, Elsa Tamez and Elizabeth Salazar.

To further a wide variety of dialogues, the assembly participants took part in one of twenty-two **ecumenical conversations**. The ecumenical conversations met three times: first, to explore trends and "signs of the times" regarding their specific

Reading the Bible together

topic of deliberation; second, to share their experiences on how churches are dealing with the issue; and third, to propose ecumenical collaboration and options for change rooted in theological and biblical imperatives. The participants could select one of the following ecumenical conversations grouped under four different theological categories addressing key issues for today's world Christianity.

A) Changing the religious and cultural context
 1. Mission as healing and reconciling communities (based on the theme of the May 2005 conference on world mission and evangelism held near Athens)
 2. Religious plurality embraced and feared
 3. Becoming a community of women and men: learning from women's ways of being church
 4. Human sexuality: body and soul; world and church
 5. Keeping the faith in a cyber-world: Christian communities and new technologies
 6. Disabled people: a church of all and for all

B) Changing the ecclesial and ecumenical context
 7. Challenges on the way to unity: seeking an ecumenical response for today
 8. Emerging forms of ecumenism
 9. Challenges to diakonia today: seeking an ecumenical response
 10. Memories and renewed quest for ecumenical formation
 11. Youth transforming the ecumenical landscape

Youth tent discussions

C) Changing the international and political context
    12. Walking in truth, speaking with power
    13. Protecting peoples' lives and human dignity
    14. Churches responding to new threats to peace and human security
    15. Building hospitable communities: responding to migration
    16. Public life, religion and politics: ambiguities and possibilities

D) Changing the social and economic context
    17. The scandal of poverty and growing inequality
    18. Overcoming health threats to humanity in the context of HIV & AIDS
    19. Witnessing to the sanctity of life: bioethics and the challenges of new technologies
    20. Co-existence in God's creation: caring for the earth's resources
    21. The agenda of racism: a priority for the churches
    22. Zero tolerance for violence against women and children

Most of the ecumenical conversations were exciting, theologically enlightening and eye-opening. The proposed linkage between these ecumenical conversations and the assembly resolutions and declarations prepared in committee, however, was not always fully achieved.

The **bate-papo** proved to be a particularly agile way to sponsor dialogue between generations. From 12:45 to 13:15 each day, a young theologian conversed with an eminent older theologian or church leader (among them Rowan Williams, Mercy Oduyoye, Adolfo Pérez Esquivel and Philip Potter) about pressing theological and

Ecumenical conversations

ecclesiological issues: the future of Christianity in the 21st century; mission in the struggles for life; the church in a globalized world; victims as healers who build peace in a context of violence; Indigenous peoples, their visions and challenges; young people as agents of change; and the theological understanding of God as a woman. These informal yet intense, focused ecumenical opportunities helped educate and promote a new generation of church theologians and leaders.

In addition to the delegates and official observers, more than 2,000 visitors and guests participated daily in hundreds of expressions of **mutirão**. An integral dimension of the assembly, the mutirão provided an opportunity for reflection and dialogue on a wide array of issues that Christians all over the world care about: the struggle of Indigenous communities, war and peace, human rights, church unity, Christian identity, liberation theologies, feminist theologies, globalization, national debt and world trade, the future of the ecumenical movement, changes in the Pentecostal churches, Orthodoxy and the ecumenical movement, HIV and AIDS, migration issues, religious pluralism, religious intolerance, interconfessionality, children as war victims, terrorism and the "war against terror", new forms of Christian diakonia, human sexuality and the churches, sexual exploitation, advocacy for persons with physical disabilities, Israel and Palestine and many others.

The mutirão took many forms – round tables, workshops, seminars, dramatic presentations, films and dances. Every day, artistic groups from various parts of the world – Sri Lanka, Bolivia, India, Botswana, Peru, Brazil, Cook Islands, Germany – performed for participants and observers. It was an opportunity for countless significant exchanges, dialogues and artistic events and created a space

27

Mutirão

for the discussion of themes – the ordination of women, homosexuality, inclusive theological language – that would have proven more divisively controversial and sensitive if raised in the official assembly sessions. The reaction of most participants was very positive. Although it is difficult to evaluate all that happened as part of the mutirão, many of the organizational difficulties of the *Padares* at the Harare assembly were overcome. Yet the desire to turn those reflections into significant contributions in the assembly decision-making process proved difficult.

From February 12 to 25, the WCC, in collaboration with the Lutheran School of Theology at São Leopoldo, the Association of Protestant Seminaries in Brazil (ASTE) and the Latin American and the Caribbean Community of Ecumenical Theological Education (CETELA) sponsored an academic **ecumenical theological seminar** titled "Ecumenical Congress 2006: Mission and Ecumenism in Latin America" for almost one hundred theological students. Fifty students came from the different regions of Brazil; 30 from other Latin American countries and the Caribbean, and another 19 came from different nations overseas. The goal was to provide an intense theological course in ecumenism in counterpoint to the assembly. Distinguished ecumenical leaders and theologians offered papers, lectures and roundtables, eliciting very positive and enthusiastic responses from students and organizers alike.

ASTE, CETELA, the Lutheran School of Theology at São Leopoldo and the Ecumenical Theological Education (ETE) programme of the WCC also coordinated a **theological café**. The café created a meeting place for theological dialogues and

Theological café

presentations of books (more than 25 books were discussed) in an informal environment. The café sponsored roundtables on the challenges to theological education in the Americas, Africa, Asia, the Middle East, the Pacific and Europe while at the same time providing a relaxed context in which participants could converse with the distinguished theologians present at the assembly.

Thematic plenary sessions

See pages 159-254

The assembly hosted six thematic plenary sessions, each focusing on a different topic: economic justice, Christian identity and religious plurality, overcoming violence, Latin America, church unity and, finally, the general theme of the assembly.

The first session on February 16 revolved around the crucial issue of **economic justice**. Rev. Dr Nancy Cardoso, a Brazilian Methodist theologian, initiated the dialogue with a stirring lecture contrasting two conflicting theological visions. On one hand, capitalist transnational corporations "want 'the kingdom, the power and the glory' by controlling the land, water and seed stocks. They are already lords of other people's work. They now control and determine the monetary value of their livelihood and their actual lives." On the other hand, "on the periphery of world Christianity, there are minorities who stress the need for a theology that liberates: that liberates God, and the earth, and the men and women whose humanity is being denied every day by capitalism." She challenged the assembly "to take up again a prophetic evangelical stance in the world."

Dr Cardoso's lecture was followed by addresses from: Prof. Veronica Araújo, coordinator of the Focolare Movement's Centre for Dialogue with Culture, on the

29

Plenary hall

"economy of communion project"; Archpriest Vsevolod Chaplin, deputy chairman of the Department for External Church Relations, Moscow Patriarchate, on the Code of Moral Principles and Rules in Economy proposed by the Russian Orthodox Church to curb the corruption and lack of ethical sensitivity in the Russian economy; Teruango Beneteri, lay member of the Kiribati Protestant Church, on the Pacific concept of the Island of Hope; and Prof. Yashpal Tandon, an economist from Uganda and the executive director of the South Centre in Geneva, who delivered a stringent critique of neoliberal globalization for widening the disparity between rich and poor. Prof. Tandon challenged the churches "to show the way of promoting a just and participatory world, where resources can be shared and the earth cared for".

See page 179

The February 17 plenary devoted to **Christian identity and religious plurality** began with an address by Dr Rowan Williams, Archbishop of Canterbury. In an articulate, forceful address, Dr Williams emphasized that when we identify ourselves as Christians, "we carry the name of Christ. We are the people who are known for their loyalty to, their affiliation with, the historical person who was given the title of 'anointed monarch' by his followers – Jesus, the Jew of Nazareth. Every time we say 'Christian', we take for granted a story and a place in history." This identity, he continued, is "both promising and risky". It is deployed in a world of aggressively competing religious claims. "When we face radically different notions, strange and complex accounts of a perspective not our own, our questions must be not, 'How do we convict them of error? How do we win the competition of ideas?' but, 'What do they actually see? and can what they see be a part of the world that I see?'" How to be

Nancy Cardoso   *Veronica Araújo*   *Yashpal Tandon*

faithful to our own identity and history as Christians while entering into a genuine and respectful dialogue with other religions has become a crucial challenge. To the applause of the audience, Dr Williams also called attention to the faithfulness and plight of Christians living as marginalized and sometimes-persecuted minorities. "Remarkable," he said, "is the courage with which Christians continue – in Egypt, in Pakistan, in the Balkans, even in Iraq – to seek ways of continuing to work alongside non-Christian neighbours. This is not the climate of 'dialogue' as it happens in the West or in the comfortable setting of international conferences; it is the painful making and remaking of trust in a deeply unsafe and complex environment."

Dr Anna May Chain, a Baptist theology professor and biblical scholar from the Karen ethnic minority in Myanmar, shared the story of her family's rescue by people of other faiths at a moment in which Karen Christians were persecuted: "At this point in my life, the neighbours, Muslims, Buddhists and Catholics, were in the place of Jesus to me. I was at my most vulnerable and weakest. They were my guard and shield. They were the risk takers and life givers. My Muslim and Buddhist neighbours may not know the name 'Jesus', but I believe God had found a path for himself to them."

Dr Assaad E. Kattan, a Lebanese professor of theology at the Wilhelms-Universität in Germany, identified himself as one who "is constantly wondering what our Christian identity over against other religions means.... It is difficult for us Christians to define ourselves unambiguously. It seems to me, however, that the event of the cross, which we all confess, can put us in the position to include in our identity foreignness, brokenness and silence. And when we reach that point, a door can be opened for the others who are standing outside."

31

Teruango Beneteri   *Rowan Williams*   *Assaad Elias Kattan*   *Anna May Chain*

See page 369 There were also pleas in favour of dialogue between religions from representa-tives of other faiths, among them Katsunori Yamanoi, chairman of the board of directors of the Buddhist organization Rissho Kosei-kai; Dr Deborah Weissman, of the Inter-religious Coordinating Council in Israel; and, in a video message, His Royal Highness Prince El Hassan bin Tabal of Jordan, moderator for the World Conference on Religion and Peace.

The February 18 plenary devoted to **overcoming violence** began with a moving mul-timedia presentation – video, music and liturgical dance – to illustrate instances of overcoming violence around the world. Then Olara A. Otunnu, president of the LBL Foundation for Children, former UN under-secretary-general and special representa-tive for children and armed conflict, described the tragic plight of children under the *See page 224* scourge of war. "When adults wage war", he asserted, "children pay the highest price... Their suffering bears many faces... Children are killed or maimed, made orphans, abducted, deprived of education and health care, and left with deep emotional scars and trauma... Girls face additional risks, particularly sexual violence." Mr Otunno emphasized the critical situation of children in the civil war in Northern Uganda: "As I review what is unfolding in northern Uganda, I cannot help but won-der if we have learned any lessons from the earlier dark episodes of history: millions of Jews exterminated during the Holocaust in Europe, genocide perpetrated in Rwanda, children and women systematically massacred in the Balkans. Each time we have said, 'never again', but only after the dark deed was accomplished... And what shall we tell the survivor children in northern Uganda, when they ask why no one came to stop the dark deeds stalking their land and devouring its people?"

Olara Otunnu   *Addressing the assembly*

The session on violence ended in a dramatic and unexpected way when the Very *See page 360* Rev. Leonid Kishkovsky, of the Orthodox Church of America, read a letter of apology, on behalf of the United States Conference for the World Council of Churches, that sternly criticized actions and policies of the US government:

> *We are citizens of a nation that has done much in these years to endanger the human family... We lament with special anguish the war in Iraq, launched in deception and violating global norms of justice and human rights. We mourn all who have died or been injured in this war... we confess that we have failed to raise a prophetic voice loud enough and persistent enough to deter our leaders from this path of pre-emptive war.*

As a sign of the assembly's intention to support the "Decade to Overcome Violence 2001-2010" WCC programme emphasis, two marches were held: one inside the Pontifícia Universidade, calling for an end of violence against women, on February 16, and a march for world peace through the city of Porto Alegre, led by the Nobel peace laureates Adolfo Pérez Esquivel and Desmond Tutu, on February 21.

In the opinion of many delegates, the February 19 plenary session devoted to **Latin America**, the geopolitical milieu of the assembly, was the aesthetic zenith of *See page 239* the assembly. In a multi-media presentation, using life-sized puppets, music and videos, actors/dancers of the Chameleon Doll Theatre Group (Grupo Camaleão Teatro de Benecos) rhythmically dramatized the conflicts, sufferings and hopes of

March for Peace

Latin American peoples. The production revolved around the question, "Where is God at work in Latin America?" That key question was explored in a creative and imaginative way by means of the various elements of the assembly logo: the hand of God, the cross, the spirit of peace, the rainbow of covenant and a transformed world. A packed assembly saw images of ethnic diversity and injustice against the peoples of the region and heard how it all began – with the cruelty of violent colonization. The presentation ended in a celebratory mood, acclaiming social inclusiveness and the struggle against injustice, "believing that the transformation of the world lies with us. God is journeying with us towards a land where everyone will live with dignity in their own place."

After that magnificent spectacle, a video featured several distinguished Latin American ecumenical leaders and theologians conversing about the dilemmas and challenges of the region and the churches. Among the interviewees were Bishop Julio César Holguín, president of the Latin American Council of Churches, Bishop Adriel de Souza Maia, president of the National Council of Churches of Brazil, Dr Elsa Tamez, feminist theologian, Rigoberta Menchú, the 1992 Nobel Prize peace laureate, Bishop Federico Pagura, WCC President, Adolfo Pérez Esquivel, the 1980 Nobel peace laureate, Rev. Israel Batista, general secretary of the Latin American Council of Churches and Rev. Juan Sepúlveda, Chilean Pentecostal theologian.

In the plenary session devoted to **church unity**, on February 20, several speakers *See page 159* were asked to react to the proposed ecclesiological declaration titled "Called to be the One Church". Fr Dr Jacob Kurien, vice-principal of the Orthodox Theological Seminary (Malankara Orthodox Syrian Church) in Kerala, India, 1) expressed con-

Latin America plenary

cern about the present ecumenical stagnation and immunity to ecumenical sensitivity; 2) voiced hope for new ecumenical spaces in local and national settings; 3) called for measures to heal painful external ecclesiastical interventions in nations like India; 4) criticized the neglect in the proposed text of holiness, one of the classical ecclesiological marks; 5) emphasized the need to add more appropriate criteria in judging "social commitment"; 6) and, quoting the poet Rabindranath Tagore – "Emancipation from the soil is no freedom for the tree" – questioned what he termed "ecclesiastical neo-colonialism".

Dr Isabel Apawo Phiri, a Presbyterian from Malawi and general coordinator of the Circle of Concerned African Women Theologians, raised several issues regarding the search for unity by African Protestant churches. She concluded that: "If indeed we believe that God is calling us to unity we need to show it in action through recognition of ordained ministers (of all races, gender, age, ability and sexual orientation) of other churches at our holy communion table; through ecumenical rites for inter-church marriages; embracing the spirituality of others through theological education and formation; and affirming the church as a communion of believers by getting rid of all that undermines this belief."

Fr Jorge A. Scampini, Dominican priest and moderator of the St Thomas Aquinas theological faculty's study centre at the Pontifical Catholic University of Argentina, reasserted the role of the WCC as a "privileged instrument" in the search for church unity and predicted that adopting the declaration "Called to be the One Church" could be a "milestone in the history of the WCC as an institution."

35

Jacob Kurien   *Isabel Apawo Phiri*

Norberto Saracco, Pentecostal pastor and scholar from Argentina, poignantly raised several issues: 1) Unity becomes difficult when other churches "treat us [Pentecostals] as sects, when they regard Pentecostals as a threat... Unity cannot be built on misrepresentation and prejudice." 2) "The religious map of the world has changed and the map of Christianity has also changed. The centre of gravity of the church has moved from the North to the South... Our impoverished peoples, our pillaged lands and our societies in bondage to sin present us with a challenge." 3) "We need to accept our diversity as an expression of the grace of God that itself takes many forms. There are different ways of being church and in recent times that diversity has multiplied." 4) We might be in the times of a new Pentecost. "Only a Spirit-filled church will see racial, sexual, economic and ecclesiastical barriers come down... The unity of the church will be a work of the Spirit, or it will not be at all."

See page 349

After a moving dialogue on church unity by two young members of the assembly, Lei Garcia, from the Philippines, and John N. Njoroge, from Kenya, Desmond Mpilo Tutu, former Anglican Archbishop of South Africa, former secretary general of the South African Council of Churches and 1984 Nobel peace laureate, gave one of the most inspiring speeches of the entire assembly. Archbishop Tutu expressed his gratitude to the WCC for its support in the struggle to dismantle the apartheid system in South Africa. He described the range of assembly delegations as a splendid multicultural and multi-ethnic kaleidoscopic foreshadowing of the diversity of the kingdom of God. Archbishop Tutu insisted that the search for unity is an essential task for all churches. "A united church is no optional extra. A united church is indispensable for the salvation of God's world..."

John N. Njoroge and Lei Garcia   *Desmond Tutu*

The final thematic plenary, on February 21, was devoted to the theme of the assembly, "**God, in your grace, transform the world.**" Although the speakers had prepared papers that were distributed, the session took the form of a television talk show, in which the moderator, the Rev. Dr Angelique Walker-Smith of the National Baptist Convention USA, Inc. interviewed a group of panelists. Gracia Violeta Ross Quiroga, representative of the National Network of Bolivian People Living with HIV and AIDS, spoke of suffering sexual abuse and being infected with HIV, but also of the strength she has found in God's grace and love. Sarah Newland-Martin, of the Ecumenical Disability Advocates Network (EDAN), who represented Jamaica in the Pan-American wheelchair games from 1972 to 1982 and in the 1980 para-Olympics, described her life as fully transformed by baptism through the grace of God. Carmen Lansdowne, an Indigenous person and member of the United Church of Canada, noted how autochthonous peoples have suffered, not only at the hands of the state but also at the hands of the church. Paula Devejian, from the United States and currently working in Armenia for the Catholicosate of All Armenians, said that she has been strengthened by meeting people from every area of the world and observing the commonality of their struggles. Korean professor Namsoon Kang, vice-president of the World Conference of Associations of Theological Institutions, said her encounter with feminist discourse and with the ecumenical movement has led to her personal transformation. Finally, the Rev. Dr Joseph (Leandro) Bosch, Argentinian theologian of the Ecumenical Patriarchate of Constantinople, expounded a Trinitarian and holistic vision of the world-transforming efficacy of divine grace.

See pages *72-111*

37

Transformations – thematic plenary   *Gracia Violeta Ross Quiroga*

Despite the repeatedly stated purpose of allowing for ample dialogue after each thematic plenary session, the time allotted for exchange among the delegates was always too brief due to schedule restrictions, with the result that many participants were unable to add their perspectives to the discussion. The words of the gospel, "many are called, but few are chosen" (Matthew 22:14), unfortunately prevailed.

The reports

See page 112

Several sessions were devoted to assess the state of the organization and project its future policies. As part of that process, the assembly received reports from the WCC moderator, His Holiness Aram I, and the general secretary, Rev. Dr Samuel Kobia. The report of the moderator included a biblical and theological interpretation of the assembly's theme.

38

> *In this Assembly, we will identify the implications of this theme to the ecumenical movement and particularly to the ecumenical witness of the World Council of Churches by reflecting and praying: "God, in your grace, transform the world". Indeed, this prayer is the cry of the poor for justice; the cry of the sick for healing; the cry of the marginalized for liberation; the cry of humanity and creation for reconciliation*

Aram I, who had been the WCC moderator for almost fifteen years since the Canberra assembly, called for the reconfiguration of the ecumenical movement, its *aggiornamento*, the invention of new forms of ecumenism and the reaffirmation of

His Holiness Aram I, WCC Moderator

the churches' commitment to remain together. He emphasized the need to resolve creatively the past tensions between the Western churches and the Orthodox in the WCC. "I hope," he added, "that the WCC-Orthodox crisis will shake and challenge all member churches in the ecumenical movement." Finally, the moderator, in what for many delegates was an implicit evocation of the most celebrated speech of Martin Luther King, Jr, concluded his report recounting his dreams for the ecumenical movement:

> *The ecumenical journey is a pilgrimage of faith and hope… In this journey of faith and hope I have had dreams: I dreamed that mutual recognition of baptism, the seal of our Christian identity and foundation of our Christian unity, would soon be realized. I dreamed that all the churches of the world would celebrate the resurrection of our common Lord together on the same day, as one of the visible expressions of Christian unity. I dreamed that an Ecumenical Assembly – if not an Ecumenical Council at this point in time – would be convened with the participation of all churches to celebrate their fellowship in Christ and address common challenges facing the church and humanity.*

39

See page 136

Alluding to the Brazilian tradition of Carnival, the general secretary invited the delegates to consider the assembly as *a festa da vida* (the feast of life) grounded in Christian spirituality. Dr Kobia emphasized the need to strengthen the spiritual ecumenical formation of youth as the proper foundation for their engagement in the struggle for transformative justice. "Spiritual discernment", he stressed, "con-

Rev. Dr Samuel Kobia, WCC General Secretary

tributes crucially to overcoming violence and building peace." Grounded upon renewed spirituality we are able, according to the general secretary, to perceive the tragic disparity between the world as it is and as it is intended to be by its Creator:

> *God has given us the gift of life and we have abused it. Human greed and thirst for power have created structures that cause people to live in poverty and systematically undermine the basis of life... In an era when there is more than enough food to go around many times over, 852 million people across the world are hungry, up from 842 million in 2003. Every single day, 25,000 people are killed by hunger. Every day, more than 16,000 children die from hunger-related causes – one every five seconds... Asymmetries of power are manifest in a thousand ways – between people, between communities, between countries. The litany of sins and suffering could go on and on.*

After pinpointing several challenges and dilemmas faced by the ecumenical movement, Dr Kobia suggested that the WCC and other Christian world communions jointly sponsor the next assembly. "I propose that this assembly give us a mandate to accelerate the dialogue with the Lutheran World Federation and the World Alliance of Reformed Churches to explore possibilities of holding our next assemblies as a combined event. And we should also invite any other world Christian body to join us in this dialogue."

See pages 285, 448

The assembly received, discussed and approved the report of the Finance Committee. It also amended the WCC Constitution and Rules in accordance with the suggestions of the Special Commission on Orthodox Participation in the World Council of Churches. The main changes consisted of the acceptance of the consensus model as the prevailing decision-making procedure and the strengthening of the theological guidelines for admitting a church into the WCC. According to the new norms, every applicant church must fulfill the following theological criteria:

1. In its life and witness, the church professes faith in the triune God according to the scriptures, and as this faith is reflected in the Nicene-Constantinopolitan Creed.

2. The church maintains a ministry of proclaiming the gospel and celebrating the sacraments as understood by its doctrines.

3. The church baptizes in the name of the one God, *Father, Son and Holy Spirit,* and acknowledges the need to move towards the recognition of the baptism of other churches.

4. The church recognizes the presence and activity of Christ and the Holy Spirit outside its own boundaries and prays for the gift of God's wisdom to all in the awareness that other member churches also believe in the Holy Trinity and the saving grace of God.

5. The church recognizes in the other member churches of the WCC elements of the true church, even if it does not regard them "as churches in the true and full sense of the word".

Resolutions and declarations

See pages 255-327

In several sessions of intense dialogue, the delegates received, amended and approved reports of the assembly committees, comprised of the public issues committee, the programme guidelines committee, the policy reference committee, the finance committee and the message committee.

Based upon the report of the public issues committee, the assembly approved declarations on Latin America, vulnerable populations at risk, the reform of the United Nations, terrorism, counter-terrorism and human rights, the need to protect the world reserves of water, the elimination of nuclear weapons and the requirement of a dialogue of mutual respect and responsibility with people of other faiths. Under the guidance of the programme guidelines committee, the assembly decided to streamline the work of the WCC in four major interactive areas of engagement: 1) unity, spirituality and mission; 2) ecumenical formation; 3) global justice; and, 4) public voice and prophetic witness to the world.

After the report of the policy reference committee, the assembly approved a resolution mandating that the WCC central committee and staff strengthen the relationships among member churches and with the Christian world communions, the regional ecumenical organizations and the national councils of churches, several specialized ministries and agencies related to the WCC, the Roman Catholic Church, the Pentecostal churches. It also instructed the WCC to continue its efforts towards the convocation of a Global Christian Forum and simultaneously to promote dialogue with representatives of other world faiths and religions.

The assembly also approved the declaration on ecclesiology proposed by the central committee, in a process organized by the Faith and Order commission. The text – "Called to be the One Church: An invitation to the churches to renew their commitment to the search for unity and to deepen their dialogue" – declares that:

> *Churches in the fellowship of the WCC remain committed to one another on the way towards full visible unity... Our churches have affirmed that the unity for which we pray, hope and work is "a koinonia given and expressed in the common confession of the apostolic faith; a common sacramental life entered by the one baptism and celebrated together in one eucharistic fellowship; a common life in which members and ministries are mutually recognized and reconciled; and a common mission witnessing to the gospel of God's grace to all people and serving the whole of creation".*

Each WCC assembly approves a solemn declaration to the churches and the world. Porto Alegre was no exception. The approved text – "God, in your Grace, Transform the World: Message of the 9th Assembly of the World Council of Churches: An Invitation to Prayer" – was drafted in the form of a solemn poetic prayer, meant to culminate what had been deemed a praying assembly.

See page 1

A consensus assembly

In the interval between the 1998 Harare assembly and Porto Alegre in 2006, the WCC central committee accepted the recommendation of the Special Commission on Orthodox Participation in the WCC to adopt a consensus model of decision-making as an alternative to the parliamentary model traditional in Western nations. The purpose was to develop a culture of dialogue that could elicit the expression of widely varying perspectives regarding the issues in debate and to design a careful process of achieving a common voice while allowing dissent to be registered and respected. Theologically, it is grounded in a view of the church as a sacramental fellowship of dialogue and caring, as the body of Christ in which every member has an intrinsic value in the divine economy.

Prior to the assembly, many delegates were haunted by the question of whether the consensus procedures would allow both for intense dialogue and the achievement of a common robust voice on key issues confronting the member churches of the WCC. At its conclusion, most people seemed inclined to answer the question affirmatively.

42

A process of hearing distinct voices, while inquiring constantly about the reaction of the assembly, was respectful to the wide array of opinions and yet attempted to achieve a meaningful denouement. Debate took place, dissenting opinions were recorded, and decisions were achieved that proved satisfactory to most delegates.

This, however, did not mean that everyone was entirely pleased. Voices of dissent were heard and recorded on several matters, such as the restrictions on inclusive theological language and imagery in the activities of common prayer and the lack of attention, in the declarations, to divisive issues of human sexuality. Some delegates thought that the assembly's final declaration was fine as a prayer but that it was not truly a message because it did not make any reference to specific issues that were afflicting humanity, like the war in Iraq or the Israel-Palestine conflict. These were significant points of dissent. However, the intention to be consensual prevailed while still allowing for dissident voices and ideas to be registered in the official documents.

Elections

The assembly approved the report of the nominations committee electing the 150 members of the central committee and eight WCC presidents. The results were mixed. The goal of electing at least 25% Orthodox members was achieved (26%), but not those of 50% women (42%), 50% lay people (35%) and 25% youth (15%). The plenary session was invaded by dozens of young people who, visibly displeased, protested the gap between promise and fulfillment. Six delegates from diverse Indigenous peoples and one member from the Ecumenical Disabilities Advocacy Network were also elected.

43

See page 434

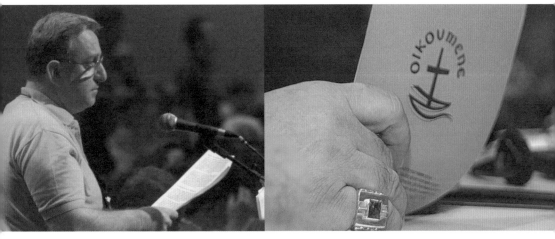

Speaking to the assembly   *Cards to show consensus*

The eight WCC presidents elected were: the Rev. Prof. Dr Simon Dossou, Protestant Methodist Church in Benin (Africa); the Rev. Dr Soritua Nababan, Protestant Christian Batak Church (Asia); the Rev. Dr Ofelia Ortega, Presbyterian-Reformed Church in Cuba (Caribbean/Latin America); Dr Mary Tanner, Church of England (Europe); the Rev. Dr Bernice Powell Jackson, United Church of Christ (North America); Mr John Taroanui Doom, Maòhi Protestant Church (Pacific); Archbishop Anastasios of Tirana and All Albania, Orthodox Autocephalous Church of Albania (Eastern Orthodox); and His Holiness Abune Paulos, Ethiopian Orthodox Tawahedo Church (Oriental Orthodox).

Immediately after the close of the assembly, the new central committee met and elected as moderator of the WCC the Rev. Dr Walter Altmann, president of the Evangelical Church of the Lutheran Confession in Brazil and former president of the Latin American Council of Churches, and as vice moderators Metropolitan Prof. Dr Gennadios of Sassima, of the Ecumenical Patriarchate of Constantinople, and the Rev. Dr Margaretha M. Hendriks-Ririmasse, of the Protestant Church in the Moluccas (Indonesia).

A whirlwind of voices

On February 11 to 13, four different pre-assembly gatherings took place in Porto Alegre. Around 250 youth, 350 women, 50 representatives of Indigenous peoples, and a similar number of affiliates of the Ecumenical Disability Advocates Network (EDAN) met to prepare their specific contributions and requests to the assembly. Symptomatic of the attitude shared by these groups were the words of EDAN

Delegates elect new Central Committee

facilitator Samuel Kabue, who is blind, to fellow Kenyan and WCC general secretary Samuel Kobia: "We will be watching you carefully."

In the main hall of the assembly, a wide variety of advocacy groups established stalls to voice specific messages, distribute literature, sell products and, occasionally, present musical or dramatic activities. Ecological groups, advocates of people suffering with HIV and AIDS, promoters of the ordination of women, EDAN, defenders of Indigenous peoples, pacifists and many others made their presence felt and contributed to the multitude of voices and views that, "like a whirlwind", strongly revolved daily within the assembly.

On the sidewalks of the Pontifícia Universidade, groups of Latin American Indigenous communities sold the crafts beautifully created by their own hands, while choirs and dance groups from different nations expressed musically the plight and hopes of their peoples. There was both serious reflection and joyful celebration in these activities that cut across the rigid schedule of the assembly. There was also, in the official programme, time allotted for regional and confessional meetings.

The event that attracted the most significant press attention was the visit and speech by the president of Brazil, Luiz Inácio Lula da Silva. Lula, as he is affectionately called, praised the WCC for the support it gave to the struggle for democracy and human rights during the epoch of military dictatorship in Brazil (1964-1985) and the shelter it provided for one of the most distinguished Brazilian exiles of those sombre years, Paulo Freire. At the conclusion of his speech, Lula congratulated the assembly for "sharing ideas, taking decisions together, exchanging experiences and strengthening one another spiritually...

See page 354

Ecumenical Disabilities Advocacy Network (EDAN)

continuing the sacred task of keeping alive the flame of fraternity and solidarity between all peoples of the world".

Closing prayers

On the evening of February 23, the Ninth Assembly of the World Council of Churches came to an end with closing prayers. The participants gathered one last time under the giant worship tent at the east end of the campus to hear the Rev. Dr *See page 65* Robina Marie Winbush of the Presbyterian Church (USA) deliver the homily, titled "For the healing of the nations", based on Rev. 22:1-5. She used the imagery of a river, drawn both from holy scripture and from a poem by Langston Hughes, to speak of God's nourishing river of life. The trees growing alongside that river, she said, produce "healing leaves". "Would you consider with me the possibility that God has been whispering to our spirits throughout this assembly, 'I am transforming the world?'" asked the preacher. The service included a prayer of commitment for the newly-elected central committee and ended with a prayer asking for God's blessing:

46

> *May the Triune God grant us grace for transformation,*
> *mercy for salvation, reconciliation for communion,*
> *so that we can fulfill together our common calling to the glory of the*
> *One Father, Son, and Holy Spirit.*

Pre-assembly youth event

Tentative assessment

Though it is too soon for a full evaluation of the significance of the Porto Alegre assembly for the World Council of Churches and the ecumenical movement as a whole, some personal assessments may tentatively be offered.

1. The churches at Porto Alegre reaffirmed their commitment to stay together in the quest for visible Christian communion. The ecclesiological declaration, "Called to be the One Church", and the final assembly message reasserted the quest for the common recognition among churches of their shared baptism, eucharist and ministry, as proposed by the 1982 Faith and Order document at Lima. The acknowledgment by many delegates that it was painful at this stage that their churches are unable to participate together in the sacramental sharing of bread and wine led the assembly to renew its quest for the visible manifestation of God's gift of unity. For, as the late Archbishop of Canterbury William Temple remarked in his celebrated opening sermon of the 1937 Edinburgh Faith and Order world conference, it is precisely the spiritual pain felt by the fragmentation of the Christian koinonia that becomes the intense source of the quest for unity. The Porto Alegre assembly could well have adopted Temple's eloquent words:

> *Our division… is a source to us of spiritual pain… God grant us that we may feel the pain of it, and under that impulsion strive the more earnestly to remove all that now hinders us from receiving together the One Body of the One Lord, that in Him we may become One Body – the organ and vehicle of the One Spirit…*

Closing prayers   *Robina Marie Winbush*

The Porto Alegre assembly also reaffirmed the integral relationship of the three traditional ecumenical concerns: the quest for church unity, the missionary proclamation of the gospel, the prophetic struggle for justice and peace. Unity, mission and justice were again conceived as indissoluble and indispensable dimensions of the ecumenical movement. The pressures to downgrade any of them were resisted.

2. Concerns voiced by the Orthodox churches in Harare seem to have been addressed adequately. Orthodox delegates played a key role at all stages of the assembly, from the opening prayer till the last plenary session. The main proposals of the Special Commission on Orthodox Participation in the WCC were put into action – consensus procedures, amendments to the WCC constitution and rules to include stricter theological and ecclesiological criteria for membership, avoidance of non-biblical, gender-inclusive language for God, the naming of devotional moments as common prayer rather than common worship, the prevention of any attempt to force eucharistic intercommunion – and the entire gathering consistently exhibited an intentional mindfulness of reconciliation and collaboration.

3. The Porto Alegre assembly took place in Brazil, one of the nations where the recent impressive and dramatic growth of the Pentecostal churches and charismatic movements has drastically altered the traditional Latin American religious landscape. The gathering also coincided with the commemoration of the first centennial of the Azusa event, considered by several historians as the trigger and matrix of the extraordinary expansion of Pentecostalism during the last century. Yet there was not much visible advancement in the rapprochement between the WCC and the Pentecostal churches. In the ardent assembly discussion about youth representation in the new central committee, not many delegates noted its most significant deficit: only one of its 150 members, the Rev. Héctor Osvaldo Petrecca, pastor of the Buenos Aires Christian Biblical Church, belongs to a Pentecostal church.

Space was given in several mutirãos to discuss Pentecostalism, but their input to the official assembly was scarce. Most Pentecostal churches are very young, still engaged in the process of drawing the frontiers of their particular ecclesiastical identity and somewhat reluctant to join the ecumenical movement. Many have emerged and developed in a social and ecclesiastical environment of contempt and disdain towards them. This atmosphere has contributed to their tendency towards isolation and their delineation of firm boundaries of separation. Some Pentecostal churches reaffirmed their membership in the WCC; several of their younger theologians were very active in the mutirão; and a few international Pentecostal organizations sent observers. Nevertheless, the predominant Pentecostal attitude towards the assembly was tepid.

It is evident that some older churches mistrust the flamboyant and enthusiastic charismatism of the Pentecostals. They also have voiced concerns about the Pentecostal proselytism that tends to disregard traditional boundaries of ecclesiastical ownership. A new breed of Pentecostal leaders and theologians is emerging, however, for whom the ecumenical movement might become as compelling as it was contemptible for their elders. As in Harare in 1998, the Porto Alegre assembly again mandated that the new central committee seek all possible means of communication and dialogue with the Pentecostal churches.

4. The churches reaffirmed their quest for a common and integral prophetic voice in a world where violence and injustice are overwhelming. An array of global social, political and economic issues was debated. Though many delegates felt that the declarations were not sharp or specific enough (some, for example, wanted the assembly to voice its approval of the US delegation's apology and censure the invasion of Iraq by the United States), in general the traditional prophetic and critical role of the WCC, which has made it a target of several right-wing religious groups, was sustained in its resolutions and declarations on international public issues.

5. The many opportunities provided to elicit ongoing theological conversations were enjoyed and highly praised by most participants. The assembly was a mettlesome bricolage of ideas and perspectives, in the ecumenical conversations, mutirão, bate-papos and the theological café, in the kaleidoscopic form of lectures, round tables, dramatic performances, plastic arts, workshops and seminars, and revolved around all possible issues of serious concern to Christians. One idea sustained and inspired those multiple theological conversations: the unity of the one Church demands an integral process of renewal of all the existing churches. However, the objective of channelling all the varied theological dialogues into assembly resolutions and declarations proved to be a daunting task not entirely achieved.

6. Though there was a serious gap between the initial promises that Porto Alegre was to be a youth-oriented assembly and the results as perceived by young participants themselves, the engagement of young people and their significant contributions should not be underestimated. Young participants were actively present in all the assembly events – mutirão, bate-papos, ecumenical conversations, musical performances and plays. This was the WCC assembly with the highest number of young participants; for the first time an assembly committee was chaired by a young person (the message committee); three young delegates were members of the business committee that monitored daily activities; and the assembly created an ongoing body of youth to strengthen their future participation in the WCC. For many of these young people, including the stewards, the Porto Alegre assembly was their first international ecumenical experience, but will not be their last. One can only hope that they will remember and cherish their time at the assembly, allowing it to serve as a building block for future ecumenical work.

We began this narrative wondering about the possible reaction of the 1948 founders of the World Council of Churches if by any sort of magical temporal transposition they could have observed the 2006 Porto Alegre assembly. Probably the most lasting impression would have been of deep spiritual joy, for despite the many adversities and conflicts, the WCC, as the main embodiment of the ecumenical movement, still kindles in the hearts and minds of many Christians a passion for the unity of Christ's church and the prevalence of peace and justice in God's world. They certainly would have joined the Porto Alegre assembly message in its prayerful appeal:

> *God, in your grace, transform the world.*
> *Transform us in the offering of ourselves*
> *so that we may be your partners in transformation*
> *to strive for the full,*
> *visible unity of the one Church of Jesus Christ,*
> *to become neighbours to all,*
> *as we await with eager longing*
> *the full revelation of your rule*
> *in the coming of a new heaven and a new earth.*
>
> **Amen**

WCC PRESIDENTS ELECTED IN PORTO ALEGRE

WCC presidents

52

Archbishop Anastasios of Tirana and All Albania | *Mr John Taroanui Doom* | *Rev. Dr Simon Dossou* | *Rev. Dr Soritua Nababa.*

| *Rev. Dr Ofelia Ortega* | *Patriarch Abune Paulos* | *Rev. Dr Bernice Powell Jackson* | *Dr Mary Tanner* |

WCC OFFICERS

Rev. Dr Walter Altmann,
Moderator

Metropolitan
Prof. Dr Gennadios of Sassima,
Vice-moderator

Rev. Dr Margaretha M.
Hendriks-Ririmasse,
Vice-moderator

Rev. Dr Samuel Kobia,
General Secretary

OPENING SERMON

ARCHBISHOP ANASTASIOS OF ALBANIA

Archishop Anastasios of Tirana and All Albania is head of the Orthodox Autocephalous Church of Albania and professor emeritus of the National University of Athens. This sermon was delivered at the service of common prayer that opened the Assembly on 14 February 2006.

I. THE TRIUNE GOD'S TRANSFORMATIVE INTERVENTIONS

1. The formulation of our Assembly theme assumes the form of a prayerful petition; if you like, it is a mystical cry, which reveals a sense of profound weakness and intense expectation. It is a contemporary variation of the prayer placed on our lips by Christ Himself: "… your kingdom come, your will be done, on earth as in heaven." It is based on the recognition that, for the transformation of the world, our human thoughts, ideas and abilities are insufficient. Yet, at the same time, it is founded on the conviction that the God, in whom we hope, is not indifferent to human history. God is immediately interested and is able, through His grace, wisdom and power, to intervene and transform the entire universe. God takes the initiative, taking action and assuming the decisive role in universal events.

The faith and experience of the Church with regard to the mystery of God are summed up in the phrase: "The Father through the Son in the Holy Spirit" creates, provides, and saves. God is incomprehensible and inaccessible in His essence. Nevertheless, His presence is perceived in the world through His grace and the manifestation of His glory. Such is the dynamic, creative and transforming energy of the Trinity that is beyond all essence. Grace is the unique gift, which contains all other gifts. It is revealed in all the divine energies. Eastern Christian thought clearly distinguishes between the created universe and the uncreated energies of God. The superessential God is not identified with any created understanding or idea, like the philosophical concept of essence. That which in the final analysis humankind is able to assume is the grace of God.

2. The most surprising transformative intervention occurred in human history when the Word of God was incarnated and assumed human nature – not only human spirit but also matter and, thereby, all of creation, since humanity is its crown. "And the Word became flesh and lived among us, and we have seen His glory, the glory as of a father's only son, full of grace and truth" (John 1:14). All the stages of Christ's life comprise expressions of divine grace as well as of divine glory. During His Transfiguration on Mount Tabor, Jesus revealed the original beauty of humanity created "in the image" of God as well as the concluding splendid glory of humanity "in the likeness" of God.

The sacrifice on the Cross and the resurrection of Christ complete the salvation of the human race by divine grace. "But God, who is rich in mercy ... raised us up with Him and seated us with Him in the heavenly places in Christ Jesus, so that in the ages to come He might show the immeasurable riches of His grace in kindness towards us in Christ Jesus" (Eph. 2:4, 6-7). Amazed before this astonishing gift, St Paul professes: "For by grace you have been saved through faith, and this is not your own doing; it is the gift of God – not the result of works, so that no one may boast" (Eph. 2:8-9). Since that time, what took place ontologically within human nature in the person of Jesus Christ continues with the ongoing presence and energy of the Holy Spirit.

The closing pages of the New Testament illumine the eschatological vision of the Church, describing a universal transformation, "a new heaven and a new earth" (Rev. 21:1). The One seated on a throne proclaims: "Behold, I make all things new." (Rev. 21:5)

What form the transformation of the world will ultimately assume in the future remains a secret of the God of surprises. After all, this is what happened in the past. If human creativity – this divine gift, which we have received – has reserved so many surprises for us, the grace of God holds incomparably more and entirely superb surprises.

The word "grace" was employed by the Seventy in the Greek translation of the Old Testament for the rendering of diverse Hebrew terms. In Greek, the original language of the New Testament, grace "denotes firstly the radiant attraction of beauty, secondly the inner radiance of goodness, and finally the gifts which bear witness to this generosity."[1]

As the energy of the Trinitarian God (Acts 13:43, 14:26; Rom. 5:15; 1 Cor. 1:4, 3:10, 15:10; 2 Cor. 6:1, 8:1, 9:14; Eph. 3:2, 7:7; etc.), grace is referred to in the New

Testament sometimes as "the grace of God", other times as "the grace of our Lord Jesus Christ", and at other times as "the grace of the Holy Spirit". In the conscience of the united Church, grace is the energy of the entire Holy Trinity. As St Athanasius the Great emphasizes: "Grace is singular, deriving from the Father, proceeding through the Son and fulfilled in the Holy Spirit."[2] And elsewhere, he writes: "They have this grace with the participation of the Word, through the Spirit and from the Father."[3]

II. WE ARE CO-WORKERS IN THE TRANSFORMING ENERGY OF DIVINE GRACE

In our petition "God, in your grace, transform the world", the immediate response that we receive is: But I want you to be with me! Your place is not to be spectators of divine interventions and actions, but co-workers. This is a direct consequence of my Incarnation, of the constitution of the Church, of my "mystical Body", where you have freely accepted to become members. All of us, then, who belong to Him have both the privilege and the obligation to share actively in the transformation of the world.

1. Beginning with ourselves. The life in Christ, to which we have been called, is a continuously transformative journey. St Paul advises: "Do not be conformed to this world, but be transformed by the renewing of your minds, so that you may discern what is the will of God – what is good and acceptable and perfect." (Rom. 12:2) "Renewing the mind" is precisely what repentance is about. And it may come through contemplative silence, which leads to the awareness of our nothingness and worthlessness. It is the result of self-criticism regarding the degree of our estrangement from the ideal determined by His will.

What is demanded is a continual gaze upon and search for God. It is not a matter of change once-and-for-all but of an ongoing transformation by the grace of the Spirit. "Now the Lord is the Spirit, ... and all of us ... seeing the glory of the Lord as though reflected in a mirror, are being transformed into the same image from one degree of glory to another, for this comes from the Lord, the Spirit." (2 Cor. 2:17-18) We are speaking of a transformative process, from purification to purification, from repentance to repentance, from virtue to virtue, from knowledge to knowledge, from glory to glory. This is a dynamic movement of unceasing renewal in the grace of the Holy Spirit. As St Gregory of Nyssa explains: a Christian "is ever changing for the better and transforming from glory to glory through daily growth, by always improving and always becoming deified and yet without ever reaching the end of perfection. For true perfection means that one never ceases to grow towards that which is better and never reduces perfection to any limit."[4]

The grace of God shapes the apostolic "being" – as St Paul explains: "By the grace of God I am what I am" (1 Cor. 15:10). And this grace in turn becomes an inexhaustible source of action (Acts 14:26, 15:40). The disciples do not remain satisfied with their personal enjoyment of grace: "And His grace towards me has not been in vain." Grace becomes service, a creative struggle for healing, reconciliation, the spreading of the Gospel for the transformation of all. Yet, St Paul again corrects himself: "Though it was not I, but the grace of God that is with me." (1 Cor. 15:11)

2. The struggle for inner transformation, in accordance with the example of Christ, takes place in the Church. The faithful Christian struggles and is sanctified as a member of the Body of Christ. Consequently, personal renewal and transformation is reflected within the entire community of the Church. "Jesus Christ, who is the same, yesterday, today, and forever (Heb. 13:8), is the head of the Church, which is His Body, sustained by the Holy Spirit, and in this sense the Church cannot sin. Therefore, we do not ask for the 'transformation of the Church'. However, if we are referring to 'the churches', specifically in the sense of communities of believers in history, we know full well that believers sometimes fail to actualize the true being of the Church. It is we sinners, personally and in community, who require transformation."[5]

The transformative journey of our church communities cannot occur on the basis of criteria occasionally proposed by fashion and vogue, but through the guidance of "the Gospel of grace". We have in practice often ascertained the substitution of many of God's commandments by the mentality of the world, by a demonic reversal of the evangelical principles. Instead of the primacy of service, we have craved the primacy of authority; instead of the power of love, the love of the power of this world; instead of respect for others, we have demanded their submission to our opinions and desires. The Church is obliged to remain at every time and in every place what its essence is: namely, the Body of Christ, "the fullness of Him who fills all in all" (Eph. 1:23), word, light, the witness of whom embraces all things with His love, transforming them. All other social and cultural actions are incidental; they are the historical expression and incarnation of love in specific circumstances and conditions.

3. Obviously, however, we cannot become a closed community of "saved ones", isolated from events on the planet. Our responsibility extends to the universe, to the journey of the entire world.

a) Since our Assembly is taking place in Latin America, the issue of poverty assumes absolute priority for all of us who worship and follow Him, who was born and died stressing the dignity of the poor and their inalienable value before God, who came "to bring good news to the poor" (Luke 4:18). In the face of all the poor – the hungry, estranged, and refugees – we are obliged to discern the face of Jesus. Woe to us if, in the 21st century, we again relinquish the initiative for social justice to others, as we have done in past centuries, while we confine ourselves to our opulent rituals, to our usual alliance with the powerful. Woe to us if we permit other forces, with different religious ideas and ambitions, to assume leadership in the struggle to overcome poverty in our world.

In our age, a globally interdependent society is taking shape, and our most fundamental problem is how we might become conscious as Christians of our obligation towards those who are deprived of the most basic goods, as well as our practical solidarity with these people within our cities and our nations, from country to country and from church to church. We can no longer claim ignorance or indifference before the millions of children that live in miserable conditions, before the one billion fellow human beings that are undernourished while another three billion survive on less than two dollars a day.

Before the challenge of economic globalization, which is solely concerned with broadening the market, while levelling cultural and popular diversities, we are called as Christians to respond with enlightened initiatives for a society of understanding, healing, reconciliation and fraternization, based on respect for each human person and each people, promoting mutual understanding and solidarity throughout the planet. We are called to promote daring initiatives and just social struggles, commencing with our own immediate environment, the family, our parish and city, our diocese and region. We are called, moreover, to practice our immediate responsibility within our specific circumstances, keeping the entire world in mind as our broader horizon.

b) On our planet, peace continues to be injured on a daily basis. The peace proclaimed by the New Testament is multidimensional: it is personal and social, yet at the same time it is sanctifying, holistic, and eschatological. With God's grace, we are obliged to struggle so that the visible and invisible conflicts may be transformed and peace may prevail in our immediate and wider environment. St Basil the Great states: "Nothing is more characteristic of a Christian than peacemaking; for that, the Lord promised us the greatest reward"[6]; that is to be called "sons of God".

Of course, peace cannot develop of itself. It is related to other significant values in life. Above all, it is related to justice. An unjust, unlawful world cannot expect peace. Genuine longing for peace on a global, local or personal level, is expressed through struggle for justice. Nevertheless, today, peace and justice have yet another name: development. And all of us, who yearn and pray for the transformation of our world, have a duty to contribute to the development of poorer nations.

c) However, even in nations that appear secure and peaceful, every now and again one observes outbreaks of violence. As a rule, those who are more powerful are also more liable to violence. This is because they have the possibility to impose their self-interested plans in a variety of means, with authoritarian methods, through the violation of information, by electronic and human brainwashing, by use of threat and blackmailing of conscience. Yet violence is not only found where powers are great, nor only where the mass media turn our attention. It is also detected in smaller nations, cities, villages, communities – even religious ones – and indeed wherever people live. Aggression is concealed within every human heart. In beseeching, then, for the transformation of our world, let us make a firm decision to struggle, with the power of the Holy Spirit, to overcome violence wherever we possibly can: in our family and society, as well as in the political and international community.

d) Finally, the ecological destruction provoked by the irrational exploitation of the earth's natural resources is creating serious concerns for the future of our planet. Therefore, Ecumenical Patriarch Bartholomew points out that "whenever we narrow religious life to our own concerns, we overlook the prophetic calling of the Church to implore God and to invoke the Divine Spirit for the renewal of the whole polluted cosmos. Indeed, the entire cosmos is the space within which transformation is enacted."[7] All our efforts in this domain will be productive when they take place in the Holy Spirit, "from whom grace and life come to all creation"[8] as we sing in the Orthodox Church. For "through the Holy Spirit spring the sources of grace, watering and reviving the entire creation."[9] St Gregory Palamas defines the duty and ethos of every faithful with regard to nature, when he states that the heart of a person illumined by the eternal uncreated light "embraces the whole of creation".

III. Inspired by the "Gospel of grace"

1. The manner in which Christ came into the world never ceases to amaze. The Saviour's entire life and preaching revealed the mystical power of humility. Our Lord "emptied Himself, taking the form of a slave, being born in human likeness. And being found in human form, He humbled Himself and became obedient to the point of death – even death on a cross." (Phil. 2:7-8)

Naturally, the ways of modern society are completely contrary to the spirit of humility. What attracts the attention of most is normally what most impresses, whatever is related to glamour, money, and illusion. Even within church circles, in spite of much talk about humility and similar things, people's ways of thinking and patterns of behaviour often betray pride and arrogance. Yet humility in Christ reveals the secret of the spiritual radiance and the transforming power of the Church. The authentic witness of the Church is borne through the centuries by the sincere humility of those dedicated to God. "For great is the might of the Lord; but by the humble He is glorified." (Sirach 3:20) In fact, Holy Scripture insists: "The Lord opposes the proud, but to the humble He shows favour." (Prov. 3:34; James 4:6; 1 Peter 5:5) When, therefore, we pray: "God, in your grace, transform the world", let us not overlook for a moment that the magnet for God's grace is humility. As a way of life, humility nourishes our thought and creativity.

2. What is able, above and beyond all else, to transform everything in the world is the sacrificial offering of love. With the entrance of the divine Word into the historical march of humanity, God's love was revealed in the most shattering manner: it was incarnated. This truth remains the root of Christian revelation, which nurtures every other Christian value and proposal. "For God is love. God's love was revealed among us in this way: God sent His only Son into the world so that we might live through Him." (1 John 4:8-9)

The fundamental mission, then, of the Church is to reveal and make manifest God's love in the here and now, in each moment and every place where it is and acts. In this way, it contributes essentially to the transformation of the world. Otherwise, it resembles "a noisy gong or a clanging cymbal", even if it possesses the gifts of prophesy, knowledge, and faith; even if it understands all the mysteries; even if it is known for great and impressive actions (cf. 1 Cor. 13:1-3).

Each cell of the visible Body of Christ, every Christian, is called to incarnate with his or her entire being and work God's love in the particular circumstances of their life. By denying ourselves and assuming the cross (cf. Matt. 16:24) in our daily life, by supporting those around us in their sorrow, their loneliness, and their need. Whoever is "in God" endeavours to love like God. God's love takes daring initiatives, knows no boundaries, and embraces all things. The conviction that "God is love" comforts us and liberates us from multifaceted fear, from fear of the other, from fear of the different, or from fear of human developments that often appear threatening. Furthermore, God's love comforts us and liberates us from fear of our failure and from fear of the abyss within our soul. "There is no fear in love, but perfect love casts out fear." (1 John 4:18)

Many of those who deny or resist the name "God" indirectly accept His other name: Love. The fact that love constitutes the supreme value of life, the mystical force of the world, is becoming increasingly acceptable even by people of other religious persuasions through diverse experiences and ways of thinking. Love becomes the mystical passage which leads people – perhaps without their even knowing it – closer to the God of love. Ultimately, it comprises the secret to the transformation of the world.

3. Finally, both our prayer and our participation in the transformative evolution of the world must take place within an atmosphere of joy and doxology. Joy is the distinctive fruit of the Holy Spirit (Gal. 5:12). It is the characteristic of those who belong to the kingdom of God (Rom. 14:17; 1 Thess. 1:6). The radiance of essential love calmly triumphs over sin, pain, and contempt. It was, from the outset, the definitive feature of the Christians. With the joy of selfless love, the joy of the perpetual presence of the Risen Christ in the Holy Spirit, the Church proceeds triumphantly amid the world. And it loses the world when it loses this joy. Christ offered us a "joy in fullness" (John 16:24), which no one can remove from us. The experience of this joy determines our daily life. St Paul incites us: "Rejoice in the Lord always; again I will say, Rejoice." (Phil. 4:4) And St Peter also insists: "Believe in Him and rejoice with an indescribable and glorious joy." (1 Peter 1:8)

Our theological reflection and our prayer concerning the transformation of the world are developed more fully within the context of doxology. With the institution of the eucharistic gathering, the Church chose from the very first moment a doxological stance to implore God's grace and proclaim "the Gospel of grace" (Acts 20:24), Christ's "Gospel of glory" (2 Cor. 4:4). Through doxology, in a harmonious synthesis with the beauty of liturgical worship, the Church powerfully expresses the acquisition of the divine grace and the appropriation of the divine glory.

This doxology of the Church is a foretaste and prelude of the eschatological hour, when the universe will be transformed within the absolute manifestation of God's glory. Each creative effort and participation in this – every ministry in the Church, every expression of love – constitutes a ray of God's loving grace and glory. It signifies a sharing in the renewal of the whole of creation.

By way of conclusion, I would like to remind you that the term "grace" in Greek denotes, among other things, the brilliance of beauty and goodness. I often recall the expression of a contemporary computer scientist, who said that just as the laws of physics support the theory that gravity, weight and mass were not distinguished in the first moments of the universe, in a similar way, I think, God did not create the world with truth, beauty and goodness separated from one another.

And I, too, believe that, in the future, this "classical triad of the beautiful, the true and the good, which has itself played a significant role in the history of Christian thought"[10] will contribute to the transformation of the world.

With our gaze firmly set on Christ, our Lord, who is the absolute truth, the boundless beauty and the incarnate love of God in the world, let us contribute, to the best of our ability, with the grace of the Holy Spirit, to the transformation of the world.

Eternal and infinite God! As we behold in ecstasy the boundlessness of the macrocosm that surrounds us and the boundlessness of the microcosm that we inhabit, we kneel humbly before You in prayer. Through Your grace, incarnate in the person of Your Son and unceasingly active through Your Spirit, transform our existence; transform our world into a world illumined by Your truth, by Your beauty, and by Your love.

Notes:
1. Léon Dufour, et. al. (Ed.), *Vocabulaire de Théologie Biblique*, Cerf, Paris, 1974, p.1.
2. Epist. ad Serapion, 1:14, PG 26.565B.
3. Three speeches against Arianos, PG 25.29A.
4. To Olympios, About perfections, Greek Fathers of the Church, Gregory Nyssa, vol. 8, Thessaloniki, 1980, p. 422.

5. Metropolitan Gennadios of Sassima (Ed.), *Grace in Abundance: Orthodox Reflections on the Way to Porto Alegre*, WCC, Geneva, 2005, p.4.
6. Epist. 113, PG 32.528.
7. "*Transformation calls for metanoia*", address on the theme of the WCC 9th Assembly.
8. Paraklitiki, Sunday Matins (Orthros), Third Tone.
9. Ibid.
10. J. Pelikan, *Jesus through the Centuries*, Yale University Press, New Haven, 1985, p.7.

FOR THE HEALING OF THE NATIONS

CLOSING SERMON ON REVELATION 22:1-5

ROBINA MARIE WINBUSH

Rev. Dr Robina Marie Winbush is director of the Department of Ecumenical and Agency Relationships of the Presbyterian Church (USA). This sermon was preached at the service of common prayer that closed the Assembly on 23 February 2006.

65

To the Moderator, Vice Moderators, Presidents, General Secretary and staff, delegates, representatives, observers, friends, my sisters and brothers in Christ and creation, I greet you this afternoon in the name of and with the awesome joy of Jesus – the One who is, now and forever, the Head of the Church.

Would you join me in prayer?

Hide your servant daughter behind the cross, that your glory might come forth, your people might be blessed, and your healing leaves might emerge; in the name of the one who is the Living Word, Jesus the Christ, we dare to pray and I dare to preach.
Amen.

I've known rivers:
I've known rivers ancient as the world and older than the flow of human blood
in human veins.
My soul has grown deep like the rivers.

I bathed in the Euphrates when the dawns were young.
I built my hut by the Congo and it lulled me to sleep.
I looked upon the Nile and raised the pyramids above it.
I heard the singing of the Mississippi when Abe Lincoln went down to New Orleans,
and I've seen its muddy bosom turn all golden in the sunset.
I've known rivers.
Ancient, dusky rivers.
My soul has grown deep like the rivers.[1]

In this classic poem by Langston Hughes, "The Negro Speaks of Rivers", Hughes writes to remind a people who had been enslaved that their history began long before 1619, when their ancestors who had been snatched from their homelands survived the horrors of the Middle Passage and were brought in chains to the United States, the Caribbean, Europe, and Brazil. He writes to remind them that theirs is not a legacy of enslavement, but that their history began along the rivers of Africa, and that they were connected to a people and carried within their spiritual DNA the rich resources of a people and land from whom they had been separated.

As we prepare to leave Porto Alegre and the 9th Assembly of the World Council of Churches, concluding a week of phenomenal worship; edifying Bible studies; challenging plenaries; long committee meetings and business sessions; motivating offerings in the mutirão; meeting, greeting and networking with sisters and brothers of a common faith and common family; we pause for just one more opportunity to see if there is one more "word from the Lord". Something that we can carry home with us – not another piece of paper, not a wristband or souvenir, not another book or media resource, but something we can carry deep within our spiritual reservoir that will allow the energy, the renewal, and the commitments not to be lost in the busyness and routines of our lives when we return home.

I was initially drawn to the Revelation text because of the baptismal and eucharistic images and the eschatological themes of a new and transformed world. I thought it would be an appropriate ending to an assembly that had prayed and sought to understand the transforming power of God. What greater transformation than a vision of the New Jerusalem and the eschatological promises given to us through John's vision!

John, the writer of Revelation, has been exiled to an island called Patmos. He writes to a people living under persecution and domination by the Roman Empire, telling them that their current reality is not the definitive word of God. They are part of a larger, cosmic plan, and he writes to remind them that theirs is not the

seduction of the empire, but ultimately the victory of the Divine and reign of Christ.
Nestor Miguez notes:

> *Revelation is written and originally read in a situation of powerlessness. John*
> *of Patmos and his readers live in a situation in which they are the subjects of*
> *an imperial power that admits no dissent ... The small communities of*
> *Christians in Asia Minor do not constitute any real challenge to Roman power,*
> *but if they manifest any kind of symbolic opposition to the Emperor's claim to*
> *unchecked dominion they are in trouble. And that is the case in Revelation.*[2]

Miguez notes that "when read under that condition Revelation gives a message that
is quite different from its use by the powerful and mighty."[3] Miguez suggests the original intention of Revelation as a challenge to imperial power was co-opted when the
Christian church became the Church of the Empire and the missionary enterprise
became the partner (willing or not) of the expansion of western culture and power.[4]

So we approach the Revelation of Jesus to John on the island of Patmos, both as
an eschatological promise of what is to come and as a socio-political-religious critique of the Roman Empire and the empty claims of empire over the eternal assur-
ances of the God of creation and the resurrected Christ who reigns in victory. John
writes of the collusion of systems of economic, military, cultural, and, yes, religious
powers that wage war against the Divine, the faithful, and all of creation that have
not bowed down to the images of the empire's temporal glory. He reminds the
churches of Asia Minor and, yes, the church universal, that their primary – no, our
only – allegiance must be to the Lamb who was slain, but now reigns upon the
throne. We must resist the temptation to be co-opted by systems of domination and
exploitation. In the midst of cosmic chaos and global imperial systems, it is a call –
a reminder – that we are never to abandon our posts as faithful witnesses to the resurrected Christ – the living Lord. Ours is never to be an easy, comfortable relationship with empire, but a relationship that measures the work of empire by the self-
sacrificing standards of the cross. Brian Blount suggest that:

> *Revelation craves witnesses as engaged, resistant, transformative activism*
> *that is willing to sacrifice everything in an effort to make the world over into*
> *a reality that responds to and operates from Jesus' role as ruler and savior of*
> *all.*[5]

Yes, to read Revelation is to understand with powerful images Paul's words to the
church at Ephesus: "For we wrestle not against flesh and blood, but against princi-
palities, against powers, against the rulers of the darkness of this world, against spiritual wickedness in high places."[6]

67

Sue Davies also reminds us, "While John's apocalypse offers fertile ground for identifying the death-dealing powers of our own day, he also affirms in the strongest terms God's sovereignty over human and earthly history."[7] It is this affirmation that I invite you to explore with me this afternoon as we finish packing our spiritual bags to go home.

Yes, Revelation is filled with eschatological hope. However, what if we were to consider that Revelation is not simply a vision of what is to come, but a vision of what is already? I have been blessed to have travelling with me a dear sister who has not been involved in the intricacies of this assembly. Whenever I get frustrated or bothered by something that has happened, she is always good to remind me, "God is not finished. God is still moving." We don't have to wait for God to be sovereign – God is sovereign now! John shares with us a glimpse of what is already in the realms beyond our reality and the limitations of our current comprehension. It becomes an invitation to live as though the reign of God and the community of God's beloved kin-dom are already.

When I was a child, there was a simple song we used to sing in my home church, Bethany Presbyterian in Columbus, Ohio. I must admit that we didn't sing it often during formal Sunday worship, but it could be heard during revival or mid-week services or any time we would dare to allow ourselves to feel the freedom and power of the Holy Spirit. The words were very simple,

God is already here. Can't you feel [God's] presence? God's already here.
All you have to do is open up your heart, for God is already here.

It carried a simple, but profound message. The God we serve is not far off in some distant realm, but because of the grace of God in the incarnation event, God has chosen to make God's dwelling in the midst of human reality. It isn't that our worlds are perfected, but in the very messiness and problems of human reality, God chooses to dwell.

We have been praying throughout this 9th Assembly, "God, in your grace, transform the world". It is a prayer that carries, as most prayers do, a confession of faith. It is a confession that we believe that the world needs to be transformed. It is a confession that we believe that the world can be transformed. It is a confession that we believe it is the free gift of God's love we know as grace that will accomplish the transformation. It is a powerful prayer and a powerful confession.

God, through the prophet Isaiah, assures us that before we call, God will answer us, and while we are yet speaking, God hears us.[8]

Would you consider with me the possibility that God has been whispering to our spirits throughout this assembly, "I am transforming the world"?

We are meeting in the same location as the World Social Forum that has previously declared, "Another World is Possible". As people of faith – as those who claim the name of the anointed one, Jesus of Nazareth – we come to give spiritual testimony to that truth. Another world really is possible.

The final vision that John records is of a world in transformation. John writes of a river not contaminated with the excess waste of the empire or the waste of cosmic catastrophes, but of a life-giving river that nourishes the earth and all creation. It is a river that cannot be privatized or exploited for the benefit of a few. Unlike Ezekiel's vision, John's vision of the river is not restricted to the Temple as God's dwelling place, but it flows freely and directly from the throne of God. Could it be possible that "the river which makes glad the city of God", as described by the psalmist, is not limited or controlled by our ecclesiastical houses, but is the free-flowing power of the Spirit of God in our midst? Could it be possible that we who are washed in the baptismal waters of God's grace and nurtured with the very life force of the Lamb – the body and blood of the crucified and resurrected Christ – are invited to be participants in God's transforming work of creation?

Unlike the Genesis narrative, the tree of life is no longer inaccessible to humanity, but as it grows alongside the river, it draws from the free-flowing Spirit that comes from the presence of God in the midst of the city. Because the tree draws from the river of life, its fruit is plentiful and sufficient. Its leaves are filled with the medicinal qualities that heal and transform nations.

Tell me, have you seen any leaves lately that God is using to heal nations and transform a world?

Before we arrived in Porto Alegre, a small group of us stopped by Salvador, Bahia. We were privileged to visit with some powerful women related to the Institute for Theological Education in Bahia (ITEBA). They have formed a group called YAMI – symbolized by cactus growing fruit in the desert. Theirs is a commitment to give voice and agency to black, indigenous, and poor women of northeastern Brazil. They invited us to visit a community centre the women are building on land that had been used as a "quilombo". Quilombos were highly organized communities of Africans that refused to be enslaved when brought to Brazil. This particular quilombo was named after a black woman named Zeferina, who was known for her strong resistance to oppression. You didn't mess with this sister! The

Zeferina Quilombo community centre is being built to give voice and agency to the women and children of the surrounding community so that they can take control of their own lives. I don't know about you, but to me that's a healing leaf!

In the nightmare of the HIV/AIDS pandemic, instead of waiting for the moral consciousness of northern and western pharmaceutical companies to be awakened, I am told that Brazil produces medicines that can be made available for use in countries that cannot afford them. That's a healing leaf!

When Cindy Sheehan, a mother whose son was killed in the war on Iraq mobilizes other mothers and families to openly challenge the Bush administration on their corrupt war policies, that's a healing leaf!

When a former US military base in Cuba is transformed into a university, training over 7,000 medical doctors in Latin America, that's literally a healing leaf.

When Palestinian Christian youth tell us they cannot be silent in the face of occupation and oppression, that they must teach hope and commit themselves to be agents of hope in the midst of violence, that's a healing leaf!

When one young person in Europe believes that they can make a difference and organizes an international movement of youth and young adults who are committed to be change makers, that's a healing leaf!

When we experience the growth of Christianity in Africa and Asia and Latin America, and the paradigm shift from a Christianity defined by the rich and powerful, that's a healing leaf!

When the World Council of Churches can break the silence and the denial and begin to talk openly and honestly about issues of human sexuality and facilitate dialogue between and within our churches, that's a healing leaf!

When the Ecumenical Disability Advocates Network can help us redefine our understanding of healing and wholeness, and while everyone may not have the same physical and mental abilities – that all are created in the image of God – that's a healing leaf!

I could go on, but I suspect everyone here could testify to the healing leaves that you have experienced and seen.

There is a question I need to ask you before you go.

God is transforming the world: Are you willing to be a leaf on the tree of life, whom God uses for the healing of the nations? Are you willing to resist bowing down to the temporal gods of exploitation and domination and allow your life and your churches to be used for the healing of the nations and transformation of the world?

Remember that the power and strength to be a leaf does not belong to you. It is a result of being attached to the tree of life whose roots are watered by the river of life that flows from the throne of God and the Lamb. When you grow weary and tired, rest assured that the river of life will nourish you. You will be reminded that you are connected to something far greater than your current reality, and the words of Langston will still speak to us: "I've known rivers – ancient, dusky rivers. My soul has grown deep like the river."

Notes:
1. *The Collected Poems of Langston Hughes*, published by Alfred A. Knopf, Inc. Copyright © 1994 the Estate of Langston Hughes. Permission requested.
2. Nestor O. Miguez, *Plurality, Power and Mission: Intercontextual Theological Explorations on the Role of Religion in the New Millennium*, ed. by Philip Wickeri, with Janice K. Wickeri and Damayanthi M. A. Niles, Council for World Mission, London, 2000, p.239.
3. Ibid.
4. Ibid.
5. Brian K. Blount, *Can I Get a Witness: Reading Revelation through African American Culture*, Westminster John Knox, Louisville, 2005, p.38.
6. Ephesians 6:12 KJV.
7. Susan E. Davies, *The Accra Confession: A View From the Belly of the Beast*. While here in Porto Alegre, Sue shared with me this paper, which was presented at a World Alliance of Reformed Churches consultation on Women and Globalization in August 2005, in Jamaica.
8. Isaiah 65:24.

Plenary "God, in Your Grace, Transform the World"

Thoughts and reflections on the Theme: "God, in Your Grace, Transform the World"

Leandro Bosch

Rev. Joseph (Leandro) Bosch, a delegate of the Ecumenical Patriarchate of Constantinople to the Assembly, is pursuing doctoral studies in Rome. This reflection was prepared for the "theme plenary" on 21 February 2006 in which the speakers were interviewed as a panel, each addressing a different dimension of the Assembly theme.

Introduction

Today's world with its convulsions could be characterized as a complex maelstrom of changes and transformations, which perhaps form one of the many-faceted peaks of its essentially multiform nature. These changes and transformations, as can be observed, come one after another and have one outstanding feature: the giddy pace driving them on and accompanying these changes that are taking place at all levels and in all areas of human life in post-modern society. We are thus experiencing constant changes at the economic, technological, cultural and social levels and, we must admit, at the religious level as well. Of necessity, humans seek to change all that has become outdated and is not equal to their high expectations, all that has consequently become an obstacle or barrier to the attainment of their aims, all that has inevitably completed its task and must now disappear in its present form so as to make way for a form more appropriate to meet present-day demands. Thus, individuals, who are anxious and even bold, are not passive links in the living chain of humankind, on the receiving end of strong pressures caused by changes in their surrounding world. They themselves are the authors and architects of the changes and alterations taking place in all aspects of life with the aim of improving it. What we thus see are human beings who are fundamentally active, energetic, diligent, prepared and expectant in face of the changes that they themselves are producing. They are, however, at the same time anxious and often fearful of the consequences of change, which does not always produce the favourable solution that they themselves have planned. In reality, not all the changes produced by humankind today have happy results: hence nature's violent reaction to the harm done to it; hence humankind's reaction against itself owing to the profound worldwide imbalances arising out of arbitrary political, economic and thus social change: famine, war, terrorism, social inequality, racism, trade in living organs, trade in children, drugs, and further numberless scourges afflicting post-modern society as a result of the changes that it itself has brought about, unavoidably or avoidably, knowingly or unknowingly, deliberately or accidentally. These changes, and their resulting methodology, manifest themselves and have repercussions on individuals and contemporary society producing controversial results, very often approaching, almost inevitably, the maximum opposite extremes of benefit or damage to individuals and their environment, since today's world is easily thrown off balance by these changes. Meanwhile, humankind and the cosmic order are increasingly at odds with each other in face of changes that are a damaging attack on the natural rhythm and nature of the life of each.

Within this convulsed and controversial world, and also over against it, we Christians also thirst for change, for transformation, but not according to the pattern of this age (John 17:16). Our desires are not according to the flesh, but according to the spirit. And so we have been brought together by divine providence for these days of blessing in this beautiful land in our diversity, yes, but first and foremost in unity, so that we may lift up our voices in prayer, or rather in a cry arising from our inmost being: "God, in your grace, transform the world!"

METHODOLOGY

Since this is an examination of the theme from the viewpoint of the Orthodox teaching of the Greek Fathers, it is necessary for me to be explicit about my theological presuppositions. They can be presented as distinctions, which are the key to understanding and interpreting the theme. These distinctions are:

The distinction between the uncreated and what is created.

The distinction between the essence of Godhead and the divine energies.

The distinction between the oneness and the distinctions within the Godhead.

The distinction of the creation into an intelligible and visible world.

The distinction between essence and energy in the world of creatures.

OBJECTIVES

My aim is to bring out the following aspects of the transformation undergone by the created world through its participation and experience in the history of the divine economy, in the drama of revelation and consequently in its experience of the divine energies.

FROM THE UNCREATED
A THREEFOLD VISION

The process of transforming and perfecting creation is necessarily closely dependent on divine providence, which rules, governs, guides and brings to fulfillment the positive process of change from what was created out of nothing at the beginning of its existence, passing through redemption in Christ, up to the second coming of Christ. These three stages – creation, redemption and the second coming (*parousia*) – provide the historic framework and also the divine framework of this process towards perfection, which is taking place in the created world. These three pillars, then, reveal in the same way the trinitarian nature of divine action upon the created world and, consequently, the trinitarian stamp on this process of transformation from the first things (*protology*) to the last things (*eschatology*).

THE CHRISTOLOGICAL COORDINATES OF TRANSFORMATION

If the process of transformation is trinitarian in nature, then it must necessarily also be, according to the Eastern Orthodox tradition, Christological in nature. The process of transformation has as its beginning in the embodiment of the *logos* – the *asarkos logos* – in the priesthood of the Old Testament. It has its pivotal point in the events of the incarnation, death, resurrection, ascension and enthronement of Jesus Christ at the right hand of the Father. Finally, it reaches its consummation in the glorious second coming of the Saviour at the *parousia*.

It can thus be seen how the process of transformation of the created world from its beginning to its end is necessarily in harmonious relation with the Christ-mystery, Christ himself being the beginning, the fulfillment and the goal of this transformation, i.e. *from* where it begins, *in* where it reaches its fulfillment, and *towards* where it comes to an end. Christ is thus the actual prototype of transformation. We are thus able to call it "Christification", or, following the Greek Fathers, "divinization".

THE PNEUMATOLOGICAL NATURE OF TRANSFORMATION

If this process is Trinitarian in nature and thus Christological, it has of necessity also to be pneumatological. The Holy Spirit is the creator of the universe, governs creation, makes all creatures divine, is the foremost guide of existence, life, wisdom and sanctification. The *Paraclete*, who proceeds from the Father and rests upon the Son, and through the Son indwells the whole of creation. By the Holy Spirit all is created, receives being, is sustained and sanctified.[1] It is the Holy Spirit who carries forward the process of transformation, jointly with the Father and the Son, in each one of the historical divinely indwelt stages referred to above: creation, redemption, *parousia*. There is however more: the Holy Spirit's action, like that of the Father and the Son, is constantly present in this ongoing ascent of humanity from the human condition towards divinity, becoming firstly human to enable humankind to attain divinization by grace.

FROM THE CREATED WORLD
THE COSMIC PLAN OF TRANSFORMATION

At the cosmic level, transformation is constantly taking place in accord with the divine economy as God disposes, towards the mysterious fulfillment of the universal divine order, which is ceaselessly being perfected until the fullness of the ages and of all things is attained in the awesome second coming of the divine Christ. This transformation process, as can be easily deduced, takes place at a universal level and depends solely on divine providence – or "economy", as the Greek Fathers called it, which is the mighty flow of the uncreated divine energies – or "emanations" – in which all created beings participate by the mere fact that they exist and live, i.e. the energies that confer being and life. Thus the whole creation – both the part of it endowed with reason and the part not – shares in the divine energies and each one of them evolves, or undergoes positive change, according to the ontological structure and form of existence proper to each of them, and consequently in accord with its capacity to receive. It is highly important to be clear that this transformation, or mutation, takes place both in beings not endowed and those endowed with reason, who share in the divine energies by virtue of being or being alive, or both, since there exists a structure of being that determines this development: they are beings created out of nothing, *ex nihilo*, i.e. by change. Thus, of necessity, they must mutate, or be transformed.[2]

TRANSFORMATION AT THE LEVEL OF PERSONS

We are by nature at the level of rational beings, humankind, created in the image and likeness of God. Transformation at this level takes place within parameters different from those of the foregoing level – although it also includes them – owing to the peculiar conditions and ontological structure belonging to persons and their consequent perfectibility. Consequently, since human beings are endowed with reason, they are also necessarily endowed with freedom – with free will.[3] They are beings with the possibility of change. Human beings change, not only in their bodies (as do those beings not endowed with reason), but also as a result of the choices that they make by virtue of their freedom. Although humans cannot extricate themselves from participating in the uncreated energies relevant to their existence and life, since these lie outside the sphere of their freedom, they are able to resist those energies that produce wisdom and divinization, since they have a direct effect on their rationality and not only on them as living beings.[4] Thus, human beings, as free beings endowed with reason, change or are transformed positively or negatively according to the choices that they make. They can take the direction leading nowhere, and thus disappear, or they can take the direction leading to the Creator and be divinized, become divine by grace through drawing on the uncreated energies. At this point, we need to concentrate our attention on the word used by the Fathers, *synergia*, which will help us to understand this process of positive transformation, from *einai* (being) to *eu einai* (well being). There must thus be constant collaboration – *synergia* – between the human and the divine. The initial stage in this collaboration is acceptance of the divine invitation, and from then on a consequent coexistence of human freedom and will with the divine. In that way, human beings, and with them all created beings, begin to conquer the upward path, the mountain that Moses had to climb to reach the presence of God, knowledge of God (*teognosia*) and participation in God (*metoche*), according to the Eastern Orthodox mystical literature, passing through the various stages involved in aspiring to the life above. This upward movement is also called *ascesis*, or spiritual exercise, since in it human beings exert themselves to experience the divine, and thus in their whole being become formed in the divine image.[5]

THE STAGES OF HUMAN TRANSFORMATION IN THIS PROCESS: METANOIA, PURIFICATION, ENLIGHTENMENT

The process of transformation, which is also called healing, or *terapia* (therapy), begins with purifying the heart, moves on to its being restored to its natural state of enlightenment, and then the whole person begins to be perfected beyond their natural capacities by the body and soul being glorified by the uncreated glory of God (*shekinah*). Following the scheme adopted by St Isaac Syrus, I propose to examine first the stage of *metanoia*.[6] God, the supreme invisible centre of all worth, presides over the whole process of:

Metanoia, transformation of the heart, leading upwards to...

Purification, catharsis of the passions, leading upwards to...

Enlightenment, attainment of the normal state, leading upwards to...

Glorification, perfection in Christ, divinization or *theosis*.

Metanoia, as Vladimir Lossky makes clear, must not only be the beginning of the process but an ongoing state throughout the whole process.[7] *Metanoia* is thus not merely one stage, but a constant posture vis-à-vis the Creator. *Metanoia* is not simply repentance, nor even penitence. It is transformation (*metamorphosis*), regeneration and new birth. According to Lossky, *metanoia* is "the gateway to grace".[8] Confronted with this "gateway of grace", human beings must turn with all their will towards the One who bestows grace through prayer. The process of healing, attainment of the normal state and perfection cannot be undertaken without prayer, since prayer is the most intimate link between God and humans. At its different levels – praxis and theory – prayer is the common denominator in all the various stages of healing.

Purification is the stage involving release from our passions and consequently the purifying of the heart. Once that release is attained through the stage of purification, the *noetic* system attains its normal state and thus follows the stage of enlightenment. In this phase, the individual sees God, but not face to face. The enlightened individual sees God vaguely, as if in a mirror, "now we see but a poor reflection as in a mirror" (I Cor. 13:12). Paul, also referring to this period writes, "now I know in part" (1 Cor. 13:12). The enlightened person is a child, "when I was a child, I talked like a child, I thought like a child, I reasoned like a child" (I Cor. 13:11).

However, on attaining glorification, he becomes adult, "when I became a man, I put childish ways behind me" (I Cor. 13:11). Now he sees God face to face, "then I shall know fully, even as I am fully known" (I Cor. 13:12). On becoming enlightened, the individual does not know Christ, but is known by Christ. But, on attaining glorification, individuals know as they are known, i.e. perfectly, since seeing or knowing Christ is seeing or knowing above and beyond one's own natural ability to see and know. Thus, paradoxically, individuals see and know without seeing or knowing, since they are in effect seen and known by the Lord of Glory.

Glorification is the result of the *noetic* system achieving normality. Divinization is the end of the healing process. The person who is glorified is able to contemplate Christ in the uncreated glory of his Father. Only those who are cured of love of self, the product of the disorder in the *noetic* system, will be capable of contemplating and participating in the uncreated glory of Christ in the coming age. St Isaac notes in this regard, "on acquiring absolute purity, the soul's movement shares in the energies of the Holy Spirit." Its nature remains in ecstatic movement, paradoxically passively active, with no memory of material things, in *apatheia*. In effect, as the spirit descends from the mind to the heart, individuals cease to be enslaved to their environment and are no longer distracted or enthralled by things of the earth. Every human faculty, now divinized, is directed towards the vision of the uncreated glory of Christ. The glory of God is present everywhere pervading the creation with its divinizing power. This uncreated glory is also present in our hearts and is available to purify and divinize us. However, not everyone responds to or accepts its life-giving transforming activity.

Once the union between the uncreated and the created is achieved love is healed. It no longer seeks itself, but is disinterested. As St Simeon the New Theologian puts it, the heart burns with compassion and the whole of creation is the object of love, an occasion for loving. And this occurs simply because it can contemplate Christ and his immaterial uncreated Glory permeating all created things regardless of whether or not they accept the action of that glory. Those who are glorified are already living in the age to come and thus become perfect beyond all known limits. The heart is enlarged through the warmth of the spirit's prayer, the force that unites heart to spirit, the force that inspires us to observe God's commandments with great delight and ease.[9]

God is an unfathomable mystery for humans and is united with them only through God's uncreated energies when humans see God face to face in this glorified state. According to St Maximus the Confessor, who in this regard is developing the thinking of Evagrius Ponticus, to know the mystery of the Trinity in its fullness is to enter into perfect union with God, achieve divinization of the human person, i.e. to enter into the divine life, into the very life of the Holy Trinity, to share in the divine nature – in the divine energy and not, of course, in its *physis* or essential nature – as expressed by St Peter (I Pet. 1:4).

CONCLUSION

The process of transformation in the created world begins in the very act of creation itself by which God creates out of a substance different from God's substance. God brings into being out of non-being, and not out of God's essence, beings that are of a different substance from the Godhead. That is the principle of transformation, which necessarily passing through the redemptive events of incarnation, passion, death, resurrection, ascension and enthronement of Christ, reaches its fulfillment in the second coming of Christ at the end of this dimension of creation. The divine historical events underlying this process of transformation are creation, redemption and *parousia*. They must be seen together in their completeness as an integral whole. They must never be regarded as separate events or phases, but as the dynamic continuous activity of the divine economy on the creation.

Thus humankind, and with it the whole of creation, freely and dynamically (and dramatically by virtue of the pivotal events referred to above) shares in the uncreated divine energies, which are guiding the process to its complete fulfillment in the end days. Thus, in constant cooperation with divine grace, we look for the day of the coming of the new heavens and the new earth (Rev. 21:1), of the heavenly Jerusalem (Rev. 21:2), which will be the completion of the plan that the Father had from the beginning, to bring all things together under Christ by the Holy Spirit (Eph. 1:10). Therefore we cry out, "God, in your grace – and with our collaboration, our *synergia* – transform the world." Therefore we cry, "Maranatha, come, Lord Jesus!"

Notes:
1. John of Damascus, *Exposición de la fe*, Ciudad Nueva, Madrid, 2003, p.54.
2. Ibid, pp.142, 143.
3. Ibid, p.142.
4. Professor Matsoukas concludes that humans have access to the energy that operates reason in a way that is not free as the two previous energies. If we regard this energy not only as operating reason but also as operating wisdom,

we can see that it operates similarly from the level of logic that it initiates, and then it can be regarded as operating once human freedom is conferred, since human freedom puts it into operation and seeks perfection through wisdom. It can thus be regarded in both ways. When it makes logical beings, it is participated in without freedom. When it makes wise logical beings, it is participated in by virtue of freedom.

5. The word *ascesis* must in no way be understood as referring to or applicable to an exclusively monastic setting. *Ascesis* is not only a product of monastic life. *Ascesis* is the way to be followed by all Christians in the pursuit of divinization, of union with their Creator and Perfector. Ascesis is simply life in the Spirit, which does not have to be lived in a monastery or in the desert, but in all places and forms where and how the Spirit itself guides them.

6. So as to understand the rich meaning of the Greek word *metanoia*, we need to examine its etymology. The word is made up of two parts, the first being a preposition, *meta* meaning "beyond" or "after". It refers to the distance between what something was and what it now is after changing, after being transformed. The second part is a noun, *nous* and is the English word "mind" or "spirit". *Metanoia* is thus a change of the spirit, a profound change in one's inner disposition, which is reflected in one's outward aspect. It is a change of attitude, a change of feelings. Is this *metanoia* then the same as repentance? Not exactly. Repentance is a phase of *metanoia*, which is an ongoing state in humans. *Metanoia* is not a conscience burden for faults committed, let alone remorse, since where remorse exists, it is impossible for repentance to exist, let alone *metanoia*. *Metanoia* involves complete knowledge and acceptance of one's own weaknesses, the cause of the fault, the object of the wrongful act, its intention and the resultant product or consequences. However, the light of the Father's love, who is waiting with open arms for his sons and daughters to return after having squandered their inheritance, attracts or draws on the soul that has moved on from (*meta*), its former state or initial fault, and the spirit (*nous*) is being enlightened by the shining light of forgiveness and remission. *Metanoia* is thus the result of a synergy between the sinful individual and the divine redeemer.

7. Vladimir Lossky, *Teología mística de la Iglesia de Oriente*, Herder, Barcelona, 1982, p.152.

8. Ibid, p.151.

9. "I will run in the way of your commandments, since you enlarge my heart." (Ps. 119:32).

Plenary "God, in Your Grace, Transform the World"

Thoughts and reflections on the Theme: "God, in Your Grace, Transform the Earth"

Carmen Lansdowne

Ms Carmen Lansdowne, a delegate to the Assembly, is a member of the United Church of Canada, preparing for pastoral ministry in rural Saskatchewan. This reflection was prepared for the "theme plenary" on 21 February 2006 in which the speakers were interviewed as a panel, each addressing a different dimension of the Assembly theme.

"Man is above, outside, and against nature. Man is part and product of nature. These two visions of man... represent the two contrasting philosophies of our time." – Mario Palmieri

This thought, articulated by Palmieri in the early 20th century, continues to hold true. Perhaps the scales have been unevenly weighted: more than focusing on our being part and product of nature, humankind has focused on being above, outside, and against nature. We have objectified, violated, oppressed and negated the earth. Not only have we been perpetrators of destruction in the name of development and progress, but we have done it despite warning signs that foreshadow the disruption of the delicate ecological balance, which supports life on earth.

I speak from the context of having grown up in North America. Not all cultures or societies share the Western worldview of economic development through domination of resources. Sadly, the world I see through 30 year-old eyes is taking lessons from the economic superpowers and their reckless endangerment of the delicate balance of life in God's creation.

This assembly's focus on "Water" as an environmental concern, as an acknowledgment of the basic dignities necessary to human life, as a symbolic metaphor used to express our faith in the Christian tradition, leads us to the impossibility of further ignoring our relationship with the earth. The call for the WCC programme emphasis on water states that reasons for the present water crisis include, "increased and unsustainable agricultural and industrial use of water, deforestation and land degradation that seriously change the water cycle, over-consumption and waste, pollution and population growth". Every one of these factors listed is the result of human behaviour affecting the earth. To pray to God for grace to transform the earth requires the ability to be accountable for our part as humankind in creating an earth that needs to be transformed.

Ecological theology has been influenced by feminist and liberation theologies. Feminist theologies would state that in order to act with integrity and justice with regard to the earth, we must stop making the earth an objectified "other" and instead allow the earth to become a subject, just as we are subjects. This subject-to-subject interaction is the basis for a sound ethical treatment of the earth – one which will embody justice without the power imbalance of humankind always acting against or on-behalf-of the earth. Renowned theologian Sallie McFague has this to say about Christian nature spirituality:

> *To those who say, "But Jesus did not extend this love to nature" we reply, "But neither did he extend it explicitly to slaves, women, or people of colour." Christians in subsequent generations have done so, however, because "the oppressed" change over time. If God the redeemer is concerned for the well-being of all creation, then we have to extend the line we have drawn which puts us* within *the circle of divine concern and the rest of creation* outside. And we must do this, first of all, for theological reasons. It is what Christian praxis demands. We do not do it because unless we care for nature, humans cannot survive or because Christianity had better get on the environmental bandwagon, but because commitment to the God of Jesus Christ demands it. A Christian nature spirituality is the logical next step away from a tribal God toward the universal God, away from a God concerned with "me and my kind", toward the One concerned with the entire creation. (Sallie McFague,* Super, Natural Christian, *Fortress Press, Minneapolis, 1997, page 12.)*

The ways in which we objectify the earth are infinite. The persistent worldview that humans are "above, outside, and against nature" has allowed us to take from God's creation at an unprecedented rate. We have created environmental catastrophes of which we even still cannot begin to comprehend the magnitude. This is becoming common knowledge. The awareness that something must change is juxtaposed against the belief (which has not significantly altered) that God has given humankind dominion over the earth. It is true that the book of Genesis states that people should have dominion over the earth. A quick look to the dictionary will define dominion as the exclusive right to have "control over". But a second definition will state that dominion can be a self-governing entity within a larger whole. Perhaps this is the definition which we ought to move towards. The earth has powerful abilities to regenerate, to recreate and to resurrect. Recognizing these powers may allow us to enter into renewed relationship with the earth recognizing that God is, and has been, always answering our prayer. If the earth is constantly transforming, then perhaps we need to pay attention to how our prayers are already being answered.

I acknowledge that the word "dominion" as translated from the Hebrew does, in fact, mean to have rule over. The western world, however, has appropriated that term for the exclusive use of economic development, when it was written as a liberation theology by the biblical writers. The people of Israel were oppressed and did not have access to land on which to subsist. It is still, then, appropriate to use the traditional definition of "dominion" in the case of the disenfranchised and oppressed in the world as a liberation text. It is no longer acceptable, however, to use it as a coercive force of human power over creation. To do so any longer is to deny that the whole of God's creation has inherent worth and is deserving of our embodied Christian love. One North American preacher wrote:

The Genesis stories were written to exemplify the deep truths about how creative and purpose-filled God's acts were, and are. That God's willingness to consult and share power, and our human responses, sometimes lead to messy and less-than-desirable outcomes and to recognize that everything does not always turn out as God planned. Yet, through it all, God remains a faithful, covenant-making, covenant-keeping God. (from www.godalming.org.uk/13-2-05.html)

The inability to see how God's spirit moves in creation is not new to us as humans. Throughout history we have often prayed for salvation, prayed for God's intercession in our lives, yet remained blind to see God's grace and radical love incarnate in the world. John 3:31-36 tells the story of John's testimony to Jesus as the messiah. The people of Israel prayed and prayed and prayed for a messiah. People were following Jesus and the disciples in their ministry, yet there were still those who could not see Jesus' true nature. It wasn't only the Pharisees and those with authority. Jesus and John's own disciples are described as being consistently unable to fully comprehend Jesus as messiah. John 3:32 states that, "He has testified to what he has seen and heard, yet no one accepts his testimony". Is this not what we are doing with our inability to see the earth as inherently worthy in God's creation?

Even our focus on nature as a means for spiritual connection to God can be, in a way, an objectification of the earth. For rather than using the earth for the extraction of resources, we are using it for the creation of personal pleasure – as if the earth exists solely for our use and sense of beauty. Even those who are responsible for decisions that create destruction in the environment have a sense of the aesthetic beauty in the world. It is not that each decision we make as individuals is catastrophic in itself, but rather the use of earth as pleasure that allows the denial of accountability for our use of the earth. If I was the CEO of a large manufacturing corporation, and my hobby was hiking in the mountains on the weekend, I can see how it would be difficult to admit that I was not loving the earth. For I would be just one person, and standing on a lush mountain top looking at the glory of God's creation below me, how could I not want to deny the fact that my actions at work were contributing to the destruction of what I held most dear?

Again, I turn to the gospel of John (6:60-63a), "When many of his disciples heard it, they said, 'this teaching is difficult; who can accept it?' But Jesus, being aware that his disciples were complaining about it, said to them, 'Does this offend you? Then what if you were to see the Son of Man ascending to where he was before? It is the Spirit that gives life'."

What the Spirit is calling us to is a re-evaluation of our global economic paradigm and how it affects God's creation. Theologians are beginning to learn that being able to speak to economists in economic jargon is a way to make progress in this area. Rather than viewing this form of dialogue as submitting to the *status quo*, it can and perhaps should continue as a form of resistance: resistance which is consistent with our Christian heritage. Post-colonialist theologian R.S. Sugirtharajah writes that:

> *Resistance... is a "rediscovery and repatriation of what had been suppressed in the natives' past by the process of imperialism". Seen within the colonial*

context, resistance meant not simply a repudiation or rejection of Western rule or Western discursive practices. Rather, it was a profitable use of paradigm provided by the colonizer, in that it was successfully turned against him. (R.S. Sugirtharajah, The Bible and the Third World, *University Press, Cambridge, 2001, page 74.)*

The work of economists such as Amartya Sen, winner of the 1997 Nobel prize in economics, encourages us as Christians to advocate on behalf of nature. If nature is not viewed as inherently worthy, then it becomes simply a utility for the use of humankind. Sen clarifies something implicit in the global economic model – economic evaluation based upon utilitarian principles excludes any non-utilitarian information. That means the exclusion of information such as the inherent worth of creation. It is sometimes easy to view the workings of global corporations as separate from the actions of individuals – indeed, that is why they were created. But the people in corporations who are making decisions that dictate our interactions with the earth are, in fact, people we know. Some of them are sitting in the pews of our congregations and worshipping with us. Our working theologies of how we take our faith out into the world need to be modernized to include a 21st century understanding that overrules the misappropriation of a utilitarian dominion-based theology. And those in our communities who are making good/healthy decisions about how to interact with the earth need to be held up as living examples of Christ's ministry.

Our faith is one based upon the rebellious love of those excluded by society. Jesus ate, served and taught with those who would have been considered to be on the margins of society – those who could not speak for themselves. The earth has, with regard to its inherent worth, become disenfranchised. Our faith, through prayer for the earth, calls us to accept what the Spirit says through our environment – to refuse to be offended by the need to look at the world as an intricately woven ecological web; to walk with grace and humility in creation; to show an incarnate love for the earth as a renewed form of Christian praxis devoted to the One concerned with the whole of creation. May it be so. Amen.

PLENARY "GOD, IN YOUR GRACE, TRANSFORM THE WORLD"

THOUGHTS AND REFLECTIONS ON THE THEME: "GOD, IN YOUR GRACE, TRANSFORM OUR SOCIETIES"

PAULA DEVEJIAN

Ms Paula Devejian, a delegate of the Armenian Apostolic Church (Holy See of Etchmiadzin), comes from the United States and is working for the Mother See of Holy Etchmiadzin in Armenia as Internet development director. This reflection was prepared for the "theme plenary" on 21 February 2006 in which the speakers were interviewed as a panel, each addressing a different dimension of the Assembly theme.

Societies today are faced with ever-increasing problems. And while tension mounts between people and between nations, complacency and apathy also abound. We become numb to the disasters, and the tragedies, which make it easy to turn a blind eye to the problems of others. Changes in society can be subtle but, over time, result in decreasing moral principles, values and standards as well as ethics.

Prior to departing for this Assembly, our delegation met as a group to prepare ourselves for the event. One of the questions asked around the table was, what did our nation, our community and our church expect out of these proceedings? I had to honestly answer to myself, that I didn't think the expectations were much. Not that there was no hope, but that there is an awareness that no one body or organization can resolve the problems of the world.

In today's society, individual responsibility is often overlooked. When we call upon God to transform our societies, we must not forget that he has already granted us the tools to make this possible. He has taught us, through the teachings of His Son Jesus Christ, the rules of life, right from wrong, good from evil. We also know that actions speak louder than words; leading by example does work; and we can make a difference, as long as we choose to do so.

When we speak out against violence, or tyranny, or poverty, we must also ask ourselves, "What do we do or not do in our own daily life to work to overcome these things?" These are hard choices we are faced with, because as humans, we are weak and the temptation to take the easy path is always great.

It is not easy to refuse or deny ourselves the new piece of clothing because it's in fashion or more modern or even looks nicer on us than three we already own. Consumer excess in the Western world is rampant and sadly, sets a standard that others long for and desire. The quest for material wealth and possessions and creature comforts has a snowball effect on society with people constantly wanting and looking for what's next, what's new and what's better.

This makes it easy to overlook the plight of others. We talk about the inequities in the world, but how many of us make a concerted effort in our everyday lives to make a difference, to not be wasteful, to set a true example for others?

God has given us the tools to change our societies, what we need to pray for is the strength, will and fortitude as individuals to use what God has already granted to us, and make it happen. The examples of God transforming the world are constantly around us.

Throughout history, the Armenian Church and nation has been shaped by God's grace of transformation. Noah's Ark landed on Mt Ararat, in the historical lands of Armenia, and is an example of God's grace giving all of humanity a second chance. Through God's grace, the Armenian nation was one of the lands visited by the apostles, and through the works of Sts Thaddeus and Bartholomew, our bishops have been graced by the unbroken chain of Apostolic succession. Through the seeds of Christianity, planted by the apostles, Armenia became the first nation to adopt Christianity in the 4th century through the efforts of our patron saint, St Gregory the Illuminator who survived insurmountable odds and converted a pagan king only through God's grace. We were forever defined as a nation when our alphabet was created in the 5th century, which allowed our people to worship and learn of God's teachings in their own language. The first sentence translated into Armenian was: "That men may know wisdom and instruction, understand words of insight" (Proverbs 1:1). Even with the first written words in Armenian, the Church encouraged her people to accept the tools of God's grace. "Wisdom", "understand" and "insight" – all words leading us to a more peaceful coexistence with one another.

Through God's grace we became a national church, preserving our faith and ethnic identity for over 1,700 years, and while we've also suffered many times for our faith, the Armenian people never stopped believing that the power of God's grace could transform the world. Our people suffered the heinous crime of genocide, not only for our faith, but also for our ethnic identity. As a result of the genocide, our people were scattered throughout the world, but our diaspora grew strong and despite adversity we found strength. We lived through 70 years of Soviet atheism and state-sanctioned oppression of our church, and even in those days we did not feel deserted by God, as his light was kept alive in the hearts and minds of the people. We have been separated from each other, those living behind the oppressive curtain of communism and those on the outside. But we remained faithful to one another, through the grace of God. Our people relying on Jesus Christ have always looked to the future, to the coming day, to the better tomorrow. And in 1991, we received our independence, and once more he transformed the Armenian lands. In 1991, Artsakh and the historical lands of Armenia were declared independent and through great sacrifice the land was liberated and today our people worship freely. We have been united once again as a nation, under the banner of the Armenian Church and our spiritual and administrative headquarters, the Mother See of Holy Etchmiadzin, and today through God's grace we believe that there are better days ahead, that our economy will improve, and that our people though denied the light of Christ for decades, will learn again of God's grace. In my lifetime, I could only dream that I would one day see the Mother Cathedral of Holy Etchmiadzin free from foreign domination, but it was a dream that I never stopped having. And now that dream has come true, and our people are a witness to God's grace and power.

The Armenian nation is an example to the world of how God's grace can transform a society. The Armenian people, given their difficult history of persecutions, invasions and oppression from the moment they accepted Christianity, should long ago have disappeared from the earth. But they have remained steadfast to their faith, and turned adversity into advantage, using the tools God gave them. While we are a small nation, our people have made an impact on the societies, wherever they have lived. By living as a nation in dispersion in foreign lands, we have coexisted with people of many faiths and cultures. We exist on every continent of the world. And even in regions where we no longer live, our positive impact on society remains. We have adapted ourselves to our new homes and made peaceful contributions to whatever society we have lived in. We have trusted in God and His Divine Grace and succeeded in maintaining our national identity while becoming contributing members of society on foreign shores. We have remained steadfast and loyal to the lofty ideal of brotherhood and solidarity, as first stated by St Augustine and confirmed by our venerable pontiff St Nerses the Graceful in the 11th century: "Unity in the Essentials, Liberty in the non-essentials, Love in everything".

God's grace is all around us, he has given us the tools to change our societies, we must find the strength and courage to use them. We talk about unity, about speaking and acting with one voice, and one mind, but we as a body are unable to achieve this among ourselves. If we, as a Christian body cannot unite among ourselves, how can we realistically expect the world to? We talk about unity, but do our actions really reflect that wish? Long after the speeches have been made, studies done, papers written, theories analyzed, what becomes of those words? When we leave this venue, leave the view of the public eye, do our actions reflect these same desires and goals that we preach?

We seek for the world to accept each other. But maybe we seek too much. We have learned through our experiences that perhaps what we should start with is tolerance. Accepting another person's view point, lifestyle, even culture is difficult and sometimes even impossible. If we can get people to first tolerate each other, then the acceptance will come later. But it is something that must be worked on every minute of every day.

God created us as individuals, with free will. And this individuality balances the effects of globalization. Our individuality is what makes us strong. Our diversity doesn't have to be something negative and can be viewed as a positive if we tolerate the differences among us.

Each of us, by the experiences and wisdom that we have received at this conference, by attending this assembly, now have the power to return to our churches, communities, neighbourhoods, family and friends, and by example, through our own actions, affect the perceptions and actions of society. We should not look to "the Church" by itself, as a separate body aside from ourselves, to solve the problems of the world, because each of us as an individual makes up the body of the Church. We have the power within our own hands to change society, we must pray for the strength to use it.

Plenary "God, in Your Grace, Transform the World"

Thoughts and reflections on the Theme: "God, in Your Grace, Transform our Churches"

Namsoon Kang

Prof. Dr Namsoon Kang, a theologian from Korea, is associate professor for world Christianity and religions at Brite Divinity School in the United States and serves as vice president of the World Conference of Associations of Theological Institutions (WOCATI). This reflection was prepared for the "theme plenary" on 21 February 2006 in which the speakers were interviewed as a panel, each addressing a different dimension of the Assembly theme.

Opening Remarks

Before I start my remarks, I would like to clarify two things. One is about the word "transform" and the other is about "churches", which are the two key components of the theme that is given to me.

First, about the word "transform".

Very often, "transform-the-churches" can easily become a catch-phrase or a kind of propaganda when it is used by those in church politics. So I would like to make clear what I mean by "transform". My use of the word "transform" is based on three sensitivities: 1) contextual sensitivity, 2) ecumenical sensitivity, and 3) sensitivity to all forms of justice. And this notion of "transform" requires a radical and fundamental change of the very framework of the churches. The meaning of "transform" is not like "reform". Transform means a fundamental paradigm shift from the old to the new. It requires a thorough scrutiny of the church as it is with these three sensitivities. "Transform" is not just adding something to what already is. It is about a fundamental change of the epistemological framework, institutional structure, practice of Christian tradition, to promote a holistic sense of justice, peace and equality for all living beings within the churches and society.

The second point that I would like to make clear is the obvious simple fact that the "churches" are not a unitary entity. There has been no unitary form of Christian church in the entire history of Christianity. We tend to have a nostalgic notion of "the church", especially in a grand ecumenical gathering like a WCC Assembly. We wish to say we are somehow "one" in the name of Jesus the Christ. This is both Yes and No – Jain (in German). In order to reflect on the issue of "transforming our churches" it is necessary for us to attend carefully not only to our similarities as believers in Jesus Christ, but also to the critical differences among the churches. There are churches, for instance, that do not allow women into ordination, while there are churches that not only ordain women but also have women bishops. There are churches that condemn the sexual minority people in the name of God, while there are other churches that allow sexual minority people even into priestly ordination in the name of God. Therefore, it is obvious that the way we deal with the issue of "transforming our churches" may take a totally different direction depending on which specific churches I refer to. Having this complexity of the theme, "transform the churches", in mind, I would like to start my remarks.

First, transforming the churches requires overcoming a "Religious Peter Pan Syndrome".

There are more and more churches that are trapped in the so-called "Peter Pan syndrome". As you may know, Peter Pan is the one who refuses to become an adult. Simply speaking, being an adult means to grow, to change, to take responsibility. Those who are trapped in the "Peter Pan syndrome" just want to enjoy receiving the tangible, materialized blessings from God but continue to refuse to take any responsibility for making a commitment to justice, peace, and the equality of society. I would like to call this the "religious Peter Pan syndrome".

Growth, both physical and mental, is the only evidence of life and to grow is to change. Transforming the church requires overcoming a "religious Peter Pan syndrome", changing their perspective of the human being, of the world and God, taking responsibility for the world, and continuously being self-critical to become mature. Many Christians in "good faith" continue to remain at the Peter Pan stage by not asking "why it is what it is", by not taking responsibility in church and society and thereby continuing to support the system of various forms of injustice and discrimination, wittingly or unwittingly.

Many churches are taking out the "question-marks" from the teaching of Christian life. And those who ask a fundamental "WHY?" are easily excluded from the faith community, being labeled "unfaithful," "unspiritual" or "less-Christian". However, not asking "why?" but saying always "Yes and Amen" is very dangerous because there is no way for Christians to see their own participation and role in fostering various forms of injustice and violence. This is the lesson from the history of the Holocaust, the slavery system, witching-burning, apartheid... There are so many examples of how so-called "good Christians" can foster such horrible practices against humanity in the name of God by not asking the fundamental WHY. The Christian's conscious or unconscious complicity in injustice must be revealed by a fundamental question-mark, "WHY?" But if this fundamental question, "WHY?", is removed, the absence of question marks in the churches may easily lead to the unwitting complicity in the maintenance and perpetuation of injustice, discrimination, exploitation, bigotry, or hate-crime.

"Charity" acts of the churches are important but not enough, because charity does not ask "WHY?", it does not question the fundamental problem of reality that requires the very act of charity. Charity acts of the churches need to be coupled with the compassionate concern for justice. Concern for justice means asking the fundamental question of "WHY?" about the reality as it is.

This question mark of "WHY?" is the beginning of transformation of churches. The churches need to move from a charity-oriented mission to a justice-oriented mission by overcoming the religious Peter Pan syndrome. And this is a way to revive a social accountability of the Christian churches today.

SECOND, TRANSFORMING THE CHURCHES REQUIRES "INSTITUTIONAL REPENTANCE". WITHOUT REPENTANCE, NO TRUE TRANSFORMATION OF THE CHURCHES IS POSSIBLE.

To grow is to change. Simply speaking, to change is first to repudiate prejudice and discrimination. This is what Christians mean by repentance, a complex activity that involves discarding wrong attitudes and publicly espousing right ones. It is certainly easier for individuals to do this than for humanity in its collective forms, but "institutional repentance" for collective or systemic sin can happen and is powerfully effective when it does. There have been several celebrated examples in Christian history.

For instance, in 1972 Pope Paul VI repudiated the ancient Christian accusation that the Jews had killed God, the sin of deicide, and thereby publicly repented for centuries of anti-Semitism in the church. An equally dramatic example of public repentance took place in South Africa in 1990, when the Dutch Reformed Church publicly repented the sin of racism and the heresy of apartheid and invited Archbishop Desmond Tutu to absolve them.

These acts of "institutional repentance" and repudiation of past sins are profoundly liberating. They reveal the fundamental nature of Christian churches. The Christian community, after centuries of indifference, publicly repented of the great evil of slavery. Thus it was that Christians in the USA publicly repented of the sin that denied African Americans their civil rights. And thus it is that many Christian men today are publicly repenting the sin of sexism in themselves and in the church. They are acknowledging that for centuries the church has discriminated against women, according women a lower status than men, thereby denying the liberating truth of the gospel. Now it is time for the churches to institutionally repent for the complicity of churches in various forms of injustice and violence, to repent for misogyny, to repent for capitalistic teaching and practice of the gospel, to repent for religious expansionism and superiority over other faiths, to repent for hierarchical clericalism, to repent for homophobia and bigotry.

Without "institutional repentance", without knowing what has been wrong in the churches, and without harshly scrutinizing the complicity of Christian churches in fostering injustice and violence in various forms, a true transformation of the churches is ever-impossible.

THIRD, TRANSFORMING THE CHURCHES REQUIRES TRANSFORMING THEOLOGICAL INSTITUTIONS AND ECUMENICAL BODIES.

Transforming the churches is inseparably interlinked with transforming theological institutions and ecumenical bodies. I would call this interlinked nature of transformation of the churches, the triangle of transformation in Christianity. These three areas are so closely interdependent and their own existence is sustained by one another's existence. Without transformation of theological institutions and ecumenical bodies, the transformation of the churches is always incomplete, and also vice versa.

Unlike "reform", "transform" requires a radical, fundamental change of the very ground. If we adopt this "radicality" as the nature of "transform", we need to look at the very ground of theological institutions that educate the pastors and leaders of the churches. We need to first scrutinize the curriculum, the composition of faculty members and also methods of teaching and pedagogy to see whether these are really reflecting the global reality and the pressing issues that we face, whether these are democratic and inclusive enough, whether these are ecumenical enough, whether these are justice-oriented in an unjust world such as we live in.

These three bodies – church, theological schools and ecumenical bodies – are like siblings. They are closely interdependent, one way or the other. We must remember that all transformations are interdependent.

Fourth, transforming the churches is also closely interlinked to transforming the WCC as an umbrella body of all churches of the world.

Transforming the ecumenical bodies entails national, regional and global dimensions. Since this is a global gathering of ecumenical bodies and Christian churches, I would like to take an example from the WCC for what I mean by transformation based on the three sensitivities that I mentioned earlier: contextual sensitivity, ecumenical sensitivity, and sensitivity to all forms of justice.

There have been various discourses on what to transform in the WCC. But there is one dimension that has hardly been challenged in a fundamental way: the very way of communication in the WCC.

An attentive communication with one another is the very starting point for pursuing the "unity" of the churches. This 9th WCC Assembly is making a very significant mark on the entire history of WCC in its adoption of a consensus-model decision-making process. By adopting this consensus-model in its way of doing business, the attentive listening to one another, exploration, consultation, questioning and reflection on the issues on the table are becoming more and more significant. I entirely welcome adopting this consensus model. Nevertheless, there is one thing that worries me very deeply, which has been a lingering dilemma that I have felt for a long time: the standardization of official language in the WCC Assembly and other international gatherings.

There is long-standing and deep-seated "rankism" in WCC. When you are on board, you realize that there are different classes among those who are on board: the first class passengers, the prestigious (business) class passengers, and the economy class passengers. On the plane, those ranks are made by the amount of money they pay for the airfare.

I sense that exactly the same mechanism has been operating in WCC meetings and assemblies. But in these WCC gatherings, ranks are made not by money but by language. The first class passengers are those who speak English as their native language. The business class passengers are those whose native language belongs to either one of the three translated languages: French, German, Spanish (sometimes Russian). Needless to say, the economy class passengers are those whose native language belongs to none of these languages, and who cannot express themselves in one of these four "official" WCC languages.

The choice of language is absolutely the issue of power. Language is not just a means of communication. It is about standardization of thinking, worldview, value-system, culture, and even one's attitude to other people around one. The choice of language is about power: power of decision-making, power of knowledge-production, power to express oneself. Language is power to express who one is, power to persuade, it is power to convey one's values and opinions.

We should ask then a fundamental, transformational question that has hardly been asked: why it is what it is now, how right it is what it is.

If someone cannot fully express his/her opinion in these four or five WCC "official" languages, decision-making by consensus is in fact the consensus of only those who hold these languages. As long as the WCC continues to adopt these four languages, the former colonial languages, it will be impossible to avoid falling into the trap of the imperialistic mentality that WCC is against. It is so obvious that a majority of people in the world do not speak English.

Today I would like strongly to suggest that the WCC needs to organize a "language committee" as one of WCC Assembly committees. The "language committee" has three roles to play: first, to examine the practice of inclusive language in all the documents and continuously theorize the theological, historical, social, spiritual, psychological and political implications of the use of inclusive language. Second, to make a suggestion and even create languages/terminologies that enhance the rights and dignity of marginalized people. And finally, persistently to seek an alternative solution to this huge dilemma of the standardization of official languages in the WCC. The WCC's decision to adopt a consensus model is not based on its "utilitarian, pragmatic" value. To find an alternative to this language issue cannot be based on the pragmatic value. It is based on the value of true unity in its biblical sense.

CLOSING REMARKS

It has been emphasized that churches need to be prophetic. One of the significant acts of the prophet is to read the signs of our time. It is hard to deny that there are signs of "moral disengagement" not only in society but also in the churches.

The churches do not seem to care about the global reality of war, violence, dislocation of the people, and furthermore there is a sort of "church-exceptionalism" that employs a religious alibi for violating even a common sense and moral code of society. We have to learn to recognize this moral disengagement of the churches and scrutinize church-exceptionalism.

"Transforming the church" is a decisive act of totally reconstructing our epistemology (way of knowing things), our value system, our way of practising the gospel, our understanding of the mission of the churches. It is a collective act of hope for a new heaven and a new earth.

Plenary "God, in Your Grace, Transform the World"

Thoughts and reflections on the Theme: "God, in Your Grace, Transform Our Lives"

Sarah Newland-Martin

Ms Sarah Newland-Martin is the general secretary of the Kingston YMCA and the national general secretary of the National Council of YMCAs in Jamaica. She is part of the Ecumenical Disability Advocates Network (EDAN). This reflection was prepared for the "theme plenary" on 21 February 2006 in which the speakers were interviewed as a panel, each addressing a different dimension of the Assembly theme.

"Grace" is that quality in the heart of God that causes him not to deal with us according to our sins or to retaliate against us according to our iniquities. God's grace pours out love, kindness and favour to all who will trust him.

The Illustrated Dictionary of the Bible indicates that "transform" means "a change radically in inner character, condition or nature". In Romans 12:2 Paul exhorted Christians "not to be conformed to this world but be transformed by the renewing of your mind."

In order to experience a transformed life, the following are of great importance.

1. Openness to God

Openness to God allows us to be frank with him and become aware of aspects in our lives we know are wrong, such as: poor decisions, bad habits, behaviour that we are ashamed of, areas we want God to change, but where we may be fearful of his condemnation. If we have received Christ into our hearts, we have been declared his own, forgiven and now under his grace. (But there is therefore now no condemnation to them who are in Christ Jesus ... Romans 8:1).

2. ACCEPTING THE INVITATION

God offers an open invitation for us to come in truth and humility. James 4:6 says "God is opposed to the proud but he gives grace to the humble." If we refuse to accept his invitation, there is no relationship. When we come to the Lord, he is willing to listen to us sharing our shortfalls in the areas mentioned and then he will meet us in that need with his grace. God is not demanding that we change ourselves. Instead he asks us to come to him in honesty and faith and cast all our cares on him (1 Peter 5:5-7).

3. RECOGNITION FOR THE CHANGE NEEDED

The story in Luke 18:9-14 which speaks of the parable (told by Jesus) of the Pharisee and the tax collector, showed that the tax collector who stood some distance away beating his chest saying "God be merciful to me a sinner" was deeply conscious of his sin and guilt and in true repentance turned from sin to God for forgiveness and mercy. So it is for us, we need to be aware of where we fall short and instead of being defensive, able to say, like the tax collector, "Lord be merciful to me, a sinner."

We can experience God's grace and transformation in our lives when we recognize our weaknesses and come to the throne of grace in truth and humility. When we are walking in God's wisdom, then we will recognize the change needed in our lives.

4. ACCEPTANCE OF THE TRANSFORMED LIFE

Hebrews 4:13, says "Nothing in all creation is hidden from God's sight. Everything is uncovered and laid bare before the eyes of him to whom we must give account." Romans 5:20 says, "where sin abounded, grace abounded all the more." We must take God at his word that his grace is there, in order to be able to receive it. There is absolutely one inescapable condition that must be met if grace is to change a person, and that is, God's grace must be believed. We have to respond to God with an answering trust. And he will act.

Lewis Sperry Chafer who wrote a comprehensive book on grace says "The overwhelming testimony of the Word of God is that every aspect of salvation, every blessing of divine grace, in time and eternity is conditioned only on what is believed."

PERSONAL EXPERIENCE

As a child I grew up in two institutions after being abandoned by my parents. I was born with both legs deformed – and which were of no use.

The first institution was one which catered to children who were from destitute families, orphans, abandoned children and a small number of children with disabilities. I fell in the last two categories.

While growing up at these institutions, the late Professor Back spoke with the late Sir John Golding who had me transferred to the University Hospital and performed surgery to remove the legs I could not use. I was sent to another institution. This one had only children with disabilities. There were some 50 other children and 30 adults at that time who were afflicted with polio after the epidemic in 1954.

I strongly believe that these men were specially identified by God to do his work in my life.

Most of the children had a family of one sort of another – I had no one to call family. I felt rejected, alone and unwanted. Many times I was afraid of not being like the other children who had legs and who were visited by their relatives. Often times I was reminded by them that I had no one. They were mean to me at times. I felt like a "nobody" and this happened for a long time.

The transformation came when I could walk on peg legs before being allowed to use artificial legs; when I started going to high school and was made to feel that indeed I was like anyone else, that I was a child of God, that I should not compare myself with others, that God made me unique with my unique role, with my own personalities, gifts, strengths and weaknesses. The day I walked through the waters of baptism in 1968 was the key point in my life.

I met my mother and father at age 24 and discovered that I had six brothers.

I found then that when I became a Christian, Jesus began to transform me in his image. I was able to forgive my parents for what happened and my thinking became moulded by God's word which is "inspired by God and is useful to teach us what is true and to make us realize what is wrong in our lives" (2 Timothy 3:16a NLT). Indeed, knowing God's word is very important because it is the objective means by which I am able to evaluate the world and myself.

A relationship with God is more powerful than anything else in the world and under grace I have more than my own resources. I have God's Holy Spirit enabling me to do his will. I am able to acknowledge my weaknesses and keep bringing them back to God and continue to take personal responsibility for my sins, asking him to transform my life on a daily basis.

Often times when I reflect on where I was and the various levels of transformation through which I have passed, I am deeply indebted to God for his limitless love in my life. As a result of my transformed life, the lives of many individuals have been positively impacted, in particular the young people.

BIBLICAL CHARACTERS WHOSE LIVES WERE TRANSFORMED

The following gives a brief account of some of the biblical characters whose lives were transformed:

- Saul (the original name of Paul) who was a prosecutor of the church became an apostle of Christ and a missionary of the early church (Acts 7:58-9:26; 11-25-13:9).

- David and Bathsheba – Although David was a righteous king, he was subject to sin, just like any other human being. On one occasion when his army went to battle, David stayed home. This led to his great sin with Bathsheba. While Uriah, the Hittite, Bathsheba's husband was away in battle, David committed adultery with her. David repented and asked for God's forgiveness. His prayer of forgiveness is recorded in Psalm 51.
- Zacchaeus was the chief tax collector of Jericho who had grown rich by over- taxing people. When Jesus visited Jericho, Zaccheaus who was "of short stature" (Luke 19:3) climbed a tree in order to see Jesus. Jesus asked him to come down and visited him as a guest. As a result of the visit of Jesus, Zacchaeus became a follower of the Lord, repented of his sins, and made restitution for his wrongdoing. Jesus showed that he came to call sinners to repentance.

SELF-EVALUATION

In evaluating our lives one can ask the following questions:

- How do I see myself?
- Do I accept God's invitation?
- Are there hindrances to my being transformed?
- Am I ready to be transformed?
- Is my life one of transformation?

CONCLUSION

When we become followers of Jesus, God begins to transform us in his image. A key part of this transformation is the transformation of the way we think.

However, it must be noted that transformation is not a one-shot experience but is likened to the salvation experience which is a process. We must guard against putting ourselves into a box by asking questions such as "Why me?" "Can I be changed?" The process of transformation allows us to ask, seek, and surrender our lives.

Transformed lives depict an outward action of what happens inside; as a result we should not wait for things to happen but instead we can pray for others such as our children, friends, fellow believers, missionaries and pastors.

One of my favourite books in the Bible is Colossians which provides many steps to living a transformed life.

In Col. 1:9-11, for example, we are told that the knowledge of God's will, results from praying and remaining in his word and in fellowship with him. It is only this kind of knowledge that will lead to spiritual understanding and transforms our hearts and lives

As we experience nearness, love, righteousness and power through prayer and the Holy Spirit, we are being transformed into his likeness (2 Cor. 4:6; Col. 1:15; Heb. 1:3). In this age the transformation is progressive and impartial. When Christ returns, we will see him face to face, and our transformation will be made complete (1 John 3:2; Rev. 22:4).

101

PLENARY "GOD, IN YOUR GRACE, TRANSFORM THE WORLD"

THOUGHTS AND REFLECTIONS ON THE THEME: "GOD, IN YOUR GRACE, TRANSFORM OUR WITNESS"

GRACIA VIOLETA ROSS QUIROGA

Ms Gracia Violeta Ross Quiroga, a member of the Christian Evangelical Church in Bolivia, is an advocate for the rights of people living with HIV and AIDS in Bolivia and serves as vice president of the association +VIDA, coordinator of Voces VIHvas and as national representative to the network of Bolivian people living with HIV and AIDS. This reflection was presented at the "theme plenary" on 21 February 2006 in which the speakers were interviewed as a panel, each addressing a different dimension of the Assembly theme.[1]

GRACE FOR GRACE, TESTIMONY OF A PASTOR'S DAUGHTER

GRACIA

My name has a meaning. Gracia in Spanish means Grace. My parents named me Gracia due to their understanding of "God's grace"; that wonderful attribute of God which enabled human beings to be saved. This essay shows how I (Gracia) received the grace of God.

When I was a child, I had many problems at school because my classmates used to make fun of me with my name saying "Gracias Gracia", in Spanish the words "thanks" (gracias) and "grace" (gracia) are different only in the "s".

Every time I had to say my name was Gracia, I had to explain to people about the grace of God and the reason why I had such a different name, I had to declare I was a Christian and I was not ready to do so with every single person I met. Therefore I decided to use my second name: Violeta, which means "violet", the flower. This name was easier to remember and did not cause so many questions.

Nevertheless, the difference between Gracia and Violeta was not only in the name but also in the attitudes and the kind of life Gracia and Violeta led. Within the church I was Gracia, living a "good" life like "the daughter of a pastor" that I am. Violeta was a rebellious teenager doing her will and ignoring God's commandments. As Violeta I did all the things Gracia was not allowed to do. This situation ended with me having two lives.

WITHIN THE CHURCH

I was born into a Protestant family. My father is a spiritual leader; both my father and my mother have founded churches in Bolivia. I grew up in the church. For a while, the church was based in our garage while we did not have a place to meet. I used to attend Sunday school, and learnt about Abraham, Joseph and Jesus and also heard about Samson and his mistake involving a woman who did not belong to God's people.

Without being completely conscious, I developed two kinds of lives. Gracia used to attend church every single Sunday making a "performance" for other people, showing that everything was good. Violeta was a different person and I can say, as Violeta, I did not belong to God's family at all. My life was being divided between two attitudes, and neither of them was real nor complete. I was playing with God and the flesh at the same time; this game can never have a good end. I was not a real Christian, I was just someone else in the church, using another seat.

BITTERNESS ROOTS

I do not pretend to justify myself but the abyss between my life and God was growing deeper every day. When I decided to do my will I never thought I could end up having HIV. I was not aware of the great risk I was in.

This history of rebellion started with my inability to forgive, and the bitterness I let grow up in my heart because I was not able to forgive my older sister when she became the fiancé of the boy I used to like. From that moment I started to think all Christian people were a fake and decided to have a boyfriend outside of the church.

My bitterness made me feel so much the need of being loved. I needed so much to have someone to love in order to show my sister that even though she was with the boy I liked, I had many others and did not need him.

This career to get more boyfriends than my sister was my death sentence. I was looking for love, for someone to take care of me, someone to understand me, to be loyal, never to lie, to support me, to be faithful, to speak the truth… I was looking in a man for what only God can give! So I never found it. Men realized I needed love and took advantage of my need. Men can love but they will ask a price for it, they will ask for the body, the integrity, they ask to have the temple of Holy Spirit. They asked for my body and I accepted.

I kept going to church every Sunday but my heart was far from God. I went to university to study Anthropology even though my father disagreed with this choice. While at university I began to drink alcohol and met friends who used to smoke marijuana and other drugs.

My family suffered a lot during this time, because they were worried about the people I had made friends with, they felt that they were bad influences on me. They could not understand how I was able to make these decisions to go out with these people, because I had been brought up knowing God, and this was not how they had brought me up.

I remember nowadays, with tears in my eyes, how much my mother and father, my sisters and little brother suffered. They tried to rescue me, they locked the doors so that I could not escape, they prayed for long nights when I did not arrive home, they forbade me access to the telephone so that I would not be able to contact those friends who took me to drink alcohol; finally they begged me to change and to remember God, crying so many times; they told me to abandon that life but I became more rebellious each time they tried to talk to me.

I asked them to forgive me and they did, but I cannot forget all the pain I caused. I understand now that my parents are the first authority settled by God himself, the rules they have were there in order to protect my life.

My life far from God

I had been taught I had to remain a virgin until I got married. My parents wanted me to marry someone from the church, but I decided to date boys outside of the church. I also decided that I wanted to play sex with them. I knew about the severe risk of getting pregnant outside of marriage, and I knew what shame this would bring on my father especially, because he was such a prestigious leader within the church. Therefore I had to find information on my own regarding issues such as avoiding pregnancy. No one in the church spoke to me about sex or sexuality and all the problems that these issues raise.

I never got pregnant but I was unaware of the risk of AIDS, and at that time I did not realize how much at risk I actually was of contracting HIV. I do not know how long I could have kept living this kind of life. I did not care about anything. I did not care about my parent's suffering or about my family's credibility within the church, I just wanted to do my will.

My chosen lifestyle had bitter consequences. One night I was coming back home from a party. I did not have any money to get a taxi home, because I had spent all my money on the ticket for the party. I went out every Saturday, without my parents' permission, they had no idea that I was going out! Honestly I only wanted to dance, and have a good time with my friends, but unfortunately wherever there is music, there is also always alcohol, at least in Latin America. That night I had crept out of my bedroom via the balcony.

It was getting really late at the party, it was 2 a.m. and I wanted to go home. I asked my friends to walk me home but they wanted to stay at the party a little while longer. I begged them to walk me home, and because they all wanted to stay, they chose one person to go with me. On the way home this "friend" told me that he wanted to have sex with me but I asked him why he was saying this. I knew it was because he was drunk; if he had been sober then he would not have asked me that. He was angry because I said "No" and he left me, right there, and I was left to walk home alone. It was only a short walk to my house from there.

My sister used to help me escaping and getting in again; that night she was not home and had not read the note I left her to open for me at 2:30 a.m. I decided to go and look for her in a pub she used to go to. I was really drunk and did not realize that two men were following me. They hit me and took me to an alleyway and they both raped me.

I could not believe this was happening to me, I was so close to home. I felt my heart was being destroyed. I was a child of God; I thought that he had a duty to protect me. I told my older sister about what had happened, but I never told my parents, I did not want to see them suffer. I was traumatized for a time. I did not want to have any man near to me. What happened should have taught me a lesson. However, I did not learn from my mistakes.

"My son do not go along with them, do not set foot on their paths; for their feet rush into sin (…) these men lie in wait for their own blood."[2]

"YOU HAVE MADE MY DAYS A MERE HANDBREADTH…"

"You have made my days a mere handbreadth, the span of my years is as nothing before you."[3]

After this experience of sexual assault I thought nothing worse could ever happen to me. I was wrong. Even though I had experienced great pain with this assault I did not change my life-style. I used to think that nothing worse could happen now, so why would I try to take care? Why? Everything was lost already, I had screwed up already.

In March 2000 I went to a little town in my country. I was preparing research for a thesis for my degree about the availability of small loans for small enterprises of peasants in Bolivia. I was bitten by a little insect and the bite got infected. I was getting tired very quickly and was having some nosebleeds. My family and I thought I had malaria because this illness is endemic in this area. I went to a specialized laboratory to take a test to find out if I had contracted malaria or another similar illness; my older sister told them to test for HIV as well.

The other tests were negative, however my HIV test came back positive. I could not believe it; I had not had more sexual experiences than most of my school friends, in fact I had had less than them! I was simply a girl from university discovering her sexuality. I never injected drugs and I was not a sex worker. My first thought was how to tell my parents. What was going to happen to me? When was I going to die? How could I face the people and their prejudices about AIDS? How could I ever tell people from church that I was HIV positive?

I cried a lot and I was sad and depressed for a very long time. Finally one day my sister told me that I had to tell my parents. How could I tell them? We had never talked about sexuality, where was I going to find the strength to tell them "I have AIDS"? The thought of telling them tortured me for many months.

I decided to tell them. I thought that they were going to reject me. I thought that they were going to throw me out of the house. I wrote a letter to them and I sent it with my sister while I was staying at a friend's. I decided that if my parents rejected me, life would not be worth living. When I saw them they were astonished with what I had told them in the letter. I will never forget their tear-stained faces, they had one question written all over their faces: why did this happen to our child?

My family did not reject me at all, they received me with open arms, they told me they did not want to know what happened, they just wanted to be with me and support me until the last day. The Bible says:

"As a father has compassion on his children, so the Lord has compassion on those who fear him."[4]

I began to understand this proof of love was a reflection of God's love in my family. This love was just one of the gifts God has prepared for me.

"LET THE BONES YOU HAVE CRUSHED REJOICE..."[5]

In my anguish due to this HIV positive diagnosis, I looked for God again. He gave me freedom from blame and shame, I found peace, forgiveness, hope and eternal life. My heavenly Father consoled me in the worst time of my life, he showed me promises of eternal life and strength to go on:

"Even though I walk through the valley of the shadow of death, I will fear no evil for you are with me."[6]

The Lord used different brothers and sisters in the faith to bring healthiness and consolation to the pain in my heart. He showed me nothing could take me away from his incomparable love, neither all the evil I had committed, nor the virus, nor the death:

"No, in all these things we are more than conquerors through him who loved us. For I am convinced that neither death nor life, neither angels nor demons, neither the present nor the future, nor any powers, neither height or depth, nor anything else in all creation, will be able to separate us from the love of God that is in Christ Jesus our Lord."[7]

Not even AIDS can separate me from the love of God!

The sacrifice Jesus made on the cross was enough to save me and enough to forgive my sins and those of people living with HIV. So much grace and mercy were difficult to believe! The Lord is faithful to me even though I was unfaithful! He had a mission for my life, even based on my mistakes!

"JESUS REACHED OUT HIS HAND AND TOUCHED THE MAN..."[8]

I reconciled with God, as king Hezekiah did[9], I humbled myself in God's presence, I repented for my sins, I asked for forgiveness and I gave God what I still had of my broken life. He forgave me, restored me, healed my body, my soul and my spirit.

I started to study the Bible again. I was not the same person any more, I needed to know what God demanded from me now.

I have met other people living with HIV and AIDS (PLWHA). The pain for their souls and bodies is terrible: they die alone, abandoned by their families, without having a ray of hope.

I discovered I was privileged among those living with HIV. I have a family who support me, they do not judge me or discriminate. I am healthy, alive and have eternal life. The Lord told me to work as a volunteer with these people.

I wanted to find what God said about illnesses like AIDS. I found that the judging role is only for God. I understood I had to put aside my prejudices if I really wanted to work with these people, specially when we are talking about sex workers and gay people.

I also discovered God gave us examples of what to do in such situations. I was impressed by Jesus' attitudes with people suffering from leprosy. While the whole society and synagogues treated them with discrimination (physical, symbolic and social discrimination), having special rules for them, asking them to use a bell to announce their presence, Jesus touched them, ate with them and healed them, both physically and spiritually[10]:

"A man with leprosy came to him and begged, "if you are willing, you can make me clean." Filled with compassion, Jesus reached out his hand and touched the man. "I am willing", he said. "Be clean!"[11]

"...HE HAS GIVEN US NEW BIRTH INTO A LIVING HOPE..."[12]

I decided it was not important to know how much time I would live. Each day lived would be for God's glory.

The Lord had a mission of hope for persons living with HIV and AIDS. God has designed a mission based on my mistakes! His mercy and grace cover my broken promises and my failures. He did not reject me but used my experiences to console in order that I console other people suffering.

"Praise be to the God and Father of our Lord Jesus Christ! In his great mercy he has given us new birth into a living hope through the resurrection of Jesus Christ from the dead..." (1 Peter 1.3).

God has a living hope for persons living with HIV and AIDS.

While most people despise and judge us,

the divine response is plenty of forgiveness and living hope.

Together with other co-workers, I decided to found a self-help group for PLWHAs. We work as volunteers in prevention, advocacy, assistance for the ill ones, information for families, society, community-based organizations and the govern-ment. The Lord has blessed our work, we have been chosen as a "successful experi-ence on HIV and AIDS" by the Pan-American Health Organization. God used us to bring hope to suffering people.

"THE AIDS CRISIS IS THE HARVEST GOD GAVE US" [13]

Among the plans God had, was the role of being a messenger to the Bolivian evan-gelical churches.

In September, 2002, I was invited to the Conference on Integral Mission and HIV/AIDS held by the Micah Network in Chiang Mai, Thailand. I met Leah Mutala at this conference. Leah is an African woman working as a volunteer, taking care of the orphans left by the AIDS epidemic. She taught me God takes up the cause of the widow and the orphan, God is a Father to the fatherless[14]; these are only some of the consequences the AIDS epidemic brings for societies. The most impor-tant thing Leah taught me was that "the AIDS crisis is the harvest God gave us."

"Do you not say, 'Four months more and then the harvest'? I tell you, open your eyes and look at the fields! They are ripe for harvest."[15].

This is the message I received for the evangelical churches:

Let's open our eyes and see, the harvest is ready.

The AIDS crisis is the harvest God gave us,

we will crop for eternal life.

"I WILL NOT DIE BUT LIVE,
AND WILL PROCLAIM WHAT THE LORD HAS DONE" [16]

It is not important for me to know how long I will live any more, because I know that if I die sooner or later, I will be with my Heavenly Father for eternity.

The time I shall live in this world,

I will proclaim the wonders God has done

in my life and the way his great love

and mercy reached me having grace in his eyes;

God taught me the meaning of my name in my own flesh.

"THIS CHURCH THAT I LOVE…"

God had even more beautiful things prepared for me. I am a public speaker on HIV and AIDS. I am leader of the community-based organization REDBOL

(Bolivian Network of PLWHA). I am on TV very often and it is not possible to keep the secrecy anymore.

So my family and I decided to tell the church about my HIV status. We were frightened of the possibility of being expelled from the church, specially considering that my father is currently the pastor of the church. There is a lack of information about HIV in Bolivia and very often we see attitudes of discrimination. We prayed a lot but I must confess we did not trust God.

We chose one Sunday to tell the church and from the moment I started speaking I could not avoid the tears in my eyes. I was so repentant for causing that pain, for being a bad testimony for my church, for the shame I brought to my father and my whole family. I had a fight in my soul, sometimes the fear was bigger than my need to confess my sin.

God had prepared a loving church who supported us from the moment they knew about my HIV status. My dear brothers and sisters pray for me every week, asking God that I finally may be healed. They support me during my trips by praying and also in my speeches and my family with words of hope. This church that I love is a gift from God.

Nowadays

My viral load (quantity of virus in the blood) is 15000 copies/ml.[17] Currently I do not take any antiretroviral medicine. These medicines are very expensive (USD1500/month) and no one in Bolivia has enough money to pay this kind of price, and still have enough money left over to live. The HIV virus reproduces itself every 37 hours in my body. A medical diagnosis would point out that I am a weaker person every day but God supports me; he said to me:

"My Grace is sufficient for you, for my power is made perfect in weakness. Therefore I will boast all the more gladly about my weakness, so that Christ's power may rest on me. That is why, for Christ's sake, I delight in weakness, in insults, in hardships, in persecutions, in difficulties. For when I am weak, then I am strong."

Notes:

1. This article was published under the title 'I have AIDS: Testimony of a pastor's daughter' in *The Church and the HIV/AIDS Crisis: Providing Leadership and Hope* (Wheaton, IL: Crossway Books, Tetsunao Yamamori, David Dageforde, and Tina Bruner (eds.) (2004). The article in Spanish *How Grace found the real Grace: Not even AIDS could separate me from God's love!*, was published in the Sunday bulletin of the Christian Evangelical Church of Free Brethren in La Paz in May, 2003.

2. Prov. 1:15-18, NVI.

3. Ps. 39:5, NVI.

4. Ps. 103:13, NVI.

5. Ps. 51:8b, NVI.

6. Ps. 23:4, NVI.

6. Rom. 8:37-39, NVI.

7. Mk 1:41b, NVI.

8. 2 Kings 20, NVI.

9. "While he was in Bethany, reclining at the table in the home of a man known as Simon the Leper…", Mark 14:3, NVI.

10. Mk 1:40 and 41, NVI.

11. 1 Pet. 1:3b, NVI.

12. Leah Mutala, Zimbabwe 2002.

13. Ps. 68:5; 146:9, NVI.

14. Jn 4..35, NVI.

15. Ps. 118:17, NVI.

16. A PLWHA can die with over a million copies/ml.

17. 2 Cor. 12:.9-10, NVI.

Report of the Moderator

Aram I, Catholicos of Cilicia

His Holiness Aram I, Catholicos of Cilicia, was Moderator of the WCC Central Committee from 1991 to 2006. This report was presented in plenary on 15 February 2006.

1. Assemblies are important stages in our ecumenical journey. Through prayer, meditation, presentations, discussion and decision, they provide a proper framework to evaluate the World Council of Churches' ecumenical witness, identify its future priorities and set a new course. Assemblies are also unique occasions to deepen our fellowship "on the way" towards the visible unity of the church. This 9th Assembly takes place in a period of world history when values are in decline, visions are uncertain and hopes are confused; when injustice is spreading and peace is almost unattainable; when violence and insecurity are becoming dominant in all spheres of human life.

"God, in Your Grace, transform the world"

2. In this turbulent world we turn to God and pray: *"God, in your grace, transform the world"*: a supplication emanating from our broken hearts; a sign of hope emerging in the midst of the uncertainties of human life; a genuine expression of faith unfolding in the context of the tensions and anxieties of the world.

3. Grace (in Hebrew *Q'en* and in Greek *Xaris*) is the core of God's revelation. It appears in the Bible with multi-faceted meanings and manifold implications. Grace is benevolence, compassion, love, mercy, gift and beauty manifested through God's "manifold gifts" (1 Pet. 4:10) and "gracious deeds" (Is. 63:7-9). St Paul's letters are rightly described as the basis of the theology of grace. In the Bible, grace displays the following basic features: a) It is God's gift of the "fullness" of life (John 10:10). It is also a quality of life sustained by obedient response to God. b) Grace is the concrete expression of God's love (2 Cor. 12:7-10), which makes the human being strong even in his weakness (2 Cor. 12:10). c) It is God's transformative power that restores

His image in human beings. d) As God's essential attribute, grace pertains both to His transcendence and immanence. God has communicated and shared His grace with us; He came to us "full of grace" and "dwelt among us" (John 1:14-16). e) Grace is God's victory over sin (Rom. 5:21). Salvation of humanity and creation is the fruit of God's intervention in Christ (Rom. 3:24). f) Grace is God's gift of justice and peace, namely, the expression of God's mercy and love towards humanity and His commitment to the covenant. g) The grace of God is His reconciliation in Christ with humanity (2 Cor. 5:17–21). Reconciliation is healing and transformation of humanity and the creation realized by God's *kenosis* in Christ (Col. 1:19-20). h) God's grace is the coming of the kingdom of heaven on earth manifested in and through Christ. God's kingdom is the reign of grace. i) Grace has replaced the law. It is God's free gift (Rom. 3:24) given to all without discrimination. However, God's preferential option is for the oppressed and marginalized (Matt. 5:1-12).

4. The biblical perception of grace is dominant in Orthodox theology and spirituality. The following aspects capture our attention:

a) Grace aims at the renewal and transformation of the whole of humanity and creation; it is new creation. Grace as re-creation starts with the "microcosm", i.e. human beings and the human community. Humanity and creation are interconnected. The blessing of elements of creation (water, fruit, land, etc.) in Orthodox churches indicates the integrity and sacredness of creation.

b) God's act of transformation has become a reality in the Christ-event. God's transformative presence with us is a continuous reality; it is both an event and a process, existential and eschatological. In the power of the Holy Spirit, God's grace becomes a living and life-giving reality in and through the eucharist.

c) The transformative action of God is trinitarian: the love of God the father, the grace of our Lord Jesus Christ and the communion of the Holy Spirit. Grace is God's all-embracing action; it permeates all dimensions and spheres of created order, which is referred to in Orthodox theology as the cosmic action of grace. Grace is God's omnipresent and omnipotent power; it transforms all aspects of human life. It comes through the sacraments of baptism, eucharist and ordination.

d) God's grace makes us all one body; it is the source of our unity in Christ and of our bond of unity with each other. In spite of worldly divisions, in the power of the Holy Spirit God's grace continuously ensures, undergirds and protects our unity, as well as the integrity and continuity of the church and leads it to *eschaton*, the second coming of Christ in glory.

e) God's grace creates communion between the human being and God. The human being is not only created by God, but also for God. The human being is co-worker (1 Cor. 3:9) with God and the guardian of His creation. The human stewardship of the creation and accountability to God are expressed through the humanity-God communion that reaches its culmination in *theosis*.

f) Accepting God's grace means sharing it with others through evangelism and diakonia. This is "liturgy after liturgy". Responding to God's grace in gratitude and faithfulness is costly; it implies *kenosis*, namely, *martyria* in life and even in death.

5. Strenuous efforts have been made in history to transform the world. All political, religious, economic, ideological and technological attempts have failed. With its new value-system, paradigms and powerful forces, globalization is yet another attempt to transform the world. As Christians, we believe that only God's grace can empower, renew and transform humanity and creation. In this Assembly, we will identify the implications of this theme for the ecumenical movement and particularly for the ecumenical witness of the World Council of Churches by reflecting and praying: *"God, in your grace, transform the world"*. Indeed, this prayer is the cry of the poor for justice; the cry of the sick for healing; the cry of the marginalized for liberation; the cry of humanity and creation for reconciliation. Empowered with the grace of the Holy Spirit (Mark 13:11; John 16:13), the church as transformed and transforming community is called to be Christ's witness to the end of the world, until in Christ all things are reconciled and the whole of creation is transformed into a "new heaven and a new earth" (Rev. 21:1).

THE LATIN AMERICAN CONTEXT

6. This is the first assembly of the WCC to take place in Latin America. With its struggle and hope for justice and dignity, this continent will, undoubtedly, have a strong impact on our deliberations and actions.

7. Latin American societies have suffered from their colonial origins. European societies, mainly Spain and Portugal, imposed their social and political systems and cultural values on the aboriginal peoples, thus destroying their cultures and religions. The colonizer's oppressive rule and culture left deep scars on the Latin American societies. The poverty, inequalities and foreign dependence continued after the transition from the colonial period to the era of independence.

8. Today, although Latin American societies differ from one another in many ways, they also share a great deal. Most of them were affected by political, economic and social turmoil throughout the 20th century. By the middle of the 1970s,

many Latin American countries were ruled by military regimes which violated human rights, persecuted and assassinated political and community leaders and outlawed political organizations. Since the 1980s, most governments of the region have adopted economic strategies that were inspired or based on neo-liberal principles and doctrines. For the last ten years, most countries in the region have suffered severe economic and political crises, which in turn have brought about social unrest and protests. Throughout this period, the Latin American people have struggled for life, dignity and human rights. Globalization has dramatically impacted the political, social and cultural aspects of the societies in the region. Because of globalization, local people have lost control over their national resources and economic activities, and the gap between rich and poor people has widened. Recently, several countries have elected governments committed to development strategies that are at odds with the policies of international institutions (IMF, World Bank, etc.).

9. Many churches have been and remain alert to these changes, developments and challenges. They believe that their pastoral and prophetic role is to participate actively in nation building. The churches' involvement in nation building has helped them to understand God's mission in a new context and in a new way. Faith is an essential reality in the daily life of the people of Latin America. Spirituality, evangelical zeal and ecumenical engagement are strong among the churches. The growth of non-institutional churches and charismatic movements is an important feature of Christianity in Latin America.

10. The Assembly theme has a special meaning at this moment in the history of this continent. Through the special session on Latin America, as well as through worship in local communities and daily contacts with the local churches and people, we will have the opportunity to learn more about the continent, in general, and Brazil, in particular.

A PERIOD OF UPHEAVALS AND TENACITY

11. The last seven years have been a complex and fragile period of world history. The report *From Harare to Porto Alegre* (1998-2006) covers the major developments and significant aspects of the Council's witness during this period. It briefly outlines the achievements made and the lessons learned during the journey from the 8th to the 9th Assembly. Attached to the report, you also have in your files the *Pre-Assembly Programme Evaluation* which is a critical, comprehensive and objective assessment of the Council's work in its various aspects and manifestations.

12. As we look at the period that is now behind us, we may rightly ask how much we have been able to move forward towards our ecumenical goals. Giving a full and exhaustive account about the journey of our fellowship is not easy, indeed. One of the words frequently used in recent years to depict the life and work of the Council is "crisis". We have gone through crises of various kinds. We have faced tremendous tensions and have carried on the Council's witness under enormous pressures. Great achievements are realized and major goals are attained through crises. Was not the incarnation of Christ due to a crisis? Was not the creation of the WCC a response to a crisis? Crises will always remain with the Council in different forms and ways. We are called to respond to crises in faith and hope and with a forward-looking vision.

13. The last seven years in the life of the Council was a period of upheaval and yet tenacity. The Council experienced the strong impact of global developments. In spite of the negative repercussions of these developments, the in-house mood of restlessness, due to a significant fall in income and the necessity of reducing programmes and staff and, in spite of the emergence of multiple concerns pertaining to Council-member churches relations, the Council largely realized the recommendations made and the programmatic priorities set by the Harare Assembly. The reflection and action of the Council were mainly organized around four foci: being church, caring for life, ministry of reconciliation and common witness and service amidst globalization. Financial constraints, programme re-adjustments and changes in staff leadership did not hamper the quality of the Council's witness. Nor did they affect the morale and dedication of the staff. Guided by the Central and Executive Committees and supported by programme-related committees and commissions, the Council's staff performed their work well. They deserve our great appreciation.

14. An assembly is primarily an occasion for the Council to be accountable by assessing its achievements, failures and deficiencies. It is also an opportunity to take a broader and realistic look at the ecumenical movement, which the Council is called to serve. Indeed, such a serious attempt to analyze the ecumenical situation, spell out the emerging new realities and concerns, and identify new expressions and challenges of ecumenism will enable us to look forward with greater confidence and clear vision. In the last decade, the ecumenical movement has witnessed significant developments, which will undoubtedly become, with their broader ramifications and far-reaching consequences, crucial for the future course of ecumenism. I would like to focus my observations on three specific areas: ecclesiology, inter-religious dialogue, and new self-articulations of the ecumenical movement.

FOR A CHURCH BEYOND ITS WALLS

15. The ecumenical movement is about "being church". It will always remind the churches to fulfill their being and vocation in the context of changing times and circumstances. In my report to the Harare Assembly, I asked: "What kind of church do we project for the 21st century: a church confined to nation-states or ethnic groups and exclusively concerned with its self-perpetuation or a missionary church open to the world and ready to face the challenges of the world?"[1]. Through its programmes, relations and activities, the Council continued to wrestle with this pertinent question. Our churches, too, each in their own way, grappled with this critical issue.

16. Mainstream Christianity is ageing and falling in number, and Christianity is re-emerging with new faces and forms. The formation of non-denominational congregations, para-church and mega-church organizations, has dramatically changed the Christian panorama. Major changes are taking place also inside the churches: the institutional church is losing much of its strength and impact on society; tensions and divisions in many churches on ethical, social and pastoral issues are creating confusion and estrangement; the divide between "belonging" and "believing" is growing; and we hear more and more in the mass media about the church in "confusion", the "polarized" church and the "silent" church. Many people, particularly the youth, seem to be disappointed with what they perceive as the incapacity of the institutional church to respond to the challenges and problems of new times. They are looking for a church that is capable of meeting their spiritual yearnings; a church that can serve their pastoral needs; a church that can provide answers to their questions.

17. These emerging trends urge the church to go beyond its institutional boundaries, to transcend its traditional forms and reach the people at the grass roots. For centuries, dogmatic, ethical, theological, ethnic, cultural and confessional walls have protected our churches. I wonder whether they can any longer defend the churches in a world where interaction and inter-penetration have become integral to human life. The church is exposed to all sorts of vicissitudes and upheavals of society. Some churches have reacted to this situation by withdrawing back into their national, confessional or institutional boundaries to preserve their specificity. In response to the changing environment, others are seeking new ways of "being church". The church can no longer stay inside the "fortress" as a self-contained reality; it must interact with its environment. The church cannot transform the world from inside the walls; it must reach out. In a new world context "being church" is, indeed, a great challenge with concrete implications:

a) It means perceiving the church essentially as a missionary reality and not a frozen institution. The church acquires its authentic nature and full meaning when it fulfills itself as a mission. The church is sent out to the world to discern and respond to the will of God in the complexities and ambiguities of the world.

b) It means going beyond itself, reaching out to the poor and outcast, sharing their concerns, identifying with their suffering, and meeting their needs. The church loses its credibility if it fails to interact with the people in the pews. It must become a "church for others", a church that empowers the marginalized.

c) It means becoming a community of and for all; where all segments of society come together within the framework of a common life and decision-making, where the voices of women are heard, the participation of youth is encouraged, and expectations of differently-abled people are met; where, in fact, all forms of discrimination are destroyed.

d) It means addressing issues related to bio-ethics, bio-technology, human sexuality and other areas of ethics and morality. The ecumenical debate has taught us that the church's being and unity are intimately related to ethics. The churches can no longer ignore these issues in intra-church and inter-church relations. Through pastoral and contextual approaches a common ground must be sought. Such an engagement will greatly help the churches avoid tensions and divisions.

e) It means bringing healing and reconciliation to broken humanity and creation. As God's transformed community, the foretaste and sign of the kingdom, the church is sent by Christ to transform the world in the power of the Holy Spirit. The church is mandated to exercise its responsible stewardship over the creation.

f) It means rediscovering the centrality of unity. A divided church cannot have a credible witness in a broken world; it cannot stand against the disintegrating and disorienting forces of globalization and enter into a meaningful dialogue with the world. Speaking with one voice and assuming together the church's prophetic vocation are, indeed, essential requirements of "being church" in a polarized world.

18. Today, new environments are being formed around the churches, calling on them to review and broaden the church's theological reflection; new ways of missionary outreach are emerging, challenging the churches to go beyond traditional norms of evangelism and diakonia; new ways of "being Christian" are being shaped, reminding the churches of the necessity to change their educational concepts and methodologies. Clearly, a self-sufficient and inward-looking church cannot survive in radically changing societies. Only a church liberated from its self-

captivity, a church in creative dialogue with its environment, a church courageous-
ly facing the problems of its times, a church with the people and for the people, can
become a living source of God's empowering, transforming and healing grace. I am
not advocating for the church an uncritical openness to the world, but a dynamic
and decisive move from self-centredness to dialogical interaction, from concern for
self-perpetuation to missionary outreach, from reactive to proactive engagement,
from self-protective to responsive action. "Being church" is an ecclesiological issue;
it means going to the authentic roots of the church's catholicity, holiness, apostolicity and unity. "Being church" is a missiological issue; it means redefining and re-
articulating the *esse* of church as a missionary reality. "Being church" is also an ecumenical issue; it means challenging and helping the church to become an efficient
and credible instrument of God's transformation in a changing world. "Being
church" must remain at the heart of the ecumenical movement.

SELF-UNDERSTANDING IN PLURALIST SOCIETIES

19. Religious plurality constitutes the very context of "being church". Our theology, our traditions, our values, and our way of life are strongly influenced by our
pluralist environment. The church is called to redefine its identity and missionary
vocation in the midst of religious plurality. The church has always lived in dialogue
with its milieu. Globalization has made dialogue even more existential and integral
to the church's daily life. Dialogue is the commitment of living our diversities as one
humanity, meaningfully and coherently in one world. It is also the attempt to work
together, irrespective of our divergences and tensions. The following considerations
merit special attention:

a) Christian self-understanding in the context of religious plurality is crucial.
   Phenomenological approaches to the question of identity in a globalized world
   and in pluralist societies are simply irrelevant. The new environment in which
   we live questions exclusivist, monological, and self-centred self-understanding,
   and calls for a dialogical self-definition. Although our identity is conditioned by
   our faith, it is tested by the specific environment in which it is experienced and
   articulated. This interactive perception of Christian identity, in spite of its
   potential risks, enriches and broadens our self-understanding; it also affects the
   way we organize Christian education and formation.

b) This approach to Christian self-understanding also helps us to understand in
   the right perspective the "otherness" of the other who is no longer a stranger,

but a neighbour. Globalization has transformed the dialogue with strangers into a dialogue of neighbours. As an expression of compassion and respect, dialogue with our neighbour is a vital dimension of biblical teachings. To discover the "other" is to rediscover oneself. But our understanding of the "other" should always be checked by the "other's" self-understanding. Our perception of the "other" is also crucial for the church's missiological self-understanding and self-fulfillment. The churches' missionary outreach must not be perceived as a reaction "against" the stranger, but as a proactive engagement "with" our neighbour. Hence, we need to explore the meaning and implications of *Missio Dei* in the context of religious plurality.

c) Addressing religious plurality from a Christian perspective is always judgmental; it is based on our faith in the Triune God and our commitment to *Missio Dei*. We must revisit the biblical theology and the Logos Christology of the early church, which help and remind us to look at the basics of our faith in a broader perspective. According to biblical teachings, God's gift of salvation in Christ is offered to the whole humanity. Likewise, according to Christian pneumatology, the Holy Spirit's work is cosmic; it reaches in mysterious ways to people of all faiths. Therefore, the church is called to discern the signs of the "hidden" Christ and the presence of the Holy Spirit in other religions and in the world, and bear witness to God's salvation in Christ.

d) In inter-religious dialogue our truth claims cannot be compromised. Affirming our faithfulness to Christ, however, must not preclude engaging in dialogue and collaboration with other religions. The specificity and integrity of each religion should be respected in dialogue. To make our dialogue credible and set it on a solid basis, we must deepen our common values and accept our differences. While the need for religions to speak together on issues of common concern from the perspective of common values is growing with acute urgency, the ambiguity of religion's role in society and misuse of religion are ever increasing. The churches are caught in this dilemma. This ambivalent situation makes inter-religious dialogue even more imperative. The churches and the ecumenical movement must take most seriously inter-religious dialogue.

FOR A RELEVANT AND CREDIBLE ECUMENISM

20. We have entered a new period of ecumenical history. The ecumenical landscape is undergoing rapid and radical change: traditional ecumenical institutions are

losing their motivation and interest; new ecumenical models and norms are emerging; new ecumenical alliances and partnerships are being formed; and new ecumenical agendas are being set. The ecumenical panorama today presents a new picture. I want to identify some of these significant developments:

a) **People-centred ecumenism**. In the last decade, institutional ecumenism began to generate indifference and even alienation, and ecumenism, as a movement pertaining to the whole people of God, started to acquire predominance. Ecumenism is steadily coming out from the narrow confines of institution and even going beyond the churches. Ecumenism is marginal for some churches, while it appears as a top priority for ecumenical agencies and action groups. Grassroots ecumenism is gaining more attraction in many regions. There is a growing awareness that if the ecumenical movement is not rooted in the life of people and is not looked at from the perspective of people, its authenticity and credibility will be considerably undermined. In fact, ecumenism is not something to be imported from the outside or developed on an institution-centred basis; rather, it must emanate from the very life of people and be owned by the people. It must touch the life of people in all its layers and dimensions. As a consequence of people-centred ecumenism, a life-centred vision of ecumenism is emerging as a feasible paradigm. Such a vision, which has all the potential to take the ecumenical movement beyond its institutional expressions, is already in formation. The movement of "Churches Acting Together" is a concrete manifestation of this.

b) **An ecumenism that is responsive to changing realities**. The ecumenical movement – for some – is getting old; for others, it has already become obsolete. The current norms of ecumenical culture and forms of ecumenical structure are no longer adaptable to new environments. Furthermore, the ecumenical agenda is, to a large degree, outdated and incompatible with present needs and concerns. In addressing issues, the ecumenical movement has perceived its role mainly as one of discerning and articulating. It is expected that the ecumenical movement go beyond its traditional role by seeking solutions, providing guidance and, when necessary, taking a strong prophetic stand. I also see a serious problem in the ability of the ecumenical institutions to respond promptly and efficiently to the churches' expectations and global crisis. Institutional ecumenism has been preoccupied with its own problems and has, therefore, lost touch with the issues facing the churches. This growing gap between institutional ecumenism and the churches must be treated critically. Rather than the reactive ecumenism that we have been developing, we must build a responsive ecumenism that transforms and accompanies the churches in their efforts for the renewal of the church, an ecumenism that questions archaic perceptions and encourages creative reflection, and one that endeavours to replace traditional styles by innovative methodologies and conservative approaches by realistic attitudes.

c) **Ensuring the complementarity and wholeness of the ecumenical movement.** More and more churches are engaging in bilateral theological dialogue (a form of ecumenical relationship favoured mainly by the Roman Catholic Church since the Vatican II Council) and in bilateral ecumenical collaboration. As a result, multilateral ecumenism is declining and conciliar ecumenism is stagnating. The ecumenical movement is developing in four directions: bilateral theological dialogue, bilateral ecumenical partnerships, institutional ecumenism and people's ecumenism. The ecumenical institutions and the churches thus far have not been able to ensure the complementarity of these directions. In fact, we are now witnessing the emerging signs of polarization, identifiable in many areas and on different levels of ecumenical life, and a steady disintegration in many ecumenical institutions. It is vitally important to establish coherence between ecumenical structures, initiatives or actions on global, regional and national levels. It is even more important to ensure the oneness, wholeness and integrity of the ecumenical movement. As the ecumenical statement on "Common Understanding and Vision of the World Council of Churches" (CUV) has stated, the WCC, as the most organized and institutional manifestation of the ecumenical movement, is obliged to engage in this major task[2]. During the last decade, the Council has made considerable efforts to strengthen the inclusiveness of the ecumenical movement; yet, in my judgment, we have not been so successful in manifesting concretely, even with the Roman Catholic Church, the oneness and the wholeness of the ecumenical movement. It seems to me that if the churches, the main owners and actors of the ecumenical movement, do not assume this critical task, the ecumenical organizations will be dominated by ecumenical partners and the churches' ecumenical work will be confined to bilateral theological dialogues.

d) **Unitive or divisive ecumenism?** When the ecumenical movement came into existence, its stated aim was to destroy the "walls of separation" (Eph. 2:14) and lead the churches to visible unity. However, due to intra- and inter-church developments and changing circumstances in the world, the ecumenical movement has become a space for new tensions and alienations. Controversies and divisions pertaining to ethical, political and social issues are often echoed in the ecumenical movement. Many churches misinterpret ecumenism; they equate it with the forces of liberalism and secularism. They fear that it threatens the church's moral teachings and will lead to proselytism and syncretism. The WCC and many regional and national councils, and even world communions, have suffered from this misperception. This situation calls for deep reflection, a comprehensive approach and careful treatment. The only way to cope with this complex situation is for churches and ecumenical institutions to listen to and trust each other, understand each other's sensitivities and respect each other's concerns. The ecumenical movement must continue to provide space for the churches to engage in honest dialogue and creative interaction in order to see their contradictions clearly. It must also assist them to strive for greater coherence and consensus, while remaining faithful to their diversities.

e) **Emergence of new models of ecumenism.** For a long time the ecumenical stakeholders and actors were limited to churches and their hierarchs; they now include donor agencies and specialized ministries. New ways of "being" ecumenical and "doing" ecumenism are unfolding: networking is replacing institutions, advocacy is substituting the programme; membership-based ecumenism is losing its importance and an ecumenism of partnership and alliance is gaining ground. More and more churches and ecumenical circles consider the ecumenical movement as a "forum" or a "space" for encounter and collaboration. These new models of ecumenism are not only strengthening non-committal ecumenism, but also sidelining the goal of visible unity. I believe that we should not waste any more time and energy on the perpetuation of vestiges of ageing ecumenism. The ecumenical movement must serve its sacred cause and not remain paralyzed within ossified structures. I also believe that any form of ecumenism that does not create restlessness and does not generate commitment is not ecumenism. "Easy-going" and "free-lance" ecumenism impedes our ecumenical journey. We need ecumenical models that constantly challenge the churches not simply to co-habit, but to grow together, to move from self-sufficient existence to interdependent existence, from unilateral witness to multilateral witness. This is the true ecumenical way.

f) **Are the institutions or the vision in crisis?** The ecumenical movement has always faced crises. Many believe that crisis is inherent in the institution. I agree.

In my view, the ecumenical vision is also facing crisis. Some maintain that the problem is not so much with the vision, but with the way its imperatives and challenges are perceived and translated into reality. Others, however, are convinced that we are already beyond CUV, and, therefore, must seek a new vision for the 21st century. The real problem, in my judgment, is twofold: the ecumenical institutions have started to lose contact with the vision; and the vision appears to be vague and ambiguous. We must not become captives of our ecumenical institutions; neither must we be trapped in our ecumenical vision. The ecumenical movement cannot be equated to the programmatic activity; it cannot be reduced to mere advocacy and networking. The institution cannot replace the spirituality, and action cannot replace the vision. As the gift of the Holy Spirit and as a future-oriented movement, the ecumenical movement transcends its institutional limitations and geographical expressions. What the ecumenical movement needs is a fresh articulation of its spirituality and vision. The horizontal dimension of the ecumenical movement must be under-girded by a vertical dimension, namely by a spirituality that will make the ecumenical movement a source of renewal and transformation. Furthermore, the ecumenical vision must be constantly re-assessed and redefined, both in faithfulness to the gospel message and in response to changing conditions.

21. These developments will continue to have an impact on the WCC and we must have the courage to accept not only the Council's strengths, but also its vulnerability and fragility; along with its achievements, we must also have the humility to recognize its deficiencies and failures. A triumphant spirit will only deepen the stagnation, and a protective spirit will further isolate the Council from the ecumenical movement. The WCC is not an organization to be evaluated only on "checks and balances". It is a fellowship of prayer and hope. The Council is called to become the sign, agent and instrument of a credible, reliable and responsive ecumenism. To achieve such a goal, the Council must undergo a profound change and renewal in its way of thinking and acting, and of organizing and communicating its work.

BEYOND THE ASSEMBLY: LOOKING FORWARD

22. An assembly is also a unique opportunity to look forward, to attempt to identify those emerging priority areas and major concerns that will determine the future agenda and course of the Council. The post-Assembly period should be marked by intensive strategic planning, the aim of which should be to reshape the programmat-

ic framework of the Council. In this process, which must start in this Assembly, I strongly believe that the following issues need to be given serious consideration:

FELLOWSHIP-BUILDING: AN ECUMENICAL PRIORITY

23. In spite of continuous efforts to fulfill itself as a fellowship of churches, the WCC has remained an organization located in Geneva. More than ever, the fellowship character of the Council faces tremendous challenges: first, with the widening gap between the member churches and the Council; second, with the increasing participation of the ecumenical partners in the life and witness of the Council; third, with the growing shift of emphasis from fellowship-building to an advocacy-oriented role of the Council.

a) For many, unity is no longer an ecumenical priority but, rather, an academic topic or, at best, an eschatological goal. In fact, as a new ecumenical methodology and strategy, the Council has linked unity to ethical, social and missiological issues. As a result, unity has lost much of its centrality and urgency. The Council must re-emphasize the vital importance of visible unity by re-embarking on convergence and reception processes, particularly through the following studies: "Baptism, Eucharist and Ministry"[3], "Confessing the One Faith"[4], and "The Nature and Mission of the Church"[5]. Yet, on the other hand, the Council must also deepen the theological conviction that the quest for unity and engagement in common witness and service to the world are not mutually exclusive, but are, rather, mutually enriching.

b) What kind of Council are we: an organization that plans activities, sets programmes and initiates advocacies, or a fellowship that strives for the visible unity of the church? I would say both. I do not see any dilemma or ambiguity; these two aspects of the Council's work condition and strengthen each other. Because we are an organization, it is imperative that we work with a broader constituency, including ecumenical partners. It is also crucial for the future of the ecumenical movement that we develop a sense of mutuality and complementarity with ecumenical partners. The Council needs their expertise and financial resources. We must bear in mind, however, that the creation of new alliances and advocacies and the growing partnership with ecumenical partners may, sooner or later, reduce the fellowship character of the Council. The WCC cannot be transformed into a global ecumenical organization that simply facilitates, networks, and organizes activities. This would deny the very nature and vocation of the

Council. The Council must remain accountable to the churches as a church-based fellowship; yet it needs more space for creative reflection and action. As the CUV has indicated, "deepening" and "widening" of the Council's fellowship are inseparable[6]. Therefore, the specificity of the Council as a fellowship of churches and its unique role as an organization within the world-wide ecumenical movement need to be balanced, re-affirmed and reshaped.

c) Some churches believe that there are other ways of articulating ecumenical engagement. Hence, they are committed to working together rather than growing together and dialoguing within the membership of the Council. How can we initiate a process of deeper ownership of the Council by the member churches? The Council is the member churches in their common commitment to the gospel and to one another. The Council must listen more carefully to the churches; its primary focus must be to deepen fellowship. And the churches must take their membership in the Council more seriously, and must recognize that being part of the WCC fellowship has spiritual, ecumenical and financial implications. Once, when I asked a church leader what his church does for the WCC, he said: "we raise money". I said: "you must also raise awareness". Indeed, building fellowship entails deepening awareness, strengthening confidence and making sacrifices. At the Harare Assembly, the churches said: "We now commit ourselves to being together in a continuing growth towards visible unity"[7]. We are called to give a new quality to our fellowship: by sharpening the Council's accountability to the churches and by enhancing the churches' ownership of the Council; by seeking new ways of reflecting, working and acting together; by initiating new ways of "being church" together. If a minimum ecclesiological basis is not ensured for the Council, our fellowship will always remain shaky and ambiguous. Is it not time to revisit the Toronto statement?[8]

FROM CHANGE OF RULES TO CHANGE OF ETHOS

24. Since the end of the cold war, the WCC and the Orthodox churches have basically followed separate directions, with different concerns and priorities. The WCC has neither fully nor correctly understood the Orthodox expectations in their attempt to recover and rediscover their identity and place in the post-communist society; at the same time, the Orthodox churches' criticism of the Council has been exaggerated to the extent of ignoring fundamental ecumenical achievements, in which it had played a significant role. Some of the WCC-Orthodox tensions and

estrangement were caused by the intra-Orthodox situation, the changing realities in new societies with a predominantly Orthodox population and the internal structure and agenda of the Council. After seven years of intensive work, the Special Commission, which was created by the Harare Assembly, has identified a number of specific areas that require serious review. The Commission's recommendations have been adopted by the Central Committee. Matters pertaining to the constitution and bylaws are on the agenda of this Assembly.

a) The consensus model in voting procedures is the most important achievement of the Commission. Through it the Council will experience a fundamental change by moving from a parliamentary voting system to consensus building. The consensus model is not only intended to change voting procedures; it is expected that it will promote participation, ownership and fellowship. Consensus does not necessarily mean unanimity; rather, it means preserving diversity and respecting differences and, at the same time, overcoming contradictions and alienation. Therefore, it is not merely a procedural matter; it is intended to challenge us to share our theological insights and spiritual experiences, as well as display our perspectives and concerns more effectively, empowering each other and seeking together the mind of the church. Initially, consensus was a move to strengthen the participation of the Orthodox churches. It must go beyond the Orthodox churches, and remind all member churches that they, together, constitute a fellowship and, therefore, are called to address issues in a non-confrontational way and in a spirit of mutual openness and trust.

b) Would the consensus model and other recommendations of the Special Commission change the ethos of the Council? In fact, the "Orthodox consultations" that we have organized, "Orthodox statements" that we have made, "Orthodox contributions" that we have offered to the Council since its creation in 1948 have, undoubtedly, had some impact; but they did not bring about any real change in the Western Protestant-dominated style, structure and methodology of the Council. This failure was mainly due to the lack of consistent and persistent engagement and follow-up on the part of the Orthodox churches, as well as to the reluctance and indifference of the Protestant churches regarding the Orthodox concerns and contribution. Here is the real problem; here is also the real challenge. The Special Commission has proposed new ways of working together in respect to controversial matters and divisive issues. It is expected that the Orthodox churches will be better heeded and understood. I hope that the Orthodox churches will,

in their turn, seize this opportunity to bring more organized and efficient participation in all areas and at all levels of the Council's life and work. The Council's
ethos cannot be immediately changed by the findings of the Special Commission.
We must be realistic and patient. The critical question remains: how can the
Council move from a change of rules to a change of ethos? All the member churches have a pivotal role to play in this long and difficult process.

c) Do the findings of the Special Commission meet the "Orthodox concerns"? Some
Orthodox churches are not fully satisfied with the work of the Commission. Some
Protestant members of the Council also have reservations about certain aspects of
the Commission's work. Besides common approaches, divergences and ambiguities
will continue to exist. What the Special Commission has thus far achieved is not
the end; it is only the beginning of a process. Further work needs to be done, particularly in respect to membership, common prayer, ecclesiology, social and ethical
issues. The times of Orthodox "contributions" have gone; and the time of
Orthodox integration into the WCC has come. This process must be primarily initiated in the Orthodox churches at the grassroots level by building awareness of the
importance of ecumenism for the life of the church. It must find its concrete
expression through the active involvement of the Orthodox representatives in programme-related committees that constitute, in a sense, the heart of the Council's
work. Consensus and the recommendations of the Special Commission facilitate
this process. I hope that the WCC-Orthodox crisis will shake and challenge all
member churches in their ecumenical commitment.

RECONFIGURATION: A PROCESS OF RENEWAL

25. The ecumenical institutions have been shaped in response to the old world
order. They are incompatible with the new world context. The present ecumenical
landscape, with its new developments and realities, may soon create confusion and
disorientation if it is not critically assessed and reordered. In the last decade, the
WCC has sought to address, through the CUV and Special Commission, urgent
and pertinent questions facing the ecumenical movement in general and the
Council in particular. The "reconfiguration" process that the Council recently
embarked on must occupy an important place on the ecumenical agenda. The following questions and factors, in my view, need to be given due attention:

a) The concept of reconfiguration has different connotations in different regions,
   and the churches and ecumenical partners look at it with different perceptions

and expectations. The common concern is that the ecumenical movement, in all its aspects and manifestations, needs a comprehensive and realistic re-evaluation, and a reshaping and refocusing. Therefore, reconfiguration must not be considered as a Council-related project with limited scope and implications. It must be perceived and organized as a global and common venture, involving all churches, including the Roman Catholic Church, ecumenical institutions, partners and different ecumenical actors.

b) Reconfiguration must not be confined to merely mapping and reordering of the oikoumene. It must basically aim to renew the ecumenical life and witness by adapting its culture to new conditions, restructuring the ecumenical institutions, reviewing the programmes and relationships, deepening the quality of growing together, establishing coherence and networking among different forms and expressions of ecumenism, and broadening the scope of ecumenical partnership. The Council has not been able to incorporate the CUV fully into its programmatic work. Although CUV, as a vision statement, still retains its relevance for the whole ecumenical movement, it needs reinterpretation. The CUV and the work of the Special Commission must be given proper attention in this process.

c) The ecumenical movement should develop an integrated approach to its institutions, agenda and goals, as well as to its way of reflecting and acting. It must also develop an integrated perspective to respond to the critical issues and major challenges of the world. The integrated approach, which opposes the unilateral and isolated initiatives by promoting an interactive and coordinated perspective, is not merely a question of methodology or strategy; it is an ontological reality pertaining to the *esse* of Christian faith. Such an approach may also ensure the effectiveness of ecumenical witness.

d) The ecumenical movement is currently in a dilemma, wavering between integration and disintegration, partnership and fragmentation, advocacy and fellowship, and bilateralism and multilateralism. By its very nature, being a growing fellowship of churches, the WCC also has a facilitating, networking and coordinating role in the world-wide ecumenical movement. This specific and privileged vocation of the Council must acquire more visibility and efficiency at this critical juncture of ecumenical history.

e) The ecumenical movement is facing a crisis of credibility and relevance. We must not respond only by reconfiguring institutions. At the dawn of the 21st century, what the ecumenical movement urgently needs in order to respond responsibly

129

and effectively to the problems of new times and the expectations of the churches, is fundamentally an *aggiornamento*, i.e. renewal and transformation.

f) The Roman Catholic Church has been calling for "clarity" concerning the theological foundation and vision of ecumenism. I share this concern. One of the most valuable contributions of the reconfiguration process could be the development of what I call a shared ecumenical vision. By shared vision I mean a comprehensive review and articulation of ecumenical goals, with which all churches, including the Roman Catholic Church and ecumenical partners can associate themselves. This shared vision must sustain our ecumenical action irrespective of its institutional or ecclesial framework. Such a step would significantly enhance the ecumenical goals. Otherwise, the growing activism may weaken the spiritual and theological basis of the ecumenical movement. Reconfiguration must also take into consideration this important matter.

VIOLENCE: A MAJOR ECUMENICAL CONCERN

26. In response to a growing culture of death, the Harare Assembly launched a *Decade to Overcome Violence: Churches Seeking Reconciliation and Peace (2000-2010) (DOV)*. In embarking on this landmark process, the Council said: "We will strive together to overcome the spirit, logic and practice of violence", and our prophetic vocation calls us to be "agents of reconciliation and peace with justice"[9]. Regional launches, annual focus campaigns (Latin America is the focus for 2006), peace to the city projects and resource materials, significantly helped raise awareness and promote values of life, tolerance, and compassion. Responding to and overcoming violence must remain a major ecumenical priority. By assessing the insights and experiences gained during the first half of the Decade, the Assembly will certainly give its direction for the period ahead of us. In this context, I want to share with you a few perspectives:

a) We have repeatedly stated that DOV, being a Council-wide focus, is basically an ecumenical process. It is, therefore, vitally important that the ecumenical movement, with all its institutional expressions, consider "overcoming violence" as an urgent priority. The Christian contribution to this global campaign against violence must be reorganized in light of new developments, and its specificity be more sharply spelled out.

b) Violence is a complex phenomenon with different faces. The DOV must address not just the symptoms or blatant eruptions of violence, but also its root causes and its surrounding ideology.

c) Overcoming violence implies understanding the "other", and promoting compassion, tolerance, and the values of co-existence. Religions can play a pivotal role in this context. Inter-religious dialogue and collaboration can serve as a proper framework to enhance community building.

d) Overcoming violence means healing memories by accepting the truth and thus moving towards forgiveness and reconciliation. DOV calls the churches to work for reconciliation. As an efficient way of conflict resolution, which is a vital dimension of Christian faith, the Council must take this particular area most seriously.

e) Often the root cause of violence is the denial of justice. Working for justice is an important way to overcome violence. On the other hand, sometimes violence is used to achieve justice. The inter-relatedness of justice and violence is a critical matter that requires a more comprehensive and deeper analysis. In this context, the study document prepared by CCIA on the protection of endangered populations in situations of armed violence[10], which was sent to the churches for reflection and reaction, must be revisited.

f) The church's approach to violence must be proactive and not reactive. Non-violence must be considered as a powerful strategy and an active approach to overcoming violence. The church must preach tolerance, mutual openness and acceptance. Our Christian vocation is to become agents of God's reconciliation, healing and transformation. Others' strategy is "war on terror"; ours is "overcoming violence"; others' objective is "security", even by military intervention; ours is peace with justice and the promotion of mutual understanding and trust.

YOUTH: THE GENERATION OF A NEW COURSE IN ECUMENISM

27. **"God, in your grace, let the youth transform the world"**. This is what the youth said with a profound sense of humility, responsibility and courage at the last meeting of the Central Committee. They called for a more open church, more relevant theology, more credible ecumenism, more participatory society. I fully associate myself with the youths' firm commitment and clear vision. As Head of church and as Moderator, I have always enjoyed and been enriched listening to the youth in my church and in ecumenical circles. Listening to the youth! What a challenge to each of us sitting on chairs of authority in our respective churches and in ecumenical institutions. Certainly, youth have an important role to play in our churches, the ecumenical movement and our societies. But, to simply state that idea is not enough.

We must engage them fully in the total life of the churches and the ecumenical movement at large. In this respect I want to make a few observations:

a) Youth have a special role in "being church". I consider the role of youth as being essentially an agent of transformation. We must help the youth to move from the fringes of our churches to the heart of the churches' life and witness, including the decision-making processes. I cannot imagine a church without its youth. They ensure the church's vitality and renewal. Youth should be actors, not merely listeners; they should be leaders, not merely followers.

b) Youth have a major role to play in "being ecumenical". They are called to become actively involved in reshaping and transforming the ecumenical movement. When we organize meetings or appoint committees, we should not regard youth as merely an appendix or a separate category. The question of youth is neither about quotas nor about programmes directed specifically at youth. I want to see youth actively present in all categories, in all places, in all areas, and at all levels of the whole life and witness of the churches and the ecumenical movement.

c) The ecumenical formation of youth is of decisive importance for the future of the ecumenical movement. The quality and quantity of persons interested in ecumenical life, both in the WCC and elsewhere, is declining. The survival of the ecumenical movement is largely conditioned on the active and responsible involvement of youth. A vision requires visionaries to dream and struggle for its realization. The preparation of a new ecumenical generation is imperative. It must become a major focus for the ecumenical movement. The future belongs to those who have the vision and courage to shape it.

d) If we do not empower our youth, they will find other "spaces" outside the churches and the ecumenical movement to create their own networks and seek other ways of expressing their concerns, their dreams and visions. The 8th Assembly was a Jubilee Assembly. This Assembly must become a Youth Assembly, not only by a strong youth presence, but also by their impact-making participation and challenging perspectives. Youth should become the pioneers of a new ecumenical order, as well as the avant-garde of a new ecumenical future.

A JOURNEY OF FAITH AND HOPE

28. I started my ecumenical journey as a youth delegate with such feelings and commitment. I was so delighted when, a few years ago, a group of young people from different parts of the world, meeting in my own church in Antelias, Lebanon, stated that

being ecumenical "belongs to the very essence of being church"[11]. This is what I myself learned out of my existential experience in the ecumenical movement.

Being ecumenical means engaging in a common mission and diakonia, and struggling for the visible unity of the church.

Being ecumenical means praying together, working together, suffering together, sharing together, witnessing together.

Being ecumenical means perceiving our essential identity not in those matters that distinguish us from each other, but in our faithfulness to the gospel imperatives.

Being ecumenical means affirming our diversities, and at the same time transcending them to discover our common identity and unity in Christ.

Being ecumenical means being a church that constantly fulfills itself as a missionary reality in response to God's call in a changing world.

Being ecumenical means being firmly committed to and responsibly engaged in a journey of faith and hope.

29. In Amsterdam, at the first Assembly of the WCC (1948), we said: "*we intend to stay together*". In Porto Alegre we must say: "*we shall stay together*" in this journey of faith and hope towards God's future.

30. When I assumed my task as Moderator in 1991, I said: "The sea is stormy; we are called by God to sail, in the power of the Holy Spirit, the ecumenical boat in the stormy sea". The ecumenical movement is a boat moving forward. The profound symbolism of this image will always challenge us. While sailing through the stormy sea, the ecumenical boat has taken on plenty of water. Some would even say that the ecumenical boat is foundering. I deeply believe that our spiritual courage to seek new visions, our profound faith to hope for a new future, our firm commitment to the ecumenical cause, will keep the ecumenical boat strong and straight in the terrible storms of the world.

31. The ecumenical journey is a pilgrimage of faith and hope. I have been on this pilgrimage since 1970 – what a short period of time for such a long journey! In this journey of faith and hope I have had dreams:

I dreamed that mutual recognition of baptism, the seal of our Christian identity and foundation of our Christian unity would soon be realized. I dreamed that all the churches of the world would celebrate the Resurrection of our common Lord together on the same day, as one of the visible expressions of Christian unity. I dreamed that an Ecumenical Assembly – if not an Ecumenical Council at this point in time – would be convened with the participation of all churches to celebrate their fellowship in Christ and address common challenges facing the church and humanity. Dreaming is an essential dimension of "being ecumenical". I am confident that new generations, sustained by renewed faith and hope, vision and commitment, will continue dreaming.

I am grateful to all those who, in this ecumenical journey, strengthened my faith, nurtured my reflection, supported my action and enriched my diakonia. I have had the privilege to work closely with three General Secretaries: Rev. Dr Emilio Castro, Rev. Dr Konrad Raiser and Rev. Dr Samuel Kobia, and four Vice-Moderators, Bishop Dr Nelida Ritchie, Bishop Dr Soritua Nababan, Dr Marion Best and Judge Sofia Adinyira, as well as with so many sisters and brothers in Christ from different parts of the oikoumene. Let God judge what I gave to the WCC. What I took from the WCC transformed my life and my ministry. I give thanks to God for granting me this privilege of serving Him through the WCC.

Recently, an ecumenical friend asked me: "Will this Assembly be the epilogue of your ecumenical journey?" I said: "On the contrary; it will become the prologue of my new ecumenical journey." Ecumenism has become integral to my very being. Enriched by many years of experience, I will become even more ecumenically engaged. With the help of God, I will continue this journey of hope and faith as one of the devoted ecumenical pilgrims praying with you and with so many people around the world:

> *God, in your grace, transform our churches.*
> *God, in your grace, transform the ecumenical movement.*
> *God, in your grace, transform the world.*

Notes:

1. Aram I, *In Search of an Ecumenical Vision*, Antelias, 2000, p.283.

2. *Towards a Common Understanding and Vision of the World Council of Churches: A Policy Statement*, Geneva, 1997, pp.8-20.

3. *Baptism, Eucharist and Ministry*, Faith and Order Paper no.111, Geneva, 1982.

4. *Confessing the One Faith: An Ecumenical Explication of the Apostolic Faith*, Faith and Order Paper no.153, Geneva, 1991.

5. *The Nature and Mission of the Church: A Stage on the Way to a Common Statement*, Faith and Order Paper no.198, Geneva, 2005.

6. *Towards a Common Understanding and Vision of the World Council of Churches: A Policy Statement*, Geneva, World Council of Churches, 1997, pp.14-15.

7. Diane Kessler, ed., *Together on the Way – Official Report of the Eighth Assembly of the World Council of Churches*, Geneva, 1999, p.3.

8. In 1950, the WCC Central Committee, meeting in Toronto, formulated a text on "*The Church, the Churches and the World Council of Churches: The Ecclesiological Significance of the World Council of Churches*" (see *A Documentary*

History of the Faith and Order Movement 1927-1963, ed. Lukas Vischer, St Louis, MO, Bethany Press, 1963, pp.167-76). This text, which is referred to in ecumenical literature as the "*Toronto Statement*", remains fundamental for any common understanding of the WCC. It is in two parts; the first part makes five declarations about what the WCC is not; the second part offers eight positive assumptions which underlie life in the Council.

9. *World Council of Churches, Central Committee, Minutes of the Fifty-First Meeting, Potsdam, Germany, 28 January – 16 February 2001*, Geneva, 2001, p.177.

10. "The Protection of Endangered Populations in Situations of Armed Violence: Towards an Ecumenical Ethical Approach", in *Central Committee, Minutes, Fifty-First Meeting, Potsdam*, pp.219-42.

11. "Vision from Youth Consultation on Reconfiguration of the Ecumenical Movement", *Consultation on Reconfiguration of the Ecumenical Movement. Convened by the World Council of Churches, 17-21 November 2003, Antelias, Lebanon.* Geneva, World Council of Churches, 2004, p.27.

Report
of the General Secretary

Celebrating Life
A festa da vida

Samuel Kobia

Rev. Dr Samuel Kobia has served as General Secretary of the World Council of Churches since 2004. This report was delivered in plenary on 15 February 2006.

1. How wonderful it is to be here in Brazil! How wonderful it is to be together! Let me add my words of welcome to all of you to this first WCC Assembly in the 21st century and the first to take place in this region. Special thanks to our Brazilian hosts for their overwhelming hospitality and excellent preparations for this Assembly.

2. God, in your grace, transform the world! This theme has come alive to me during my visits to member churches in the past two years. And, as we meet here on this continent, we celebrate with the people in South America the recent election of Mme Michelle Bachelet as the first woman President of Chile and Evo Morales as the first Indigenous President of Bolivia. Commenting on these historic developments, one Latin American ecumenical friend told me: "This signifies that the seeds of peace, justice and democracy which were planted twenty or thirty years ago have grown up through the years and are now blooming." He went on to thank the WCC for contributing to the struggles that led to the fruits they are now reaping.

3. That reminded me of the moving experiences I had during my visit to South America in November, 2004. One particular moment was in Buenos Aires, Argentina. The leadership of the Mothers and Grandmothers of the Plaza de Mayo told me that under the dictatorships of the mid-1970s churches and ecumenical organizations provided the "safe place" where the relatives of those who disappeared could meet to share their sorrow and hope. One of them could not hold back her tears as she narrated what the support of the WCC had meant to them. She said if it had not been for such accompaniment, most likely she would not be there to tell her story. But what was really impressive for me were the testimonies of those mothers and grandmothers of the disappeared persons. For over thirty years they have lifted up the flame of hope seeking truth and justice. The crucible of their spirit is matched only by their incredible resilience.

4. In my travels I have witnessed again and again such surprising signs of hope. People celebrate life in places where humanly speaking one could only see death and despair. It is this capacity to celebrate together and to strengthen life in community that has kept Africa going. It reminds me of what links my own experiences as an African with the history of Brazil and of this continent. In the lively and vital celebration of the carnival, I catch glimpses of the African heritage!

5. As a Christian, I discern the gift of God's grace in those moments, when life is transformed and a glimpse of hope becomes reality. It is against such a backdrop that I dream of an ecumenical movement as a movement of people who are messengers of God's grace, a people open to each other and discovering the presence of Christ and of God's grace in the other. To see Christ in the other is so much stronger than all that separates us. The reward in the search for visible unity of the churches in Christ is to discover the presence of the grace of God in each other on the common journey as we walk together.

6. In my report to you today, I would like to make five assertions of an ecumenical movement open to these signs of God's transformative grace as a movement of life. I will talk a bit about this assembly and essential dimensions of the challenge that the WCC is engaging. I speak of an ecumenical movement which:
 • is grounded in spirituality
 • takes ecumenical formation and youth seriously
 • dares to work for transformative justice
 • puts relationships at the centre
 • takes risks to develop new and creative ways of working

137

AN ECUMENICAL MOVEMENT, DAILY GROUNDED IN SPIRITUALITY

7. We come together here in Porto Alegre to reflect, to deliberate, to discuss, and to make decisions. But most of all, we come together to pray for unity of the churches and for the world, to rejoice in the shared experience of glorifying God in Christ, and to affirm the deep spiritual bond that holds us together across many divides. Imagine a time ten years from now when this assembly has long been over, when the reports have been written and the decisions duly noted. What will you remember above all else? Most probably, the common prayers in the worship tent, the murmur of the Lord's prayer being said in 100 different languages; and the exhilarating feeling of this assembly, in all of its glorious diversity of those who have come together to praise God, the one who has given us life.

8. I invite you to think of the spiritual base of the ecumenical movement as the festa da vida – the feast of life. The invitation to the feast comes from God and we are all welcome. This feast, this *festa*, comes to us as grace. The wonder of grace is that it is a gift, which we don't deserve, a reward which we don't earn, but it is freely given and is ours for the partaking. In the Christian tradition, grace is defined as a spiritual, supernatural gift which human beings receive from God without any merit on their part. Grace can better be defined as signs and, indeed, acts of divine love. Grace reveals itself as God communicating God-self.

9. In an Easter sermon, the father among the Saints, St John Chrystom, said it wonderfully:

The table is full, all of you enjoy yourselves. The calf is fatted let none go away hungry. All of you enjoy the banquet of the faith. All of you enjoy the richness of God's goodness… Let no one bewail their faults: for forgiveness has risen from the tomb. Let no one fear death: for the Saviour's death has freed us.

10. Festa da vida. Fiesta de la vida. The feast of life. Fête de la vie. Fest des Lebens. Karamu la maisha!

11. As churches, we celebrate the life-giving presence of God among us in the holy eucharist. It is at the Lord's table that the broken body of Christ and the blood shed on the cross create a new community reconciled with God. This eucharistic vision of the world, reconciled and united with God in Christ, is at the heart of the visible unity of the church which we seek. This vision is rooted in faith.

12. Spiritual discernment is essential for our way towards unity. When I talk of spirituality, I want to make it clear that I am not referring merely to contemporary religious or quasi-religious responses to the felt lack of a deeper meaning in the val-

ues of affluent societies – although the spiritual hunger in those societies is real. I point here to the subject and origin of all life: God's Holy Spirit. All our efforts will be meaningless and powerless if they are not blessed by God and not driven by God's loving grace. After receiving such blessings, one's spiritual life is fully transformed. One's intellect, will and memory are ever more focused on God, thus creating space for a meeting point at which God's love is shared with us. The ecumenical movement is rooted in a common recognition that we are spiritual beings who long to know God and the knowledge that our spiritual quest is enriched by the fellowship we share.

13. Spiritual discernment grounds us. It gives us strength, conviction, and the courage to withstand the harsh realities of power. In this fractured and insecure world the forces of globalization and militarism threaten life itself. Being in touch with the word of God and experiencing the presence of God in the other makes us able to withstand the day-to-day rigours of working for peace and justice.

14. Spiritual discernment also allows us to step back from the immediate issues and to see the larger picture. We all get so wrapped up in specific issues, in details of our particular programmes, organizations, issues, and constituents that sometimes we lose sight of the big picture. A process of spiritual discernment can get us back on track.

15. I am suggesting that we take a different approach to the "business" of our meetings: our business is part of the process of spiritual discernment and is embedded in the *festa da vida*. Let us look at the assembly as a spiritual experience and not just as a business meeting that has to fulfill a constitutional mandate.

16. This assembly is the first to use consensus procedures. Consensus is an effort to build the common mind. The differences among us reflect the realities of our congregations and the lives that we share with people around us. In fact, these differences help us to see the multi-faceted realities and lead us to search for the truth that is not ours, but the truth of the Holy Spirit among us (1 John 5:6). It is this truth that ultimately lies in God that will transform us and make us free (John 8:32). We need to approach consensus these next 10 days not as a technique to help us make decisions, but as a process of spiritual discernment.

TAKING ECUMENICAL FORMATION AND YOUTH MORE SERIOUSLY

17. We live in a world of proliferating Christian churches and related organizations, resurgent confessionalism, a shift in the centre of Christianity towards the South, painful internal struggles within church families, the growth of

Pentecostalism and of evangelical, conservative and charismatic churches. In mainline Western churches that have been a mainstay of ecumenical councils, we find complex patterns of shifting membership and renewal. A clear vision of what these churches may become is still emerging. All of these trends and uncertainties have made the ecumenical movement fragile.

18. Young people are growing into this reality, struggling for orientation and meaning. The ecumenical movement emerged from the same search for new meaning by an earlier generation of young people. The heritage of those who came before us is too precious to be kept just for us. It must be transmitted to the next generation. We pledge to devote energy and commitment to nurturing a new generation, knowing that this is not just a matter of education and formation, but of trust and participation.

19. Ecumenical formation must be based on the formation of faith. Ecumenical learning is experiential. Young people need opportunities to experience the joy of working and praying with others from different traditions and different contexts. They need support and mentoring to participate fully in ecumenical gatherings with their sometimes intimidating elders. We need to go out to where young people are – to the schools and universities. We need to be willing to change to respond to the demands of young people. We must offer opportunities to know and learn from others through scholarships and travel. At a time when information technology is forever advancing, we must enable our youth to interact more deeply and to discover creative ways of using virtual spaces for ecumenical formation.

20. The time has come when we must not only open opportunities to young people for their ecumenical growth and leadership, but where we must learn from the innovative and dynamic models of ecumenical relationships that youth can teach us. As an ecumenical and intergenerational family, we need to humble ourselves and to listen to young people. It was with young people that the ecumenical movement was born. It is young people's passion and insight today that will ensure the relevance and vitality of it. Without young people our ecumenical family is incomplete. At this time we need to nurture meaningful relationships and shared leadership between the generations. Young people need to know that they are important partners and that we are open to learning from their ecumenical experience.

21. They can help all of us to understand better where we are going and what kind of response is required of us. It is young people today who increasingly have little patience with the divisions among us and who reach out to others with similar values. There is a widespread hunger for spirituality in young people, even though there

may be a rejection of church structures. Out of desperation, one of my colleagues enlisted her 22-year-old daughter to format the mutirâo schedule over last Christmas. When she finished the tedious work with Excel spreadsheets, she said excitedly to her mother, "I want to come to this assembly. The workshops are so diverse and so interesting – I had no idea that this was what ecumenism is all about. It makes me want to get involved." The issues that engage the ecumenical movement today are the issues which attract young people. But they need to be invited in. And they need to be equipped and supported to participate.

22. We hope that this assembly is a wonderful experience of ecumenical formation for the participants – both the young and the "formerly young" – and that it becomes a part of our ongoing life. The *festa da vida*, the feast of life, is a call to young people. The *festa da vida* is an open feast, but sometimes participating in an open feast means that others must step back. I challenge all of you church leaders here at the assembly to look at ways that your young people can participate. I call on all of us – ecumenical organizations, denominational structures, international and regional ecumenical bodies – to commit ourselves to youth. We have tried very hard to make this a youth assembly, but we have only partly succeeded. It needs the will and commitment of all of us.

WORKING FOR TRANSFORMATIVE JUSTICE

23. It is in Jesus Christ that God's loving grace transforms the world from within. Christ became flesh, lived among us and shared human suffering and joy (John 1:14). In Christ we have all received "from God's full store grace upon grace" (John 1:16). In him and through him all were created and all are called together in unity, in justice and peace. In him, all are to be reconciled, transformed, transfigured and saved (Col 1:15-23): a new humanity and a new heaven and new earth (Rev 21:1). The whole world is filled with God's grace in the life-giving power of the Holy Spirit.

24. The assembly theme is an invitation to look at the world as a place loved by God and permeated by God's grace. Such emphasis on God's transformative grace corresponds to a new emphasis on transformative justice in our work for change and transformation. Seen with the eyes of faith, we ourselves, and this world, can and must be transformed.

25. God has given us the gift of life and we have abused it. Human greed and thirst for power have created structures that cause people to live in poverty and systematically undermine the basis of life. Our very climate is in jeopardy. In an era

when there is more than enough food to go around many times over, 852 million people across the world are hungry, up from 842 million in 2003. Every single day, 25,000 people are killed by hunger. Every day, more than 16,000 children die from hunger-related causes – one every five seconds. Threats to life – here in Latin America and in the world – abound. Globalization both brings us closer together than ever before – and exacerbates disparities of power and wealth. Violence continues to cause untold suffering – violence in the homes, on our streets, in our countries, sometimes even in our churches. Asymmetries of power are manifest in a thousand ways – between people, between communities, between countries. The litany of sins and suffering could go on and on.

26. Something is gravely wrong when at the beginning of the 21st century, the wealth of the three richest individuals on earth surpasses the combined annual GDP of the 48 least developed countries. Political arguments and economic rationalizations cannot counter the basic immorality of a world with this degree of inequality.

27. Something is gravely wrong in the world when there is still a real risk that nuclear weapons will be used in our lifetimes. Nuclear proliferation is an outrage to all humanity. The recent reports of countries acquiring nuclear weapons technology are frightening. But it is equally a scandal that countries which possess vast arsenals of nuclear weapons are unwilling to renounce their use.

28. Something is horribly wrong when children are sold into prostitution, when babies are aborted because they are girls, and when people of a certain ethnicity or race or caste continue to be oppressed. We need to be spiritually centred to confront such realities.

29. As churches, we are called to plan together, to speak together and to take action together in the face of conditions that we know to be wrong in this world.

30. A belief in God's call for abundant life means, first and foremost, affirming human dignity and the right of the poor to liberate themselves from unjust conditions. The struggle for life must be rooted in the experiences and the actions of those who are oppressed and excluded. When the poor as social actors begin to disappear behind "poverty" as defined by the statistics of the international financial institutions, our whole understanding changes. Poverty becomes an abstract term, divorced from the reality of what it means to be people who are poor. We must struggle to hold up the voices of the poor, to recognize them as actors in their own struggles, and to continually strive to enable them to advocate on their own behalf, to tell their own stories in their own language.

31. The *festa da vida* – the feast of life – is not a party. It is a celebration of life, which will sometimes be painful. The *festa da vida* invites you all into the household of God, to experience the pain and the suffering of others, and to feel yourself a part of the fragile and imperfect community of humanity. The vision of Christians gathered around a table in celebration recalls the gospel accounts of the last supper. There the people of God received God's gifts directly from the hands of Jesus, sharing one loaf and one cup. This is the source of our eucharistic vision, an occasion for joy.

32. And yet at the very same time, the disciples sensed that something was amiss. There was a failure of mutual trust, a prophecy of betrayal, a conviction that something was terribly wrong. When Jesus confirmed that one of them would betray him, the response on the lips of each was, "Is it I, Lord?" And this question was not directly answered – for even though eleven of the twelve would not betray him, all would deny him. In today's world, we find that our celebration of being together is also marked by contradictions, by a lack of mutual trust, by failure to live up to the gospel call. *Is it I, Lord? Is it we? Teach us to pray "God, in your grace, transform the world".*

33. As part of humanity we must constantly ask why the world is in such a mess. Too often we have been silent or too quick to blame others, while failing to recognize our own responsibility to each other. We need to move from resignation to indignation to righteous anger in confronting these life-denying forces.

34. If we are to transform the world, we have to change our paradigms. For example, it is common practice these days to talk about the United States as the world's sole superpower. And yet we know that the powers of this world and the empires they form come and go in history. At the end, the Bible tells us, they are built on feet of clay. They are vulnerable in many ways. How can we talk of any country as a superpower when the government cannot protect its people from terrorism, from natural disasters, from preventable diseases? Our conceptual tools are inadequate to understand the ambiguities of power. As we are recognizing, power is not only expressed in different forms of empire. The rapid development of newly emerging technologies is a very powerful tool with great potential impact on people and nature.

35. When there are such enormous inequalities and unequal access to different means of power, it counts in what part of the world one lives. Our churches and the stance they take on matters of economic justice and many other ethical challenges often reflects the realities surrounding them and impacting on the lives of their members. Some churches tend to see the present phase of economic globalization as the continuation of 500 years of oppression through colonialism and

changing empires. Others emphasize change and discontinuity based on their experience of the rapidly changing political landscape. These different perspectives cannot be easily reconciled. We need to continue wrestling with these tensions because they help us to see the realities surrounding us more clearly and to identify the different entry points for both, advocacy and dialogue.

36. At this assembly we are celebrating the mid-term of the Decade to Overcome Violence. The goal of DOV is not so much to eradicate violence as it is to overcome the spirit, the logic and the practice of violence by actively seeking reconciliation and peace. This is an ecumenical task – because, as we are learning, preventing violence cannot be accomplished by any one particular group. Preventing and overcoming violence must be done collaboratively by churches together, and jointly in cooperation with governmental and civic institutions and people's grassroots initiatives.

37. In the second half of the Decade, several issues must be considered if we want to remain both realistic and hopeful.

38. Firstly, globalization is a reality on every level, not just economic. Terrorism appears to be globally networked, as is the war on terrorism. The consequences of this affect people in their activities and dignity almost everywhere. We must, therefore, take globalization and its many implications into consideration as we plan our common actions towards proclaiming the good news of peace.

39. Secondly, interfaith dialogue and cooperation is significant and imperative in the process towards overcoming violence, seeking peace and promoting reconciliation. Churches and religious people of all walks of faith recognize the imperative of interfaith action in response to the pressing needs and concerns of the societies in which they live. More and more people see interfaith action as an integral part of the ecumenical task. The vision of many today is that God's oikoumene includes not just Christians, but people of all living faiths.

40. Dialogue is often called upon to assist in resolving many ongoing conflicts that seem to be framed by religious language or have religious overtones. However, contacts between people of different faiths built quietly by patient dialogue during peacetime may in times of conflict prevent religion from being used as a weapon. Contacts across communal divides may prove to be the most precious tool in the construction of peace.

41. Thirdly, spirituality contributes crucially to overcoming violence and building peace. I believe that prayer and contemplation together form the foremost discipline for overcoming violence. The joint exercise of that spiritual discipline is an

ongoing challenge for our fellowship. We must make space for this exercise to inspire and shape our individual and joint actions.

42. Within this dimension of spirituality, I am grateful to our Orthodox brothers and sisters in helping the ecumenical movement to recognize the dimension of the earth and nature more consistently. Our spirituality is robbed of a crucial dimension if it does not include our being part of creation as well as co-creators in an intimate relationship with God's earth and all that fills it.

43. The theme of the 9th Assembly – God, in your grace, transform the world, reminds me very much of the theme of the 1st Assembly in 1948 in Amsterdam: *Man's disorder and God's design.* The theme of the Amsterdam Assembly reflected both the violent past and the new hopes of the time. The colonial conquest of European nations had reached into the most distant corner of the world, epitomized by the British Empire where the sun never set. European nations themselves had turned against each other in violence in the so-called World Wars I and II. With the development and use of the atomic bomb, humanity had acquired the terrible capacity to destroy life on this planet. The vital question of the new era was whether God's design of the web of life of a transformed world would mark the future or whether human disorder where life is threatened and millions suffer would prevail.

44. The Amsterdam Assembly dared to speak of "God's design". This was an ethical statement par excellence in such troubled times. The theme reminded the churches and the world that when God created the world, the world was good. There was reason to become engaged for justice and peace. There was reason to work for a responsible society despite human sin and the quest for power. There was not only the hope, but also the ethical imperative for a new United Nations to provide a basis for peace, human rights and development for all.

45. The theme of the Amsterdam Assembly reflected a certain optimism that responsible leadership mindful of God's design would correct the disorder of human societies. Somehow the basic assumption of the Christendom era that progress in history would lead by itself to a world united by a powerful Christian civilization was not yet broken. Such optimism – often unaware of its contextual origins in Europe and North America and its colonial and imperial connotations – was fuelled by the rapid development of new technologies as the cutting edge of economic, political and military power.

46. Just as in Amsterdam, we too are on the threshold of a new era, conscious of the enormous gap between God's will for humanity and the present reality. In the

run-up to the Amsterdam Assembly, the world stood on the brink of a human-generated disaster; in the run-up to the Porto Alegre Assembly, the world stands on the brink of seemingly natural disasters. According to God's design nature has an in-built self-regulatory capacity and cannot destroy the earth's entire life. But, driven by insatiable greed for self-aggrandizement, human beings have interfered with God's designed natural order to such an extent as to induce natural disasters capable of annihilating all life, including humankind.

47. Today we have become much more aware that the crisis we are confronted with goes much deeper and manifests itself beyond injustice and war among human beings, but affects all life. In particular, I point to the challenge to this planet and its inhabitants of climate change. Just as atomic weapons changed the very way we thought about life, so too the potential of major climatic changes puts life as we know it in danger.

48. Climate change is, arguably, the most severe threat confronting humanity today. This is not an issue for the future: severe consequences are already being experienced by millions of people. We can prevent catastrophic climate change – at least, we know enough to reduce the degree of human-induced climate change – if we find effective ways of combining the voice of the churches with others who can make a difference. We must call on all Christian churches to speak to the world with one voice in addressing the threat of climate change.

49. This divided world needs a church living as one body of Christ. Archbishop Desmond Tutu once said "apartheid is too strong for a divided church". I say that this planet, where life is threatened, needs a church which lives unity in diversity as a sign and foretaste of the community of life that God wants to be – God's household of life, the inhabited earth, the *oikoumene*. Even though our differences may at times divide us, deep in our hearts we know very well that we belong to each other. Christ wants us to be one. We are created one humanity and one earth community by the grace of God.

FOCUS ON AFRICA

50. Together with the Decade to Overcome Violence, the Africa Focus was a major mandate from the 8th Assembly. In response to the call from the African plenary at the Harare Assembly, the WCC committed itself to accompany the churches and the people of Africa on their journey of hope for a better Africa. In the intervening years the Ecumenical Focus on Africa provided the framework for

coordinated programmatic work in the areas of women and youth, peace-building, governance and human rights, reconstruction, HIV and AIDS, people with disabilities, theological education and ecumenical formation, inter-religious relations, church and ecumenical relations and economic justice. (The full account is found in the official report *From Harare to Porto Alegre.*) In our ecumenical engagement with Africa in these last seven years, we have also learnt to listen to the African churches and to the people of Africa concerning the continent's situation: pain and cries as well as joy and hope.

51. The insights gained from our experience with the Ecumenical Focus on Africa suggest that overcoming poverty in Africa, which should be a high priority in our future ecumenical accompaniment, will require addressing two root causes: one systemic and structural, the other ethical and political in nature. On the systemic level, there are four factors that combine to militate against food sufficiency, which is a prerequisite to overcoming poverty: the economic policies which are unfavourable to investment in agriculture and rural community development. Rural-urban migration continues to empty rural areas of educated and able-bodied young people who contribute the core of human resources for rural transformation. The third factor is violence. This includes civil war and senseless inter-personal violence at the domestic and community level. The fourth and most recent is HIV and AIDS in Sub-Saharan Africa. For aid to make a dent on poverty in Africa it must be an integ-ral part, and not given in isolation, of a holistic and comprehensive approach addressing all those factors.

52. It is possible to formulate and have in place good policies for development. It is also possible to increase foreign financial aid to Africa. It is also possible to provide mechanisms for good governance. But the experience so far has shown that overcoming poverty and achieving social transformation is more than a mechanical approach to sustainable development. A vital ingredient that lacks is the moral will on the part of African leadership. For far too long African leaders have accepted the unacceptable and tolerated the intolerable.

53. Progressively, Afro-pessimism is being replaced by guarded optimism on the part of African churches and African people. The transformation from the Organization for African Unity to the African Union, the creation of new partnerships in Africa's development, the ongoing transforming of the All Africa Conference of Churches into a strategic ecumenical instrument, peace initiatives of women in Sierra Leone and Sudan and the recent election of the first woman pres-

ident in Africa, Mme Ellen Johnson-Sirleaf as President of Liberia, are signs of hope. In the last seven years, most of the African countries have moved from one-party dictatorships to parliamentary democracies.

54. But, in the final analysis, Africa remains a paradoxical continent: Africa is extremely rich yet full of extremely poor people. Certainly, the outside world, the ecumenical movement included, has accompanied Africa in many and diverse ways. One of them is by providing aid. In the last thirty years a staggering $330 billion have been poured into Africa. So why is Africa in its present predicament? This one thing we have observed: financial aid alone is not the answer to overcoming poverty in Africa; it is too easily misconceived, misdirected, misregulated or misapplied. It will take a level and depth of anger, indeed of righteous indignation, similar to that which produced the spirit of Pan-Africanism in the struggle against colonialism and apartheid, to overcome poverty in Africa. The Africans on the continent and the African diaspora will have to come together again under the rubric of a kind of *global Africana* and say: it cannot go on like this because what is at stake is the core of what it means to be African - the African soul! And that requires more than material aid to recover.

IT'S ALL ABOUT RELATIONSHIPS

55. Why is it so difficult to overcome what separates us? Why do we fall still short in our relationships with other human beings despite the technological advances of our age that defy imagination? It is incredible to think of our ability to manipulate genes and to send rockets to the far edges of our solar system – while we are still engaged in wars.

56. There is a common element in the social, economic and environmental threats to life we are confronted with and the ambiguous experience of growing interdependence that provokes greater fragmentation and enmity instead of better cooperation. Those whose power thrives on our fears and anxieties exploit this situation. Fears and anxieties prevent us from a common witness. They pit us against each other, undermine our trust and confidence in each other, and force us to become defensive and reactive to the realities that surround us.

57. The biggest challenges that we face today, it seems to me, all converge at their roots in the lack of human capacity to relate to each other, to creation, and to God as we ought to. Whether we talk about our social realities, issues of power and politics, and even about the realities within and among the churches, we can

see that the quality of our relationships has suffered considerably not just today, but for decades and centuries.

58. We live in a diverse world – a world of ethnic, racial, linguistic, cultural and religious differences. The migration of people has meant that almost all of our societies have become multi-cultural. And yet our capacity to relate to the other is sadly limited. We lash out and accuse those who are different from us. We are too often fearful of newcomers. We draw lines between ourselves and others in ways that are hurtful. Racism continues to rear its ugly head; xenophobia and Islamo-phobia spread to more and more places; anti-Semitism has revived where it was expected to have died years ago. And yet the commonalities that unite us are far greater than those that divide us. We are all capable of love, we all revere our families, we all depend on the environment, we all have a vested interest in making this planet a loving and hospitable place.

59. If we focus on our capacity to relate to each other, to creation and to God, we realize that our ethical challenges have a profoundly spiritual dimension and vice versa. We can no longer separate ethics and ecclesiology, the search for unity of the church and the unity of humankind. They are closely intertwined with each other. What aggravates our divisions and the inequality among us and what can contribute to healing and reconciliation has, indeed, a common centre.

60. This should not surprise us. The reality of sin reflects the reality of broken relationships with God, the fellow human being and creation. Sin – so teaches the Bible – is first and foremost a matter of broken relationships in all of these three dimensions of our existence. Sin is real. Sin has its social and practical expressions, which breed death instead of life and undermine our fellowship. It is this reality that is directly targeted, redeemed and transformed by God's grace. Taking the toll of human sin on himself in his death on the cross, Christ restores life and heals and reconciles relationships distorted by sin. We celebrate this mystery of life renewed in Christ in the eucharist that transforms us as members of the one body of Christ. In our daily lives, this liturgy of the eucharist continues in the healing of relationships, in sharing life with life.

61. The life that God gives us and that sustains us, all of us, is the food that creates a new community of sharing, a community justified and reconciled with God by God's grace. The *festa da vida* is an open feast. It welcomes those who come and it builds community through relationships. For Christians, the "Agape" – the fellowship meal that often follows the eucharistic service – is a celebration of this community. It too anticipates the kingdom which is to come.

62. We will be best equipped to promote human relationships in the world around us if as churches we shall learn how to share with one another all the gifts of grace which we have received from God. To a very large extent our disunity as churches is due to our incapacity to practise this genuine sharing of gifts. One way of enriching our fellowship of sharing is by transforming the way we relate to each other as churches and as ecumenical organizations – a kind of horizontal sharing of the gifts of grace. Today, more than ever before, we need each other as churches. We must find new ways of deepening our fellowship as churches within the WCC fellowship. A new paradigm of being church to each other is an imperative in the 21st century work on ecumenical and ecclesial relationships. This is needed for the churches' self-empowerment, not for their own sake, but for the sake of each other and in order to gain the capacity to contribute to the world in dire need of learning to build better ways of relating. But as churches we can also learn from many communities that have developed ways of sharing the richness of who they are in spite of what they are.

63. During my travels to different regions of this world, I have seen that in many places worship continues in a common Agape meal – a celebration of shared life for all. I remember poor Indigenous women in Bolivia sharing the little they had after worship and creating a festive meal for everybody on the basis of the different varieties of potatoes they had brought to church. There, in that deprived community, the communal joy radiated as life met life in earnest. By sharing the little each had, the women did not become poorer than they had been; rather, they each became happier for each other because none went back home hungry. The miracle of feeding five thousand (without counting women and children!) is a reality on a daily basis among the poor. That is how they still survive in this otherwise cruel and merciless world.

64. Carnival here in Brazil is exactly such a sprawling and over-abundant celebration of life against a backdrop of poverty and marginalization. Poor communities continue to nurture the creativity and capacity to celebrate life together in the midst of the destitute and desperate situation that confronts them. Such celebrations of life among the poor remind me also of all the other parables of the invitation to the festive table that are told by Matthew, Mark, Luke and John in various ways. They all have in common that the host is deeply disappointed by the negative response of those invited in the first place. In an act of transformative justice, he extends the invitation to those from the streets and the fences at the margins of society. Jesus' sermon in the

synagogue of Nazareth speaks to their lives: the good news to the poor (Luke 4:18f). They want to celebrate the new, empowered community in Christ by worshipping together in song and prayer. They want to experience the healing power of the gospel in their daily lives. And this is for sure: they will celebrate with God when the usual patterns of exclusion and marginalization are turned upside down!

65. The *festa da vida* invites us to look afresh at the quality of our relationships and to put these relationships at the centre of the ecumenical movement.

66. The Common Understanding and Vision (CUV) policy statement adopted at the Harare Assembly called on the WCC and its members to deepen their relationships with one another. To some extent, this has taken place, as in the important work of the Special Commission on Orthodox Participation in the World Council of Churches. Pastoral visits and "living letters" have offered churches the opportunity to express solidarity and compassion with one another in different difficult situations. We need to deepen our mutual accountability to one another, and do it in concrete and visible ways.

67. The CUV also recognized that the ecumenical movement is broader than the World Council of Churches and called on the WCC to develop its relationships with other Christian bodies, notably the evangelical and Pentecostal churches and other ecumenical organizations.

68. Our relationship with the Roman Catholic Church has matured over the years. The WCC and the Roman Catholic Church are very different bodies, but both are deeply committed to the ecumenical enterprise. For the last forty years we have worked together fruitfully through the Joint Working Group. The WCC is grateful for the direct involvement of the Roman Catholic Church in our work to overcome the theological, historical and social divisions among the churches; in mission; in theological education; in the witness for justice in our world; in inter-religious dialogue; and in other ways.

69. Perhaps sometimes there have been unrealistic expectations – and that on both sides. But we have always had the will to clarify the issues in order to resume a common search for the *kind* of unity which is Christ's will for his church.

70. There is a natural tension between efforts towards deepening, and those towards widening, the fellowship of the churches constituting the World Council. This assembly gives an opportunity to re-focus attention on the quality of relationships within the fellowship, to explore together what it means to be in fellowship towards greater unity, and to challenge one another to manifest that unity more

deeply. The assembly also gives us the opportunity to reaffirm our readiness to widen this fellowship through dialogue, inter-action and cooperation with sisters and brothers in Christ beyond the intimate circle of membership in the World Council of Churches. One concrete example is that of the Global Christian Forum, which brings together followers of Jesus Christ from a broader range of traditions and expressions than has ever been seen. The World Council of Churches is pledged to do everything in its power to continue to facilitate this process which, so far, has been very encouraging.

71. There is, as we know, a natural tension between the various institutional expressions of the ecumenical movement. All ecumenical organizations are struggling today with the question of how to respond to the changing ecclesial and ecumenical landscape. This is why we have begun to address together the major challenges to ecumenism in the 21st century – a process that goes beyond a narrow institutional focus that the term "re-configuration" might suggest. There is the constant need for spelling out together the theological and spiritual basis of our common ecumenical commitment. Just as there is the urgent need to work out mechanisms for coordinating our ecumenical response to diakonia, advocacy and development. Many actors in the ecumenical movement underline the need for defining together the common ecumenical vision and not only "the common vision of the WCC". I expect that this assembly will affirm the Council's role within the one ecumenical movement and encourage the Council to become the leading force, the facilitating agent for this important ecumenical task in serving the ecumenical movement of the 21st century.

72. In addition, there is some tension in regard to inter-religious relationships. Many ask if this is integral to the ecumenical quest for Christian unity. We all recognize that we live in a multi-faith world, and we need to learn more about relating to people of other faiths, particularly at the community level. Beyond that, in addressing a broad range of world issues – and not just those involving conflicts between peoples of different religions – we need to learn how to relate, learn about the ways people of other faiths believe and see the world, and learn to act together for the good of our communities and of the world. Religion is increasingly recognized as playing a major role in international affairs, and we need to build relationships with other faith communities on all levels. This was affirmed by the Critical Moment on Religious Dialogue Conference which the Council organized last June. The meeting brought together participants from all major world religions in all parts of the world.

One of the main conference recommendations was to call on the WCC to put in place mechanisms for bringing world religious leaders to address together the problems facing the human community today. Inter-religious relationships should be given a high priority in the next period, and we look to this assembly to advise on the best ways of achieving this objective.

73. The *festa da vida*, to which we are all invited, is also an invitation to reach out to those we know and to those whom we don't yet know.

74. We have long recognized that all of the WCC's programmatic work is grounded in relationships and yet the reality is that different staff or teams are responsible for programme and for relationships. In our work after this assembly, I hope for a more integrated and interactive approach to programme and relationships where our programmes strengthen the quality of our relationships and where our constituency feels more ownership of the programmes. The significance of this deep inter-relatedness was emphasized by the main findings of the Pre-Assembly Evaluation Report.

CREATIVE WAYS OF WORKING

75. As we begin this assembly, I hope and pray that we celebrate this extraordinary opportunity given to us as a moment of sharing with each other what we bring to this place and celebrating together a *fiesta of life*. We hope that the assembly plenaries, the series of ecumenical conversations and mutirâo events will help us to identify the main challenges and priorities the churches should address worldwide through their common instrument, which is the World Council of Churches. We hope that the Programme Guidelines Committee will arrive at a relevant and workable agenda for transformation and that the Policy Reference Committee will move our relationships forward. And we hope that the Finance Committee will offer practical advice on how to develop a concept of dynamic stewardship which undergirds the management of our financial, human and physical resources as an integral part of the Council's overall work. Beyond that, we will focus on adopting a plan of work and programme for ecumenical spirituality that will be inspired and strengthened by our common commitment to praying together and fully owned and implemented by member churches. Several pre-assembly events have already highlighted the contributions of those often on the periphery of the ecumenical movement: youth, Indigenous Peoples, dalits, women, and people with disabilities. Their challenge and perspectives continue to be an important entry point not just for critiques of injustice and exclusion but for new and creative understandings of transformation. The

fact that we are meeting in Latin America will shape our discussions and we look forward to deepening our understanding of this continent through the Latin American celebration and plenary.

76. In what has been described as "the information age", our ecumenical movement is challenged to proclaim God's eternal Word and interpret its meaning across a wide range of cultures and technologies. As we seek creative ways to communicate, we remain committed to telling the love of Jesus, building trust and supporting the growth of base communities – both actual and virtual – in which spiritual fellowship may mature and lives may be transformed.

77. The present context challenges us to re-think the following four current emphases of the ecumenical movement. They should not be seen as a proposal of a new WCC programme structure because there are many different ways of dealing with them.

78. **Faith and spirituality**: The central question of our time, as I have indicated in my remarks, is the question of faith and the presence of Christ in the other. This is at the basis of our understanding of unity and mission. Faith must be central to our life together and must be the foundation for our ecumenical vision and engagement. How do we make visible and effective the unity which is given us in Christ?

79. What does Christian faith in the 21st century entail? This question is relevant to the Northern and Eastern churches as well as to the churches in the global South. It is no longer a realistic expectation that Christian faith formation takes place in the Christian families, in the churches and Sunday schools, and in the schools or even in the society at large. Deliberate efforts must be made to ensure that basic facts about the Christian faith are understood by those who confess Christianity. However, it is also necessary to understand the emerging Christendom in the 21st century because Southern Christianity is not just a transplant of Christendom of yester-centuries. New expressions of non-denominationalism and post-denominationalism are increasing in all parts of the world. Our Christian self-understanding in an increasingly multi-faith society will gain greater currency in the next period. What all this challenges us to do is to see our faith in a radically new perspective. This we could do if we considered Christianity as a global reality, i.e. seeing it with new eyes and not just with the eyes of one particular region or theological perspective. What must be our theological response to the poverty and deprivation of so many, to the affluence of others, and to the link between the two? All these phenomena have implications for the way we do and teach theology, how we do mission,

and how we witness in the 21st century.

80. At a time when issues of identity characterize political, social and interpersonal relationships, dialogue and cooperation between faiths become even more imperative. The more firmly we are grounded in our Christian faith, and the more we speak with one voice, the more effective we shall become as participants at the table of inter-religious dialogue.

81. **Ecumenical formation**: This is one of those areas that surfaces forcefully, not merely as need or priority but as a real ecumenical imperative, as a determining factor that can have a decisive influence on the ecumenical movement throughout the 21st century.

82. In many member churches, a new generation of leadership – though committed to ecumenical principles – seems not to be fully informed about the rich legacy and experience of the modern ecumenical movement. In this crucial moment of generational transition, leadership should be given the opportunity to profit from this body of knowledge and wisdom.

83. If contemporary Christians, including church leadership and staff, are to participate creatively and responsibly in the search for unity, and grow together, appropriate means of ecumenical formation must be offered to enable better, richer contributions to our common life. We must bring together human resources and educational materials, from the churches and from ecumenical organizations.

84. If we look at the Ecumenical Institute in Bossey, Switzerland, a model for ecumenical formation, we may discover two further challenges. First, in recent years, evangelicals and Pentecostals have been manifesting a clear interest in ecumenical courses and seminars, including programmes of graduate study. Second, young people have been pressing for more inter-religious encounters and seminars. Both these trends are suggestive of the way forward, and a cause for hope.

85. **Transformative justice**: In response to those who suffer the consequences of injustice that split the world along the lines of poverty and wealth, work in the area of transformative justice is needed which integrates the care of creation, the transformation of unjust economic and social structures, a clear prophetic voice in global advocacy and prophetic diakonia.

86. In the period since Harare, the WCC has explored the concept of transformative justice particularly in the area of overcoming racism. Instead of the more commonly used "restorative justice", the concept of transformative justice is based on the understanding that it is not possible to simply reinstate, re-establish, bring back,

return – what has been lost. Centuries of injustice in any form cannot be erased – either historically, collectively or individually. People's lives and cultures, languages, lifestyles, worship and spirituality cannot again be as they were. Transformative justice deals with the past in the present. Its goal is to overcome oppression and domination so as to achieve healing, reconciliation and the re-establishment ("to put things right") of people's relationships.

87. My vision for the future is that we will explore this further as we continue to address issues of justice and diakonia, advocacy and dialogue. This will require creative new ways of addressing how the church's mission history has sometimes been interwoven with the breaking down of traditional forms of healing and reconciliation. It will include more direct processes of liberation and healing through encounter and dialogue between perpetrators of injustice and those who are victimized.

88. This calls for a paradigm shift in our work, for *metanoia*, that will allow structures, culture, and defining values to be transformed. It will require us to re-direct our programmes towards more intentionally building truly inclusive and just communities which safeguard diversity, where different identities and unity interact, and where the rights and obligations of all are fully respected in love and fellowship. Transformative justice calls on the churches to make a costly commitment to overcome the divisions within their own life – our communities need to be transformed to fully live the diversity of their peoples and cultures as a clear reflection of God's creation and image in humankind. To be the church today is to be healing, reconciled and reconciling communities.

89. **Being a moral voice to the world**: With growing recognition of the role of religion in public life, we have new opportunities to influence decisions on global policies. This changing context with a renewed emphasis on the role of religion introduces new perspectives in dealing with issues of the churches' social responsibility.

90. In fulfilling our historic responsibility we are challenged to become a strong, credible moral voice to the world: a voice that is grounded in spirituality, and therefore is distinguished and distinguishable from the many competing voices in a world where ethical values are too often found wanting.

91. All these are common concerns for member churches and ecumenical partners. I hope that in the future we can develop fresh and creative ways of working which strengthen our relationships with churches and a wide range of ecumenical partners. These ways will take different forms with different partners. For example, I would like to see an interaction with Christian world communions, especially

those whose membership largely overlaps with the membership of the WCC, in our common commitment to visible unity and our common readiness to develop relationships with those churches and Christian families that do not actively participate in the ecumenical movement. I would like to see a closer programmatic relationship between the WCC and the regional ecumenical organizations, which builds on our respective strengths and constituencies. I would like to see more intentional collaboration with the international ecumenical organizations, which are often working on the same issues. I hope that initiatives to develop new ways of working in the field of development and diakonia with specialized ministries will bear fruit in the coming months and years. And as I have previously indicated, I hope that a renewed focus on ecumenical spirituality will transform the way we work.

92. But I want to go beyond these suggestions and renew the proposal that, as a concrete step, the next assembly of the WCC should provide a common platform for the wider ecumenical movement. If we are ready to take such a significant, concrete step we could envisage together, instead of the many different global assemblies and general conferences organized by the various world communions and other bodies, just one celebration of the search for unity and common witness of Christian churches. To be even more specific, and as a minimum next step, I propose that this assembly give us a mandate to accelerate the dialogue with the Lutheran World Federation and the World Alliance of Reformed Churches to explore possibilities of holding our next assemblies as a combined event. And we should also invite any other world Christian body to join us in this dialogue.

93. Such a proposal obviously requires careful consideration of many details. But I am fully convinced that we can do this, and that the ecumenical movement will be stronger with a common global platform. This could be a means of beginning to plan together, so that we may even more effectively speak and act together.

In closing...

94. Dear friends, sisters and brothers in Christ, the delegates to the Ninth Assembly of the World Council of Churches are entrusted with a significant responsibility. It is a responsibility alive with potential. In Porto Alegre we are challenged to face up to the sharp-edged realities of this world, and to discern the signs of the time. In the same moment, we are challenged to pray with all our hearts, "God, in your grace, transform the world!" And renewed through prayer, in the power of the Holy Spirit, we expect to be sent again from this place as messengers of God's grace

and of God's will for the transformation of this world, as messengers of hope for our children, for our grandchildren, for the future.

95. The Word of God is a word of hope, the good news of transformation by grace. It is the proclamation of a new heaven and a new earth, where former things are no more. It is God's invitation to participate in *a festa da vida*, to rejoice in the feast of life!

96. In the course of this assembly, may God's Spirit spark an unquenchable flame of hope within our spirits, illuminating a creation restored to goodness, revealing us as God's children, members of the one human family and one earth community.

97. At this gathering, may God's Spirit kindle within us the deepest desire of our predecessors in the ecumenical movement, the conviction that there is and must be one church – holy, catholic and apostolic – the undivided body of Christ in service to the world, united at one table in the presence of our living Lord.

98. With God, all things are possible. And so we take up our responsibility, relying on God's transforming grace. All are welcome to the *festa da vida*, therefore, let us keep the feast!

PLENARY
"CHURCH UNITY – CLAIMING A COMMON FUTURE"

"INVITATION" ON ECCLESIOLOGY STATEMENT AN ORTHODOX VOICE

JACOB KURIEN

Dr Jacob Kurien, of the Malankara Orthodox Church, is Vice-Principal of the Orthodox Seminary, Kottayam, Kerala, India. This reflection was prepared for the plenary on "Church Unity" on 20 February 2006.

Moderator, Sisters and Brothers,

There is a proverbial statement in the Harare Report: "Any vision which does not inspire new forms of acting remains a distant utopia". The strength of the Ecclesiology statement entitled "Called to be the One Church" is an inspiring vision and a new form of acting for the manifestation of Christian unity.

As an Oriental Orthodox, I am delighted to notice a trinitarian image of unity and an emphasis on the faith of the early undivided Church as embodied in the Nicene-Constantinopolitan Creed. As an Indian Christian living in a multi-religious and dominantly non-Christian environment, I see in the text a commitment for inter-religious dialogue as integral to the unity we seek. A theological self-understanding on religious plurality and a common stance against religious extremism and violence are central to our vision of Christian unity.

My reflections and comments on the text are summed up in seven observations especially from an Orthodox, Indian perspective.

OBSERVATION 1.
AN ANXIETY: OVER THE PREVAILING CULTURE OF "STAGNATION".

Our text begins with an affirmation on "our commitment on the way towards visible unity". But are the churches, including my own, really serious about this commitment? Are we not living in an age of ecumenical "stagnation"? (For this term "stagnation" I am indebted to Prof. Nikos Nissiotis, a former moderator of the Faith and Order Commission). No doubt we have been accustomed to a culture of stagnation, with no spectacular unity-concerns for decades. Let me touch on my own context. Despite theological agreements on almost all theological issues, the two families of the Orthodox churches still remain divided! Many people, especially youth, have lost hope and confidence in "official" deliberations for unity. They have been seeking alternate channels of Christian unity. Our text is, in fact, inviting the churches to rethink the legitimacy of our self-complacency; we have become immune to ecumenical sensitivity and have delegated the unity-concerns to the WCC and similar bodies.

OBSERVATION 2.
A HOPE: FOR NEW "ECUMENICAL SPACES" AT THE NATIONAL AND THE LOCAL LEVELS TOO.

The second paragraph of the text very much underscores the fact that the church is manifested "in each place" through the local eucharistic koinonia, and the koinonia of such eucharistic communities is the manifestation of unity which is the ideal conciliarity of the early ecumenical councils. Today we, however, experience this koinonia and conciliarity in limited horizons only. Such experiences give us the hope for wider "ecumenical spaces". It is hoped that the recently-suggested ecumenical space – the Global Christian Forum – can provide new levels of conciliarity in the national and local situations too where the experience of conciliarity has so far been limited.

OBSERVATION 3.
AN OPPORTUNITY: TO HEAL THE PAINFUL MEMORIES OF DIVISIVE ECCLESIASTICAL INTERVENTIONS.

The third paragraph of our text highlights the beauty and gift of diversity in church life. The Orthodox churches in general, and the Orthodox Church in India in particular, witness to an underlying unity in the midst of cultural diversities. We in India have been experiencing it in two contexts: that of the same koinonia in diverse cultural traditions and that of the same cultural group in diverse ecclesiastical traditions. We can observe here that it is not the cultural diversity that became divisive, but the ecclesiastical interventions. This calls for measures of healing the painful memories of divisive ecclesiastical interventions from outside and seeking ways of returning to the once-enjoyed unity.

OBSERVATION 4.
A MISSING NOTE: ON "HOLINESS".

The text on ecclesiology has substantial elaboration on Oneness, Apostolicity and Catholicity of the Church (paragraphs 3 to 6). But its comparative silence on "holiness" is conspicuous. Is this symbolic of the growing signs of unholiness becoming legitimized in the churches? Is not this "missing" element a reminder to rethink the churches' preoccupation with money and power-politics?

OBSERVATION 5.
A THREAT: OF PROSELYTISM.

161

Two paragraphs of the text (paragraphs 8 and 9) seek to underline our common belonging to Christ through baptism. We should thank the Faith and Order Commission, the JWG and other study groups for the theological consensus on "Baptism" as a basis for our common belonging to Christ. Our belonging to Christ through "Baptism" will be the basic ground for mutual accountability. However, it remains a fact that wherever proselytism is practised with or without (re-)baptism in inter-Christian belongingness, the quality of the common belonging is seriously threatened.

OBSERVATION 6.
A NEED: FOR MORE APPROPRIATE CRITERIA IN JUDGING "SOCIAL COMMITMENT".

Paragraphs 10 and 11 in the text project the mission of the church as a "reconciling and reconciled" community. In my Indian context, the mutual reconciliation of the churches has to take place largely in the area of mutual apprehensions over each other's social commitment. Social commitment is often judged by such inadequate criteria as the weight given to Brahminic Hinduism, solidarity with the Dalits and the approach to the ordination of women, etc. The apprehensions on the basis of such criteria have branded certain churches as "caste-oriented" and affected local initiatives on church unity. Therefore, the already existing social apprehensions have to be sorted out, and more appropriate criteria have to be evolved.

OBSERVATION 7.
A CHALLENGE: OF CHOICES AND PRIORITIES IN THE MATTER OF CONFESSIONAL ALLEGIANCE.

When we finally address the nine (and similar) questions in the unity text, are we once again driven back to the pre-Uppsala situation of "comparative ecclesiology"? The reason for this doubt is that the possible answers may again be "confessionally" conditioned. In the Asian context, especially that of mine, local initiatives and enthusiasm for visible unity have been controlled by the confessional identities created by a so-called "ecclesiastical neo-colonialism". Here, the churches have a challenge indeed to make choices and set priorities in favour of local fruits of visible unity, always bearing in mind the words of the Indian philosopher-poet, Rabindranath Tagore: "Emancipation from the soil is no freedom for the tree."

God, in Your Grace, transform not only the world, but also the churches – Amen.

PLENARY
"CHURCH UNITY – CLAIMING A COMMON FUTURE"

"CALLED TO BE THE ONE CHURCH": THE FUTURE OF ECUMENISM A PROTESTANT VOICE

ISABEL APAWO PHIRI

Dr Isabel Apawo Phiri is the current head and professor of African theology at the School of Religion and Theology, University of KwaZulu-Natal. She is general coordinator of the Circle of Concerned African Women Theologians. This reflection was prepared for the plenary on "Church Unity" on 20 February 2006.

INTRODUCTION

In this presentation I attempt to present only "one" perspective of the Protestant voice as a response to the text: "Called to be the One Church" as an impulse for the churches' search for visible unity in faith, life, witness and action. This perspective is shaped by my own context as a Malawian Presbyterian, living in South Africa. In addition, it is informed by my work in theological education in ecumenical and multi-faith environments and my commitment to social justice issues through the work of the Circle of Concerned African Women Theologians.

UNITY – A DIVINE GIFT AND CALLING

"Is the Holy Spirit present in these ecumenical gatherings that you attend?"

I was recently asked by my minister's spouse whether the Holy Spirit is present in ecumenical gatherings, as she understood ecumenical gatherings to be simply about what she called "head knowledge". When reflecting on her question I realized that this is a view that is shared by a significant number of Christians across the denominations in Africa who think that the Holy Spirit is not present in ecumenical gatherings, let alone among ecumenical believers. What is missing in this understanding however is that church unity is indeed both a divine gift and calling. It is the Holy Spirit that guides the Church, both at a global and local level, to be obedient to the command of Jesus that all Christians should be one.

As part of a charismatic Presbyterian church, my own congregation shows signs of visible church unity by broad acceptance of: a) a variety of different types of baptism; b) invitation to all believers in Christ from all churches to partake of the holy communion; c) ordained ministers of other denominations to share the pulpit; and d) allowing ministers of other denominations to preside over the holy communion.

KOINONIA/COMMUNION THROUGH THEOLOGICAL EDUCATION AND FORMATION

The document "Called to be the One Church" has affirmed that we confess one, holy, catholic and apostolic Church. The School of Religion and Theology at the University of KwaZulu-Natal in Pietermaritzburg, South Africa, is an example of an attempt to live out the consequences of this unity through the formation of a cluster of theological institutions that offer theological education and formation to the Roman Catholic Church, the Evangelical Churches, the Lutheran Church, the Moravian Church, the Congregational Church, the Anglican Church and soon the Methodist Church. At a time when many ecumenical institutions are closing in favour of denominational ones, Pietermaritzburg is thriving again as the hub of visible unity of the church as a witness of Christ. The school also engages in multi-faith dialogue and collaboration. This is a clear affirmation and example that ecumenism goes beyond "church unity". This is a very important angle in our witness as one Church because Africa is home to many religions.

The fact that many more churches in South Africa, the African continent and other continents are sending their students to be part of this ecumenical body of Christ is promising for the future of ecumenism in our region and strengthens the urgent need for ecumenical theology to guide the theological institutions and the church in Africa.

CHURCH UNITY THROUGH ECUMENICAL RITES OF MARRIAGE

I come from a family of six children. Despite our Presbyterian background, through inter-church marriages the Assemblies of God Church, the Seventh Day Adventist Church, the Church of Christ, the Roman Catholic Church, the Living Waters Church, and the Anglican Church have found their way into our family and we embrace them all. Our family has resisted the assumption that women follow their husband's denomination. Inter-church marriages have been a thorny issue in the body of Christ due to our different church doctrines, especially among the Catholic, Orthodox and Protestant churches. To some, marriage is a civil or social contract, while to others it is a sacrament. However it is what happens at grassroots level that calls for the church in Africa to heed the call for ecumenical rites of marriage, as one visible symbol of the obedience of the church in Africa to Jesus' call for one church. Ecumenical marriages should be a place to celebrate the spirit of fellowship and Christian unity.

THE CHURCH AS A COMMUNION OF BELIEVERS

The document "Called to be the One Church" has reminded us that the Church is a communion of believers. In practice, the marginalization of people on the basis of gender, race, ethnicity, sexual orientation, age and ability undermines and challenges what we have been given by God.

Several publications of the Circle of Concerned African Women Theologians (which is both an ecumenical and a multi-faith movement) illustrate gender challenges to the unity of the churches. For example, many women express the frustration that gender difference is used "to divide women from men and assign their gifts an inferior value". This can be seen in the inability to deal with gender-based violence in the church, and in the difficulties which women who are already ordained experience in the church as they carry out their ministry. A continuing source of tension is the fact that some churches ordain women, and others do not.

CONCLUSION

The topic of church unity is far too broad to have done justice to it in this short presentation. Notwithstanding, I have attempted to home in on my own context to frame the discussion. I have highlighted some of the possibilities that exist for further exploration such as the potential for unity which exists in all the Protestant churches in Africa. If indeed we believe that God is calling us to unity we need to show it in action through recognition of ordained ministers (of all races, gender, age, ability and sexual orientation) of other churches at our holy communion table; through ecumenical rites for inter-church marriages; embracing the spirituality of others through theological education and formation; and affirming the church as a communion of believers by getting rid of all that undermines this belief.

Thank you.

PLENARY
"CHURCH UNITY – CLAIMING A COMMON FUTURE"

REFLECTING TOGETHER ON THE TEXT "CALLED TO BE THE ONE CHURCH"

JORGE A. SCAMPINI

Father Jorge Scampini is a Dominican priest and is the moderator of the St Thomas Aquinas University theological faculty's study centre. He teaches systematic theology at the centre and at the Pontifical Catholic University of Argentina. This reflection was prepared for the plenary on "Church Unity" on 20 February 2006.

As a Roman Catholic, I approach the text "Called to be the One Church" in a particular way. The text is an "invitation" addressed to the member churches of the World Council of Churches, which is not the situation of the Catholic Church, although it has entered into a considerable network of working relationships with the WCC in the course of the forty years of existence of the Joint Working Group, and through participation in the Commissions on Faith and Order and World Mission and Evangelism. Despite the peculiarity of this relationship, all that is affirmed and achieved within the WCC takes place within the one ecumenical movement, which the Catholic Church acknowledges as a gracious gift from God, and to which it is irrevocably committed. This invitation thus concerns us. Within that framework of reference I now offer the following observations.

Any title is an attempt to express the thrust of a document's contents. Thus the title "Called to be the One Church" expresses a vision of the Church and, consequently, a way of conceiving the goal of the ecumenical movement. Without forgetting that we are dealing with what "we at this point on our ecumenical journey can say together about some important aspects of the Church", this vision is a yardstick for discernment that should allow the WCC, at the beginning of a new stage in its life, to evaluate what has been achieved, where there has been slowness and uncertainty in the past, and to discern challenges and determine priorities for the coming years.

The invitation is being issued at a particular ecumenical time and place, characterized by the grace of God, who "transforms the world", and the churches' response to that gracious gift. Beginning with its identity as an institution, as expressed in its doctrinal basis (section 1), it moves on to an understanding of unity as koinonia, as stated by the Canberra Assembly, and appreciated in Catholic circles for its theological rigour. That is done without ignoring what lies ahead concerning the understanding of "the meaning of unity and catholicity, and the significance of baptism" (section 2). In fact, this tension between what has been achieved ecumenically and issues awaiting clarification is present as the central themes of the invitation unfold: the Church (sections 3-7), baptism (sections 8-9), and the Church's service in the world (sections 10-11).

In dealing with the subject of the Church, the invitation begins with a confession of faith, which is a way of saying that everything that follows should be seen in the context of dynamic faithfulness to the gracious gift given us. This is the context of the affirmations concerning the Church. As regards convergence, Catholics could assent to what is stated in the invitation. It is clear that they would do it in full awareness that a mere listing of the elements that, put together as a whole, express the mystery of the Church, can be understood and articulated in different ways, resulting in different ecclesiologies.

Thus, working through the document and by way of example, in addition to the questions in section 14, we could ask ourselves the following questions:

a) Is it possible for us all to state, baldly, that "the Church as communion of believers is created (only) by the Word of God" (section 4)?

b) What are we to understand by "Each church is the Church catholic and not simply a part of it" (section 6)? Are we referring to each "local" church or to each "confessional" church? And, if each local church, what do we mean by that?

c) How long will it be possible for us to go on speaking of Christ's reconciling ministry without clarifying the basis on which certain moral decisions are made?

As the Catholic Church understands it, the unity of the Church as a mystery of communion is expressed by a threefold bond: the bond of the faith that is professed (vinculum symbolicum); the liturgical and sacramental bond (vinculum sacramentale); and the hierarchical and social bond (vinculum hierarchicum). While the first two bonds constitute the Church and are its foundation and origin, the third represents its task of witness and guarantees its continuity. For the Catholic Church that is an integral part of its vision of faith. Thus the divergences referred to in the invitation (section 14) are real obstacles lying in the way of achieving visible unity. That explains why the Catholic Church attaches such importance in theological dialogues to the themes relating to sacraments, ministry and the Church.

We who are on this journey and trust in the risen Christ look back to the past and live in hope for the future. At the level of ecumenical memory, it is important to point out that the issues in the invitation – in a condensed form by the nature of the document – are reminiscent of Faith and Order studies: *Baptism, Eucharist and Ministry* (1982), *Confessing the One Faith* (1991), *Church and World* (1990), and *The Nature and Purpose of the Church* (1999); and are also related to studies by the Joint Working Group: *The Church: Local and Universal* (1990), *Ecumenical Dialogue on Moral Issues* (1996) and *Ecclesiological and Ecumenical Implications of a Common Baptism* (2004). This recognition of the ground already covered should give rise to a renewed commitment to make these studies more widely known and to study them in depth, with the aim of encouraging the reception of them by the churches. These studies, which are the fruit of long careful theological work, still have a word to say to us on some of the questions that await a response.

These very questions give me the hope that God's gift to us will not be in vain, thanks to the acceptance and willingness of the churches and the WCC:

a) …of the churches, because the invitation is being addressed to them as the real protagonists on their common journey in response to the grace of God. They should enter into a renewed conversation "about the quality and degree of their fellowship and communion, and about the issues which still divide them" frankly and thoroughly, because God, in love, is calling God's people to discernment and to the fullness of koinonia;

b) …of the WCC, because in service of the cause of unity, it must continue to

have the role of "privileged instrument" (section 12) and that in two ways...
- ...by stating that one of its priorities is taking up the theological issues arising out of the present invitation and effectively supporting the continuance of the programmes dealing with the differences "dividing the churches", particularly the Faith and Order studies on ecclesiology, baptism and theological anthropology.
- ...by adopting as an assembly the text before you as your own word addressed to the churches. This can be a milestone in the history of the WCC as an institution, taking relations between the member churches on to a new stage, as was the case at New Delhi, Nairobi and Canberra, and thereby being of service to the whole ecumenical movement.

Plenary
"Church Unity – Claiming a Common Future"

New Possibilities in the Quest for Visible Unity
A Contribution from the Evangelical Churches of Latin America

J. Norberto Saracco

Dr J. Norberto Saracco is a Pentecostal pastor and scholar. He is the founder of Argentina's International Faculty of Theological Studies. This reflection was prepared for the plenary on "Church Unity" on 20 February 2006.

You belong to the same church as me,
If you stand at the foot of the cross.
If your heart beats in time with my heart,
Give me your hand. You are my brother, my sister.

For decades the words of that chorus have been sung by millions of evangelicals throughout Latin America. It has been a sort of theme song in meetings and activities at which brothers and sisters of different denominations met. Its ecumenical theology is simple: if you are at the foot of the cross, you belong to the same church as I do; if your heart beats in time with my heart, you are my brother, my sister.

That simple statement reduces centuries of ecumenical discussion to the barest minimum, but it also glosses over our real divisions.

Diversity and plurality, values which are a legacy from our Protestant history, have drifted towards fragmentation and polarization. These have been features of the life of the evangelical churches and, for the Pentecostals, almost a measure of their spirituality!

However, today it is different. In recent years, it has been the evangelical churches, and particularly the Pentecostal churches, that have worked hardest in the quest for the visible unity of the Church. The strengthening of the National Alliances and Federations of Churches, the establishment of Pastoral Councils in thousands of cities, and joint mission and evangelism projects are only some examples of this. We know that it is not the same in all places and that there is still much to be done, but it would be wrong not to acknowledge the truth of this.

For the evangelical churches, unity comes out of their faithfulness to the Word of God and out of mission. In the Lausanne Covenant, it is put like this: "We affirm that the visible unity of the Church in the truth is the will of God. Evangelism is also an invitation to unity, since unity strengthens our witness, just as disunity is a denial of our gospel of reconciliation."

For evangelical churches, unity is not based on the recognition of a hierarchical authority, nor on dogmas, nor on theological agreements, nor on alliances between institutions. We have to accept that that way of doing ecumenism has gone as far as it can. We know one another better than ever before, we have said to one another all that we have to say, and we understand exhaustively the causes of our divisions. What is the next step to be? The ecumenical agenda must disentangle itself from the past and become open to the ecumenism of the future. In a dynamic and lively church, like the church in Latin America, there is an ecumenism of the People of God, which declares, like the song I mentioned to begin with, that if you and I are at the foot of the cross, then we belong to the same church, so, give me your hand, let us walk together, you are my brother, my sister. I admit that this ecumenical simplicity may be disturbing, but its sole aim is to help an ecumenism that has come to a standstill to break out of its inertia.

Why can we not listen to the millions of Christians who have no understanding of our divisions? In recent decades, we have in fact witnessed the weakening of denominational structures. There has been a globalization of religious experience. The lines of authority, loyalty and spirituality cut across the different denominations. We cannot ignore the dangers in this new situation, but we must also ask: Will this not be, perhaps, the breath of the Spirit? Will it not be that God is creating something new without our being aware of it?

We are being asked, "How can the evangelical churches relate to the fellowship of churches which belongs to the World Council of Churches?"

When the question is asked in that way, the diversity among the evangelical churches and the diversity among the WCC member churches make an answer impossible.

I can, however, suggest some possible ways in which they can relate to one another...

1. We need to regard one another honestly with mutual respect and appreciation. In the past, we evangelical churches in Latin America have (in inverted commas) "evangelized" by exposing the weaknesses of the Catholic Church. Today it is different. In the 1970s we were also not able to understand the struggle of our brothers and sisters who, at that time, were risking their lives by being witnesses to Jesus Christ, his justice and his truth. Since then, we have, more than once, publicly and privately, repented of this. Unity becomes, however, difficult when our brothers and sisters treat us as sects, when they regard Pentecostals as a threat, and see in the growth of evangelical churches an advance of the pro-war right. Unity cannot be built on misrepresentation and prejudice.

2. We need to understand that the religious map of the world has changed and that the map of Christianity has also changed. The centre of gravity of the church has moved from the North to the South. The fact that this assembly is taking place in this city of Porto Alegre is not a coincidence. We, the Christians from this part of the world, therefore have this not-to-be-missed opportunity to make our unity in Christ visible in our day-to-day commitment to mission. Our impoverished peoples, our pillaged lands and our societies in bondage to sin present us with a challenge. An ecumenism of mission is possible in so far as Jesus Christ is proclaimed as Saviour and Lord and the gospel presented in its entirety. We believe that the centrality of Jesus Christ points up the difference between the mission of the church and religious compassion. We need to be clear. Latin America needs Jesus Christ and we should come together in mission to declare that truth.

3. We need to accept our diversity as an expression of the grace of God that itself takes many forms. There are different ways of being church and in recent times that

diversity has multiplied. It would be a good ecumenical exercise to find out what are the limits to diversity that we are prepared to accept. But we need to accept one another without reservation, without dividing churches into first-class and second-class. It needs to be an acceptance without ecclesiological word-play (communities of faith, ecclesial communities, churches, and so on), which is an attempt to conceal our inability to acknowledge others as part of the one Church.

4. Allow me to end with a question. Suppose we were to give the Spirit a chance? We have used oceans of ink and tons of paper in writing about unity. That has not been a waste of time, effort or money. But it has brought us as far as we can go. Is not this the time for a new Pentecost? Only a Spirit-filled church will see racial, sexual, economic and ecclesiastical barriers come down. Only Spirit-filled lives will stop calling "impure" or "unclean" what God has called holy, and stop regarding as sacrosanct what is "unclean".

The unity of the church will be a work of the Spirit, or it will not be at all.

PLENARY
"CHURCH UNITY – CLAIMING A COMMON FUTURE"

DESIRE FOR A COMMON FUTURE

LEI GARCIA AND JOHN NGIGE NJOROGE

Ms Lei Garcia is a member of the United Church of Christ in the Philippines. Mr John Njoroge is a member of the Greek Orthodox Patriarchate of Alexandria and All Africa. John and Lei met at the WCC Assembly in Porto Alegre. They began talking about their vision of the ecumenical movement and the Church. Both share their visions and discuss the challenges of achieving visible unity. They tell of their hope amidst the challenges brought by the fragmentation of the world and the Church. This reflection was prepared for the plenary on "Church Unity" on 20 February 2006.

SCENE 1

John	:	Good to see you again Lei!
Lei	:	Hey John, how are you?
		(John and Lei hug each other)
Lei	:	It's so good to see so many people here at the Assembly!
John	:	Yeah! It's amazing. So, how do you feel to be a participant?
Lei	:	Well, I'm very glad to be part of this important juncture in the life of the WCC. And of course, it is my joy to be among those who are praying with Christ for the unity of the divided church. (John 17:20-21)

John : That's great, and speaking about the divided church, it is challenging when we look beyond into the texture of the unity we seek, its quality and significance.

Lei : (nodding) So, are you saying that the texture of unity means the value and relevancy of the visible unity in our churches? If so, I think this calls for a common Christian identity that invites our churches to a visible unity, which is an expression of a common faith, common mission, and a common witness to the world.

John : Aha! But would a common identity mean anything to the diversified local Christian churches on the ground, when it comes to their spiritual, economical and political struggles?

Lei : I believe so. For example, in the Philippines, our very own pastors, priests and religious workers were not spared in the recent political killings and repressions because they took the side of the poor and exercised their prophetic voice. So, I firmly believe that a united church is an instrument by which our churches, which constitute the household of God, seek to live and witness to all peoples that the oikoumene may become the oikos of God. The WCC was created precisely to be an instrument to build the household of God.

John : And it shall take place through our collective and mutual involvement.

Lei : You are absolutely right! This could mean that it is in the creation of a better world that we begin to know what it means to be part of the oikoumene. The clearest theological statement we can make is our active involvement in the struggles of the people. Therefore, the heart of ecumenism is being immersed in the world – that way churches find their unity.

John : Wonderful reflection. But is it possible to achieve this vision with all the fragmentation and brokenness inside and outside our churches?

Lei : Of course, it is possible! Don't you think so?

John : (silently thinking) Well, yeah! I think so, it's just that...

Lei : Come on John, I know you are more optimistic than I am.

John : Okay, I think…. Our common faith in the Triune God, God the Father, the Son and the Holy Spirit, goes beyond our current divisions and requires us not to limit the unity we seek only to the level of dialogue but to make it practical in the reality of our everyday life.

Lei : Right, it is possible, first and foremost through the grace of God and our commitment to work collectively for the realization of these visions. And I also think that we can achieve this vision of unity by reordering our relationships, at all levels, into images of wholeness, mutuality and interdependence.

John : Well, realization of these visions calls us to worship together as a community of believers. This confirms God's presence and action in the midst of his people. It renews and keeps alive the relationship between God and his people, which creates harmony and unity among us.

Lei : Do you think worship, with its widely diverse liturgical practices, is the focal point of the existing divisions among us?

John : Yes, sure, but in the future I hope that we will participate truly in the spirit of worship without pointing at each other as liturgically "right" or "wrong" but rather listen and benefit spiritually from each other's liturgical practices.

Lei : And also, we can achieve this vision of a truly united church if we internalize that Jesus Christ is the central focus of our being together and any divergences in understanding of who we are as a Church and even the style of worship or faith expressions are all peripheral.

John : That's a good observation, Lei - centre and periphery. But of course we also have to recognize that our search for unity is not simple and to achieve it, it needs a lot of trust, understanding and respect for each other.

Lei : I absolutely agree! Thanks John!

SCENE 2

(Sound of drums)

(John and Lei move closer to each other)

J & L : As younger members of the ecumenical movement

J & L : we offer our VOICES

Lei : to speak the truth in love

John : to tell the stories of the unknown, outcast, downtrodden, and marginalized

J & L : we offer our EARS

Lei : to listen to each other with respect

John : to listen carefully to the wisdom of the elders

J & L : we offer our FEET

Lei	:	to tread the path of righteousness and to go to the ends of the earth proclaiming God's redemptive love and justice
John	:	to dance and celebrate for every gift God has given us
J & L	:	we offer our HANDS
Lei	:	to support and be in solidarity with those who suffer
John	:	to create instruments of peace, not war
J & L	:	we offer our MINDS
Lei	:	to think of innovative and creative approaches to deepen our dialogue and to realize mutual accountability
John	:	to dream of a just world
J & L	:	we offer our HEARTS
Lei	:	to beat the rhythm of forgiveness, healing and reconciliation
John	:	to love God above all and our neighbors as ourselves, and to receive each other as Christ has received us in his Church.

(John and Lei link arms)

J & L : Finally, we commit ourselves to a common future of Christian life and witness.

We commit ourselves to our continuing journey in calling one another to visible unity in one faith and in one eucharistic fellowship, expressed in worship and common life in Christ, through witness and service to the world, and to advance towards that unity in order that the world may believe (WCC Constitution).

We commit ourselves, through God's grace and our collective response, to transform the world.

We are ready.

Together, sisters and brothers, let us walk towards that beautiful day full of love, justice, and peace.

Let us do it!

Amen.

PLENARY
"CHRISTIAN IDENTITY AND RELIGIOUS PLURALITY"

ROWAN WILLIAMS
ARCHBISHOP OF CANTERBURY

Archbishop Rowan Williams is the Anglican primate of all England and leader of the Anglican Communion. This reflection was prepared for the plenary on "Christian Identity and Religious Plurality" on 17 February 2006.

If someone says to you "Identify yourself!" you will probably answer first by giving your name – then perhaps describing the work you do, the place you come from, the relations in which you stand[1]. In many cultures, you would give the name of your parents or your extended family. To speak about "identity", then, is to speak about how we establish our place in the language and the world of those around us: names are there to be used, to be spoken to us, not just by us; work is how we join in the human process of transforming our environment; and who we are becomes clear to those around when we put ourselves in a map of relationships. Before we start thinking about what is essential to Christian identity in the abstract, it may help us just for a moment to stay with this element of simply putting ourselves on the map.

So in these terms how do we as Christians answer the challenge to identify ourselves? We carry the name of Christ. We are the people who are known for their loyalty to, their affiliation with, the historical person who was given the title of "anointed monarch" by his followers – Jesus, the Jew of Nazareth. Every time we say "Christian", we take for granted a story and a place in history, the story and place of those people with whom God made an alliance in the distant past, the people whom he called so that in their life together he might show his glory. We are already in the realm of work and relations. We are involved with that history of God's covenant.

As those who are loyal to an "anointed monarch" in the Jewish tradition, our lives are supposed to be living testimony to the faithfulness of God to his commitments. There is no way of spelling out our identity that does not get us involved in this story and this context. Explaining the very word "Christ" means explaining what it is to be a people who exist because God has promised to be with them and whom God has commanded to show what he is like.

And to say that we are now under the authority of an anointed monarch whose life on earth was two millennia ago is also to say at once something about that "monarch". His life and presence are not just a matter of record, of narrative. There are groups that identify themselves by their founders – Lutherans, Marxists – but the name Christians use of themselves is not like that because of what the title "Christ" means. We do not look back to a founder; we look now, around, within, for a presence that has authority over our lives and is active today. And so we already imply the ways in which we shall be thinking theologically, doctrinally, about the story of the resurrection and ascension of Jesus.

But as we go further, the identity we are sketching becomes fuller still. What does the anointed king tell us to do and how does he give us power to do it? We are to reveal, like the Jewish people, that the God whose authority the king holds is a God of justice, impartial, universal, and a God who is free to forgive offences. But we are also to show who God is by the words our king tells us to address to God. We are to call him "Father", to speak in intimate and bold words. Our identity is not just about relations with other human beings and our labours to shape those relationships according to justice and mercy. It is about our relation to God, and the "work" of expressing that relation in our words and acts. In Greek, the word leitourgeia first meant work for the sake of the public good, before it came to mean the public service of God. Christian identity is "liturgical" in both senses, the work of a people, a community, showing God to each other and to the world around them, in daily action and in worship. Our "liturgy" is both the adoration of God for God's own sake and the service of a world distorted by pride and greed. It is expressed not only in passion for the human family, especially in the middle of poverty and violence, but in passion for the whole material world, which continues to suffer the violence involved in sustaining the comfort of a prosperous human minority at the cost of our common resources.

"Identify yourself!" says the world to the Christian; and the Christian says (as the martyrs of the first centuries said), "We are the servants of a monarch, the monarch of a nation set free by God's special action to show his love and strength in their life together, a monarch whose authority belongs to the present and the future as much as the past. We are witnesses to the consistency of a God who cannot be turned aside from his purpose by any created power, or by any failure or betrayal on our part. We are more than servants or witnesses, because we are enabled to speak as if we were, like our king, free to be intimate with God; God has stepped across the distance between ourselves and heaven, and has brought us close to him. When we speak directly to God, we speak in a voice God himself has given us to use."

So, as Christians spell out, bit by bit, what is the meaning of the name they use of themselves, they put themselves on the map of human history. Before they start analyzing the doctrines that are necessary for this identity to be talked about and communicated abstractly, they speak of themselves as belonging in this story and this set of possibilities. Creed and structure flow from this. And it can be put most forcefully, even shockingly, if we say that Christians identify themselves not only as servants of the anointed king but as Christ. Their place in the world is his place. By allowing themselves to be caught up into his witness and doing what his authority makes possible for them, in work and worship, they stand where he stands. The Christian Scriptures say that believers bear the name of Christ, that this name is written on their foreheads, that their life together is a material "body" for the anointed king on earth.

Christian identity is to belong in a place that Jesus defines for us. By living in that place, we come in some degree to share his identity, to bear his name and to be in the same relationships he has with God and with the world. Forget "Christianity" for a moment – Christianity as a system of ideas competing with others in the market: concentrate on the place in the world that is the place of Jesus the anointed, and what it is that becomes possible in that place.

There is a difference between seeing the world as basically a territory where systems compete, where groups with different allegiances live at each other's expense, where rivalry is inescapable, and seeing the world as a territory where being in a particular place makes it possible for you to see, to say and to do certain things that aren't possible elsewhere. The claim of Christian belief is not first and foremost that it offers the only accurate system of thought, as against all other competitors; it is that, by standing in the place of Christ, it is possible to live in such intimacy with God that no fear or failure can ever break God's commitment to us, and to live in such a degree of mutual gift and understanding that no human conflict or division need bring us to uncontrollable violence and mutual damage. From here, you can see what you need to see to be at peace with God and with God's creation; and also what you need to be at peace with yourself, acknowledging your need of mercy and re-creation.

This perspective assumes from the beginning that we live in a world of plural perspectives, and that there is no "view from nowhere", as philosophers sometimes express the claim to absolute knowledge. To be a Christian is not to lay claim to absolute knowledge, but to lay claim to the perspective that will transform our most deeply rooted hurts and fears and so change the world at the most important level. It is a perspective that depends on being where Jesus is, under his authority, sharing the "breath" of his life, seeing what he sees – God as Abba, Father, a God completely committed to the people in whose life he seeks to reproduce his own life.

In what sense is this an exclusive claim? In one way, it can be nothing except exclusive. There is no Christian identity that does not begin from this place. Try to reconstruct the "identity" from principles, ideals or whatever, and you end up with something that is very different from the scriptural account of being "in Christ". And because being in Christ is bound up with one and only one particular history – that of Jewish faith and of the man from Nazareth – it is simply not clear what it would mean to say that this perspective could in principle be gained by any person anywhere with any sort of commitments. Yet in another sense exclusivism is impossible here, certainly the exclusivism of a system of ideas and conclusions that someone claims to be final and absolute. The place of Jesus is open to all who want to see what Christians see and to become what Christians are becoming. And no Christian believer has in his or her possession some kind of map of where exactly the boundaries of that place are to be fixed, or a key to lock others out or in.

In the nature of the case, the Christian does not see what can be seen from other perspectives. He or she would be foolish to say that nothing can be seen or that every other perspective distorts everything so badly that there can be no real truth told. If I say that only in this place are hurts fully healed, sins forgiven, adoption into God's intimate presence promised, that assumes that adoption and forgiveness are to be desired above all other things. Not every perspective has that at the centre. What I want to say about those other views is not that they are in error but that they leave out what matters most in human struggle; yet I know that this will never be obvious to those others, and we can only come together, we can only introduce others into our perspective, in the light of the kind of shared labour and shared hope that brings into central focus what I believe to be most significant for humanity. And meanwhile that sharing will also tell me that there may be things – perhaps of less ultimate importance, yet enormously significant – that my perspective has not taught me to see or to value.

What does this mean for the actual, on-the-ground experience of living alongside the plurality of religious communities – and non-religious ones too – that we cannot escape or ignore in our world? I believe that our emphasis should not be on possessing a system in which all questions are answered, but precisely on witness to the place and the identity that we have been invited to live in. We are to show what we see, to reproduce the life of God as it has been delivered to us by the anointed. And it seems from what we have already been saying that at the heart of this witness must be faithful commitment. Christian identity is a faithful identity, an identity marked by consistently being with both God and God's world. We must be faithful to God, in prayer and liturgy, we must simply stand again and again where Jesus is, saying, "Abba". When Christians pray the eucharistic prayer, they take the place of Jesus, both as he prays to the Father and as he offers welcome to the world at his table. The eucharist is the celebration of the God who keeps promises and whose hospitality is always to be trusted. But this already tells us that we have to be committed to those around us, whatever their perspective. Their need, their hope, their search for healing at the depth of their humanity is something with which we must, as we say in English, "keep faith". That is to say, we must be there to accompany this searching, asking critical questions with those of other faiths, sometimes asking critical questions of them also. As we seek transformation together, it may be by God's gift that others may find their way to see what we see and to know what is possible for us.

But what of their own beliefs, their own "places"? Sometimes when we look at our neighbours of other traditions, it can be as if we see in their eyes a reflection of what we see; they do not have the words we have, but something is deeply recognizable. The language of "anonymous Christianity" is now not much in fashion – and it had all kinds of problems about it. Yet who that has been involved in dialogue with other faiths has not had the sense of an echo, a reflection, of the kind of life Christians seek to live? St Paul says that God did not leave himself without witnesses in the ages before the Messiah; in those places where that name is not named, God may yet give himself to be seen. Because we do not live there, we cannot easily analyze let alone control how this may be. And to acknowledge this is not at all to say that what happens in the history of Israel and Jesus is relative, one way among others. This, we say, is the path to forgiveness and adoption. But when others appear to have arrived at a

183

place where forgiveness and adoption are sensed and valued, even when these things are not directly spoken of in the language of another faith's mainstream reflection, are we to say that God has not found a path for himself?

And when we face radically different notions, strange and complex accounts of a perspective not our own, our questions must be not "How do we convict them of error? How do we win the competition of ideas?" but, "What do they actually see? and can what they see be a part of the world that I see?" These are questions that can be answered only by faithfulness – that is, by staying with the other. Our calling to faithfulness, remember, is an aspect of our own identity and integrity. To work patiently alongside people of other faiths is not an option invented by modern liberals who seek to relativize the radical singleness of Jesus Christ and what was made possible through him. It is a necessary part of being where he is; it is a dimension of "liturgy", staying before the presence of God and the presence of God's creation (human and non-human) in prayer and love. If we are truly learning how to be in that relation with God and the world in which Jesus of Nazareth stood, we shall not turn away from those who see from another place. And any claim or belief that we see more or more deeply is always rightly going to be tested in those encounters where we find ourselves working for a vision of human flourishing and justice in the company of those who do not start where we have started.

But the call to faithfulness has some more precise implications as well. In a situation where Christians are historically a majority, faithfulness to the other means solidarity with them, the imperative of defending them and standing with them in times of harassment or violence. In a majority Christian culture, the Christian may find himself or herself assisting the non-Christian community or communities to find a public voice. In the UK, this has been a matter largely of developing interfaith forums, working with other communities over issues around migration and asylum and common concerns about international justice, about poverty or environmental degradation, arguing that other faiths should have a share in the partnership between the state and the Church in education and, not least, continuing to build alliances against anti-Semitism. The pattern is not dissimilar elsewhere in Europe. There is a proper element of Christian self-examination involved here as Christians recognize the extent to which their societies have not been hospitable or just to the other.

However, the question also arises of what faithfulness means in a majority non-Christian culture; and this is less straightforward. For a variety of reasons, some based on fact and some on fantasy, many non-Christian majorities regard Christian presence as a threat, or at least as the sign of a particular geopolitical agenda (linked with the USA or the West in general) – despite the long history of Christian minorities in so many such contexts. One of the most problematic effects of recent international developments has been precisely to associate Christians in the Middle East or Pakistan, for example, with an alien and aggressive policy in the eyes of an easily manipulated majority. The suffering of Christian minorities as a result of this is something which all our churches and the whole of this Assembly need constantly to keep in focus.

Yet what is remarkable is the courage with which Christians continue – in Egypt, in Pakistan, in the Balkans, even in Iraq – to seek ways of continuing to work alongside non-Christian neighbours. This is not the climate of "dialogue" as it happens in the West or in the comfortable setting of international conferences; it is the painful making and remaking of trust in a deeply unsafe and complex environment. Only relatively rarely in such settings have Christians responded with counter-aggression or by absolute withdrawal. They continue to ask how they and those of other commitments can be citizens together. It is in this sort of context, I would say, that we most clearly see what it means to carry the cost of faithfulness, to occupy the place of Jesus and so to bear the stresses and sometimes the horrors of rejection and still to speak of sharing and hospitality. Here we see what it is to model a new humanity; and there is enough to suggest that such modelling can be contagious, can open up new possibilities for a whole culture. And this is not simply a question of patience in suffering. It also lays on Christians the task of speaking to those aspects of a non-Christian culture which are deeply problematic – where the environment is one in which human dignity, the status of women, the rule of law and similar priorities are not honoured as they should be. To witness in these things may lay Christians open to further attack or marginalization, yet it remains part of that identity which we all seek to hold with integrity. Once again, where this happens, all of us need to find ways of making our solidarity real with believers in minority situations.

The question of Christian identity in a world of plural perspectives and convictions cannot be answered in clichés about the tolerant co-existence of different opinions. It is rather that the nature of our conviction as Christians puts us irrevocably in a certain place, which is both promising and deeply risky, the place where we are called to show utter commitment to the God who is revealed in Jesus and to all those to whom his invitation is addressed. Our very identity obliges us to active faithfulness of this double kind. We are not called to win competitions or arguments in favour of our "product" in some religious marketplace. If we are, in the words of Olivier Clément, to take our dialogue beyond the encounter of ideologies, we have to be ready to witness, in life and word, to what is made possible by being in the place of Jesus the anointed – "our reasons for living, for loving less badly and dying less badly" (Clément, *Anachroniques*, p.307). "Identify yourself!" And we do so by giving prayerful thanks for our place and by living faithfully where God in Jesus has brought us to be, so that the world may see what is the depth and cost of God's own fidelity to the world he has made.

Note:
1. This reflection is copyright Rowan Williams, used with permission.

CHRISTIAN IDENTITY AND RELIGIOUS PLURALITY – A RESPONSE

MY PLACE, MY IDENTITY

ANNA MAY CHAIN

Dr Anna May Chain is a theology professor and biblical scholar from Myanmar. This reflection was prepared for the plenary on "Christian Identity and Religious Plurality" on 17 February 2006.

The Archbishop of Canterbury, Rowan Williams, has stimulated us with many critical issues relating to "Christian Identity and Religious Plurality". I want to concentrate on one point and that is the place Jesus is in, and as followers of Jesus that we are in – in relation to a loving and forgiving God and in relation to the world, both human and non-human.

For a start I would like to begin by identifying myself as a Karen Baptist from Myanmar, a minority group among the Burmese Buddhists who form 92 percent of the population. Further, I would like to describe my place as a Karen Christian at a time of political chaos in our homeland, that is, in 1949.

After the Japanese occupation of Burma ended with the allied victory in 1945 we all thought that with independence from the British, Burma could now build "*Pyi Daw Thà*" (a peaceful nation). But our peaceful world again erupted into flames with the Karen insurrection in 1949. The background for this conflict was the British colonial policy of "divide and rule", which pitted the Buddhist Burmese against the ethnic minorities who were mainly Christian, such as the Karens. As ethnic Karen Christians we suddenly became the enemy to our Burmese Buddhist neighbours. The Karens tried to find safety anywhere they could amidst cries of "Kill the Karens. Kill the Christians". When a mob met a person they asked, "Are you a Karen Christian?" To say "yes" most often led to death.

In this life and death situation, our family desperately looked for help. At this point, Muslim neighbours offered us sanctuary. My father and brothers were hidden in the mosque and I and other women were taken from one safe house to the next. These Muslim neighbours, at great risk to their lives, kept us hidden and fed us out of their meagre food supply. Later, we were taken to prison for safety.

Burmese Buddhist friends had been trying to get news of us. When it was against the law to help the enemy they forgot their own safety to demonstrate their solidarity with us by bringing food, medicine and clothes to the prison.

From jail, Father Perrin, a French Roman Catholic priest, came and took us to St Joseph's Convent. In those days, for the Baptists, the Catholics were outsiders. To get help from the Catholics was unimaginable for the Baptists. However, sisters and brothers warmly welcomed us, gave us a place to sleep and food to eat. Father Perrin tried to rescue both Karen Christians and Burmese Buddhists and said, "Stop this fighting!" On one of his missions of rescue Father Perrin was killed. All of us who had been brought to a safe place through the love of this man forgot our differences for one day and joined together in mourning him. In times of conflict and war the worst is brought out of us as well as the best.

At this point in my life, the neighbours – be they Muslim, Buddhist or Catholic – were in the place of Jesus to me. I was at my most vulnerable and weakest. They were my guard and shield. They were the risk-takers and life-givers. My Muslim and Buddhist neighbours may not know the name Jesus but I believe God had found a path for himself to them.

MY NEIGHBOURS' PLACE

Next, I want to talk about "my neighbours' place", the place where they come from, their perspective on life today and the future.

When I say neighbours, I mean my close friends. There are six of us, all women who meet irregularly. We have been friends since we were in grade 1 at a mission school. Two of us are Christians, three are Buddhists and one is Muslim.

We have taken part in each others' festivals and family rituals. Talking is an important activity in our get-togethers. As teenagers we talked about make-up, clothes, movie stars and boys. As young adults our interests were on college, work, husbands and children.

Now, as senior adults our talk turns more on serious subjects. All six of us are committed to empowering women. We find things in our religions that are liberating for women and others that oppress us. For instance, in Theravada Buddhism as practised in Myanmar, although the path to enlightenment is open to all, a woman cannot be a Buddha unless she is reborn as a male. To be a son is to be valued. My friend Miriam, the Muslim, also finds some restrictions against women in Islam. As a Christian, I find the evangelical tradition prevalent in our country limiting the leadership and status of women in the churches. As women, although from different faith traditions, our commitment to the empowerment of women unites us.

In another area, we do not agree but are learning from each other. Last June one of us, Than Nwe, died unexpectedly in Phnom Penh, Cambodia. She was the first in our group to die. We thought we were invulnerable, special. But one of us, still relatively young, was dead. We five gathered in sorrow and remembrance. At one point I asked my Buddhist friends, "At Buddhist funerals, when the dead person leaves the house for the last time, the eldest son breaks a pot of water. What does it mean?" Tin Tin, who had lost her husband three years ago, tried to explain, "For Buddhists it signifies that the person as we know him is no more. The stream of his life which had mixed and flowed with ours has ended. As the spilt water from the pot cannot be gathered together again, that person no longer can be the person he was". Aye, another Buddhist added, "The person we know as Than Nwe no longer exists. Depending on her thoughts and deeds she will have another reincarnation." Marjorie, the other Christian in the group asked, "Then there is no way we can meet each other after death?" A Buddhist friend replied, "No, for us death is the end. So our life here together is precious." Marjorie said, "Last Christmas my eldest son died. This year my little granddaughter died. It would be unbearable for me as a Christian if we had no hope of a future." As a Christian I respect my friends' spirituality, their commitment to live each day mindfully, to work to improve other peoples' lives today and not wait for tomorrow.

The Archbishop of Canterbury, Rowan Williams, has said we should not turn away from those who see from another place, which is not ours. So I will continue to walk and to talk together intimately with my friends. Our lives are intertwined. As I have learned from them to value living life today mindfully, my conviction is that they will also learn from me about the loving-kindness, the forgiveness and mercy of God. God in loving relationship with us and in infinite love and compassion for us, may have a plan for us, my friends and I, to continue this walk even beyond death.

Christian Identity and Religious Plurality – A Response

Thoughts of a Protestant Missionary

Assaad Elias Kattan

Prof. Dr Assaad E. Kattan is professor in Orthodox theology at the Wilhelms-University in Münster, Germany. This reflection was prepared for the plenary on "Christian Identity and Religious Plurality" on 17 February 2006.

A missionary's story...

I am a missionary. My father was a missionary, as was my grandfather. I am a Protestant missionary. However, I could just as well be a Catholic or Orthodox missionary. Today it seems that the confession to which one belongs is of no great consequence. For in this third millennium which Christian confession is the most numerous will certainly be far less important than whether Christianity itself can actually set the pace.

I am a missionary. My family is almost entirely made up of missionaries. One of my ancestors came to the Near East – where we all later lived – to preach the gospel to the Muslims there. Unfortunately – or perhaps fortunately – the Western missionaries had hardly any success with the Muslims. As a result my ancestors turned their attentions to the local Christians. Doubtless they meant well. They were full of enthusiasm, although at that time they did tend to identify the gospel with the form it had taken in their own culture. Many people in the Middle East today acknowledge that the missionaries have left an enduring legacy, in the form of education, freedom and democracy. My ancestors did mean well, so well that some of them even came to the opinion that only the local Christians could succeed in evangelizing Muslims, for they shared the same language and culture with them. For that to happen, however, the local churches had themselves to be reformed, for in the course of time the gospel had been replaced with many traditions. Particularly the fact that local Christians were attached to images of Jesus, Mary and the saints was considered by my ancestors to be a serious obstacle to persuading Muslims of the self-evident truth of Christianity. That is an approach which certainly no intelligent Protestant would have today, since the days of Protestant iconoclasm and Christian glorification of one's own culture are long past. None the less, my ancestors did mean well. However, they overlooked one thing – a considerable number of local Christians did in fact consent to be reformed, but few of them had any interest in making Muslims into Christians. Of course, their experience with the Muslims was not always milk and honey. And many of them, who in debates with the West are today attempting to idealize this history, are simply creating a myth that must be demythologized. Nonetheless, despite tensions with the Muslims, despite occasional instances of persecution and massacres, the local Christians were content with their Muslim neighbours as they were. And these neighbours often visited them, not only to be able to have a secret drink of wine with them, but sometimes to pray together with them.

I am a missionary. It is indisputable that our missionary activity has been of benefit to the local peoples of the Middle East, whether Christians, Muslims or Jews. We translated the Bible into Arabic, which resulted in a revival of Arabic language and literature. We established schools, universities and hospitals and thereby communicated the values of the gospel through people who were inspired by God's living Spirit. I have to admit, however, that the process of learning was mutual. On this subject I could tell you many things that I have heard from my father and grandfather, but I will limit myself to my personal experiences. As a missionary in the Middle East I have often come into contact with Arabic literature. An Arab Christian has written a beautiful novel in which he refers to a liturgical song that is sung in the Orthodox Church of the Byzantine Rite on Good Friday. In the song, Joseph of Arimathea approaches Pilate to ask him for the body of Jesus, with nonbiblical words, in which the dead Jesus is described as a foreigner...

Give me the foreigner,
Foreign as a foreigner from childhood,

Give me the foreigner,
Killed as a foreigner,
Give me the foreigner,
I am amazed that he is held by death.

What I find striking in this song is that Jesus is perceived as a foreigner, not only on the day of his death – as if all living people had rejected him, as if no alternative were left him but to find hospitality in the kingdom of the dead – but that he is also portrayed as a foreigner from his childhood on. Jesus' foreignness was thus not dependent on his situation but was a permanent condition. I think that the reason why I remember this image is because being a missionary also means being "foreign". We are foreign, we live in a foreign land, we are perceived as foreigners. And the context to which we have to relate is also foreign. There will always be an element of foreignness remaining in us despite all our efforts to become part of this foreign world, to familiarize ourselves with it. Jesus, however, who in this song is presented as a foreigner, identifies not only with us missionaries, who in any case live in a foreign land, but also with those people whom we meet and who seem foreign to us, to whatever culture they may belong.

I am a missionary, who – probably like many other missionaries – is constantly wondering what our Christian identity over against other religions means. What is the relationship between one's own perspective and the perspective of others, one's own position and the position of others, one's own belief and the belief of others. And just like so many other missionaries, despite my full trust in the gospel, I have no clear answer, but have an inner feeling mainly of brokenness, interwoven with hundreds of questions, such as "Did Jesus reveal himself by concealing himself and did he conceal himself by revealing himself?" I do know one thing, however. When people are baptized into the death of Jesus Christ, then they meet the Crucified One. We can draw a picture of this encounter in our imagination... Those baptized are taken to Golgotha. They seek Jesus of Nazareth, the Crucified One, in order to die his death. And what do they see there? On the cross Jesus of Nazareth is not alone. There are two other crosses, one on either side of him, two crosses with unknown faces. Everything happens very quickly – the bitter drink, the abandonment by God, the cry of dereliction. And then all three crosses are caught up into God's silence, like in the Old Testament cloud that accompanied a foreign people through the desert, and was an anticipation of the light of the resurrection. Some missionaries have over the course of time developed an ability to sense the power of

God, which for a moment makes itself known, as at the cross, through silence… in our silence, in the silence of events that have not been significant enough to be mentioned in the history books, in the silence of our failing church institutions, in the silence that comes out of the foreignness of other religions.

It is difficult for us Christians to define ourselves unambiguously. It seems to me, however, that the event of the cross, which we all confess, can put us in the position to include in our identity foreignness, brokenness and silence. And when we reach that point a door can be opened for the others who are standing outside. Any attempt to determine a Christian identity must never skirt around or must never avoid taking the way of the cross.

Plenary
"Economic justice"

Introduction:
The Signs of the Times

Wolfgang Huber

Bishop Wolfgang Huber is the bishop of the Evangelical Church in Berlin-Brandenburg in Germany. This reflection was prepared for the plenary on "Economic Justice" on 16 February 2006.

In recent days in Peshawar, a city in Pakistan, 70,000 people have been demonstrating against cartoons published in Copenhagen. The offices of a Norwegian mobile phone company there have been set on fire to demonstrate outrage against a Danish newspaper. These are alarming signs of the global reality in which we live. But it is also in Pakistan that more than 11,000 fair trade footballs for the World Cup in Germany are being produced for our church; some of these fair trade footballs have found their way to Porto Alegre. That's also a sign of the global reality in which we live. To what extent does the globalization of our world challenge us to readjust our trade according to the yardstick of justice? My introductory remarks concentrate on this issue.

Globalization has many aspects. One aspect is that hatred can be organized and spread throughout the world. But another aspect is that global humanitarian action for the victims of the tsunami around the Indian Ocean was organized within a few hours. Another aspect is that economic relations can promote prosperity and enable people to have decent work. But it also means that economic power can be organized selfishly, thereby standing in the way of economic justice. Anyone who wants to interpret the signs of the times needs to look at both sides: both the opportunities and the dangers of the current developments in the world.

We live in an age in which the world economy as a whole is growing, leading to an improvement in living standards, an increase in life expectancy, and improvement in levels of education in some parts of the world. But at the same time the blatant and inhumane poverty experienced by more than a billion people continues. The United Nations in its World Social Report makes it clear that in many parts of the world social inequalities are increasing. The natural foundations of life are being exploited in a way that is incompatible with the most basic requirements of sustainability. For all Christians, increasing poverty in many parts of our world is a scandal. For those of us in Europe, Africa and Eastern Europe are two examples that challenge us particularly. Our assembly directs our attention to the increasing poverty in Latin America. Such a scandal will jolt us even more in that we, as no generation before us, have the possibility to overcome structural poverty and to make the world a more just place.

In issues of economic justice the Christian faith is not neutral. It does not conform to the economy's claim to be omnipotent, because its allegiance is to Christ as the only Lord of the world. It does not leave economic trade to follow its own laws, because it is based on God's commandments. Human dignity, human rights and social justice are basic values against which economic activity is to be measured both today and tomorrow. As Christians we judge the globalization of our world according to whether it promotes dignity of life, serves human freedom, and enables the expression of cultural diversity. That is why we name the injustices that are linked to current economic relationships of power.

A globalization worthy of its name includes everyone and does not divide humanity into winners and losers, into rich and poor. That is why we are mobilizing as a worldwide fellowship of churches linked by the prayer of Jesus, through the Lord's Prayer that includes the request for daily bread for everyone. In the World Council of Churches we are not a global player but a global prayer. It is through the power of prayer that we work for economic structures that benefit all.

In recent days many Christians have been remembering Dietrich Bonhoeffer, the theologian of the Confessing Church in Germany who encouraged us as Christians to pray, to do justice, and to wait on God. A few days ago on 4th February we marked the 100th anniversary of Dietrich Bonhoeffer's birth. The key experience that made him a Christian, as he himself acknowledged, was the encounter with the

195

Sermon on the Mount. The corollary he wrote in a letter: "There are things for which an uncompromising stand is worthwhile. And it seems to me that peace and social justice, or Christ himself, are such things."

In the perspective of this commitment the economy is only part of life, not the whole of life. The debate about the issues linked to globalization should not be limited to economic aspects alone. As Christians and as representatives of the churches we must not surrender to the pervasive economic thought around us. Economic decisions do not create moral values. Solidarity cannot be created by the market. Economic justice is only possible when civil society maintains its own independence and develops new strength. It can develop only when the state promotes the conditions for human solidarity and supports those who are weaker. Appropriate political conditions are needed to create social equality and promote social cohesion.

The ecumenical movement has been intensively discussing the process of globalization since the Harare assembly. This was inspired by the word "Agape", the word which means love for one's neighbour. Many people are now waiting for us to get beyond making statements, to show that there are alternative possibilities for action. The key issue is how the biblical option for the poor can be related in a more meaningful way to economic thought. Young people in particular, including youth at this assembly, are clamouring for alternative perspectives for action to be developed that can be implemented and find resonance in the worldwide debate. Even Christians in positions of responsibility in the economy or international institutions are hoping to hear the voice of their churches. They want to be part of a globalization of justice and solidarity. I hope that this afternoon will serve this purpose.

Is there an Agape economy, an economy of love? That is what we have to discuss this afternoon. We will hear the perspectives of a theologian and of an economist. The theology part will be the first part and the economy part the last part of our session. Then we shall hear about three examples for alternative action in our churches. At the end of this plenary session is the Agape call that is intended to stimulate thought and action. But first we shall see a video about the ways in which the ecumenical movement in the past dealt with issues of economic justice and what answers it found.

Plenary
"Economic Justice"

Empire and Religion Gospel, Ecumenism and Prophecy for the 21st Century

Nancy Cardoso Pereira

Rev. Dr Nancy Cardoso Pereira is a Methodist pastor from Brazil and a member of the Pastoral Land Commission. She is professor of ancient history at the Porto Alegre Institute of the Methodist Church. This reflection was prepared for the plenary on "Economic Justice" on 16 February 2006.

When Janis Joplin sang in the distant 1960s, "O Lord, won't you buy me a Mercedes Benz?" it seemed a piece of harmless fun, but in a way it was a prophetic condemnation, in advance, of a trend in Western Christianity: voracious consumerism.

Today this spirituality of the market economy has taken complete possession of some sectors of Christianity, and prayers alternate between continuing to pray to God for a Mercedes Benz and, already in some cases, "O Mercedes Benz, buy me a god!" or even, "Mercedes Benz, be my god!'" – as if material goods themselves could be the way to fullness of life.

The divine beings vying to bring "our daily bread" to our tables feed not only on the total control of the processes of food production and distribution, but are also gobbling up the forms of consumption represented by quick-moving fast-food outlets. Today, world trade in agricultural products – especially cereals, meat and dairy products – is controlled by no more than twenty oligopolistic groups of transnational corporations located in the United States and Europe. "Give us this day our daily bread, O Monsanto, Cargill, Swift, Anglo, ADM, Nestlé, Danone, Syngenta, Bunge!"

So, "on earth as in heaven", globalized capitalism in national capitals – an unfathomable metaphysical mystery – is punishing farmers in poor countries, whom they are treating as permanent debtors, while at the same time the debts of agriculture in rich countries are being cancelled in the form of subsidies, tariffs and free trade treaties – and there is no one who "can deliver us from that evil". The last WTO round in Hong Kong showed that the farming capitals in the United States and Europe will not be "led into temptation" and will continue to defend the interests of their agricultural, industrial and service sectors. The peasant workers of Korea, India and Brazil, and other countries, know that the governments negotiating in Hong Kong had no legitimacy to negotiate on their behalf.

Capitalist transnational corporations want more: they want "the kingdom, the power and the glory" by controlling the land, water and seed stocks. They are already lords of other people's work. They now control and determine the monetary value of their livelihood and their actual lives. "Hallowed be the name" of patents and technologies that make inroads into people's inner being, their possibilities and their vulnerability, and then make fresh profits out of medicines, chemical products, biological products and genetically modified products.

"Hallowed be the name" of the business campaigns that declare themselves to be environmentally friendly, community-building, child-friendly, educational sponsors who by complex sleight of hand attempt to disguise the voracious appetite of the profit motive. False NGOs, promotional moral talk, funding of campaigns and community initiatives, with no questions asked about profits or motives.

Regardless of life, war fulfills its role of ensuring access to cheap materials and labour, of expanding and protecting markets for capital's consuming hunger and its passion to enslave. Money passionately loves profits and will not tolerate any obstacle, restriction or regulation. "My kingdom come!" cries capital, seated on its divine throne at the heart of the world, making itself out to be god.

In the pride of its heart, capital says, "I am a god; I sit on the throne of a god in the heart of the seas." "You think you are wise… and no secret is hidden from you. By your wisdom and understanding you have gained wealth for yourself and amassed gold and silver in your treasuries. By your great skill in trading you have increased your wealth, and because of your wealth your heart has grown proud... You think you are wise, as wise as a god... Through your widespread trade you were filled with violence and you sinned... Your heart became proud on account of your beauty, and you corrupted your wisdom because of your splendour... By your many sins and dishonest trade you have desecrated your sanctuaries" (Ezekiel 28:2-6; 16-18).

Ezekiel's prophecy is forceful and amounts to saying simply and directly, "You are only human! You are not God!"

Who today knows how or is able to produce such theology and prophecy?

Who is able to condemn and combat this spiritual aura conferred on a social phenomenon, this illusion that things, that economic systems are natural or eternal? The dominant economic system becomes before our eyes no longer a historical social phenomenon: rather the world and its beings, personal relationships and human creations become commodities; business takes on an impetus and existence of its own that cannot be questioned, a movement that sweeps us along to perpetuate inequality and violence, without our even realizing it. The economy and economic relationships rule humankind, instead of being seen and appreciated as the product of humankind in history, and for that reason capable of being overcome, criticized and reinvented.

Our theologies and pastoral policies are tired and exhausted. The economic system has taken over Western religious language, leaving more or less generous margins for the churches that have before them the easiest option, which is to become an integral functional part of the whole package presented by capitalism, offering religious goods as commodities, and services in the form of powerful fundamentalisms and charismatic spectacles of marketing and prosperity.

We need to choose the difficult option and learn to say again, "By your many sins and dishonest trade, you have desecrated your sanctuaries" (Ezek. 28:18). The world and its living beings, peoples and their cultures, the earth, water and seeds – everything that moves is sacred! And no economic system that produces injustice and dishonest dealing can be blessed or legitimized or tolerated in the name of God.

The gospels, the Law and the prophets, which are accepted in our Christian tradition, demand that we confess God throughout the inhabited world – the oikoumene – but that we give that confession concrete form, in the struggle for law and justice as the full accomplishment of the world and our humanity.

However, the theology that we are doing today is sterile, because it attempts to hide behind systematic exegetical generalizations that fail to name, choose, opt, state preferences, take a stand, refute, be outraged, condemn or resist.

At the beginning of all things, the world order was divided into sky, water and land, setting up relationships within the whole created world: weather, night and day; dry land and water; land creatures and the birds of the air; living beings in their animal and plant forms.

"Then God said, 'Let the land produce vegetation: seed-bearing plants and trees on the land that bear fruit with seed in it, according to their various kinds.' And it was so" (Gen. 1:11).

So God said, "Let them live!" and all came to life, as an exercise in similarities and differences, as question and response, consecutively or simultaneously. Everything is alive and everything is good.

The whole book of Genesis examines again and again the issue of the highly delicate relationships between living creatures and the constraints placed on them by land, water and fire; between the constraints placed on the earth, on the plants and on the beasts, and the human mouth and its hunger. The hunger of the world, the hunger of the human body, produces new relationships within the created world. Hunger produces contemplation, observation, work and its technologies. Hunger is the world's yearning, the longing for more, for life. It is hunger that establishes the critical creative relationship between living beings and their surrounding environment. And God saw that it was good.

Starting with this ordering of creation the text goes on to emphasize the essential but difficult relationships between the physical world and its vegetation and human bodies and their hunger. The book of Genesis describes crisis situations of food shortages at the beginning of the narratives of the wanderings of Abraham, Isaac and Jacob. Going to Egypt is always represented as a consequence of a shortage of food: "Now there was a famine in the land, and Abram went down to Egypt to live there for a while because the famine was severe" (Gen. 12:10).

In the following narrative, we read that "The land could not support them" (Gen. 13:6), giving limited access to resources for survival as a reason for remaining in small family groups engaged in animal husbandry. Thus human groups and their memories are also marked by issues of food insecurity within the wider framework of the farming and land policies of empires.

In this context the story of Cain and Abel is fundamental. The text recalls different ways of life and work and relationships with God. Abel was a keeper of sheep and Cain tilled the soil. That is the one piece of information that we are given: two different ways of organizing people's relationship with the earth, work and relationships with other people.

The offering is made. Cain offers the fruits of the soil as his offering and Abel offers some of his animals: fat portions from some of the firstborn of his flock. God looked with favour on Abel and his offering, but God did not look with favour on Cain and his offering. Simply that. Various explanations have been given to explain this situation. Why did God prefer Abel and his offering?

The gauchos here in Rio Grande do Sul would like to interpret this story by seeing God as a gaucho whose favourite food was a barbecue, but perhaps we ought to look elsewhere for alternative interpretations!

I take it to be possible that this text recalls two ways of life, two ways of organizing work and relationships in antiquity. If Cain represents agriculture, he should be seen as part of an economic system of exploitation based on forced labour and tribute, probably in the setting up of the city-states in Canaan under Egyptian influence.

Abel would thus represent human groups engaged together in different economic activities that were not the monopoly of the city-states with their tribute and forced labour. Abel, the keeper of sheep, would be found among the Canaanite population of the high plateau, who resisted and survived on the basis of smallholdings, nomadic sheep-rearing, the activities of bands of mercenaries or groups involved in trading, either as merchants or carriers of merchandise.

The significant fact is that God chooses, elects, prefers the latter way of life to the former. That explains the conflict. Cain is angry and his face downcast. God says, "If you do what is right, will you not be accepted? But if you do not do what is right, sin is crouching at your door... You must master it" (Gen. 4:6-7).

This description of the two offerings could mask the violence, hiding the wild beast... If only God would accept both offerings! But the God in this narrative refuses to legitimize the offering that is the fruit of violence and sin. Cain comes out of the ritual offering with his face downcast. He has been rejected. No. Cain is incapable of mastering the violence inherent in his way of life, because it is systemic violence. That is the function of the ritual act: it assesses, scrutinizes, sheds light on production methods, and it opts, states a preference.

Cain cannot cope with living without divine approval. He invites Abel out into the country – and, in the final definition, that is what it is all about: land! Cain kills Abel. Simply that. Apparently, Cain decided to kill Abel because he, Cain, had been rejected by God. Seen in that way… God could be to blame!

Or, rather… the violence against Abel was already an integral part of Cain's offering and that is why it was not pleasing to God. Cain's way of life and production involved denying life to Abel and to other human groups with him. That is why Cain's offering was rejected.

Offerings do not simply offer themselves. The function of religion in economic exchange does not consist of establishing regulations and procedures, but of determining value, i.e. formulating economic values, shaping structures and strengthening assessment mechanisms.

This ritual exchange or offering contains the cultural mechanism for calculating value, i.e. what can be given and exchanged and what is kept and retained. It is not the intrinsic value of beings or things that determines the difference between what is retained and what is acceptable in the form of an offering, but it is society that confers value and produces the scale by which to measure the meaning and function of ritual exchanges.

God reappears in the narrative, asking the key question, "Where is your brother?"

Cain's reply is well known, "I don't know. Am I my brother's keeper?"

God replies, "What have you done? Listen! Your brother's blood is crying out to me from the ground."

It is one of the most probing narratives in our tradition. It is a dialogue between God and the violent brother and the other brother who, as a victim of violence, is speaking in the form of blood spilt on the ground.

For some reason or other, this narrative has remained dormant in our theologies. This radical understanding of a God who prefers, who discriminates, who chooses, has given way before a co-opted theology that no longer knows how to ask the difficult questions. It is a community life that no longer sees itself as a space where life is assessed and true worth established.

Alas for us! God is no longer asking, "Where is your brother?" We have made a god who whispers sweet messages of forgiveness and reconciliation, without the critical courage that makes the violent bow their heads in shame, unable to claim any human or divine qualities. They are cornered wild beasts prepared to destroy!

This god is no longer able to hold a conversation with the ground. This god now does not hear the cry of the blood of people and beings who are being downtrodden by an economic model that knows no limits, accepts no regulation and brooks no opposition.

On the periphery of world Christianity there are minorities who stress the need for a theology that liberates: that liberates God, and the earth, and the men and women whose humanity is being denied every day by capitalism. This World Council of Churches has been a privileged and sensitive space where voices can be raised that are not heard in our countries, in national churches or in regional councils. Men and women who no longer wish to repeat again and again the North American and European theology that ceaselessly pores over itself and its dearly loved theologians, what they have said, what they have written. Throughout the world young theologians are silenced by a dominant North American and European theological model that is weary of becoming good news, that is cosying up to the knowledge industry in the service of an economic model which gives privileged place to its comfortable, stable consumerist societies.

They no longer want to know about a God who asks questions, who causes the powerful to bow their heads in shame and encourages the weak to announce the Kingdom of Justice. They no longer ask after their brothers and sisters, because they have created NGOs and agencies that fund works of charity but do not ask questions about the system.

The blood crying out from the ground becomes a case study, an experience mentioned in the course of the liturgy, but it does not provoke the anger that refuses to continue to tolerate ways of life and production based on violence and inequality.

Together with many brothers and sisters here in this space I have learned not to refrain from asking these questions. I have learned with brothers and sisters from different churches and different countries to organize campaigns and efforts to opt constantly for a way of life and production based on justice that will enable us to walk with straight backs, open minds and tranquil hearts.

This Assembly must acknowledge and identify its tasks so as to commit our churches to take up again a prophetic evangelical stance in the world. "No one can serve two masters," said Jesus. It is either God or money, life or death and all the difficult issues contained in that question, "Where is your brother? Where is your sister?"

We need to listen to what the Spirit is saying to the churches, what the Spirit is saying through the blood spilt on the ground, through our brothers and sisters not present here! We need to listen to the earth, to learn to engage in conversation with the blood of people who are being destroyed.

We need to listen to what the Spirit is saying to the empires of this world: "You are not God. Bow your heads in shame." Let the wild beasts be mastered: Mercedes

Benz, Volkswagen, Monsanto, Cargill, Swift, Anglo, ADM, Nestlé, Danone, Syngenta, Bunge.

We are not motivated by an all-embracing missionary project for the whole world. Our passion comes from what we learn in the gospel of Jesus Christ and from our lively faith, which is able to live with differences without being afraid of being destroyed or disappearing.

The faith that affirms God's grace in the building of another possible world is not like the strength and wealth of the successful but is like an adventure of love, caring for life, for the world, for ourselves.

"As servants of God we commend ourselves in every way: in great endurance; in troubles, hardships and distresses; in beatings, imprisonments and riots; in hard work, sleepless nights and hunger; in purity, understanding, patience and kindness; in the Holy Spirit and in sincere love; in truthful speech and in the power of God; with weapons of righteousness in the right hand and in the left; through glory and dishonour, bad report and good report; genuine, yet regarded as impostors; known, yet regarded as unknown; dying, and yet we live on; beaten, and yet not killed; sorrowful, yet always rejoicing; poor, yet making many rich; having nothing, and yet possessing everything"(2 Cor. 6:4-10).

PLENARY
"ECONOMIC JUSTICE"

THE ECONOMY OF COMMUNION PROJECT

VERONICA ARAÚJO

Prof. Veronica Araújo coordinates the work of the Focolare Movement's Centre for Dialogue with Culture. This reflection was prepared for the plenary on "Economic Justice" on 16 February 2006.

Mr General Secretary, Dr Samuel Kobia,
Honourable delegates from all over the world,

Allow me first of all to convey Chiara Lubich's greetings, the foundress of the Focolare Movement whom I am here to represent.

Since she could not be here as she so desired, she assures you of her prayers and best wishes for the success of this Assembly.

My task is that of briefly outlining the project referred to as "the Economy of Communion", born within the sphere of the Focolare Movement from an inspiration that Chiara Lubich had while travelling here in Brazil in May 1991.

While staying at the small city of witness of the Focolare close to São Paulo, Chiara was directly exposed to the social-economic inequity of this immense nation. She was informed that numerous members of the Movement lived in the *favelas* of many Brazilian cities, immersed in poverty and want. The communion of goods that had been practised among the members of the Movement since its inception was no longer enough to cover the basic needs of many of them.

After living days marked by a high spiritual climate and great brotherhood among people of different social backgrounds, she then had an inspiration: to give life to businesses, entrusting their management to competent people who would run them efficiently and render them profitable. Then – and herein lies the novelty – these profits would be divided into three parts: the first part for those in need; the second for the formation of *new people*, that is, people oriented to the culture of giving and inspired by it for their economic endeavours, because without such people, it is impossible to build a new society. And finally, the third part would be invested in the business, to strengthen and further develop it.

It was a simple idea, linear and very innovative because it introduces on the economic plane the principle of gift, of gratuity.

Today there are about 750 businesses that follow the principles of the Economy of Communion (EOC) worldwide. In responding to their primary mission to help the poor, every year they share their profits and thus alleviate many people's needs, providing employment for them, helping them rediscover the dignity that they had lost or never experienced.

This initiative is managed by a central commission that compiles the requests of needs and distributes the profits to those people, through the help of the directors of the Focolare Movement throughout the world. The people who receive them are also committed to living the culture of giving and mutual love.

This is a new way of giving: it is not a matter of philanthropy or social benefits, but of living in communion with the poor through the shared brotherhood experienced among the business members and those who are disadvantaged.

In these 15 years, then, we have understood and experienced that the EOC project, in embracing the principles of the spirituality of unity of the Focolare as values to be lived out in concrete economic activity, is now developing its own method of business management. This practical experience has germinated guiding principles of a technical-ethical nature with which to orient business practice towards social co-responsibility, the mentality of giving.

These businesses, while operating in the current "for profit" market, function with a different logic than the traditional market model insofar as they follow a logic of sharing and communion.

Industrial parks have grown around the small cities of witness of the Movement as further developments of the EOC in these years. These parks give visibility to the project, bringing different firms together who have mutual love at the core of their business dealings, giving each other advice, supporting one another… Seven of these industrial parks have already been built, in several nations: three in Brazil; one, respectively, in Argentina, Belgium, Portugal, and Italy.

Chiara Lubich has received two honorary degrees in economics as a result of this project. Many scholars are beginning to deepen new ideas that emerge from these businesses, such as the concept of relational goods, trust, communion, and so on.

Many people are asking how businesses that are so attentive to anthropological and ethical issues can actually survive in our current market. I will let Chiara respond to that question: "In this type of business, one leaves room for God's intervention even in its concrete economic management. One then experiences that with each decision made counter-culturally to normal business practice, He never fails to send that hundredfold that Christ had promised: perhaps in the form of an unexpected revenue, a new window of opportunity, the support derived from new collaborations, an idea for a new product, and so on."[1]

This then, in brief, is the Economy of Communion Project which is raising considerable interest in the business sector and academic circles.

Thank you for your kind attention.

Note:
1. C. Lubich, The experience of the Economy of Communion: from spirituality a new proposal for business practice". Report given during the conference organized by the Council of Europe in Strasbourg, entitled "Market economy, democracy and solidarity: a space for comparison?"

PLENARY
"ECONOMIC JUSTICE"

THE ISLAND OF HOPE:
AN ALTERNATIVE TO
ECONOMIC GLOBALIZATION

TERAUANGO BENETERI

Ms Terauango Beneteri is a lay member of the Kiribati Protestant Church in the Pacific. This reflection was prepared for the plenary on "Economic Justice" on 16 February 2006.

We, as the Pacific island churches, wish to contribute the Pacific concept of the Island of Hope to the assembly.

Pacifically, on the Island of Hope, life is significant, valued and celebrated. There is a celebration of life over material wealth. The Island of Hope is sacramental, self-contained, independent, and in tune with nature. It is an island marked by sharing and caring, to which people want to journey in order to celebrate life in all its fullness (Isa. 25:6). The Island of Hope has the "mana" (power) to draw human beings together.

The Island of Hope, like the Kingdom of God, is praiseworthy and unique, boundary-less and sought after.

The Island of Hope is a reality of people together braving the attacks of religio-social, political and economic tyrannies.

The Island of Hope is biblical-theological and is inclusive of the idea of smallness in partnership uniting people and making them strong. Jesus is the Island of Hope who gave the whole world what it hopes for. Jesus' passion and the cross (resurrection) is the Island of Hope for humanity.

As Pacific Islanders, there is awareness that the Island of Hope is not spared from the forces of globalization. Yet, in the face of its onslaught, the following defences remain firm and intact:

- The ethos of communal life and of communal economic and social relations.
- Communal ownership of resource bases.
- The strength of family and kinship ties.
- High levels of intra-community interaction and solidarity.
- A wealth of living languages and of ceremonies, rituals and other practices rich in meaning.
- Traditional structures like fale, bure-Kalou (house of worship) and material culture producing both functional exchange or gift items.

The Island of Hope offers an alternative to the negative effects of globalization. The Island of Hope is founded on godly values as opposed to economic globalization, which is erected on the value of material goods. The Island of Hope is sustainable, wholesome, peaceful and all-embracing, whereas globalization is unsustainable, damaging, conflict-ridden, and excluding.

The concept of the Island of Hope is not merely a dream. It is founded in reality and has been our normal life in our islands. The institutions and values embedded in the Island of Hope may not create wealth on a massive scale but they will never be responsible for creating second class citizens, destroying the environment at will, causing poverty, the debasement of humanity and denial of human dignity, as economic globalization is doing.

- The Island of Hope will never entail economic tyranny.
- Spirituality, family life, traditional economy, cultural values, mutual care and respect are components of the concept of the Island of Hope which prioritizes relationships, celebrates quality of life and values human beings and creation over the production of things.
- The Island of Hope is an alternative to the project of economic globalization which entails domination through an unjust economic system.
- The Island of Hope represents life-centred values deeply rooted in Pacific communities, which provide an orientation for a just and sustainable economy and a life of dignity.

Plenary
"Economic justice"

Post-Soviet Countries: The Need for New Morals in Economy

Vsevolod Chaplin

Archpriest Vsevolod Chaplin of the Russian Orthodox Church is deputy chairman of the Department for External Church Relations of the Moscow Patriarchate. This reflection was prepared for the plenary on "Economic Justice" on 16 February 2006.

After the demise of the totalitarian Communist system the economic and social life in the countries of the former Soviet Union found itself in the hands of radical neo-liberal reformers and their Western advisers. The initial public support for these people's policies was almost unanimous: the population of the USSR knew very well all the disadvantages of the state-controlled, absolutely centralized and heavily militarized totalitarian economy which suppressed any independent initiative. The idea of the free market's "omnipotence" in solving not only economic, but also political and social problems, occupied the public space at the beginning of the 1990s.

Unfortunately, the results of the unwise policies of radical neo-liberals proved very soon to be dramatic. Dozens of millions of people, including young and energetic ones, started to find themselves living below the poverty level. Their savings turned into nothing, many of them lost jobs or were paid only symbolic salaries. The Soviet social system which guaranteed for many people a predictable future started to gradually disappear. Alcoholism, drug abuse and suicide became widespread. Social marginalization (e.g. the number of street children) reached levels unknown since the civil war of 1917-1923.

At the same time many economic players started to "preach" unlimited wealth and moral cynicism in the context of the absolute poverty of millions. Several families who started to "own" post-Soviet countries as a result of questionable privatization of state properties, pretended to hold the political power as well. One of their representatives said on TV: "Population doesn't matter"; another one said "I can elect even a monkey president here". In the eyes of many simple people the very word "economy" became a sort of synonym of crime, injustice, manipulation and oppression. Schoolchildren, when asked about their plans for the future, identified "prostitute" and "gangster" among the most prestigious professions. The very idea of economic ethics was declared outdated and linked to the Communist past. Still, at the turn of the new century many economic actors started to realize that economy without ethics is not only immoral, but also counterproductive.

The Russian Orthodox Church, uniting many dozen million Christians in different post-Soviet countries and other regions of the world, raised its voice many times against economic injustice in the 1990s and since 2000. Its leadership spoke to the government, the businessmen and the common people, criticizing late payments of salaries, unemployment, inadequate financing of social benefits and many other phenomena which brought suffering to our compatriots.

In February 2004, at the initiative of my church, the World Russian People's Sobor (Assembly) adopted the Code of Moral Principles and Rules in Economy, which was offered to the state, entrepreneurs and workers. Although it does not speak in direct Christian terms (the document was later supported by Jews, Muslims and Buddhists), the Code is based on the Ten Commandments of the Bible. Allow me to quote just a few paragraphs from this document.

"Historically the Russian spiritual and moral tradition has been inclined predominantly to give priority to the spiritual over the material, the ideal of personal selflessness for the sake of the good of the people. However, the extremes of this option would lead to terrible tragedies. Remembering this, we should establish such an economic order as to help realize in a harmonious way both spiritual aspirations and the material interests of both the individual and society."

"The greater one's property, the more powerful one is over others. Therefore, the use of property in economy should not be of a narrow egotistic nature and should not contradict the common interest... Poverty, like riches, is a test. A poor person is obliged to behave in a dignified way, to seek to make his work effective, to raise his professional skills so that he may emerge from his misery."

"Political power and economic power should be separated. The participation of business in politics and its impact on public opinion should be open and transparent. The entire financial support given by business to political parties, public organizations and the mass media should be made public and verifiable. Any secret support is to be condemned publicly as immoral."

"Individuals and structures guilty of grievous crimes, especially those involved in corruption, should be unacceptable as business partners or participants in the business community... Those who fail to pay salaries, who delay them systematically and allow them to stay below the subsistence wage, are to be censured by society."

Now the Russian Orthodox Church is working to promote and implement this Code. It was well received by several economy-related state institutions, and leaders of nation-wide trade unions. Several big companies (for example, the Sistema financial corporation, the Itera oil company and the Ingosstrakh insurance company), have indicated that they will follow in their activities the rules and principles outlined in our document. The Code has been widely discussed by researchers and journalists, as well as the broader public. Some have criticized the church for "interfering in a non-religious area". But I am deeply convinced that it is the task of the church to call and work for moral renewal, truth and justice in the economy.

PLENARY
"ECONOMIC JUSTICE"

WEALTH AND POVERTY: CHALLENGE TO THE CHURCHES

YASHPAL TANDON

Mr Yashpal Tandon, an economist from Uganda, is the executive director of the South Centre in Geneva, Switzerland. This reflection was prepared for the plenary on "Economic Justice" on 16 February 2006.

Brothers and Sisters,

The greatest challenge of our time is the increasing disparity between wealth and poverty, both between and within nations. The chasm between the poor and the rich is widening. From the monetary point of view over three billion people are classified as poor, living on less than two dollars a day. This is 50 percent of the global population. The neo-liberal approach in economics, particularly how trade and finance is handled globally, is responsible for this human tragedy.

Global inequality has grown exponentially. The ratio between the richest and the poorest 20 percent of the world's population was 30:1 in 1960, and 114:1 in 2002. If this is not addressed, humanity risks gross social and political chaos, unprecedented in world history. Ecologically, we are destroying our mother earth to a degree never experienced before. Churches and social movements have alerted the world over and over again, but actors of corporate globalization have decided not to heed this warning. Instead, the driving forces of economic globalization continue to promote more growth without limits. One country which has five percent of the world's population consumes a quarter of the world's oil. Global trade is dominated by corporations. They pay lip service to poverty eradication and the protection of the public good and the environment. Profits, not public welfare, are their raison d'être.

If we all go down this road, we shall need seven more planets like ours. This assembly comes at the right time. We are at the crossroads between continuing to live or die with our earth. I therefore challenge the churches who are the custodians of ethics and morals, I believe, to show the way to promoting a just and participatory world, where resources can be shared and the earth cared for. We need a world without poverty and this should be possible if we rethink the way we consume, produce and distribute resources.

THE NEO-LIBERAL DEVELOPMENT PARADIGM –
THE CURSE OF OUR TIMES

The AGAPE document which I have read defines neo-liberalism. You need to say loud and clear that the free market system is a myth – it never existed, nor will it ever. It is in truth an ideology of the corporations paraded as the "science of economics" by the neo-liberals. They are a kind of sect in the academic community, employed in large numbers by global trade and financial institutions, major universities in North and South, and most finance ministries in third world countries. They use a one-size-fit formula as their development paradigm. In the Greek legend, the bandit robber, Procrustes, used to waylay travellers and chop short their legs if these did not fit into a "one-size-fit" bed. It may be said with justification that the neo-liberal economists are the "Procrustean economists" of our time; they chop the legs of poor nations when they do not conform to their economic programmes. The poor in the South are these chopped legs that do not fit the one-size-fit formula of the neo-liberal economists.

Malaysia, to give one example, has been able to develop better than larger countries like Indonesia and the Philippines. Why? Because Malaysia made its own policies, often in defiance of the IMF and the World Bank and the neo-liberal economists. Most of Africa, on the other hand, has adopted neo-liberal strategies as part of the Structural Adjustment Programmes and Africa is the continent suffering the worst. In Latin America, on the other hand, things are changing. Argentina followed the neo-liberal strategy with dedication in the 1980s and '90s. Then came the financial crash of November 2001, and the country imploded like a powder keg. The present government negotiated with the IMF and got away with writing off 75 percent of the debt. The IMF could do nothing about it. In Venezuela the people, in popular elections, overthrew the ruling oligarchy, declared a Bolivarian revolution, and took control of the nation's resources. In Bolivia, they are doing the same – taking control of the nation's oil and gas resources.

WHERE DO WE GO FROM HERE? REASONS FOR HOPE IN THE FUTURE

The challenge to the churches is to offer the people alternatives to neo-liberalism. They do not have to go far. People everywhere are engaged in working out their own partial solutions on the basis of their experiments in survival strategies. These have to be acknowledged, made more systematic, and given support, but in a different environment. For example, credit institutions for people's self-help projects have been tried by the thousands all over the third world. But they have failed to lift people out of poverty. Why? Because the environment was not conducive. Within the reigning capitalist framework, these self-help projects simply got absorbed into the dominant patterns of production and finance.

So the foremost challenge of our epoch is to change the whole edifice of global production and exchange. In order to do this, the churches have to work at various levels:

• At the global political and ideological level;
• At the national and regional levels;
• At the level of the people on the ground.

Starting at ground zero, people are learning from the past, and taking matters into their own hands. Against Thatcher's famous dictum that "There is No Alternative" (TINA), people are saying "There Are Hundreds of Alternatives" (TAHA). People are experimenting with creating their own currencies, or exchanging goods and services using the barter system. They are pooling their labour together to build boreholes and damming rivers to generate electricity. They are growing food on abandoned land to fight against hunger and poverty, collecting waste and turning it into assets for survival. They are now even taking to politics, and putting in power their own leaders who will respond to their demands for a total overhaul of the national and global system of production, and ownership as well as distribution and welfare systems.

At the national and regional level, some Latin American and Asian countries are defying the IMF and neo-liberal orthodoxy. The churches have to support such acts of unilateral defiance by the nations and regions of the South. Argentina paid only 25 percent of its external debt and got away with it. In Bolivia the people are taking control of their natural resources. For Africa, the Bolivarian type revolution could be a start. But it may not be enough. Africa may have to seriously contemplate active disengagement from globalization in a sequenced selected manner and then, once they build African unity within sub-regions and continentally, negotiate its re-entry into the global system from a position of strength. The churches in Africa may have to look at this possibility seriously. Already, an innovative section of the trade unions in the SADC region has launched a movement called ANSA – Alternatives to Neo-liberalism in Southern Africa. They have a ten-point programme on an alternative strategy that the churches may want to study and support.

At the global level, there is now a paradigmatic confrontation between the World Economic Forum (WEF) and the World Social Forum (WSF), or what may be described as the "development camp" and the "free trade" camp. The latter believes that the objective of development is best served through giving free rein to the forces of the market, and creating conditions in which each country engages in international trade on the basis of its comparative advantage. This position has been challenged for the last twenty years, and now there is enough evidence on the ground that contrary to the self-perception of the free market theorists, they are actually anti-development. The practical effects of their policies lead to the negation of development and the creation of extreme wealth on one side and extreme poverty on the other. In 2001, here in Porto Alegre, began a process that challenged the rich people's club at Davos in Switzerland. As opposed to looking at the world from the perspective of those in citadels of power and privilege (which is what Davos does), the Porto Alegre process does so from the perspective of the marginalized and disempowered people of the world.

Where governments and intergovernmental organizations – even including the United Nations – are still bogged down in discredited theories of the past, some church organizations such as Christian Aid, and secular organizations such as Oxfam, are taking the lead to draw attention to the inequities of the system, and challenging neo-liberal theories that are servicing the greed of corporations. But these efforts are still in the margins of society. They have to become mainstream. The churches are positioned well in society to make this happen.

Some people and institutions in the North are realizing that the problem of poverty is not confined to the South. Globalization, and with it the erosion of social welfare in Europe and America, is creating a new wave of the unemployed, a new generation of the poor in the North as well. Furthermore, the South's poor are jumping walled fences across the Rio Grande in Mexico, and crossing from Africa to Europe over land and sea, half of them perishing on the way or exploited by unscrupulous agents who all want to get rich. The minorities from the South in the North are becoming the racial and religious underclass that is threatening the peace and prosperity of Western nations. At the same time, the wanton exploitation of the soil, minerals, forests, seas, oceans, mountains, wild-life, all this for the greed of corporations, is creating a doomsday scenario for the world.

The warning that the time bomb is ticking has been sounded a thousand times before. It has been either largely ignored, or palliatives thrown at some problems, such as making corporations responsible to the poor and to the environment. These have not worked; these will not work. The world needs a more thorough-going transformation of the way it is organizing life on this planet – the only planet we have.

I hope that from here the churches will go with two messages: how to deliver the world from the curse of neo-liberalism, and how to strengthen the hundreds of alternatives (TAHA) of the people for a different world. In the words of the World Social Forum: Another World is Possible! We can make it!

Plenary
"Economic justice"

Alternative globalization addressing people and earth

AGAPE
A call to love and action

This document is the result of work on economic globalization from Harare to Porto Alegre. It was prepared by the Commission for Justice, Peace and Creation under the direction of the WCC Central Committee. Its final version was received by the Executive Committee in September 2005 which also approved the use of the document in the "Economic Justice" plenary.

Introduction

We, representatives of churches gathered at the Ninth Assembly of the World Council of Churches (WCC), emphasize that a world without poverty is not only possible but is in keeping with the grace of God for the world. This conviction builds on the rich tradition of ecumenical social thought and action, which is centred on God's option for the poor as an imperative of our faith. It captures the results of a seven-year global study process of the churches' responses to economic globalization with contributions from all regions of the world and involvement of a number of Christian world communions, particularly through the 2003 assembly of the Lutheran World Federation (LWF) and the 2004 general council of the World Alliance of Reformed Churches (WARC).

This process has examined the project of economic globalization that is led by the ideology of unfettered market forces and serves the dominant political and economic interests. The international financial institutions and the World Trade Organization among other such institutions promote economic globalization. The participants in the AGAPE process shared their concerns about the growing inequality, the concentration of wealth and power in the hands of a few and the destruction of the earth – all aggravating the scandal of poverty in the South and increasingly in the North. In recent years the escalating role of political and military power has strongly surfaced. People all over the world experience the impact of imperial forms of power on their communities.

Meeting in Porto Alegre, Brazil, the home of the World Social Forum (WSF), we are encouraged by the constructive and positive message of the movements gathering in the WSF that alternatives are possible. We affirm that we can and must make a difference by becoming transformative communities caring for people and the earth.

We recognize that the divisions of the world are present among us. Since we are called to be one in Christ, we are called to be transformed by God's grace for the sake of all life on earth, overcoming the world's division. Challenged to monitor and transform economic globalization, we call ourselves to action as churches working alongside people of faith communities and movements.

AGAPE Call – FOR LOVE AND ACTION

God, Creator, endowing your creation with integrity and human beings with dignity;
God, Redeemer and Liberator, freeing us from slavery and death;
God, Holy Spirit, transforming and energizing us.
Father, Son and Holy Spirit let us witness to your love, life and transforming grace.
All: God, in your grace, transform the world.

We have become apathetic to suffering and injustice. Among us are many who suffer the consequences of economic globalization; women, abused and yet caring for life; children who are denied their rights; youth living in economic insecurity and unemployment; those labouring under exploitative conditions; the many caught in unjust trade relationships and debt slavery. There are people with disabilities and those living at the margins of society, people of colour often the first and most painfully hit by poverty, those pushed away and alienated from the land, the earth – battered, depleted and exploited. Denied of their sustenance, these people are often the most vulnerable to diseases such as HIV/AIDS. We confess that many of us have failed to respond in solidarity.

All: God, in your grace, transform the world.

We are tempted to give in to comfort and its empty promises when we ought to choose costly discipleship and change. We are driven to accept oppression and suffering as a given, when we should keep our hope and advocate for justice and liberation. We confess that many of us have failed to take a stand in our faith and act against economic injustice and its destructive consequences on people and the earth. We are tempted to give in to materialism and the reign of money. We play to the rules of greed and conform to political and military power when we should align ourselves with the poor and excluded people.

All: God, in your grace, transform the world.

God, we ask your forgiveness.

All: God, in your grace, transform the world.

God, let our economic structures be inspired by the rules of your household of life, governed by love, justice and grace.
Let us not be afraid of change, or to seek alternatives.
Let us work for justice by resisting destructive economic structures,
proclaiming with hope the jubilee year of the Lord, the cancellation of debt, the release of the captives and rest for the land,
let us work for an agape economy of solidarity.

All: God, in your grace, transform the world.

God, you send us out,
to care for the earth and to share all that is necessary for life in community;
to resist and to denounce all that denies life,
to love our neighbours and to do what is just,
so that where there was death, there will be life.

We call each other
to respond to your love for all people and for the earth
in our own actions and in the witness and service of our churches;
to work for the eradication of poverty and the unconditional cancellation of debts;

to care for land, water, air – the entire web of life;

to build just and sustainable relationships with the earth.

In the world of labour, trade and finance, to study and engage power in its different forms and manifestations, remembering that all power is accountable to you, God. God in your grace, help us to be agents of your transformation and to hear your call to act with courage.

All: Creator God, may the power of your grace transform us,

Christ, give us courage and hope to share our life with each other and the world,

Holy Spirit, empower us to work for justice for people and the earth.

God, in your grace, transform the world. Amen.

In the spirit of this uniting prayer, we challenge ourselves to have the courage to take action. The AGAPE call invites us to act together for transformation of economic injustice and to continue analyzing and reflecting on challenges of economic globalization and the link between wealth and poverty.

1. POVERTY ERADICATION

We recommit ourselves to work for the eradication of poverty and inequality through developing economies of solidarity and sustainable communities. We will hold our governments and the international institutions accountable to implement their commitments on poverty eradication and sustainability.

2. TRADE

We recommit ourselves to work for justice in international trade relations through critical analyses on free trade and trade negotiations, and to collaborate closely with social movements in making those agreements just, equitable and democratic.

3. FINANCE

We recommit ourselves to campaign for responsible lending; unconditional debt cancellation and for the control and regulation of global financial markets. Investments should be redirected towards businesses that respect social and ecological justice, or in banks and institutions that do not engage in speculation, nor encourage tax evasion.

4. SUSTAINABLE USE OF LAND AND NATURAL RESOURCES

We recommit ourselves to engage in actions for sustainable and just patterns of extraction and use of natural resources, in solidarity with Indigenous Peoples, who seek to protect their land, water and their communities.

We recommit ourselves to challenge the excessive consumption of affluent societies so that they will shift towards self-restraint and simplicity in lifestyles.

5. PUBLIC GOODS AND SERVICES

We recommit ourselves to join the global struggle against the imposed privatization of public goods and services; and to actively defend the rights of countries and peoples to define and manage their own commons.

We recommit ourselves to support movements, groups and international initiatives defending vital elements of life such as bio-diversity, water and the atmosphere.

6. LIFE-GIVING AGRICULTURE

We recommit ourselves to work for land reforms in solidarity with landless agricultural labourers and small farm holders; to advocate in various ways for self-determination over food concerns; to oppose the production of genetically modified organisms (GMOs) as well as trade liberalization as the sole directive. We commit ourselves to promote ecological farming practices and to stand in solidarity with peasant communities.

7. DECENT JOBS, EMANCIPATED WORK AND PEOPLE'S LIVELIHOODS

We commit ourselves to build alliances with social movements and trade unions that advocate decent jobs and just wages. We commit ourselves to advocate for those workers and bonded labourers who work under exploitative conditions and are deprived of their rights to form trade unions.

8. CHURCHES AND THE POWER OF EMPIRE

We recommit ourselves to reflect on the question of power and empire from a biblical and theological perspective, and take a firm faith stance against hegemonic powers because all power is accountable to God.

We acknowledge that the process of transformation requires that we as churches make ourselves accountable to the victims of the project of economic globalization. Their voices and experiences must determine how we analyze and judge this project, in keeping with the gospel. This implies that we as churches from different regions make ourselves accountable to each other, and that those of us closer to the centres of power live out our first loyalty to our sisters and brothers who experience the negative impacts of global economic injustice every day of their lives.

This AGAPE call is a prayer for strength to transform unjust economic structures. It will guide our reflections and actions in the next phase of the ecumenical journey. Our engagement will build on the findings, proposals and recommendations to the churches from the AGAPE process as outlined in the AGAPE background document.

PLENARY
"OVERCOMING VIOLENCE: LIVING A CULTURE OF PEACE"

SAVING GOD'S CHILDREN FROM THE SCOURGE OF WAR

OLARA A. OTUNNU

Mr Olara A. Otunnu is the president of the LBL Foundation for Children and former UN under-secretary-general and special representative for children and armed conflict. This reflection was prepared for the plenary on "Overcoming Violence" on 18 February 2006.

The theme for my presentation this morning is: *Saving God's Children from the Scourge of War.* I believe that few missions could be more compelling for the world today. This is a central issue of peace and justice.

When adults wage war, children pay the highest price. Children are the primary victims of armed conflict. They are both its targets and increasingly its instruments. Their suffering bears many faces, in the midst of armed conflict and its aftermath. Children are killed or maimed, made orphans, abducted, deprived of education and health care, and left with deep emotional scars and trauma. They are recruited and used as child soldiers, forced to give expression to the hatred of adults. Uprooted from their homes, displaced children become very vulnerable. Girls face additional risks, particularly sexual violence and exploitation.

I can think of no group of persons more completely vulnerable than children exposed to armed conflict. Yet, until very recently, their fate did not constitute specific and systematic focus and response by the international community. Indeed when policymakers convened to discuss issues of peace and security, the fate and well-being of children did not feature in their deliberations. This has now changed.

Children do not only deserve but, indeed, have a right to protection and well-being. Those who brutalize children and deny them schooling and medical care in situations of war, are committing two crimes simultaneously – they are destroying the present as well as the future.

These violators need to be identified, named and held accountable by the international community.

In post-conflict situations, it is imperative to invest in the healing, rehabilitation and development of children. This should constitute a central concern, reflected in the setting of priorities, the formulation of policies and programmes, and the allocation of resources. When they are constructively engaged and are active participants, war-affected youth can be an important force for rebuilding their societies. But when they feel marginalized, alienated, embittered and without hope, the same youth can easily turn into an army of spoilers, and a recruiting pool for other warlords to fight new wars. Such youth also become much more vulnerable to radical indoctrination and enlistment by terrorist entrepreneurs.

Ensuring protection for our children and investing in their education and development is therefore among the most important and effective means for building durable peace and justice in society.

CAMPAIGN TO PROTECT CHILDREN FROM THE SCOURGE OF WAR

Over the last several years, I have led a UN-based campaign to mobilize international action on behalf of children exposed to war, promoting measures for their protection in times of war and for their healing and social reintegration in the aftermath of conflict. I undertook this mission by developing and implementing specific strategies, actions and initiatives. The campaign was organized in four phases, namely: *laying the foundation; developing concrete actions and initiatives; instituting a "naming and shaming" list of offenders; and instituting the CAAC compliance regime.*

The first phase – laying the foundation – consisted of defining and framing the CAAC agenda, gaining acceptance and legitimacy for the new agenda, establishing a network of stakeholders within and outside the UN, and laying the groundwork for broader awareness-raising and advocacy.

DEVELOPING CONCRETE RESPONSE AND ACTIONS

In the second phase, I led initiatives and efforts (involving in particular UN entities, governments, NGOs and regional organizations) to develop concrete responses and actions and initiatives.

During this period, our initiatives and advocacy yielded significant advances and innovations, most notably: significant rise in awareness, visibility and advocacy on CAAC issues; the protection of war-affected children has been firmly placed on the international peace-and-security agenda; a comprehensive body of protective instruments and standards has now been put in place; a systematic practice of obtaining concrete commitments and benchmarks from parties to conflict has been developed; children's concerns are being included in peace negotiations and peace accords, and have become a priority in post-conflict programmes for rehabilitation and rebuilding; Child Protection Advisers (CPAs) have been integrated in peacekeeping operations; key regional organizations have incorporated this agenda into their own policies and programmes; this issue has been integrated and mainstreamed in institutions and mechanisms, within and outside the UN; and war-affected children are coming into their own, through their active participation in rebuilding peace and "voice of children" programmes. These efforts and initiatives created strong momentum.

EMBARKING ON THE "ERA OF APPLICATION"

Yet, in spite of these impressive gains, I remained deeply preoccupied by one phenomenon. On the one side, we had now developed these clear and strong standards for protection, and important concrete initiatives, particularly at the international level. On the other side, atrocities and impunity against children continued on the ground. In effect, the international community and the children were now faced with a cruel dichotomy. This dichotomy is not unique to the CAAC agenda; it is a perennial problem of UN and other multilateral efforts at moving from creation to enforcement of international instruments, norms, and standards.

In my view, the key to overcoming this gulf lay in embarking on a systematic campaign for the "era of application" – for transforming international instruments and standards into an actual protection regime on the ground. The "era of application" had to be developed and anchored within a formal and structured compliance system or mechanism. Words on paper alone cannot save children and women in danger. To my mind, the time had come for the international community to redirect its energies from the normative task of the elaboration of standards to the compliance mission of ensuring their application on the ground. I have spent the last three years working to crack this conundrum.

INSTITUTING A "NAMING AND SHAMING" LIST

The third phase was to institute a "naming and shaming" list. This also became the first concrete step in the "era of application" campaign. The purpose of the "naming and shaming" list was to institute a practice to identify, name and publicly list offending parties for grave abuses against children. This would underscore accountability and exact public pressure on the offending parties. The idea was not only to publish the list but to submit it officially to the Security Council. This was a controversial project in uncharted territory. It would take a lot of lobbying and negotiations before the proposed listing was accepted by the Security Council.

We proceeded to develop the listing practice in stages, building block by building block. The first list, compiled in 2002, named only parties in situations of conflict which happened to be under consideration by the Security Council. The violation for which the parties were cited was limited to the recruitment and use of child soldiers.

The second list, compiled in 2003, was expanded to include all offending parties, governments as well as insurgents, and in all conflict situations, whether or not their particular conflict happens to be on the agenda of the Security Council.

The third and latest list, published in January 2005, was the subject of protracted and difficult negotiations at all levels. But in the end we were able to realize our most important objective – a comprehensive listing practice. The "naming and shaming" list now incorporates all offending parties, in all situations of armed conflict or concern, and with respect to all major violations against children.

This became the basis for the development of a full compliance regime, discussed below.

ESTABLISHING A FORMAL CAAC COMPLIANCE REGIME.

The fourth and last stage in our campaign was the task of developing a full-fledged compliance regime. Two years ago, I embarked on an intensive process of designing, drafting and holding extensive consultations with all stakeholders, particularly, governments, UN agencies, regional organizations, and NGOs. Last January I put forward a detailed action plan,[2] proposing a structure and a series of measures necessary for a formal compliance regime. This was subsequently submitted to the Security Council for formal approval. The action plan identified the international instruments and standards that constitute the basis for monitoring – the yardsticks for judging the conduct of parties to conflict and the basis for "naming names". It specified the particular violations to be monitored and the entities that should undertake the gathering, scrutiny and compilation of information at various levels. Much of this work is designed to be undertaken by the Secretariat-level task force, working with similar monitoring and reporting bodies at the country-level. The Office of the Special Representative for Children and Armed Conflict, UNICEF, UN peacekeeping missions and UN country teams are to play the key roles in the implementation of the compliance regime.

It took six months of intensive and protracted negotiations within the Security Council and with other delegations, before the Security Council, in a major and ground-breaking development, unanimously adopted Resolution 1612 on July 26[3], endorsing the structure and the series of far-reaching measures contained in the action plan. This marks a turning point of great consequence. For the first time, the UN has established a formal, structured and detailed compliance regime of this kind.

The compliance regime breaks new ground in several respects. First, it establishes a "from-the-ground-up" monitoring and reporting system, which will gather objective, specific, and timely information – "the who, where and what" – on grave violations being committed against children in situations of armed conflict. UN-led task forces in conflict-affected countries will focus on six especially serious violations against children: killing or maiming; the recruitment or abduction of children for use as soldiers; rape and other sexual violence against children; attacks against schools or hospitals; and the denial of humanitarian access to children. Under this new mechanism, UN-led task forces will be established in phases, ultimately covering all conflict situations of concern, to monitor the conduct of all parties, and to transmit regular reports to a central task force based at UN headquarters in New York. These reports will serve as "triggers for action" against the offending parties.

Second, all offending parties, governments as well as insurgents, will continue to be identified publicly, in what has been called the "naming and shaming" list, which I have prepared and submitted annually to the Security Council since 2003. The latest report lists 54 offending parties[4] in 11 countries. These include: the LTTE (Tamil

Tigers) in Sri Lanka; the FARC in Colombia; the Janjaweed in Sudan; the Communist Party of Nepal; the Lord's Resistance Army in Uganda; the Karen National Liberation Army in Myanmar; and government forces in DRC, Myanmar and Uganda.

Third, the Security Council has ordered offending parties, working in collaboration with UN Country Teams, immediately to prepare and implement very specific action plans and deadlines for ending the violations for which they have been listed. Typically, these should include: immediate end to all violations by the listed party; commitment by the listed party to the unconditional release of all children within its ranks, within a time-frame agreed with the United Nations team; time-bound plans and benchmarks for monitoring progress and compliance, agreed with the United Nations team; and agreed arrangements for access by the United Nations team for monitoring and verification of the action plan.

Fourth, where parties fail to stop their violations against children, the Security Council will consider targeted measures against those parties and their leaders, such as travel restrictions and denial of visas, imposition of arms embargoes and bans on military assistance, and restriction on the flow of financial resources.

And, finally, in order to monitor compliance with Resolution 1612, the Security Council has established its own special Working Group, composed of all 15 members, to review reports and action plans, and consider targeted measures against offending parties, where insufficient or no progress has been made.

Clearly the information compiled and transmitted in monitoring reports is only useful if it serves as a "trigger for action" on the part of key decision-making bodies such as the Security Council, the International Criminal Court, the Commission on Human Rights, regional organizations and national governments, to take necessary and concrete measures to end documented grave violations against children. The monitoring reports are designed to serve this specific purpose.

It is also crucial that the issue of compliance be taken up beyond the corridors of the United Nations, by concerned public opinion. That is why it is important to mobilize an international public campaign in support of compliance. With Resolution 1612 we have a solid base and springboard for this campaign, particularly on the part of legislators, religious leaders, women's organizations, the media, non-governmental organizations, and children themselves. There is a need and important role for a civil society network of "Friends of 1612".

BUILDING LOCAL CAPACITY FOR ADVOCACY, PROTECTION AND REHABILITATION

In order to build a viable regime of protection on the ground, international actors need to do much more to support the efforts of local actors, in particular, to strengthen the capacities of defenders of children who are labouring at the very frontline of this struggle – national institutions and local and sub-regional civil society networks for advocacy, protection, and rehabilitation. This is the best way to ensure local ownership and long-term sustainability for the protection of children.

I believe that we should strongly support local communities in their efforts to reclaim and strengthen indigenous cultural norms that have traditionally provided for the protection of children and women in times of war. In addition to international instruments and standards, various societies can draw on their own traditional norms governing the conduct of warfare. Societies throughout history have recognized the obligation to provide children with special protection from harm, even in times of war. Distinctions between acceptable and unacceptable practices have been maintained, as have time-honoured taboos and injunctions prohibiting indiscriminate targeting of civilian populations, especially children and women. These traditional norms provide a "second pillar of protection", reinforcing and complementing the "first pillar of protection" provided by international instruments.

In these efforts to build and strengthen local capacity for advocacy, protection and rehabilitation, I see communities of faith playing a particularly important role.

CAN WE INFLUENCE INSURGENTS?

The question is often raised as to how the international community can influence the conduct of all parties to conflict, particularly insurgents. In fact, insurgent groups have grown increasingly sophisticated in their political and financial operations and in their external connections. This means that carefully chosen and calibrated measures can have significant impact on insurgencies.

The imposition of carefully calibrated and targeted measures can have the desired impact on governments as well as insurgents. At political and practical levels there are levers of influence that can have significant sway with all parties to conflict. The viability and success of their political and military projects depend crucially on networks of cooperation and goodwill that link them to the outside world – to their immediate neighbourhood as well as to the wider international community. In this context, the force of international and national public opinion, including particularly the voice of the communities of faith; the search for acceptability and legitimacy at national and international levels; the demand for accountability as represented, for example, by the ICC and ad hoc tribunals; the external provision of arms and financial flows; and illicit trade in natural resources; the growing strength and vigilance of international and national civil societies, and media exposure – all of these represent powerful conditions and levers to influence the conduct of parties in conflict. From this list, "pressure points" can be determined and a carefully targeted sanction regime can be constituted against a given offending party. That the imposition of such carefully calibrated and targeted measures can have the desired impact on insurgents as well as governments is demonstrated by the recent examples of effective sanction measures imposed on UNITA in Angola and RUF in Sierra Leone.

In today's inextricably interdependent world, parties to conflict do not and cannot operate as islands unto themselves.

NORTHERN UGANDA: THE WORST PLACE IN THE WORLD TO BE A CHILD TODAY

As we focus this morning on the fate of children being destroyed in situations of war, I must draw your attention to the worst place on earth to be a child today. That place is the northern region of the Republic of Uganda.

The situation in northern Uganda is far worse than that of Darfur, in terms of its duration, its magnitude, and its deep and long-term consequences for the society being destroyed.

Witness the following:

20 years of war. The human rights and humanitarian catastrophe in northern Uganda has been going on, non-stop, for twenty years.

10 years in concentration camps. For over 10 years, a population of almost 2 million people, of whom 80 percent are children and women, have been herded like animals into concentration camps, some 200 camps in all* in abominable living conditions, defined by staggering levels of squalor, disease and death, humiliation and despair, appalling sanitation and hygiene, and massive overcrowding and malnutrition. As a relief official in Gulu stated, "People are living like animals. They do not have the bare minimum."

Although the camps are predominantly concentrated in Acoli since 1995, Lango (particularly Lira district) and Teso (Katakwi, Kaberamaido, and Soroti) are also gravely affected; and the living conditions in all the camps in the region are abominable.

Staggering death levels in the camps. These camps have the worst infant mortality rates anywhere in the world today. A recent survey by WorldVision reported that about 1,000 children die every week because of the conditions imposed in the camps; the director of WV in Uganda stated, "When I first saw these findings, I though it was a lie. But let us face it. We have reached the worst category an emergency can ever reach." This situation was underscored by the UN in a November report which stated that the mortality rates are in northern Uganda double those of Darfur. As the Gulu NGO Forum noted, "The camp population is not coping anymore but only slowly but gradually dying."

Healthcare, non-existent. As reported recently by the international agency, Internal Displacement Monitoring Centre, "Access to healthcare is almost nonexistent."

Malnutrition and stunted growth. Chronic malnutrition is widespread; 41 percent of children under 5 years have been seriously stunted in their growth.

20 years without education. Two generations of children have been denied education as a matter of government policy, they have been deliberately condemned to a life of darkness and ignorance, deprived of all hope and opportunity. Imagine this in the land that produced Archbishop Janani Luwum, the martyred primate of the Anglican church in Uganda, Rwanda, Burundi and Boga-Zaire (Eastern DRC) who was murdered by Idi Amin in 1978.

Children abducted and brutalized. Over the years, over 20,000 children, unprotected, have been abducted and brutalized by the rebel group, Lord's Resistance Army (LRA). Some 40,000 children, the so-called "night commuters", trek several hours each evening to sleep in the streets of Gulu and Kitgum towns (and walk back the same distances in the morning) to avoid abduction.

Suicide and despair. In the face of relentless cultural and personal humiliations and abuse, suicide has risen to an alarming level. Suicide is highest among mothers who feel utter despair at their inability to provide for their children or save them from starvation and death from preventable diseases. For example, in August, 13 mothers committed suicide in Pabbo camp alone.

Rampant rape, sexual abuse and HIV/AIDS. As several reports have documented, rape and generalized sexual exploitation, especially by government soldiers, have become "entirely normal". As noted in a recent report by Human Rights Watch, "Women in a number of camps told how they had been raped by soldiers from the Ugandan army… It is exceptionally difficult for women to find protection from sexual abuse by government soldiers." From almost a zero base, the rate of HIV infection among these rural communities has galloped to staggering levels: 30-50 percent compared to national infection of 5 percent. Last June, the medical superintendent of Gulu Hospital reported that 27 percent of children who were tested there were found to be HIV-positive; 40 percent of pregnant women attending Lacor Hospital for routine prenatal visits tested HIV-positive. Journalists John Muto-Ono p'Lajur and Wendy Glauser reported that, "Awer camp leader Benjamin Oballim believes HIV infection is close to 50 percent among adults living in his camp. A 2004 study in Lira found out of 4,026 IDPs who went for testing, 37 percent were positive."

This is the face of genocide.

In the sobering words of a missionary priest working in the region, "Everything in Acoli is dying". Or, as MSF has reported, "The extent of suffering is overwhelming…according to international benchmarks this constitutes an emergency out of control."

Following a recent visit to the region, the Ugandan journalist, Elias Biryabarema, wrote: "I encountered unique and heart-stopping suffering… shocking cruelty and death stalking a people by the minute, by the hour, by the day; for the last two decades… These children, these women, have committed no crime to deserve this. They deserve an explanation from their president: they deserved it yesterday, they do today and will tomorrow." Or, in the words of another Ugandan journalist, P.K. Mwanje, "Ugandans south of the River Nile and their friends do not know of the genocide taking place in northern Uganda."

The population of northern Uganda has been rendered totally vulnerable; they are trapped between the brutality of the LRA and the genocidal project, atrocities and humiliations which are being systematically committed by the government. The LRA have been responsible for brutal atrocities, including massacres, abduction of children and gruesome maiming, for which they must be held accountable. However, it is clear that the LRA factor and presence is being cynically manipulated to divert attention from the genocide unfolding in the camps and other atrocities being committed by the government itself. A carefully scripted narrative is promoted, according to which the catastrophe in northern Uganda begins with the LRA and ends with their demise. In this respect, the LRA and the "war" have become both the cover and the pretext under which genocide is being conducted in the region.

In his Easter message last year, the Catholic Archbishop of Kampala, Emmanuel Cardinal Wamala, stated "There will be genocide in the north if the international community does not intervene to end the war." In an anguished plea, Bishop Macleord Baker Ochola II, retired Anglican Bishop of Kitgum Diocese in northern Uganda, recently said "All these cries from the people of Uganda show very clearly that a slow but sure genocide has been taking place in Northern Uganda, while the world is looking on, as was the case in the Rwanda genocide."

When faced with genocide, we have a moral, religious and political obligation to recognize it, denounce it, and stop it, regardless of the ethnicity or the political affiliation of the population being destroyed.

We look particularly to you as spiritual and religious leaders to provide that prophetic voice and leadership. We look to you to denounce the genocide in northern Uganda. We look to you to mount a campaign to end the genocide and to dismantle the concentration camps.

As I review what is unfolding in northern Uganda, I cannot help but wonder if we have learned any lessons from the earlier dark episodes of history: millions of Jews exterminated during the Holocaust in Europe, genocide perpetrated in Rwanda, children and women systematically massacred in the Balkans. Each time we have said, "never again", but only after the dark deed was accomplished.

The genocide unfolding in northern Uganda today is happening on our watch, with our full knowledge. And tomorrow, shall we once again be heard to say that we did not know what was going on for all these years? And what shall we tell the survivor children in northern Uganda, when they ask why no one came to stop the dark deeds stalking their land and devouring its people?

Notes:
1. CAAC is used as shorthand to denote "children and armed conflict" and "children affected by armed conflict".
2. Olara A. Otunnu. *Ensuring the 'Era of Application' for the Protection of Children Exposed to Armed Conflict: A Plan of Action for Establishing a Monitoring, Reporting and Compliance Mechanism for CAAC.* January 10, 2005.
3. S/RES/1612. July 26, 2005.
4. For a full list of the 54 offending parties, see Report of the Secretary-General to the Security Council (S/2005/72).

PLENARY
"OVERCOMING VIOLENCE: LIVING A CULTURE OF PEACE"

MID-TERM OF THE DECADE TO OVERCOME VIOLENCE 2001-2010: CHURCHES SEEKING RECONCILIATION AND PEACE

CALL TO RECOMMITMENT

This document attempts to capture the learnings, the dynamics and the results of the first part of the Decade. Moreover, it is a reminder that the Decade is by no means over. In September 2005 this document was submitted to the executive committee which affirmed its content with the understanding that it be given to the assembly delegates in the context of the plenary on the Decade to Overcome Violence as a call to recommitment for the churches.

Nothing is so characteristically Christian as being a peace-maker. (St Basil the Great) Five years have passed since the World Council of Churches launched the Decade to Overcome Violence. The assembly at Porto Alegre marks the mid-term and offers an opportunity to celebrate what has been achieved, share experiences, make an interim assessment, and refocus the course to be followed during the second five-year period.

The goals of overcoming violence and building a culture of peace imply spiritual, theological and practical challenges for our churches which touch us in the centre of what it means to be church. The debate about the whole spectrum of the spirit and logic of violence has started, but the course we have entered requires persistence and endurance.

It is encouraging that the impulse of the Decade has been taken up in an ever-growing number of churches and regions. Bonds of ecumenical solidarity in the search for reconciliation and peace have been built and strengthened: new initiatives around the world have started, new alliances in peace-building have emerged, new theological reflection is being undertaken and a growing number of Christians are rediscovering a spirituality of non-violence.

Interreligious dialogue about the hidden connections between religion and violence has become one of the foci of the Decade. This is true in particular for dialogue between Christians and Muslims. The trust that has been built through patient dialogue and practical cooperation for the common good may prevent religion from being used as a weapon.

During the first half of the Decade we were confronted with cruel terrorist attacks, which have provoked wars in Afghanistan and Iraq. The spirit, logic and practice of violence manifested themselves again in an unexpected dimension. The massive efforts for strengthening security in the context of the so-called "fight against terrorism" have led to noticeable arms proliferation and a growth in the general militarization of the world. While we are beginning to discern in more depth the ethical demands of the responsibility to protect those who cannot protect themselves, we are convinced that international terrorism is not being overcome with military means. At the same time we acknowledge that more people are becoming victims of violence in civil and local conflicts which are being fought with light and small weapons. This remains a strong challenge to the churches together.

The concern for security has become the dominant motif for individual as well as social and political decisions. "Human security" is the fruit of just relationships in community. We acknowledge that security is increasingly being threatened through the effects of economic globalization. Therefore, the search for an "Alternative Globalization Addressing Peoples and Earth" has to be understood as a decisive contribution to the continuation of the Decade.

The respect for human dignity, the concern for the well-being of the neighbour and the active promotion of the common good are imperatives of the gospel of Jesus Christ. Men and women are created equally in the image of God and justified by grace. Therefore, human rights are a basic element in preventing violence at all levels, individual, interpersonal and collective, and especially violence against women and children. This must include the effort to build and develop the rule of law everywhere. We shall further pursue the understanding of "restorative" or "transformative" justice with the aim of establishing viable and just relationships in communities.

To relinquish any theological and ethical justification of violence calls for discernment that draws its strength from a spirituality and discipleship of active non-violence. We have committed ourselves to a profound common ethical-theological reflection and advocacy for non-violent conflict prevention, civilian conflict management and peace consolidation. The praxis of non-violence must be rooted in a spirituality that acknowledges one's own vulnerability; that encourages and empowers the powerless to be able to face up to those who misuse their power; that trusts the active presence of the power of God in human conflicts and therefore is able to transcend the seeming lack of alternatives in situations of violence.

During the second half of the Decade we will increase our efforts to work towards firmer alliances and more effective links between churches, networks and movements. We will support and coordinate common projects, which are aimed at building up structures, instruments and communities of non-violent, civilian conflict management. The "ecumenical space" offered by the Decade needs to be shaped through mutual encounters, including governmental and non-governmental organizations.

Our goal remains to move the search for reconciliation and peace "from the periphery to the centre of the life and witness of the church". Peace-building in non-violent ways is a Christian core virtue and an imperative of the gospel message itself. We are determined to become what we are called to be: "ambassadors of reconciliation" (2 Cor. 5). This is the mission of healing, including responsible accompaniment for those who are voiceless as well as speaking truth to those in power. We will reject every attempt to use violence and fear as tools of politics.

The ecumenical fellowship of churches strongly manifests the conviction that the communion of all saints, which is a gift from God and rooted in God's triune life, can overcome the culture of enmity and exclusion which continuously leads into the vicious circles of violence. It has become in itself an image for the possibilities of reconciled living together while recognizing continuing diversities. If this community becomes an advocate of reconciliation for all people in all places who suffer from violence, and presents active non-violent ways of resolving conflict, we will indeed become a credible witness for the hope that is within us, building a culture of peace and reconciliation for all of creation.

There is no need to tell how the loving-kindness of Christ comes bathed in peace. Therefore we must learn to cease from strife, whether against ourselves or against one another, or against the angels, and instead to labour together even with the angels for the accomplishment of God's will, in accordance with the providential purpose of Jesus who works all things in all and makes peace, unutterable and fore-ordained from eternity, and reconciles us to himself and, in himself, to the Father. Concerning these supernatural gifts enough has been said with confirmation drawn from the holy testimony of the scriptures. (Dionysius the Areopagite)

We pray: God, in your grace, transform us, transform the world.

PLENARY
ON LATIN AMERICA

WHERE IS GOD AT WORK
IN LATIN AMERICA?

A key to understanding the Plenary on Latin America which took place on 19 February 2006.

The Brazilian anthropologist Darcy Ribeiro speaks of three major sources that have shaped race and culture in Latin America.

- There are *the surviving indigenous people* of the south of Mexico, Guatemala, Ecuador, Peru and Bolivia, who maintain the pre-Colombian legacy of the Aztecs, Mayas and Incas.

- There are *the new people*, including inhabitants of Venezuela, Colombia, the Guyanas, Brazil, Central America and the Caribbean, and Paraguay, mixed race descendents of Indigenous, European and African ancestors, whose distinctive identity is still being shaped.
- There are *the transplanted people*, European immigrants living in Argentina, Uruguay, the south of Brazil, and the south of Chile, who swamped the earlier Indigenous and mixed race populations. This group has been responsible for the second major wave of religious diversification in the continent, marked by the presence of all the forms of Protestantism brought by immigrants, various types of European Catholicism, the ancient Orthodox versions of Christianity from the East, plus other religions, such as Islam, Buddhism and Shintoism. The first wave was the distinctive cultural and religious diversity of the more than 2,500 indigenous peoples, which was smothered by the imposition of Christianity.

An important aspect is that our continent was built on the foundation of colonial political domination, confiscation of the land of indigenous peoples, their massacre, or their economic and social exploitation as forced labour; and the imposition of Spanish, Portuguese, French, English and Dutch culture, and of Catholic and Protestant Christianity.

The main challenge facing Christianity is the inequality and injustice that it has shared in and legitimized – and at times prophetically condemned. An important contribution by Christianity follows in the line of this more prophetic tradition. It has surfaced in the last forty years in the form of cooperation with popular movements, has nurtured the ecumenical movement, and has contributed to the flourishing of Latin American theology and its various accompanying strands taking up the cries of the poor and the cry of the earth for the integrity of creation.

At the beginning of the 20th century, the Pentecostal movement made its appearance in Latin America, formed by communities that, in the great majority of cases, have a strong sense of their calling to evangelize, an immense capacity to welcome the sick and the overburdened, and who celebrate their faith in cultural ways close to everyday life. These experiences, albeit with their inconsistencies, together with those of many churches in Latin America, have shown that Christianity has a great contribution to make towards affirming a spirituality and pastoral approach rooted in the life of the people. The basis of these movements and theologies is the popular reading of the Bible, which is both prayerful and liberating, and can be seen in the words of our various characters.

In our presentation we have indigenous faces (an indigenous woman and an elderly indigenous man), an Afro-Latin American face (our pilgrim), and the faces of transplanted peoples (a teenager and a revolutionary). The presentation using puppets is an attempt to show that fun and humour are part of our way of life and are elements in the struggle for survival and love of life.

We realize that the whole diversity and richness of the peoples of Latin America cannot be shown here in all their detail. However, we wish to invite you, the participants in this Plenary, to enter into this short experience of the Latin American way of being and living and, above all, of surviving, of struggling for life and of dreaming of better days to come. In that way we shall be showing where God is at work in Latin America…

RESUMÉ

In a multi-media presentation, using dummies, music and videos, different characters reflect on the question, "Where is God at work in Latin America?" Five individuals – puppets – offer their reflections on the most important historical events in Latin America, emphasizing the role of the churches and the ecumenical movement. Nine individuals from the region will also share their thoughts on these issues. The question, "Where is God at work in Latin America?" is explored by examining the various elements of the Assembly logo:

- **The hand of God** illustrates the present situation of the continent with its various social contradictions (poverty, wealth, deprivation).
- **Creation and the Cross** symbolize the cruelty of colonizers towards the Indigenous and Black peoples. The cross, although violently forced on Latin America, is also the symbol of a Christianity that, despite its inconsistencies, has promoted a holistic and liberating gospel.
- **The spirit of peace** reflects the richness of the different peoples living in the region, with their cultures and traditions which, despite the wounds of the past, make it possible for them to live together in plural societies.
- **The rainbow** symbolizes the commitment of men and women of faith who have struggled for justice and life; people who believe in the importance of combining prophetic with pastoral activities; men and women forming the churches that have become healing communities.
- **The transformed world** shows that the humblest of people, with faith as their foundation, are building pathways of hope in our continent.

241

CHARACTERS (NARRATORS)

TEENAGER (15 years old) – inquisitive, sensitive, naïve and with a sense of humour. She represents the persistent hope that a society with more justice and freedom can be built. She wants an answer to the question, "Where is God at work in Latin America?"

OLD INDIGENOUS MAN – the oldest character (70 years old), who easily shows his feelings and has lived through some of the most moving moments in the history of the continent. He represents suffering, resistance and longing for freedom. He is in favour of accepting people who are different, the quest for an inculturated Christianity, the demand for the conversion of the conquistadors and a plea for forgiveness from them, so that communion with them can come into being.

INDIGENOUS WOMAN – she represents the struggle of women and the reinstatement of the indigenous presence in Amerindia (45 years old). She describes the important campaigns of women in defence of human rights at various moments in the history of our continent. Her long plaits portray the legacy of other women who have responded to the challenges of being a woman in Latin America.

THE REVOLUTIONARY – (a reference to the revolutionaries of the 1950s-70s) – a character who swings between anger and fun (55 years old). His appearing here points to the activity and ideas of those who acted against military repression, and to the continuing popular struggles in Latin America. He believes that democracy is one of the greatest achievements in Latin America and must be maintained.

THE PILGRIM (35 years old) – he is black. He represents the awareness that in vast areas of Latin America the economy and society were based on traffic in black people and slave labour, which was responsible for almost everything that was built and produced. His intention is to discover the challenges arising out of his own people, whose ancestors were so violently destroyed. His remarks show his concern with breaking the chains of injustice, and building up faith in the continent, with the God of the poor and the little ones, the God of life, as its foundation. He recalls the role of the churches and the ecumenical movement.

VIDEOTAPED TESTIMONIES INCLUDE:

- Julio Cesar Holguin, Bishop of the Episcopal Church of the Dominican Republic, and President of CLAI, the Latin American Council of Churches.
- Adriel de Souza, Bishop of the Methodist Church of Brazil, and President of CONIC, the National Council of Churches.
- Elsa Tamez, a Latin American theologian and Professor at the Latin American Biblical University.
- Nora Cortiñas and Estela Carloto of Asociaciones de Madres y Abuelas de la Plaza de Mayo, the Plaza de Mayo mothers and grandmothers.
- Rigoberta Menchú, an indigenous women from Guatemala who, thanks to her personal struggle for justice as well as for her people, received the Nobel Prize for Peace in 1992.
- Antônio Olimpio de Sant'Ana, Pastor and Director of CENACORA, defender of the rights of Blacks in Brazil and Latin America.
- Federico Pagura, Bishop of the Methodist Church of Argentina, and President of the WCC.
- Adolfo Perez Esquivel, Argentina, who was arrested by the military dictatorship in 1977 and was counted among the missing persons until he reappeared alive 14 months later thanks in part to the efforts of the ecumenical movement. He was awarded the Nobel Prize for Peace in 1980 for his work on peace and reconciliation.
- Juan Sepúlveda, a Pentecostal theologian and a Professor of Theology in Chile.

CREDITS

Main contributors

World Council of Churches/Latin American Working Group

National Assembly Committee in Brazil

Ecumenical Forum in Brazil/KOINONIA, Ecumenical Presence and Service/Anivaldo Padilha, Methodist University of São Paulo

Latin American Advisory Group composed of the WCC and CLAI: Eugenio Poma, Benjamín Cortéz, Rui Bernhard, Juan Sepúlveda and Marta Palma.

Production

Methodist University of São Paulo (Rectorship, Department of Communication and Marketing, Department of Technology and Information, Faculty of Theology, Faculty of Multimedia Communications, Department of the Arts)

Programme
Maria Aparecida Ruiz

Creator and General Director
Alvaro Petersen Jr

Acting and Musical Director
Álvaro Petersen Jr

Coordination
Magali do Nascimento Cunha

Production in Porto Alegre
Marcelo Schneider

Audio-visual production:
Methodist RTV Agency
Marcio Kowalsk
Michelle Dantas Garcia

Audio Technician
Gustavo Cotomacci

Technicians
Moacyr Vezzani
Video assistant
Guilherme Bravo Alves

Filming
Marcelo Moreira
Márcio Antonio Kowalski
Michelle Dantas Garcia

Actors /Puppeteers:
Chameleon Doll Theatre Group
Andréa Perez
Adriana Azevedo
Carlos Azevedo
João França
Tânia de Castro

Doll Makers
Jesus de Moraes

Models
Antonio Rabadan

Scene design
Rafael Silva

Support
Vera Lucia Potthoff da Silva

Programme Collaborators
São Paulo Methodist University
  Working Group
Álvaro Petersen
Claudia César da Silva
Davi Betts
Fábio Josgrilberg
João Plaça Jr
Lauri Emilio Wirth
Luciano Sathler
Luiz Carlos Ramos
Magali do Nascimento Cunha
Paulo Roberto Garcia
Paulo Roberto Salles Garcia
Rui de Souza Josgrilberg
Tércio Bretanha Junker
Anivaldo Padilha, KOINONIA,
  Ecumenical Presence and Service
José Oscar Beozzo, Comissão
  Ecumênica sobre História da Igreja
  na América Latina

Content Advisors
Benjamin Cortés
Eugenio Poma
Juan Sepúlveda
Lucio Flores
Marta Palma
Rui Bernhard
Anivaldo Padilha

Production Advisor in Porto Alegre
Rui Bernard

Picture transmission
Benjamin Cortés
Humberto Shikiya
José Oscar Beozzo
KOINONIA, Ecumenical Presence
  and Service
Secretariat for Latin America/WCC

Song selection
Álvaro Petersen Jr with the collaboration
  of Anivaldo Padilha

Picture selection and digitalization
Priscila Munhoz
Thiago Siqueira

**Ecumenical Journey Pictures and
Testimony**
Felipe Oscar Ino
Michele Dantas Garcia

PLENARY ON LATIN AMERICA

SERIES OF TESTIMONIES AND STATEMENTS FROM THE PLENERY VIDEO

BISHOP JULIO CESAR HOLGUIN, CLAI PRESIDENT, HONDURAS
(Soundtrack – Spanish)

On behalf of the Latin American Council of Churches I want to repeat our warmest welcome to all the delegates who are participating in the Ninth Assembly of the World Council of Churches. I wish to repeat our welcome to Latin America, to Porto Alegre, to this dark-haired America. We ask you to come with open minds, ready to change what has to change. Just as we pray to God that, in God's grace, God will transform the world, we pray also that God, in God's grace, will transform our churches, transform the ecumenical movement and equip us with his grace better to proclaim our faith through our diaconal service. May God in his infinite goodness, mercy and grace be with us always.

BISHOP ADRIEL DE SOUZA MAIA, PRESIDENT OF CONIC, BRAZIL
(Soundtrack – Portuguese)

The National Council of Christian Churches in Brazil has great pleasure in welcoming delegates from throughout the world to Brazil and, in particular, to Porto Alegre for this Ninth Assembly of the World Council of Churches. This is a key moment in the life of Brazil, a time when we are consolidating the ecumenical movement. It is our hope that this Assembly, especially inspired by the theme "God, in your Grace, Transform the World", will send out an appeal worldwide, so that, in Jesus' words, we might have life in abundance, and that the churches might bear effective witness to the grace of God to a world where there is so much exclusion, in order that the world may believe in the gospel and in transformation.

Nora Cortiñas, a Mother of the Plaza de Mayo, Argentina
(Soundtrack – Spanish)

The last time I saw my son was at Easter 1977, on Easter Day. I shall never see him again, and I shall never know what happened to him. Today, it is almost 29 years ago, and I still do not know to this day what happened to him, or where his body is, for Gustavo is certainly not alive. But, even so, I and all the mothers are hoping that the State will at some time respond to our legal demands and give an account of the events that have happened. From the moment my son disappeared I began to go out into the streets, and there I met the first group of mothers who went to the Plaza de Mayo for this imaginative campaign by Açucena Villa Flor de Vinzente. And so we began to meet one another, the mothers of the Plaza de Mayo, and all of us began to make one demand, all of us for all our sons and daughters. The mothers began to stop taking individual action and began to campaign together, because they had taken away from us dissidents and leaders of people's movements. They took our children away from us, they held on to the children born of pregnant women, whom they kept for themselves, and they even arrested mothers who were looking for their sons and daughters. All of that shows what we have been condemning for years and years – a system that is perverse. And then, it shows that there are no limits, no boundaries, no frontiers, to the economic plan that the United States implemented here in the Southern Cone of Latin America, with the arrival of Kissinger to prepare the path for the military dictatorships. It also shows why and for what purpose they took away our sons and our daughters. It is obvious – it was because they were militants, militating for human rights, militating for life, militating for change. They took them away from us, so that they could implement fully this neo-liberal policy that is still with us today.

We began to understand this, and we took up the cause for which our sons and daughters had struggled, and we widened the call that we were making for them to be restored to us alive, with the guilty being justly punished, to take up also the cause of the defence of rights, economic, social and cultural rights. On this long journey, we have had many disappointments, but we have also had the joy of knowing that others have been with us. That is the case with the Catholic Church, local priests who had been friends of our sons and daughters, who had worked in poor areas alongside them. The Protestant churches have also been very generous in their solidarity, such as at times when the priests of the Catholic Church who were with us were being persecuted and being forbidden to associate with the movement of the

Mothers and celebrate mass for the disappeared. We received, particularly from the Methodist Church, unqualified support and friendship and solidarity which deserve to be remembered still today.

ALBA LANCILLOTTO, A GRANDMOTHER OF THE PLAZA DE MAYO, ARGENTINA
(Soundtrack – Spanish)

I am very much involved in the struggle for life, because I struggle for our sons and daughters, I struggle for the disappeared, so that there will be no more disappearances. This is a struggle for life and for justice. I believe that the Christian churches have a duty to be involved in this struggle for, if they did not, it would be a denial of the gospel. I had the good fortune as a practising Catholic to be part of a committed church that was faithful to the gospel, and to be very close to the Protestant churches, the Methodist Church, and various groups that have been and still are our friends. They have taught us many things. I believe that the churches have to be involved in this because it is part of their faithfulness to the gospel, and I believe that faithfulness to the gospel obliges us, and obliges the churches, to be present in the struggle for life, because God is a God of life. They have to be present in the struggle for life and in the struggle for justice. I could not be part of a church that did not think in that way.

RIGOBERTA MENCHÚ, NOBEL PEACE PRIZE WINNER, GUATEMALA
(Soundtrack – Spanish)

The Nobel Prize is a symbol of peace. Beyond any doubt, it was a sign of hope for the struggles of the Indigenous peoples throughout the continent, freedom for Indigenous peoples, wherever they are in Latin America and worldwide. For as long as they are alive, there will be a gleam of hope and original thinking for life.

"I crossed the frontier full of sadness. I felt immense pain at this dark rain-sodden early morning, that goes beyond my own existence. Our mother earth is in mourning and is bathed in blood. She weeps day and night , she is so sad."

The so-called discovery (of Latin America) has above all resulted in a long night of darkness, quite apart from how we have survived in the ashes of 500 years. They have been for us 500 years of silence, marginalization and much oppression. And that is why we cannot rejoice in, nor celebrate the elimination of our ancestors in this long night of darkness.

These 500 years of oppression directed against the Indigenous peoples have had different forms, different methods, but a common feature has been the cruelty with which the voice of our people has been repressed and silenced.

As regards discrimination, it is not only lack of respect for people and their knowledge, their values and their opportunity to make a rich contribution to culture, but we also feel lack of respect and appreciation even for our art, our dress, our way of life.

There are many things that unite us as the Indigenous peoples of America. There are aspects that unite us, such as love of the earth, the concept of Mother Earth as the source of culture, as the source of our roots.

We have survived the destruction of the earth, we have survived discrimination, the sterilization of women. In the same way we have felt the teaching that produces discrimination, oppression, and the denial of access to a life of greater dignity.

This is also the first time that as Indigenous Peoples we come together once again – a reaffirmation of our Indigenous pride. The Indigenous peoples not only demand adequate food and good housing. We also lay claim to our historic memory, we lay claim to our language, we lay claim to our Indigenous status.

This is a search for our roots, this moment in time is a search for our identity, which will strengthen the struggles of the Indigenous people and strengthen our cause.

The Nobel Peace Prize represents a recognition of all that the people of Guatemala have lost.

REVD ANTÔNIO OLIMPIO DE SANT'ANA, COMBAT AGAINST RACISM, BRAZIL
(Soundtrack – Portuguese)

CENACORA is devoted to struggle, as its title suggests, the struggle against racism, discrimination, intolerance, prejudice and xenophobia. We defend women and children, who are the main victims of violence – social, racial, physical and psychological violence. In our land we are committed to this task, working mostly with the churches, seeking to involve them in the struggle against these social evils.

In our population, which is 45.4 percent made up of black people, it is important to note that this is where the most poverty is concentrated, where there are the most poor people. Those who are the poorest are precisely those who are members of the black community. This is a classic picture mirrored again and again throughout Latin America. Poverty is quite normal where there are black people. The same situation is experienced mainly by black women, who are victimized because they are black, because they are women and, when they get old, throughout Latin America they become victims of a third prejudice: that of being old. All the black countries of Latin America have a black population that is naturally victimized because of the colour of their skin. In our land, as in all Latin America, we need to fight against what we call inequality.

Differences are natural, but inequality is not. Our struggle, which has been taking place since the beginning of the last century, is making progress, but despite all this, while we are making progress in our struggle, our oppressors are also perfecting their schemes of racism, their schemes of discrimination, their schemes of intolerance, of prejudice and xenophobia. We are all fully aware that our struggle must continue and that it is a hard struggle so that racism can be overcome. What I want to do is to express our pleasure that we, the black community of Brazil, have in welcoming all the members of the Assembly of the World Council of Churches.

ELZA TAMEZ, METHODIST THEOLOGIAN, COSTA RICA
(Soundtrack – Spanish)

The theme of this Assembly is grace. Obviously this setting needs grace, the grace of God, full of justice – transforming, liberating, tender grace – which is what was given as a tool to our people to be what we are, as sons and daughters of God, who are full of dignity. Why? Because grace is not abstract, but grows out of real life situations. Thus, as a woman, I do my theology based on the experience of women. What is this experience of women?

In today's world women are being killed at a terrible rate. I have to take this into account as I do my theology. We know that the classical categories of Christian theology were based on Western patriarchal categories, that the Bible is a book written in a patriarchal culture. That presents great challenges to women, because all we women have to be creative as we do theology.

We women have a great contribution to make to the church, to help it become another way of being church, because at the moment it excludes women and, in the world of theology, which is generally a discipline in which men engage, women have not been present as subjects, as creators of theology. Theological studies have not been part of their world. But a new possibility is opening up in Latin American theology.

Poverty has a woman's face. That means that, in this sinful economic system that is increasingly separating rich and poor, having a woman's face means that there is a very close connection between the patriarchal system and the economic system. We cannot skirt around this reality of sin. Can we speak of grace without also speaking of sin? That would be to undervalue what grace is. The situation in Latin America challenges men and women to think about God, including speaking about God out of our situation, which cries out for justice, and for transforming grace.

Juan Sepúlveda, Pentecostal theologian, Chile
(Soundtrack – Spanish)

We have already said this is not a complete or final description. We are not dealing with a closed truth, but with a truth in change. New actors appear on the religious scene and raise questions and demand discernment. That is the case with the so-called neo-Pentecostal movement. We need to acknowledge that it is a new, but legitimate, face of a diverse and multi-centred Christianity. This is a question that is still open and the reply will depend in large part on the way in which these movements themselves regard or approach the traditional Christian families.

Depending on how we experience it and on how we understand it, diversity could be something that we know, appreciate and celebrate. But it could also be a threat to unity, both Christian unity and social unity.

If we take an honest look at history, none of the faces we see can claim to be completely blameless with regard to the divisions, prejudices and intolerance that separate us. However, we wish to give thanks to God because little by little we are learning to get to know one another, to recognize one another as brothers and sisters, to pray together and to be together. We can thus venture to say that these are some of the faces with whom God is journeying in Latin America, bringing joy, confidence, hope and vitality to a people who, in the midst of great adversity, are seeking a new land in which all men and women will have their own space and live a dignified life.

Bishop Federico Pagura, WCC Latin America President, Argentina
(Soundtrack – Spanish)

Human rights have been one of the basic issues that have concerned me. Some people might ask, why human rights? We are researching, studying, proclaiming, sharing the gospel, the good news of Jesus' message, the message of the kingdom. Because human rights have been violated many times in my lifetime. But there was a key moment in my life, which was when I went to Central America, which we, proud people from the River Plate, in our prejudiced way, used to call "banana republics". In Mexico, in El Salvador and in Guatemala, I could see the suffering of the Indigenous people, the suffering of the peasants. I could see the fear in the faces of Costa Rican women and I also saw the oppression by the banana companies. The result was that my life took on a new direction, a new vision inspired by that Central American experience. I was led to a stronger commitment to the gospel, including the gospel of the kingdom, which includes the quest for justice, the quest for truth, for authentic freedom, and also the hope for a new world, the hope that a new world is possible.

As a President of the World Council of Churches I have tried to be the voice of Latin America within the life of this much loved institution. In the midst of all that, I have also had the experience of being pastor in a city such as Mendoza, on the border with Chile. There thousands of refugees came to the hostels, where we Methodists, with the Lutherans and the Catholics – only those three churches – had the courage to commit ourselves, to serve our refugee brothers and sisters.

We campaign together in peace and justice organizations with our Nobel Prize winner Perez Esquivel. It is a task, a movement for justice and peace, without separating those two elements, because justice and peace have met, have kissed one another, and together they are the only possibility for a permanent and lasting peace for our peoples.

For all this I give thanks to God, for having been able for almost 83 years to be part of this great adventure that never ends, but that does end on a note of hope, for "I know whom I have trusted, and am confident of his power to keep safe what he has put into my charge until the great day", until the final victory of his kingdom. For all this, I give thanks to God.

ADOLFO PEREZ ESQUIVEL, NOBEL PEACE PRIZE WINNER, ARGENTINA
(Soundtrack – Spanish)

We continue working to solve conflict and support popular organizations, a work of faith and social action. In doing so, we are creating spaces of freedom, understanding, life and development. We are a people who are subjected and dominated, and inevitably we have to find answers in order to live in human dignity. That is the message of the gospel. It is a message of life, not a message of death. In so doing we are working to build, to contribute consciously to building the human person, to building a vision of the human person and, naturally, to building as far as we can in our own countries. I believe that the church is the people of God, the people of God on a journey, who are building and attempting to do the will of the Father in the kingdom, this kingdom which is the kingdom of life, the kingdom of the human person, which with God transcends all.

Here in Argentina, some bishops – and I am speaking of the Catholic Church – collaborated with the military dictatorship. And there were others who were consistent with the message of the gospel, and accompanied the people, supporting them in their struggles and their demands.

In the Protestant churches it was more or less the same. Pastors in the Church of the River Plate, of the Methodist Church were very committed to social action. That is because Christ is our brother and sister and on that basis we can build new possibilities and a purpose to life based on faith. Sadly, we meet other groups who do not make this commitment.

I believe that the churches have an essential role. It is a role that has to do with critical consciousness, with values, with building a new dimension to the human person, and I believe that this is more effective when grounded in faith. I believe that out of our culture we can form relationships and reach understanding. I believe that in the ecumenical movement we must also have a deep sense of prayer, since without prayer we cannot be truly and concretely committed to express the word of God in our lives and in our communities.

BISHOP CARLOS POMA, METHODIST, BOLIVIA
(Soundtrack – Spanish)

God is journeying on in the midst of God's people. God has always been in the midst of God's people, and God is also journeying in the midst of his people. God is raising up these peoples that for a long time have been excluded and forgotten and whom the powers that be have also forgotten and never paid attention to. But among these excluded people, there is God, journeying on with them. Here, in unity and diversity God is journeying on in Latin America.

REGINA DA SILVA FERREIRA, LUTHERAN (IECLB), BRAZIL
(Soundtrack – Portuguese)

I think that God is everywhere. I think that he lives in people's hearts, God is with those who are suffering, with those who are happy. I think that sometimes people close their hearts a little to God but despite that God enters in, because we are God's dwelling place. God is everywhere, in the world of nature, in the air, in the wind.

I believe that God is always with us, in everything, in every place, at all times.

FRANCISCO PERNAMBUCANO, MOVEMENT OF THE HOMELESS, BRAZIL
(Sountrack – Portuguese)

God is present in Latin America, in social movements, with the poor, with the homeless, with the landless. God is to be found particularly in the favelas, under the bridges where the beggars are, with the hungry, with those who have no justice, no peace, here in Brazil and throughout Latin America.

REVD GUADALUPE GOMEZ, BAPTIST, NICARAGUA
(Soundtrack – Spanish)

God is to be found in the midst of the conflicts taking place in Latin America, in the midst of brothers and sisters who have no hope, who struggle day after day and work for a better society, who proclaim the gospel, who denounce wrongdoing.

REVD ISRAEL BATISTA GUERRA, GENERAL SECRETARY OF THE LATIN AMERICAN COUNCIL OF CHURCHES
(Soundtrack – Spanish)

God is to be found today in Latin America among those who do not belong and immigrants. God is journeying on and invites us to join him to renew our hope.

BISHOP NELIDA RITCHIE, METHODIST, ARGENTINA
(Soundtrack – Spanish)

I believe that God is present and is to be seen in the faces of the little ones, the vulnerable of all times, and among the vulnerable there are those who, for our society and for the interests of this world, are often faceless, invisible, anonymous. God gives a name and dignity to people, and through the preaching of the gospel we give a face and a dignity to people.

REVD MILTON MEJIA, PRESBYTERIAN, COLOMBIA
(Soundtrack – Spanish)

God is to be found in the churches that are committed to all those who are asking for the life in abundance which Jesus promised us. As churches we need to give signs that life in abundance is possible.

CHRISTINA TAKATSU WINNISCHOFER, EPISCOPAL-ANGLICAN, BRAZIL
(Soundtrack – Portuguese)

God is to be found everywhere in Latin America, in the recovery of cultures, for example the cultures of Indigenous peoples, of Afro-Latin Americans, bringing back to light all the experience of their ancestors, all their culture.

REVD JORGE JULIO VACCARO, PENTECOSTAL (CHURCH OF GOD), ARGENTINA
(Soundtrack – Spanish)

The Lord is dwelling among us and is to be found among the excluded, the homeless, and those who are about to become homeless – those who have no food, those who are hungry, those with no work. God is among them, is alongside them, blesses them, heals them, frees them, and also is doing it through other men and women, whether Christian or not. God is also present among Christians, in the churches, and at this particular time to enable us not to succumb to the temptation of theologies that come from the Empire.

Statements and reports adopted by the Assembly

Called to be the One Church

Text on Ecclesiology

An Invitation to the Churches to Renew their Commitment to the Search for Unity and to Deepen their Dialogue

WCC Assemblies have adopted texts offering a vision, or identifying the qualities, of "the unity we seek".[1] In line with these texts the 9th Assembly in Porto Alegre has adopted this text inviting the churches to continue their journey together as a further step towards full visible unity. The purpose of this "Invitation to the Churches" is two-fold: (a) to reflect what the churches, at this point on their ecumenical journey, can say together about some important aspects of the Church; and (b) to invite the churches into a renewed conversation – mutually supportive, yet open and searching – about the quality and degree of their fellowship and communion, and about the issues which still divide them.[2]

I

1. We, the delegates to the Ninth Assembly of the World Council of Churches, give thanks to the Triune God, Father, Son and Holy Spirit, who has brought our churches into living contact and dialogue. By God's grace we have been enabled to remain together, even when this has not been easy. Considerable efforts have been made to overcome divisions. We are "a fellowship of churches which confess the Lord Jesus Christ as God and Saviour according to the scriptures, and therefore seek to fulfill their common calling to the glory of the one God, Father, Son and Holy

Spirit".[3] We reaffirm that "the primary purpose of the fellowship of churches in the World Council of Churches is to call one another to visible unity in one faith and in one eucharistic fellowship expressed in worship and in common life in Christ, through witness and service to the world, and to advance towards that unity in order that the world may believe".[4] Our continuing divisions are real wounds to the body of Christ, and God's mission in the world suffers.

2. Churches in the fellowship of the WCC remain committed to one another on the way towards *full visible unity*. This commitment is a gift from our gracious Lord. Unity is both a divine gift and calling. Our churches have affirmed that the unity for which we pray, hope and work is "a *koinonia* given and expressed in the common confession of the apostolic faith; a common sacramental life entered by the one baptism and celebrated together in one eucharistic fellowship; a common life in which members and ministries are mutually recognized and reconciled; and a common mission witnessing to the gospel of God's grace to all people and serving the whole of creation".[5] Such koinonia is to be expressed in each place, and through a conciliar relationship of churches in different places. We have much work ahead of us as together we seek to understand the meaning of unity and catholicity, and the significance of baptism.

II

3. We confess one, holy, catholic and apostolic Church as expressed in the Nicene-Constantinopolitan Creed (381). The Church's oneness is an image of the unity of the Triune God in the communion of the divine Persons. Holy scripture describes the Christian community as the body of Christ whose interrelated diversity is essential to its wholeness: "Now there are varieties of gifts, but the same Spirit; and there are varieties of services, but the same Lord; and there are varieties of activities, but it is the same God who activates all of them in everyone. To each is given the manifestation of the Spirit for the common good" (1 Cor. 12:4-7).[6] Thus, as the people of God, the body of Christ, and the temple of the Holy Spirit, the Church is called to manifest its *oneness in rich diversity*.

4. The Church as communion of believers is created by the Word of God, for it is through hearing the *proclamation of the gospel* that faith, by the action of His Holy Spirit, is awakened (Rom. 10:17). Since the good news proclaimed to awaken faith is the good news handed down by the apostles, the Church created by it is *apostolic*. Built on the foundation of the apostles and prophets the Church is God's household,

a *holy* temple in which the Holy Spirit lives and is active. By the power of the Holy Spirit believers grow into a holy temple in the Lord (Eph. 2. 21-22).[7]

5. We affirm that the apostolic faith of the Church is one, as the body of Christ is one. Yet there may legitimately be different formulations of the faith of the Church. The life of the Church as new life in Christ is *one*. Yet it is built up through different charismata and ministries. The hope of the Church is one. Yet it is expressed in different human expectations. We acknowledge that there are different ecclesiological starting points, and a range of views on the relation of the Church to the churches. Some differences express God's grace and goodness; they must be discerned in God's grace through the Holy Spirit. Other differences divide the Church; these must be overcome through the Spirit's gifts of faith, hope and love so that separation and exclusion do not have the last word. God's "plan for the fullness of time [is] to gather up all things in him" (Eph. 1:10), reconciling human divisions. God calls his people in love to discernment and renewal on the way to the fullness of koinonia.

6. The *catholicity* of the Church expresses the fullness, integrity and totality of its life in Christ through the Holy Spirit in all times and places. This mystery is expressed in each community of baptized believers in which the apostolic faith is confessed and lived, the gospel is proclaimed, and the sacraments are celebrated. Each church is the Church catholic and not simply a part of it. Each church is the Church catholic, but not the whole of it. Each church fulfills its catholicity when it is in communion with the other churches. We affirm that the catholicity of the Church is expressed most visibly in sharing holy communion and in a mutually recognized and reconciled ministry.

7. The relationship among churches is dynamically interactive. Each church is called to mutual giving and receiving gifts and to *mutual accountability*. Each church must become aware of all that is provisional in its life and have the courage to acknowledge this to other churches. Even today, when eucharistic sharing is not always possible, divided churches express mutual accountability and aspects of catholicity when they pray for one another, share resources, assist one another in times of need, make decisions together, work together for justice, reconciliation, and peace, hold one another accountable to the discipleship inherent in baptism, and maintain dialogue in the face of differences, refusing to say "I have no need of you" (1 Cor. 12:21). Apart from one another we are impoverished.

III

8. All who have been baptized into Christ are united with Christ in his body: "Therefore we have been buried with him by *baptism* into death, so that, just as Christ was raised from the dead by the glory of the Father, so we too might walk in newness of life" (Rom. 6:4). In baptism, the Spirit confers Christ's holiness upon Christ's members. Baptism into union with Christ calls churches to be open and honest with one another, even when doing so is difficult: "But speaking the truth in love, we must grow up in every way into him who is the head, into Christ" (Eph. 4:15). Baptism bestows upon the churches both the freedom and the responsibility to journey towards common proclamation of the Word, confession of the one faith, celebration of one eucharist, and full sharing in one ministry. There are some who do not observe the rite of baptism in water but share in the spiritual experience of life in Christ.[8]

9. Our common belonging to Christ through baptism in the name of the Father and of the Son and of the Holy Spirit enables and calls churches to walk together, even when they are in disagreement. We affirm that there is one baptism, just as there is one body and one Spirit, one hope of our calling, one Lord, one faith, one God and Father of us all (cf. Eph. 4:4-6). In God's grace, baptism manifests the reality that *we belong to one another*, even though some churches are not yet able to recognize others as Church in the full sense of the word. We recall the words of the Toronto Statement, in which the member churches of the WCC affirm that "the membership of the church of Christ is more inclusive than the membership of their own church body. They seek, therefore, to enter into living contact with those outside their own ranks who confess the Lordship of Christ". [9]

IV

10. The Church as the creation of God's Word and Spirit is a mystery, sign and instrument of what God intends for the salvation of the world. The grace of God is expressed in the victory over sin given by Christ, and in the healing and wholeness of the human being. The kingdom of God can be perceived in a *reconciled and reconciling community* called to holiness: a community that strives to overcome the discriminations expressed in sinful social structures, and to work for the healing of divisions in its own life and for healing and unity in the human community. The Church participates in the reconciling ministry of Christ, who emptied himself, when it lives out its *mission*, affirming and renewing the image of God in all

humanity and working alongside all those whose human dignity has been denied by economic, political and social marginalization.

11. Mission is integral to the life of the Church. The Church in its mission expresses its calling to proclaim the gospel and to offer the living Christ to the whole creation. The churches find themselves living alongside people of other living faiths and ideologies. As an instrument of God, who is sovereign over the whole creation, the Church is called to engage in dialogue and collaboration with them so that its mission brings about the good of all creatures and the well-being of the earth. All churches are called to struggle against sin in all its manifestations, within and around them, and to work with others to combat injustice, alleviate human suffering, overcome violence and ensure fullness of life for all people.

V

12. Throughout its history the World Council of Churches has been a privileged instrument by which churches have been able to listen to one another and speak to one another, engaging issues that challenge the churches and imperil humankind. Churches in the ecumenical movement have also explored divisive questions through multilateral and bilateral dialogues. And yet churches have not always acknowledged their *mutual responsibility* to one another, and have not always recognized the need to give account to one another of their faith, life and witness, as well as to articulate the factors that keep them apart. Bearing in mind the experience of the life we already share and the achievements of multilateral and bilateral dialogues, it is now time to take concrete steps together.

13. Therefore the Ninth Assembly calls upon the World Council of Churches to continue to facilitate *deep conversations* among various churches. We also invite all of our churches to engage in the hard task of giving a candid account of the relation of their own faith and order to the faith and order of other churches. Each church is asked to articulate the judgments that shape, and even qualify, its relationship to the others. The honest sharing of commonalities, divergences and differences will help all churches to pursue the things that make for peace and build up the common life.

14. Towards the goal of full visible unity the churches are called to address recurrent matters in fresh, more pointed ways. Among the *questions to be addressed* continually by the churches are these:

a. To what extent can your church discern the faithful expression of the apostolic faith in its own life, prayer and witness and in that of other churches?

b. Where does your church perceive fidelity to Christ in the faith and life of other churches?

c. Does your church recognize a common pattern of Christian initiation, grounded in baptism, in the life of other churches?

d. Why does your church believe that it is necessary, or permissible, or not possible to share the Lord's Supper with those of other churches?

e. In what ways is your church able to recognize the ordered ministries of other churches?

f. To what extent can your church share the spirituality of other churches?

g. How will your church stand with other churches to contend with problems such as social and political hegemonies, persecution, oppression, poverty and violence?

h. To what extent will your church share with other churches in the apostolic mission?

i. To what extent does your church share with other churches in faith formation and theological education?

j. How fully can your church share in prayer with other churches?

In addressing these questions, churches will be challenged to recognize areas for renewal in their own lives and new opportunities to deepen relations with those of other traditions.

VI

15. Our churches *journey together* in conversation and common action, confident that the risen Christ will continue to disclose himself as he did in the breaking of bread at Emmaus, and that he will unveil the deeper meaning of fellowship and communion (Luke 24:13-35). Noting the progress made in the ecumenical movement, we encourage our churches to continue on this arduous yet joyous path, trusting in God the Father, Son and Holy Spirit, whose grace transforms our struggles for unity into the fruits of communion.

Let us listen to what the Spirit is saying to the churches!

Notes:
1. The present "Invitation to the Churches" was produced at the request of the Central Committee of the WCC (2002), in a process organized by the WCC's Faith and Order Commission. A first draft was written at a meeting in Nicosia, Cyprus in March, 2004; this was revised (on the basis of extensive comments received from WCC gov-

erning bodies, the Faith and Order Commission, and the Steering Committee of the Special Commission) at a second meeting in Nicosia in May, 2005. Faith and Order extends on behalf of the WCC its appreciation to the Church of Cyprus, which graciously hosted these preparatory meetings. A final revision took place at the Faith and Order Standing Commission meeting in Aghios Nikolaos, Crete, in June, 2005.

2. To assist this process, Faith and Order has produced and sent to the churches a new Study Document, "The Nature and Mission of the Church: A Stage on the Way to a Common Statement", Faith and Order Paper No. 198.

3. Basis, WCC Constitution, I.

4. Purposes and Functions, WCC Constitution, III.

5. "The Unity of the Church as Koinonia: Gift and Calling", The Canberra Statement, 2.1.

6. The scripture quotations contained herein are from the New Revised Standard Version of the Bible, © 1989, 1995, by the Division of Christian Education of the National Council of Churches of Christ in the United States of America, and are used by permission. All rights reserved.

7. "The Nature and Mission of the Church", § 23.

8. Cf. "The Unity of the Church as Koinonia: Gift and Calling", The Canberra Statement, 3.2.

9. The Toronto Statement, IV.3.

STATEMENTS AND REPORTS ADOPTED BY THE ASSEMBLY

REPORT OF THE PROGRAMME GUIDELINES COMMITTEE

The following report was presented to and received by the Assembly. Its resolutions were proposed by the Programme Guidelines Committee and approved by the Assembly through consensus. Dissent expressed by Assembly delegates is recorded as endnotes.

INTRODUCTION

1. One of the primary tasks of each Assembly of the World Council of Churches is to review the work and activities of the Council since its last Assembly and to set directions and priorities for the Council's programme in the future.

2. The Programme Guidelines Committee (PGC) of this Assembly has taken its tasks seriously, using as a starting point the report *From Harare to Porto Alegre*, the Pre-Assembly Programme Evaluation and Recommendations from the 2005 Central Committee, and a background paper, entitled "A Changing World", prepared by WCC staff. Each of the PGC members also attended an Ecumenical Conversation to listen to Assembly delegates about future WCC priorities. Finally, the PGC shared in dialogue and reflection on the reports of the Moderator, the General Secretary, the thematic plenaries, hearing sessions, and many suggestions and ideas coming from mutirão participants and constituency groups seeking to discern the mind of the Assembly and the call of God related to the unique role of the WCC within the ecumenical movement.

3. In presenting this report, the PGC has been aware that the work of the Policy Reference Committee has reviewed, and will address, several important programme initiatives since the Harare Assembly related to strengthening and deepening relationships among the member churches (e.g., the Special Commission on Orthodox Participation in the WCC), with ecumenical partners and with other Christian

churches (e.g., the Joint Working Group with the Roman Catholic Church, Pentecostals, etc.).

4. While the wealth of the input gathered by the PGC cannot be included in our Report to the Assembly, substantive documentation – including the reports from the 22 Ecumenical Conversations; the statements coming from constituency groups (youth, Indigenous Peoples, and persons with disabilities); the various proposals on specific issues from Mutirao workshops – will be referred to future governing bodies of the WCC in the important work of developing specific future programmes for the WCC. That documentation will inform them in their task of translating the broad policy directions included in this Report into programme.

RESOLUTION:

5. The Ninth Assembly *receives* with appreciation the report *From Harare to Porto Alegre* and the "Pre-Assembly Evaluation and Recommendations from the 2005 Central Committee"[1].

THE CONTEXT OF OUR WORK

6. The Porto Alegre Assembly has taken place against the backdrop of a rapidly changing world. It is on this stage, even as the drama of changing contexts unfolds, that the churches are called to fulfill their mission and calling. Changes are taking place everywhere, and all are related: the changing ecclesial and ecumenical contexts (including church geography, statistics, and secularization), as well as the changing political, economic and social contexts (including growing inequalities, environmental destruction, migration, violence and terror). These changes present immense challenges to the churches and to the WCC that call for courageous visions of hope and greater commitment to make visible God's gift of unity and reconciliation in Christ before our divided churches, societies, and world. We were greatly encouraged by how our Latin American hosts presented their history of struggle and hope in responding to the challenges their continent is facing. However, concerns were expressed about the marginalization of Indigenous Peoples and Afrodescendants in the life of the church and in society in Latin America.

7. We have been reminded that, "A divided church cannot have a credible witness in a broken world; it cannot stand against the disintegrating and disorienting forces of globalization and enter into meaningful dialogue with the world" (Moderator's Report, para. 17). We turn to God and pray, "God, in your grace, transform our

lives, our churches, our nations and world". All programmes and activities of the WCC are thus to be responsive to this changing context in seeking to be a faithful expression of God's justice, peace, care for creation, healing, reconciliation and salvation: the "fullness" of life for all.

OUR VISION AND OUR GOALS

8. In its work at this first WCC Assembly in the 21st century, the PGC reaffirmed the stated purpose and functions of the WCC (as expressed in the Constitution, para. III) as the basis for its work: "*The primary purpose of the fellowship of churches in the World Council of Churches is to call one another to visible unity in one faith and one eucharistic fellowship, expressed in worship and common life in Christ, through witness and service to the world, and to advance towards that unity in order that the world may believe.*" In addition, that paragraph affirms as goals of the Council that it will:

- promote the prayerful search for forgiveness and reconciliation in a spirit of mutual accountability, the development of deeper relationships through theological dialogue and the sharing of human, spiritual and material resources with one another;
- facilitate common witness; express their commitment to diakonia in serving human need;
- nurture the growth of an ecumenical consciousness;
- assist each other in relationships to and with people of other faiths; and,
- foster renewal and growth through unity, worship, mission and service.

9. These purposes and functions demonstrate the breadth of the vision of the WCC, and provide a foundation for the programmatic work of the Council.

RESOLUTION:

10. The Ninth Assembly *re-affirms* the document "Towards a Common Understanding and Vision of the WCC" (referred to in *From Harare to Porto Alegre*, pp. 175-181) as an expression of the vision of the WCC as a fellowship of churches and as a servant of the one ecumenical movement. Ways need to be found to make the content of the CUV document more accessible and understandable in order to facilitate greater ownership by the churches and by the ecumenical movement at large.

GUIDING PRINCIPLES AND METHODOLOGICAL RECOMMENDATIONS

11. Building upon the very helpful material and recommendations in the "Programme Evaluation Report from the 2005 Central Committee" (referred to in

From Harare to Porto Alegre, pp. 203-216), and receiving a strong and sobering recommendation from the Finance Committee of this Assembly related to the anticipated financial situation of the WCC in the coming years, the PGC identified seven basic principles to guide the WCC in setting its programme priorities in the future:

- to keep its focus upon what the WCC uniquely might do as a global fellowship of churches in providing leadership to the whole of the ecumenical movement;
- to do less, to do it well, in an integrated, collaborative and interactive approach;
- to lift up its central task of the churches calling one another to visible unity;
- to keep in tension the work of dialogue and advocacy, of building relationships and promoting social witness among churches and with different sectors in society;
- to foster greater ownership and participation by the churches in building as much as possible on initiatives of the churches and partner organizations;
- to bring a prophetic voice and witness to the world in addressing the urgent and turbulent issues of our times in a focused way;
- to communicate WCC activities to the churches and the world in a timely and imaginative way.

12. The PGC also identified several methodological elements in defining how future WCC life and work would be carried out, including:

- articulating a clear theological basis for all of its work;
- developing a comprehensive planning, monitoring and evaluation process that will include a clear time-line and goals;
- designing a strategy for communication, engagement and ownership by the churches;
- facilitating the coordinating role of the WCC in seeking partnerships in networking and advocacy with other ecumenical organizations, including Christian World Communions, REOs, NCCs, Specialized Ministries, faith-based organizations, and NGOs (as appropriate) – with the hope that many of these programmes can be implemented in collaborative ways of working;
- encouraging capacity-building of member churches and ecumenical partners;
- accompanying churches and peoples in critical situations and enabling and facilitating their action.

RESOLUTION:

13. The Ninth Assembly *endorses* these guiding principles and methodological elements as the basis for establishing the Council's future programme priorities.

Major Areas of Engagement

14. In light of the changing context, the vision and purpose of the WCC, and the guiding principles and methodological elements, the PGC offers four major interactive "areas of engagement" for shaping the future life and work of the Council. Each of these emphases is already reflected in the current programmes of the WCC. What is being proposed here is that there be greater integration among the programmes and standing Commissions (Faith and Order, Mission and Evangelism, International Affairs), while exploring greater collaboration with current ecumenical partners and specialized ministries in development of these emphases in the future.

15. Three additional words of introduction to these areas of engagement:

• the PGC strongly endorses promoting ecumenical leadership development of youth in the life of the WCC, including the full participation of youth in all programmes of the WCC. Youth voices, concerns and presence must be brought more directly into the decision-making and leadership of the work and governance of the Council.

• the PGC continues to affirm and celebrate the role and contributions of women in all areas and arenas in the life of the WCC, and endorses the continued participation of women in the whole of the WCC.

• the PGC urges that the WCC seek the full inclusion of Indigenous Peoples and Dalits, people of African descent, persons with disabilities and marginalized people all over the world in its life, work and decision-making.

Unity, Spirituality and Mission

16. Seeking unity and engaging in common mission and evangelism have been foundational elements in the ecumenical movement. New understandings of both unity and mission have continued to develop in the life of the WCC as member churches have engaged each other in responding to their growing relationships and expanding encounter with the diversity of theologies, ecclesiologies, and traditions. Future work in the area of mission and evangelism should engage the churches in their commitment to explore new ways of ecclesial life, fresh ways of experiencing the Christian faith, and the discovery of new contextual ways of proclaiming the gospel, including a critique of competitive missional activities.

17. Here in Porto Alegre, the need of the WCC and its member churches to focus upon the nature of Christian spirituality and the work of the Holy Spirit in the church and the world has become ever more urgent and obvious, both for the

integrity of our work for visible unity and in our mission to the world. Unity, spirituality and mission are interrelated, and their mutuality is dependent upon each receiving distinct and dedicated attention by the WCC and its member churches.

Ecumenical Formation

18. One of the issues that challenges the whole of the ecumenical movement today is that of ecumenical formation. As reported by the General Secretary in his report to this Assembly, "If contemporary Christians, including the church leadership, are to participate creatively and responsibly in the search for unity, and grow together, appropriate means of ecumenical formation must be offered to enable better, richer contributions to our common life." This is especially true for the students, young adults, laity and women in our churches as they increasingly take on leadership roles in the ecumenical movement for the 21st century.

19. The Ecumenical Institute of the WCC at Bossey was highlighted as a model for ecumenical formation, especially in its efforts in recent years in expanding its programme to include evangelicals and Pentecostals in its courses and seminars, as well as reaching out to provide greater inter-religious encounter. Providing a platform for churches and ecumenical partners working on challenges of science and technology to faith in cooperation with other parts of the WCC could be another opportunity. These trends are suggestive of the way forward, and a cause of hope.

20. Ecumenical formation also includes the role of the WCC in creating "safe spaces" for cross-cultural and cross-theological encounter so as to engage in honest encounter around issues that divide our churches and our communities, in particular, to continue the dialogue on issues such as family life and human sexuality.

Global Justice

21. Throughout this Assembly there has been the urgent call to work together in the ecumenical movement for a dynamic, global understanding of justice. Justice requires transformation of relationships at all levels of life in society and in nature towards life in dignity in just and sustainable communities (transformative justice):

- responding to those who suffer the consequences of injustice, racism and casteism,
- denouncing the scandal of a world divided along lines of wealth and poverty and contributing to the transformation of unjust economic and social structures,
- integrating the care of creation and faith perspectives and the use and mis-use of

science and new technologies such as bio-technologies, information technologies, surveillance and security technologies, energy technologies, etc.,

- challenging and facilitating the church's response to HIV and AIDS,
- including a clear voice in prophetic diakonia as an inseparable part of Christian identity and witness to societies, starting from life in family and community,
- engaging in efforts and processes aiming at conflict resolution and reconciliation.

Such work will require the WCC and its member churches "to re-direct our programmes toward more intentionally building truly inclusive and just communities which safeguard diversity, where different identities and unity interact, and where the rights and obligations of all are fully respected in love and fellowship" (Report of the General Secretary, p.14).

PUBLIC VOICE AND PROPHETIC WITNESS TO THE WORLD

22. In fulfilling its historic responsibility on behalf of its member churches, the WCC is challenged to be a strong, credible ethical voice as it offers a prophetic witness to the world. This voice and witness must be spiritually and theologically grounded if the churches are to be heard among competing voices in the world. Churches have a contribution to make to strengthen multilateral international cooperation and the international rule of law in dealing with human rights, militarism and peaceful resolution of conflicts.

23. At this Assembly the urgent need for churches and the WCC to engage in inter-religious cooperation and dialogue was strongly affirmed. In its future engagement with other religions, it is important for the WCC to continue its work in the context of religious plurality and to further develop dialogue and common action related to political, social, theological or ethical issues.

24. This Assembly marked the mid-term of the initiative launched at the Harare Assembly on the Decade to Overcome Violence. For the second half of the decade, the PGC affirmed that the style of networking local and regional initiatives in peacemaking should increasingly shape the WCC's programmatic life and work. In addition to the regional foci, the DOV should be attentive to situations of deep crisis, such as Northern Uganda and Haiti.

RESOLUTION:

25. The Ninth Assembly *affirms* these four areas of engagement in shaping the WCC's future life and work.

RESOLUTION:

26. In particular, in regard to specific programme areas that have been identified in pursuing these four "areas of engagement", the Ninth Assembly:

- *affirms* that comprehensive attention be given to unity, spirituality, and mission, both theologically and practically. The WCC and its member churches are encouraged to address the sharp ecclesiological questions set out in the report of the Special Commission on Orthodox Participation in the WCC, and to give priority to the questions of unity, catholicity, baptism and prayer;
- *encourages* churches on local, national, regional and global levels to commit themselves to the task of continuing ecumenical formation for all. In this role, the WCC should facilitate and initiate dialogue and possible cooperation between religious and political actors on the role of the church in civil society and between religions in areas of mutual understanding [2];
- *affirms* that a follow-up of the AGAPE process be undertaken and expanded, in collaboration with other ecumenical partners and organizations, to engage in (1) the work of theological reflection on these issues that arise out of the centre of our faith; (2) solid political, economic and social analysis; (3) on-going dialogue between religious, economic and political actors; and (4) sharing practical, positive approaches from the churches [3];
- in looking to the second half of the DOV, *endorses* that the regional foci be continued; that more sharing of successful examples be developed to encourage churches and local congregations to respond to overcoming violence in their own contexts supported by international mutual visits; that a process of wide consultation be undertaken towards developing an ecumenical declaration on "just peace"; and finally, that the conclusion of the DOV be marked by an international Ecumenical Peace Convocation.

269

POST-ASSEMBLY PLANNING

27. The period between the Assembly and the 2006 Central Committee meeting will be a time of intensive reflection led by the WCC leadership in consultation with churches and key ecumenical partners to receive the policy guidance from the Assembly and shape its programmatic work.

RESOLUTIONS:

28. In looking to its task of shaping future programmes for the WCC, the Ninth Assembly *approves* the following process:

- a working group made up of the leadership of the Assembly's Programme Guidelines Committee, Policy Reference Committee, Public Issues Committee and Finance Committee be asked to accompany the WCC leadership in developing future programme recommendations;
- clear, well-functioning planning, monitoring and evaluation mechanisms be established for each programme;
- a clear distinction be made between issues that are either long-term, time-bound, or specific/urgent;
- a two-way communication strategy be developed for each programme and carried out with the various constituencies;
- clear exit strategies be established in phasing out, reconfiguring, or reshaping programmes taking into account both the limited human and financial resources of the WCC and also the possibilities to cooperate and share responsibility with other ecumenical partners;
- sustained dialogue with member churches and specialized ministries regarding ways of generating additional financial support to programmatic work of the WCC.

29. The Ninth Assembly *affirms* that the WCC should claim a clearer and stronger public profile in its witness to the world. To that effect it is hoped that the WCC will focus its energy and attention on a limited number of issues that cry out for response by the churches together. HIV and AIDS (including the ecclesiological implications of this pandemic in most parts of our world) should be one of these issues.

Notes:
1. Dissent was registered from Bishop Bärbel Wartenberg-Potter, delegate from the Evangelical Church in Germany, who feels that the Central Committee's decision on "common prayer" hinders God's Spirit from speaking in diverse and inclusive images and symbols.
2. Dissent was registered from:
  - Hulda Gudmundsdottir, delegate from the Evangelical Lutheran Church of Iceland, who wished to insert the words "focusing also on dividing issues such as human sexuality" at the end of the first sentence.
  - Four delegates who wished to insert the words "focusing especially on youth, women, persons with disabilities, Indigenous Peoples, Dalits, and people of African descent" at the end of the first sentence. The four delegates were: Carmen Lansdowne, delegate from the United Church of Canada; Rev. Robina Winbush, Presbyterian Church (USA); Rev. Dr Tyrone Pitts, Progressive National Baptist Convention Inc.; and Mr David Palopaa, Church of Sweden.
3. Dissent was registered from Herr Klaus Heidel, delegate from the Evangelical Church in Germany, who wished to put the main emphasis of the recommendation on concrete activities and action.

STATEMENTS AND REPORTS ADOPTED BY THE ASSEMBLY

REPORT OF THE POLICY REFERENCE COMMITTEE

The following report was presented to and received by the Assembly. Its resolutions were proposed by the Policy Reference Committee and approved by the Assembly through consensus.

MANDATE AND OVERVIEW

1. "Behold, I make all things new." (Rev. 21:5)

The ecumenical movement, inspired by the Holy Spirit, seeks to promote the renewal of our churches and God's whole creation as integral to the growth towards unity. It is in this broad framework that the Policy Reference Committee (PRC) did its work.

2. The PRC has been asked to work in an integrated way with the Programme Guidelines Committee and Public Issues Committee of the Assembly to offer one coherent outcome within their three reports that will guide future policies and the programmatic work of the World Council of Churches (WCC). The PRC was specifically directed to consider the changing ecclesial context and the relational dynamics in the wider ecumenical movement while proposing policy guidelines for the future on the fundamental and strategic questions of relationships.

3. The reports of the Moderator and the General Secretary were received with appreciation by the PRC, in particular, the deeply spiritual tone of both reports reflecting upon the theme of the Assembly "God, in your grace, transform the world". The vision for the Ninth Assembly and also for the ecumenical movement in the twenty-first century derives from our self-understanding as a faithful, praying community of Christians dedicated to witnessing to the world together, in relationship with one another by the grace of God. The quest for the visible unity of the church remains at the heart of the WCC.

4. Our ultimate vision is that we will achieve, by God's grace, the visible unity of Christ's Church and will be able to welcome one another at the Lord's table, to reconcile our ministries, and to be committed together to the reconciliation of the world. We must never lose sight of this dream, and we must take concrete steps now to make it a reality. The report of the Moderator articulated specific hopes and dreams related to work already begun around (i) the common date for Easter, (ii) Baptism, Eucharist and Ministry, and (iii) preparations for a single ecumenical assembly, dreams that echo those stated by the founders of the WCC.

RESOLUTION:

5. The Ninth Assembly *sets* as its goal that we will have made substantial progress towards realizing these hopes and dreams by the Tenth Assembly. Witness to the world of the progress made towards visible unity can include agreement among all of the Christian churches for calculation of the annual date for celebration of the feast of the Resurrection of Our Lord, for mutual recognition by all churches of one baptism, understanding that there are some who do not observe the rite of baptism in water but share in the desire to be faithful to Christ, and for convening an ecumenical assembly that would assemble all churches to celebrate their fellowship in Jesus Christ and to address common challenges facing the church and humanity – all on the way towards visible unity and a shared eucharist.

EMERGING TRENDS IN THE LIFE OF THE CHURCHES
AND THEIR ECUMENICAL IMPLICATIONS
ECUMENICAL RELATIONSHIPS IN THE TWENTY-FIRST CENTURY

6. Understanding the rapid and radical changes in the shape of global Christianity and the life of the churches is essential to addressing the shape of ecumenical relationships in the twenty-first century. The PRC suggests that a report on changing ecclesial and ecumenical contexts be prepared and updated on a regular basis in advance of meetings of the Central Committee during the next period.

7. The Assembly was called upon by the General Secretary to put "relationships in the centre of the ecumenical movement". The PRC echoes this call, understanding the creative tension that exists at the various levels of relationship engaged by the WCC, particularly between being a fellowship while also responding to the changing ecumenical landscape and responding to the world.

8. The process of reconfiguring the ecumenical movement is in large part an effort to "choreograph" the intricate relationships among the various ecumenical instru-

ments and new ecumenical partners, so that clarity, transparency, communication and cooperative efforts mark those relationships, allowing the ecumenical movement as a whole to offer to the world and to the regions and local churches the coherent grace-filled spiritual message of Christianity. The PRC took note of the messages coming from many sources gathered in the Ninth Assembly, as well as the theme at the heart of the Assembly. The process that has been called "reconfiguration" should be understood not as patching up the existing ecumenical structures, but as a dynamic process to deepen the relationship of the ecumenical movement to its spiritual roots and missionary identity, reaffirm the relationship of the ecumenical instruments to the churches, clarify the relationships among the various ecumenical instruments and ensure that the message and the effort be coordinated and coherent.

9. The PRC noted with appreciation the efforts towards this end, including the two consultations that have taken place with broad participation, the mapping process that described the various ecumenical actors, the recommendations that resulted from those consultations, as well as the continuing dynamic, inclusive dialogue that has followed from that work.

273

RESOLUTION:

10. The Ninth Assembly:

a) *calls upon* the member churches and ecumenical instruments to encourage the WCC in its role as leader of the process engaging the wider ecumenical movement in constructive collaboration (reconfiguration), including WCC member churches, Christian World Communions, Regional Ecumenical Organizations, National Councils of Churches, World Mission Bodies, Specialized Ministries, as well as Christian churches not currently in membership in the WCC, in order to assess the strengths and weaknesses of the current status of the ecumenical movement and offer strategies for enhancing the strengths and addressing the weaknesses;

b) *affirms* the appointment of a continuation committee as recommended during the consultation on "Ecumenism in the Twenty-first Century" (Chavannes-de-Bogis, December 2004) that will report to the Central Committee to continue this process during this next term, maintaining a primary role for the member churches;

c) *requests* that the WCC explore the implications of new forms of mission and ecumenism for the reconfiguration process, building on the method and results of the Conference on World Mission and Evangelism, Athens (2005).

Strengthening and Deepening the WCC and Relationships Among Member Churches

Who We Are and How We Work Together

11. The Common Understanding and Vision document (CUV) serves as a foundational statement of the nature of the fellowship among the member churches of the WCC and as the churches relate to other ecumenical partners. The committee affirms the centrality of this statement, urges that the CUV be more fully incorporated into the life and witness of the WCC at all levels, and continue to guide the programmatic work and relationships of the WCC.

Resolution:

12. The report of the General Secretary to the Ninth Assembly articulated urgent calls for deep change – not incremental change – in the way the WCC conducts its work during the next term. The most important is the call by the General Secretary for "a more integrated and interactive approach to programmes and for relationships" in the Council's future work. In the spirit of this report, therefore, the Assembly *instructs* the General Secretary, in consultation with the Central Committee, to implement clear and consistent changes to the working style, organizational structure and staffing of the WCC necessary to meet the current and future challenges to the ecumenical movement. The PRC is particularly interested in ensuring that all programmes, consultations, visits or statements initiated by the WCC are integrated and coordinated with the work being undertaken by staff in other programme areas.

13. The PRC affirms the importance of providing possibilities for young adults to participate in meaningful decision-making roles both in the churches and in the WCC, and urges that member churches provide additional opportunities for their young adults to benefit from ecumenical formation, including theological training at the Ecumenical Institute, Bossey.

Resolutions:

14. In light of the meeting of the Moderator and the General Secretary with young adult delegates to the Ninth Assembly, and the Statement on Youth Contribution delivered to the Assembly, the Assembly *directs* the Central Committee to create a representative body of young adults who would coordinate the various roles of

young adults connected to the WCC and facilitate communication between them. Such a body would create space for a meaningful participation of young adults in the life and decision-making of the WCC, and would be able to hold the WCC accountable to its goals regarding young adults.

15. The PRC noted the persistence of references to "persons with disabilities" which can be an acknowledgement of their absence in leadership and in decision-making processes. The PRC will, however, note that this can serve to mark the continuing marginalization of those persons living with different disabilities. The Assembly *recommends* that the WCC work with representatives of the Ecumenical Disabilities Advocates Network to articulate in an even more bold and creative way, consistent with Christian theology, ways to make the churches fully inclusive communities and the ecumenical movement a more open space for all human beings.

16. The PRC affirmed the recent actions of the Central Committee on human rights, Indigenous Peoples and language loss. The Assembly *recommends* to strengthen the participation and visibility of Indigenous Peoples within the WCC. The Assembly considers this an essential step for deepening the relationships among WCC member churches. The Assembly in particular urges the WCC to address the main areas which are problematic for Indigenous churches in its policy directions. The Assembly considers strengthening relationships with Indigenous Peoples an opportunity for the fellowship to gain new insights on the importance of place, land, language and theology of creation, as well as creative perspectives on grace and transformation.

17. The PRC appreciates the new consensus style of discernment for reaching decisions in the WCC and notes the opportunity this offers to the churches. A particular concern was expressed that the length of the reports of the Moderator and the General Secretary on the one hand, and the schedule of the Assembly on the other, limited meaningful discussion despite the stated goals of the consensus process, either during the presentation plenary or in committee. The PRC suggests that the shift to a consensus process in decision-making also requires changes in methodology and process in order to create adequate space for consensus to occur. This requires an evaluation of current models of reporting.

18. The Central Committee engaged in a process of self-evaluation in the months immediately preceding the Ninth Assembly. The PRC thanks those who conducted that evaluation and receives with appreciation the report of the Evaluation Committee. The PRC suggests that clear mechanisms for planning and evaluation

of the programmes and work and for transparent and mutually accountable working methods between the WCC and its member churches be established in advance of the second full meeting of the Central Committee, with particular attention to evaluating the transition to consensus and its consequences for working methods.

Relationships among Member Churches

19. Work of the Special Commission on Orthodox Participation in the WCC marked this past term of the WCC. The PRC affirms this important achievement of the Council that deepens the relationships among member churches and helps dispel misperceptions between families of churches. In particular, the Committee urges the WCC to stress the importance of this work as it implements the policies adopted by the Central Committee, grows into the consensus process of discernment for decision-making, and engages in the reconfiguration of the ecumenical movement. The committee welcomed the revisions to the Constitution and Rules of the WCC, including especially the new ways of relating to one another in our work as member churches working towards consensus in discerning ways to work together, clarified understanding of membership in the WCC, and the new opportunities for relationship to the WCC through the category of "churches in association with the WCC".

20. The PRC noted that each new term of the Central Committee provides an opportunity for informal encounters between and among representatives of member churches, to deepen understanding of the ecclesial commonalities and particularities of each member church. The PRC urges the WCC to make space for this type of interaction at every opportunity, to encourage the practice of "Living Letters" that provides an opportunity for personal encounters with churches in their own contexts, so that the churches come to know one another, and to encourage local collaborative consultations of Faith and Order documents.

21. The PRC also urges the WCC to listen to the member churches and strive towards greater coherence in the various relations with them, increasing cooperation, exchange of information and consultation among all involved persons (including WCC staff) and ecumenical partners.

The Call to be the One Church

22. The PRC has received with deep appreciation the document entitled "Called to be the One Church" (the Ecclesiology Text).

RESOLUTION:

The Ninth Assembly:

a) *adopts* the Ecclesiology Text as an invitation and challenge to the member churches to renew their commitment to the search for unity and to deepen their dialogue;

b) *calls upon* each member church to respond to the ten questions at the conclusion of the Ecclesiology Text with the expectation that, by the Tenth Assembly, each member church will have so responded;

c) *directs* the WCC, through the Commission on Faith and Order, to prepare periodic reports to the Central Committee of the number and content of responses received, so that responses can inform the direction of work towards deepening the understanding among member churches and furthering progress towards the visible unity of the Church. Such a process would go some way to addressing the fundamental ecclesiological issues raised by the Special Commission on Orthodox Participation in the WCC.

RELATIONSHIPS WITH ECUMENICAL PARTNERS
CHRISTIAN WORLD COMMUNIONS

23. The WCC is strengthened by interaction with the Christian World Communions. Its spirituality, witness, and work are enhanced by cooperative efforts with Christian World Communions towards building Christian unity. Multilateral and bilateral dialogues have contributed to a number of unity agreements and have enhanced understanding and cooperation among churches. Cooperative efforts in areas of witness, mission, diakonia and ecumenical formation are integral to the life of the WCC. The importance of strengthening this relationship is articulated in the Common Understanding and Vision document and affirmed by the Harare Assembly.

24. The PRC notes that the various structures and self-understanding of the Christian World Communions and of the member churches of the WCC results in a variety of ways of relating to the WCC, and welcomes the ongoing relationship with the Conference of Secretaries of Christian World Communions, whilst recognizing that not all member churches find themselves represented in this body. Some Christian World Communions and the General Secretary have called for new ways of relating CWCs to the WCC, including new possibilities related to future WCC Assemblies, expanded space in the structure of WCC Assemblies for confessional meetings, and the vision ultimately of a broadly inclusive ecumenical assembly.

RESOLUTION:

25. The Ninth Assembly:

a) *affirms* the important specific role and place of the Christian World Communions in the ecumenical movement and as partners of the WCC, and particularly acknowledges the importance of the role of Christian World Communions in both multilateral and bilateral dialogues and reconfiguration of the ecumenical movement;

b) *directs* that the WCC jointly consult with the Christian World Communions to explore the significance and implications of overlap of membership, coordination of programmes, and other common efforts between the WCC and the Christian World Communions;

c) *directs* that the WCC initiate, within the next year and in consultation with the Christian World Communions, a joint consultative commission to discuss and recommend ways to further strengthen the participation of Christian World Communions in the WCC;

d) *directs* that the WCC explore the feasibility of a structure for WCC assemblies that would provide expanded space for Christian World Communions and confessional families to meet, for the purpose of deliberation and/or overall agendas. Early in the term of this next Central Committee, a decision would be expected as to whether the next WCC Assembly should be so structured;

e) *directs* that United and Uniting churches be included in this process.

REGIONAL ECUMENICAL ORGANIZATIONS AND NATIONAL COUNCILS OF CHURCHES

26. The Regional Ecumenical Organizations and National Councils of Churches worldwide comprise expressions of the ecumenical movement with a wide variety of structures and varying degrees of relationship with the work and programmes of the WCC. These independently constituted organizations have a composition of membership that is broader than that of the WCC, some including as full members representatives of bishop's conferences of the Roman Catholic Church and Evangelical and Pentecostal churches that are not members of the WCC. The current relationship between the WCC, Regional Ecumenical Organizations and National Councils of Churches, is mutually enriching and important to their common work and witness to the world, yet lacks clarity as to the specific character, role and particular strengths of each ecumenical instrument and the relationship

of each to the local churches, and also lacks coherence of common vision and cooperative efforts.

RESOLUTION:

27. The Ninth Assembly:

a) *affirms* the specific and important relationship between the WCC and the Regional Ecumenical Organizations and the National Councils of Churches as essential partners in the work of the ecumenical movement;

b) *encourages* the WCC to continue to facilitate the annual meetings of leaders of Regional Ecumenical Organizations in order to (i) bring more clarity to the specific character of each ecumenical instrument, (ii) improve the process of consultation, particularly in areas in which work and programmes might overlap and where statements or efforts of the WCC might have particularly sensitive local ramifications, (iii) articulate an agreement of shared values, and (iv) improve cooperation in programming and coherence of message so that each instrument of the ecumenical movement is undertaking the programmes and tasks most effectively suited to their strengths, the process to be overseen by the continuation committee formed following the consultation on Ecumenism in the Twenty-first Century (Chavannes-de-Bogis, 2004);

c) *endorses* the recommendation of the Joint Working Group between the Roman Catholic Church and the WCC that the WCC and the Pontifical Council for Promoting Christian Unity be asked to co-sponsor a consultation of representatives of National Councils of Churches, Regional Ecumenical Organizations and episcopal conferences from places where the Roman Catholic Church is not in membership. The consultation should consider the document "Inspired by the Same Vision" and reflect on the experience others have gleaned regarding Catholic participation;

d) *directs* that this consultation be held within the next two to four years, in order to (i) bring more clarity to the specific character of each ecumenical instrument, (ii) improve the process of consultation, particularly in areas in which work and programmes might overlap and where statements or efforts of the WCC might have particularly sensitive local ramifications, (iii) articulate an agreement of shared values, (iv) enhance relationships with the Roman Catholic Church by inviting the leadership of national bishops' conferences, and (v) improve cooperation in programming and coherence of message so that each instrument of

the ecumenical movement is undertaking the programmes and tasks most effectively suited to their strengths, on the principle of subsidiarity, that is, ensuring
that decisions are made closest to the people affected, and with the priority that
programmes are preferable when they interconnect with regional, national or
local initiatives.

SPECIALIZED MINISTRIES AND AGENCIES RELATED TO THE WCC

28. The PRC received with interest and for information a report of the proposal
for a new alliance of churches and church and ecumenical agencies engaged in development work (Proposed Ecumenical Alliance for Development, PEAD), and understands that the formation of such a global alliance and its identity as an agency related to the WCC and its member churches, and/or related to the work of Action by
Churches Together (ACT) and the Ecumenical Advocacy Alliance (EAA), is still in
progress.

RESOLUTION:

29. The Ninth Assembly:

a) *affirms* with appreciation the work and role of Specialized Ministries and their
relationship to the WCC and to the diaconal work of the WCC and the member churches;

b) *asks* the WCC to continue its leadership role in exploring with the agencies
which have proposed the new alliance the most appropriate structure for that
alliance to take in relating to the other ecumenical partners, particularly as the
alliance would relate to and serve the specific diaconal tasks of member churches and relate to ACT and other existing ecumenical instruments, including
Regional Ecumenical Organizations, taking into account the priorities that have
been articulated;

c) *directs* that the Central Committee encourage the continuing leadership role of
the WCC in relation to this proposal.

RELATIONSHIPS WITH OTHER CHRISTIAN CHURCHES
THE ROMAN CATHOLIC CHURCH

30. The PRC received with appreciation the Eighth Report of the Joint Working
Group between the Roman Catholic Church and the WCC and acknowledges with
deep appreciation the past forty years of collaboration between the Roman Catholic

Church and the WCC. Since the Second Vatican Council, major studies have resulted from this joint effort, deepening the mutual understanding and the relationship
between the Roman Catholic Church and the churches of the WCC. Joint responsibility for preparing the Week of Prayer for Christian Unity, full membership in the
commissions on Faith and Order, Mission and Evangelism, provision for staff in
areas of mission and at the Bossey Ecumenical Institute have enhanced that collaboration, even while the Roman Catholic Church declines membership in the WCC.
The member churches of the WCC continue to encourage and hope for an even
more organic relationship with the Roman Catholic Church in the quest towards
the visible unity of the Church.

RESOLUTION:

31. The Ninth Assembly:

a) *receives* the Eighth Report of the Joint Working Group between the Roman
Catholic Church and the WCC and the report of the consultation, that marked
the forty years of collaboration, and expresses its appreciation to the members of
the JWG for their work in the period 1999-2006;

b) *endorses* the continuation of the Joint Working Group and its recommendations for future direction, but also asks the Joint Working Group, working with
Faith and Order, to include in their agendas concrete steps in that context to
realize the dreams described in the Moderator's report: for a common date for
the celebration of the Resurrection of our Lord and mutual recognition by all
churches of one baptism, understanding that there are some who do not observe
the rite of baptism in water but share in the desire to be faithful to Christ, and
convening a common ecumenical assembly, including offering ways to deepen
the theological basis of all ecumenical work and engage in work towards resolution of the theological divergences that still keep us apart.

PENTECOSTAL CHURCHES

32. Porto Alegre, Brazil, provided a dynamic setting for the Ninth Assembly to
receive the Report from the Joint Consultative Group between the WCC and
Pentecostal churches, which the PRC forwards to the Assembly with appreciation
for the work of that Group. This six-year effort is an example of efforts of the WCC
to broaden the Council and the ecumenical movement and to respond to the
dynamically changing landscape of Christian expression, whilst being mindful of the

ecclesial realities that make formal partnerships difficult. The PRC appreciates the extraordinary effort that has accompanied this process to provide the safe ecumenical space for this mutually beneficial open dialogue.

RESOLUTION:

33. The Ninth Assembly:

a) *receives* the Report of the Joint Consultative Group between the WCC and Pentecostals including the recommendations and the direction for future work, expresses its appreciation to the members of the Joint Consultative Group for their work in the period 2000-2005, and endorses the continuation of the Joint Consultative Group;

b) *recognizes* the visible contribution of the Pentecostal churches in the dynamically changing Christian landscape, and the importance to the ecumenical movement of engaging in mutual learning and sustained dialogue with the Pentecostal churches.

GLOBAL CHRISTIAN FORUM

34. The Harare Assembly affirmed the proposal that the WCC facilitate the process identified in the Common Understanding and Vision document as the "Forum proposal". This process has included a series of meetings preparatory to gathering a broader representation of Christian churches than currently are members in the WCC for consultation on issues common to all Christian churches and inter-church organizations. Several regional consultations have taken place, with participation from a wide range of Evangelical and Pentecostal churches not represented in the WCC, the Roman Catholic Church, and from representatives of WCC member churches, gathering together at a global level representatives of all four main streams of Christianity. Demonstrating the timeliness of this initiative, given the changing global Christian landscape and to enhance a common Christian witness and solidarity in a fractured world, the Global Christian Forum process offers a fluid model of initiatives that can be facilitated by the WCC to welcome broader participation in the ecumenical journey.

35. The PRC noted the tension that will continue to be present as the WCC proceeds on the one hand to deepen its relationships among the member churches and explore the areas of theological convergence and divergence, while on the other hand encountering ecclesial challenges presented by engaging with the broader Christian

community. The committee reaffirms the centrality of the fellowship of member churches, the Common Understanding and Vision of the WCC, and the particular accomplishments of the Special Commission in deepening the relationships among the member churches, and notes the urgent need for the WCC to continue to facilitate gathering the broader Christian community in consultation and dialogue.

RESOLUTION:

36. The Ninth Assembly:

a) *receives* the report on the Global Christian Forum including the direction for future work and expresses its appreciation to the organizers of the consultations and the forum event;

b) *instructs* that the WCC participate in the global forum event scheduled to take place in late 2007, and following that event conduct a formal and comprehensive evaluation of the concept and the process.

RELATIONSHIPS WITH OTHER FAITHS

37. The WCC has committed itself to engaging in dialogue with partners of other faiths that is aimed at building trust, articulating common values, promoting mutual understanding, meeting common challenges and addressing conflictive and divisive issues. Inter-religious dialogue is now more than ever an expression of the Council's essential identity engaging in the world, diffusing tensions, peacemaking, protecting human dignity and the rights of religious minorities. The PRC appreciates the strong reaffirmation of this work of the Council that was contained in the reports of the Moderator and the General Secretary and concurs that forming and deepening constructive, respectful, intentional relationships with others in this pluralistic world is one of the most important efforts the WCC can model for its ecumenical partners and for member churches at the international and the grassroots levels.

RELATIONSHIPS WITH NATIONS AND WORLD EVENTS

38. The WCC expresses its fellowship by engaging in the world as we have been called by Jesus Christ to engage the world – as witnesses to His love. The WCC is in a unique position to articulate values that signify human dignity. The WCC has made a mark in its history by providing prophetic response to this calling. Participants in the Ninth Assembly were moved by the various plenary presentations

and interactions with the local churches to recommit to engage together with issues of economic justice and globalization, to fight against the HIV and AIDS pandemic, to reaffirm solidarity with people living with HIV and AIDS and to promote a culture of peace through the programmes of the Decade to Overcome Violence. The PRC acknowledges the essential significance of the work of the WCC interacting as the voice of Christian churches with secular world bodies. The PRC recognizes the significance of this expression of the WCC's responsibility for the churches towards the world as a privileged instrument of the ecumenical movement.

CONCLUSION

39. The PRC received with deep appreciation the reports of the General Secretary and the Moderator of the WCC, and thanks the Moderator, especially on this occasion of his final report to an Assembly of the WCC as Moderator, for his years of dedicated leadership of the WCC.

40. The PRC received with deep gratitude the various reports of efforts to initiate, maintain and deepen the relationships of the WCC with its member churches, with its ecumenical partners, and with other Christian churches. It suggests a full and closer reading by anyone involved in the ecumenical movement. Recommendations from those reports are offered as recommendations of the PRC with the understanding that priority be given to programmes that strengthen the WCC in the search for visible unity, enhance its ability to represent the member churches, and build new bridges for relationships and trust with other Christian churches not currently within its fellowship.

41. We give thanks to God for our relationships with Christian World Communions, the Roman Catholic and Pentecostal Churches, Regional Ecumenical Organizations and National Councils of Churches, Specialized Ministries, and the emerging Global Christian Forum. We request that the Assembly call on them all to join in a fresh commitment with the WCC and one another to create a renewed and unified ecumenical movement as we begin the third millennium of Christian history that will strengthen and deepen the fellowship of churches and enable us to be faithful in our common calling to the glory of God, Father, Son and Holy Spirit.

Statements and reports adopted by the Assembly

Report of the Finance Committee

*The following report was presented to and received by the Assembly.
Its resolutions were proposed by the Finance Committee and
approved by the Assembly through consensus.*

1. Financial stewardship and management issues:
From Harare to Porto Alegre

The accomplishment of the WCC's work during the seven year period depended
on the generous contributions by member churches, specialized ministries, congregations and individuals, contributions whether great or small, whether in money terms
or by other means. To all who have contributed, the assembly finance committee
(AFC) expresses its profound gratitude.

Since 1999, total income of WCC has decreased by 30%, from CHF 61 million
to a budget of CHF 41 million in 2006. Membership income has remained stable;
the income category which decreased most significantly was income channelled

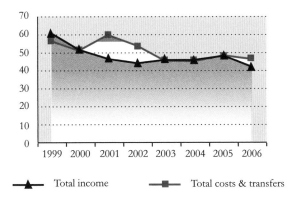

through the WCC to ecumenical partners. A framework budget for 2007 estimates CHF 39 million available income.

During the period 1999 to 2005, the funds and reserves of WCC also decreased by almost CHF 20 million, or 30%. There were at least three factors which caused this. Firstly, following investment gains of CHF 7 million in 1999, investment losses of CHF 6 million were incurred in total from 2000 to 2002. Secondly, in 2000 and 2001 operating deficit budgets were approved and subsequently realized as such. Finally, with CHF 23 million programme fund balances accumulated by 2000, it was necessary that programme funds be used for the purposes for which they were intended.

In response to the decrease in funds and reserves, a new programme structure with activity-based costing was implemented in 2002, and there was a reduction in staff. The central committee's policy statements of 2003 defining and clarifying funds and reserves categories and reducing investment risk, together with its firm targets for the rebuilding of general reserves, then helped to produce breakeven results from 2003 to 2005.

The actions taken fulfilled important recommendations from the AFC report from Harare which identified the need to establish funds and reserves policies, and to work to improve financial planning.

In 2006, programme funds are estimated to close at CHF 4 million in contrast with the position of CHF 23 million seven years ago. The overall mandate to use accumulated programme funds has been accomplished and therefore the practice of relying on funds to cover current year expenses is at an end. Reinforced planning and accurate budgeting will be essential skills for effective programme management in the forthcoming period.

The AFC thoroughly concurs with the recommendations of the central committee that the WCC do less, and do it well. In keeping with the work on the reconfiguration of the ecumenical movement, the WCC is encouraged to sharpen its focus and to communicate its unique role and responsibilities as a global fellowship of churches.

RESOLUTION:

The Ninth Assembly *recommends* that:

- the new central committee continue to set realistic and responsible annual budgets, reviewing annually the required level of the general reserves, and the long-term capital expenditure and treasury plans. In addition, programme and project plans including clearly documented three-year and one-year objectives and expected outcomes should be submitted for approval as part of three-year rolling plans;

- the focus on the unique role played by the WCC, and the manner in which each of the programmes proposed fulfills aspects of that role, be clearly stated in the plan for 2007 to 2009 which will be presented to the central committee in September 2006;
- to meet this target, an action plan be developed by the staff leadership group immediately following the assembly. Elements of the plan will include the programme priorities identified; consideration of the staffing required for each of these plans; responsible conclusion of certain project work in 2006; and discussion with Regional Ecumenical Organizations and National Councils of Churches of possible options for the transfer to and continuity of other programme projects within the church and ecumenical networks;
- in the light of the Pre-assembly Evaluation, the WCC implement a programme planning, monitoring, evaluation and reporting process led by the staff leadership group, permeating the working culture and including the assignment of a professional coordinator, the development of database programme management tools and general staff training.

2. MEMBERSHIP INCOME

Membership contributions of CHF 6.4 million make up only 13% of WCC total income in 2005. Membership income has remained stable, in itself an achievement given the financial difficulties faced by many churches since 1999. The membership campaign reports progress in the increased number of members contributing. At the end of 2005, 75% of member churches contributed, compared with 55% in 1999. Success in this area depends on the building of relationships and clear communication with churches.

The membership campaign target set in Harare of CHF 10 million has proven to be unrealistic in the time period specified. The assembly finance committee expresses its appreciation to the central committee for the implementation of the new membership calculation system, based on fairness and transparency. Under the new system, the target should be attainable in the longer-term.

The AFC affirms that all member churches should contribute at least the minimum fee of CHF 1,000, as a demonstration of their commitment to the fellowship.

RESOLUTION:

The Ninth Assembly *recommends* that:

- efforts continue to increase the number of churches paying their membership fee;
- the central committee amend the sanction for non-payment of membership contributions, such that a member church be declared non-active after three consecutive years of non-payment (instead of seven) during which no response has been made to WCC communications;
- the target of CHF 10 million be retained for the long-term, while a target of CHF 7 million should be set for the three-year period 2007 to 2009;
- assembly delegates encourage their churches to work towards attainment of the short-term and long-term targets.

3. NEW WORK METHODS

During 2003 to the present, the WCC has continued to develop new work methods based on networking, including the establishment of two new subsidiaries in Lebanon and Fiji; the appointment in host organizations of staff whose positions are funded by WCC programmes; and the development of international ecumenical initiatives which operate through a structure of consultants under contract from the WCC, placed with host organizations in Africa and Jerusalem. These initiatives also report both to international reference groups and to the programme teams in the WCC, creating some uncertainties as to the responsibilities for management decisions. At the same time, there are no reporting lines to the management teams in Geneva.

While finance and administrative staff have been reduced in Geneva, services are now being required for new organizations-in-formation in the ecumenical centre.

The AFC recognizes that there are considerable advantages in working methods which leverage the resources in the ecumenical fellowship.

RESOLUTION:

The Ninth Assembly *recommends* that:

- the WCC perform cost-benefit analyses of using small, external structures to accomplish our work, taking into account the increased risks highlighted by the WCC's auditors;

- policies be developed for both the recruitment and management of staff and of staff benefits in the external structures; and
- the WCC increase the capacity and competence of programme leadership and the management team staff to manage the new work methods.

4. STAFFING ISSUES

The WCC has also adopted the current market trend of offering temporary contracts to recruits, while almost automatically re-approving extension of contracts for long-serving executives. In 2005, over 32% of staff was over age 55, while only 11% was under 30.

Total salaried staff and consultants on longer-term contracts total 210 headcount, compared with 204 in 2002. If consultants are considered together with staff, a real increase in both headcount and full-time equivalents is reported. This trend is in contrast with guidelines issued by the finance committee in 2001 to keep staff numbers at a steady level.

Staff and consultants' costs in relation to contributions rose from 40% in 1999 to 50% in 2002; after the programme readjustment, the ratio dropped to 46% in 2003. In 2006, the ratio is set to rise to about 57%. The finance committee recognizes the WCC's evolution towards knowledge-based working structures, but considers that this ratio is relatively high.

RESOLUTION:

The Ninth Assembly *recommends* that:
- the WCC review its staff rules and regulations and personnel policies, covering in particular the following aspects:
  renewal of contracts, including reaffirmation of the concept that programme executive staff contracts are not normally renewed more than once (at present, four years plus three years);
  encouragement of the recruitment of competent younger staff who may thus also have their role in the transformation of the organization;
  recruitment procedures be transparent and open to external applicants;
- statistics on staff costs, headcount and full-time equivalents be reported regularly in a consistent manner, with written definitions of the staff and consultant categories concerned.

5. INCOME STRATEGY

Programme contributions from churches and specialized ministries of CHF 31.3 million make up 65% of WCC total income in 2005. Twenty funding partners provide approximately 90% of the programme contributions. Of those twenty, five contribute almost 60%.

Although a certain stability was achieved between 2003 to 2005, there is an anticipated decrease of 4% in programme contributions in 2006. The approved budget framework for 2007 anticipates a further reduction of 6%.

Income strategy continues to work on maintaining relationships with the principal funding partners, efforts which reach an annual focal point at the WCC round table. In addition, staff is also developing strategies for fund-raising among the US constituents and focusing some initial effort on non-traditional funding sources.

The AFC affirms the importance of the continued work in building common understanding and trust with the funding partners.

6. BUILDINGS

The Ecumenical Institute at Bossey has been entirely renovated during the last three to four years, including renovation of the student residence. The entire cost of the project was CHF 8.4 million, principally financed by long-term fixed interest mortgage loans. Increased income at the Institute has financed the interest expense, and loan repayments over the next five years have been scheduled in WCC's longer-term treasury plans, with the first payments met over the last two years.

Maintenance plans at the Ecumenical Centre have lagged behind. Action is now required to be taken to ensure satisfactory compliance with local building regulations.

RESOLUTION:

The Ninth Assembly *recommends* that the central committee address both the funding for the deferred maintenance of the Ecumenical Centre and a further financial plan for improvements for maximizing both the use of the building and its income generation potential.

7. AUDIT COMMITTEE MANDATE

The assembly finance committee received a draft audit committee mandate which had been prepared and submitted by the WCC audit committee. The assembly finance committee recognizes the contribution of the professional volunteers who have contributed to the audit committee's work over the last seven years.

RESOLUTION:

The Ninth Assembly *recommends* that the finance committee at its first meeting review the audit committee mandate for adoption by the central committee and appointment of the new committee.

8. WCC PENSION FUND

Further to the request of the executive committee, the assembly finance committee received a report on the current status of the WCC Pension Fund. The WCC Pension Fund had reported a slight lack of coverage of its obligations, and in accordance with Swiss law and further to the advice of the actuaries, the Pension Fund Board has restructured the pension plan, introducing new regulations effective from 2006. While staff benefits earned up until 2005 are guaranteed, from 2006 staff retirement benefits are accrued at a reduced rate.

The AFC recognizes with thanks the work of the members of the Pension Fund Board, and agrees that the WCC should remain in solidarity with the Pension Fund Board, sharing communications where appropriate.

Statements and reports adopted by the Assembly

Report of the Public Issues Committee

The following report was presented to and received by the Assembly. Its resolutions were proposed by the Public Issues Committee and approved by the Assembly through consensus. Dissent expressed by Assembly delegates is recorded as endnotes.

The Public Issues Committee (PIC) was asked to work on draft proposals for five statements and one minute prepared in advance through a series of consultations and reflections and endorsed by the Executive Committee of the World Council of Churches in its meeting on 13 February 2006. These were:

- Statement on Latin America
- Statement on the Responsibility to Protect
- Statement on Terrorism, Human Rights and Counter-terrorism
- Statement on Reforming the United Nations
- Statement on Water for Life
- Minute on the Elimination of Nuclear Arms

In addition, the Public Issues Committee received from the assembly participants within the stipulated 24 hours after the announcement of the proposal of the Executive Committee, seven proposals for statements endorsed by at least ten member churches. After careful examination of the proposals in the framework of the existing policy and criteria for public issues actions by the general assembly of the World Council of Churches, the Public Issues Committee proposes:

- A Minute on Mutual Respect, Responsibility and Dialogue with People of Other Faiths.

In response to the six other proposals and issues raised, the Public Issues Committee judged the following actions to be more appropriate:

TRAFFICKING OF WOMEN

The Public Issues Committee received a proposal about the issue of **trafficking of women** and a request to pay special attention to the upcoming Football World Cup taking place in June 2006 in Germany which will potentially bring tens of thousands of prostitutes, mainly from Central and Eastern European countries, to Germany.

The Public Issues Committee noted that in its meeting from 15-22 February, 2005, the WCC Central Committee issued a statement on uprooted people "Practising hospitality in an era of new forms of migration". The statement underlines human trafficking as one new trend in migration that *"involves recruiting and/or transporting people using violence, other forms of coercion, or providing misleading information in order to exploit them economically or sexually (through for example, forced prostitution and bonded labour). Trafficked persons are often in conditions of slavery and are no longer free to move or to decide on their destinies. Women and children are particularly vulnerable to trafficking".* The statement further recommends that churches should *"combat the trafficking of human beings, particularly women and children for sexual exploitation; to work with governments, churches and concerned non-governmental organizations to ensure that the victims of traffickers receive the necessary treatment and respect; and to oppose efforts by governments to use the existence of trafficking as an excuse to restrict further immigration".*

Follow-up actions on human trafficking have been initiated in the regions and taken up by some member churches. The Public Issues Committee recommends that the WCC general secretary and staff work in collaboration with their regional and international contacts to continue to monitor the situation closely, give further support to member churches and take appropriate actions.

POVERTY

The Public Issues Committee received a proposal for a statement on **poverty**. Poverty is indeed a major issue in our world and fighting poverty a priority for the World Council of Churches. The WCC gathered at its Eighth Assembly in Harare strongly stated that the "reality of unequal distribution of power and wealth, of poverty and exclusion challenges the cheap language of our global shared community". The lack of a strong ethical and moral approach in responding to poverty is sinful in the eyes of God. The Public Issues Committee agrees that the issue of poverty in our world is a challenge that the churches and the wider ecumenical family are called to address in the 21st century. This, however, must be an intentional on-going process.

Considering seriously the implications of poverty on the lives of God's people, the Public Issues Committee is presenting to the assembly three statements where the issue of poverty is addressed. These statements, carefully written after many consultations and reflections, call upon churches and governments to address the various causes of poverty in our world. The statements on water for life, Latin America and on reforming the United Nations speak firmly and specifically on issues of poverty and how to fight poverty in different contexts.

INCARCERATION OF THE ORTHODOX ARCHBISHOP IN SKOPJE, FYROM

The Public Issues Committee received a proposal to **condemn the incarceration of Archbishop Jovan of Ochrid and Metropolitan of Skopje** (FYROM). The World Council of Churches has addressed the situation of Archbishop Jovan by sending, on 31 August, 2005, a letter to H.E. Branko Crvenkovski, the President of the Former Yugoslavian Republic of Macedonia, expressing deep concern for the imprisonment and reiterating that the WCC considered that inter-church disagreements and disputes should be resolved through discussion and dialogue and that a judicial approach should be used only as a last resort.

The Public Issues Committee recommends that the general secretary and staff continue to closely monitor the situation and take appropriate measures as needed.

PROTECTION OF DISCRIMINATED WCC MEMBER CHURCHES[1]

The Public Issues Committee received a proposal on the **protection of discriminated WCC member churches** making special reference to the Hungarian-speaking minority churches in East-central Europe.

On the particular situation of these minorities, the Public Issues Committee noted the report of the Central Committee in February 2005 where the situation of **Vojvodina** in Serbia-Montenegro was taken up as an area of great concern. Several church and government delegations have recently visited the region. The WCC programme executive for Europe visited Serbia-Montenegro in April 2005, meeting the leadership of the minority churches. In addition, the regional secretary and the WCC Commission of Churches on International Affairs (CCIA) monitor and follow up the general situation in the region, paying special attention to minority situations in light of the WCC policy to give priority to the respect for human rights for all people, and the unity between the different member churches in the region.

Actions are being taken, when appropriate, with government institutions. This is done by listening to and respecting the diverse perspectives of majority and minority churches. The Public Issues Committee recommends that the CCIA and the programme executive for Europe, in consultation with the Conference of European Churches (CEC), follow the developments in the region, continuing to listen to all member churches, ensuring that different perspectives are taken into account, and considering further actions as appropriate.

The proposal highlights the issues of persecution, discrimination and oppression of member churches of the WCC also in general terms. The Public Issues Committee affirms that supporting member churches in these situations, acting on behalf of the whole WCC fellowship, is at the core of the mandate of the CCIA, and whenever such situations arise the WCC will act to protect members of the body, taking up the issues in government relations and inter-governmental meetings.

INDIGENOUS PEOPLES AND LANGUAGE LOSS

The Public Issues Committee received a proposal for a minute on **Indigenous Peoples** and language loss. The WCC Central Committee, meeting in Geneva in February 2005, issued a statement on **Human Rights and Languages of Indigenous Peoples**. In that document, the Central Committee called on member churches to urge the establishment of a UN International Year of Indigenous Languages in 2006, or a subsequent year, and to appeal to their governments to remove discriminatory laws against indigenous languages, to work towards removing the layers of educational and social pressures arrayed against indigenous languages, and to actively pursue compliance with international conventions and treaties that regard the use of the language of heritage as a basic human right. The Public Issues Committee regards the Central Committee statement of February 2005, mentioned herein, as important and relevant and requests the churches to consider practical ways in which they can respond to this world-wide crisis, calling attention to the critical issue of language loss and working towards remedies both at the local and international level. The Central Committee reminds churches and the Christian community of the diversity of spoken languages as a sign of the presence of the fullness of the spirit of God in Acts 2 and the full diversity of languages as an integral part of the vision of worship in the presence of God in Revelation 7:9. These concerns have also been shared with the Programme Guidelines Committee of the assembly.

Peaceful reunification of the Korean Peninsula

The Public Issues Committee received a proposal for a statement on **reunification of the Korean peninsula**. During the Korean War when the peninsula was divided, the WCC adopted the UN position which laid the entire blame on the Democratic Peoples Republic of Korea and resulted in enormous suffering of the Korean people.

The World Council of Churches continued to monitor the developments in the Korean peninsula. In October 1984, the WCC, at the request of the Korean churches, organized a consultation on Peace in North East Asia. Amongst others the consultation spoke of the peace and reunification of the Korean peninsula and its people. This took place in Tozanso, Japan.

Subsequent to the Tozanso meeting there was a series of visits by Korean Christian Federation (KCF) and National Council of Churches-Korea (NCC-K) leaders in Glion, Switzerland. These meetings continued in Kyoto and Macau. The WCC, in cooperation with the churches in Korea, prepared a framework for unification. Throughout the 1980s and 1990s there were visits and exchanges between member churches in Canada, the USA and the Democratic Peoples Republic of Korea, including meetings with separated families.

The WCC continues to monitor developments in the Korean peninsula including the six-party talks. Last year the Korean working group comprised of the NCC-K, the National Council of Churches in Japan (NCC-J), the Christian Conference of Asia (CCA) and the WCC reiterated support for six-party talks and agreed to continue to monitor bilateral relations between North and South. The WCC will continue to support the Korean peoples' efforts for a peaceful reunification according to the 15 June 2000 joint declaration.

In September 2004 the WCC executive committee meeting in Seoul made a statement on the unification issue but also on human rights and nuclear concerns. The WCC will continue to monitor the developments and take necessary action in cooperation with the member churches in Korea.

Resolution:

The Ninth Assembly *accepts* the responses of the Public Issues Committee to the requests for additional statements.

Additional proposals, after deadline

Furthermore, the concern for the WCC to address the grave human rights violations in northern Uganda, as well the destruction of Armenian Christian monuments in Azerbaijan, were brought to the attention of the Public Issues Committee. The Public Issues Committee refers both issues to the general secretary and WCC staff for appropriate action.

STATEMENT ON LATIN AMERICA

1. The WCC Assembly meets for the first time in Latin America and would first like to express its deep thanks to the Latin American churches for having hosted the Assembly, to the Latin American Council of Churches (CLAI) for its work in the construction of unity among the Christian churches and to the National Council of Christian Churches in Brazil (CONIC) who generously invited the WCC to hold the Assembly in this country. The present statement reflects issues and concerns received from Latin American churches.

2. The Assembly theme "God, in your grace, transform the world" recalls the different transformations the region has experienced throughout its history; a history where hope, life and joy prevail through the centuries as characteristics of the region and signs of God's grace; a history of transformations which continue to take place even now. Recent elections in Latin American countries have resulted in the first Indigenous person to be elected as President of Bolivia and the first woman to be elected as President of Chile. These new political signs in the region follow other changes, which need to be interpreted in the context of Latin American history if the presence of God who renews the whole creation (Rev. 21:5) is to be discerned.

RECALLING LATIN AMERICA'S HISTORY

3. After millennia of different indigenous cultures, with outstanding developments by, for instance, the Inca, Mayan and Tiwanacota civilizations, the "*conquista*" by the Spanish and Portuguese crowns in the 16th century gave a common recent history to this continent. This history, with a special recognition of the massacres of various indigenous populations and the introduction of slavery by the colonizers, was especially recalled in 1992, during the commemoration of the five hundred years of the colonization by the Europeans. In the 18th century, wars against the Spanish and Portuguese paved the way to freedom for most Latin American states. Hence, during the first half of the 19th century, most of the countries achieved independence. However this political independence left different nations still economically dependent.

4. Since the wars of independence, many political leaders have called for the unity of the different Latin American states and in the last two hundred years many

attempts to develop a Latin American unity have been made. Today, in the framework of the global political trends, which support regional integration, such unity is vital. Churches in the region have clearly stated that current efforts to build bridges between states should be based not only on economic trade agreements but should also respond to the needs and rights of the people, especially the weak and vulnerable. In this way, the path towards unity may be a sign of the brotherhood and sisterhood to which God calls all human beings.

5. Several voices in the Assembly pointed to the struggle for life and dignity, which has been a constant experience of Latin American people. Throughout history they have faced wars within and between states, confrontations, authoritative regimes and dictatorships, as well as irresponsible policies by governments and multinational corporations which have irreparably damaged their environment. Tribute should be paid to the testimony of thousands of Christians and other people of good will who gave their lives for human rights, dignity and care for the creation. Monsignor Romero from El Salvador, Mauricio López from Argentina, Chico Mendes from Brazil and Yolanda Céron from Colombia, are a few names among thousands, most of them unknown. The blood of these martyrs has helped to fertilize the seeds of God's kingdom, which have borne the fruits of solidarity, life and democracy.

OVERCOMING POVERTY AND INJUSTICE

6. Unjust distribution of wealth, natural resources and opportunities has generated poverty, which dramatically affects the region. According to UN statistics, now as for decades, more than 40 percent of the population still live in poverty, while 20 percent live in extreme poverty. This cannot be considered separately from the implementation of structural adjustment programmes developed by the governments as a requisite from the International Financial Institutions like the World Bank and the International Monetary Fund. The privatization of state companies brought in short-term relief and economic welfare in a few cases, but in the medium and long-term perspective, many judge that the implementation of these kinds of policies has worsened the situation of the region, with huge economic crises in the late '90s and early 2000s occurring in several countries. Though in the last years, at the macroeconomic level, the region seems to have recovered from these crises, poverty continues to be a challenge for governments and societies and a scandal for the churches. Even in those countries where poverty is relatively less, the gap between the rich and the poor is enormous and the distribution of wealth continues to be unjust.

7. The external debt has been a heavy burden for decades. Churches in the region have clearly stated the debt is unjust, illegitimate and immoral because it had been contracted during dictatorships with the complicity of International Financial Institutions and has already been paid. However, the need to continue to pay the service of the debt has prevented the implementation of effective social policies in most of the countries, seriously affecting education, health and work conditions. Furthermore, as a consequence of the economic crises, migration has increased and millions of Latin Americans are now living in other countries in the region, the United States or in Europe, their remittances to family members back home becoming one of the most important sources of income in some Latin American countries.

8. This economic situation further increases the exclusion of vulnerable groups such as Indigenous Peoples, African descendants and rural populations. Indigenous Peoples continue to struggle for the recognition of indigenous rights. African descendants in Brazil, as well as in other countries in the region, still carry the consequences of slavery, which has prevented them from fully exercising their rights as they continue to suffer racism, violence and discrimination. In a region where poverty has often been related to issues of land ownership, landless movements in different countries, particularly in Brazil, have been claiming access to land. Churches and the ecumenical movement cannot be deaf to the cries of the poor and excluded in the region. Poverty is unacceptable in a region which is extremely rich in natural resources. The tragedy is that these have often been exploited in a way that has destroyed the environment through, for example, the contamination of rivers in large areas. Indeed the whole planet is threatened through the deforestation of the Amazonian region.

HEALING THE WOUNDS OF VIOLENCE

9. Violence continues to be a major problem of the region. Some countries continue to face the consequences of political violence. In Colombia, for example, the armed conflict between political actors has largely affected the civil society. Because of this confrontation, thousands, mostly innocent people, have died and more than three million people have been internally displaced. The conflict has gone beyond national borders, having a serious impact on neighbouring countries. Colombian churches have strengthened their work with victims and have clearly asked the government of Colombia and armed groups to look for a negotiated solution of the conflict which could bring peace with justice.

10. Close to the region and to the Latin American churches' concern, Haiti is another country which has experienced extreme violence during the last years and experienced a political crisis, because of internal and external factors. Despite the presence of a UN stabilization force, violence continues, especially in Port-au-Prince. The recently-held elections, after many postponements, although important in the need to re-establish democracy in the country, have not brought peace. There is still an urgent need for a broad national dialogue and a process of reconciliation to heal the wounds of the country. The international community should strengthen its support to the Haitian people in their struggle against poverty, for the reconstruction of democratic institutions and care for the environment.

11. The dramatic situations in which these countries live cannot be considered in an isolated way. They reflect a larger phenomenon, which affects the whole region. The new dynamics of militarism that have developed in the last years in the region threaten to become even more apparent with the establishment of new US military bases in different countries, such as Ecuador and Paraguay. However, the influence of the United States in the region is not new. For decades the US has influenced decision-making processes in politics, economics and culture, has supported dictatorships and authoritative regimes, and under the concern for hemispheric security the US has trained the Latin American military.

12. A particular focus of the US agenda for the region has been Cuba. A blockade imposed in the sixties by the US government has continued to seriously affect the Cuban population. This blockade, condemned several times by the WCC, has been hardened during the current US administration. Nevertheless, Cuba has managed to develop effective policies regarding health, education and culture. Civil and political rights need to be further improved if the country is to respond to the process of economic transformation which is occurring. Spaces for dialogue between the different sectors of the society and the government are urgently necessary.

13. Urban, domestic, ethnic, gender or youth violence is also experienced in Latin America on a daily basis. Youth gangs (*maras*) are spreading in most Central American countries. The churches have especially addressed the major problem of the proliferation of small arms. The Decade to Overcome Violence during 2006 will be the opportunity in the region to tackle some of the faces of violence and bring the efforts of the churches together to build a culture of peace.

STRUGGLING FOR LIFE AND DIGNITY

14. The peoples of Latin America have struggled hard to build peace with justice and achieve democratic regimes. Victims' and Human Rights organizations, together with churches in many countries, have been at the forefront of this struggle. The Inter-American System should be strengthened to contribute to implement the rule of law and to deal more effectively with human rights violations and impunity in several countries.

15. Moreover, in recent years many countries have made significant changes through presidential elections, as an expression of participatory democracy of the people. Candidates and parties who have shown more sensitivity to the needs and rights of the peoples have often been elected. New governments have stood up in a stronger way in confronting International Financial Institutions, Trade Agreements and subsidized agriculture in northern countries. Internal policies, more respectful of human rights and addressing poverty, hunger and other social needs have been developed. These governments have raised hope in the region and beyond, though the strong limitations they are facing, and the contradictions and corruption which threaten some of them, should not be overlooked.

CHURCHES ACCOMPANYING THE PEOPLES OF LATIN AMERICA

16. Christianity was brought to the region with the colonizers during the XVIth and following centuries and has not been without controversies. Many times the persecution of those who did not accept the Christian faith caused thousands of casualties. But through their history, the faith experience of the indigenous, African, *mestizo* and European descendants has developed a Latin American face of Christianity.

17. For a long time, Latin America has been known as the Roman Catholic continent. But the composition of Christianity has changed over the centuries. In the 19th century, for instance, the Protestant and Anglican churches came to serve in the continent and the Orthodox Church was established and has contributed to build the social fabric of different communities. In the last decades, Evangelical churches, mainly Pentecostal ones, have been growing systematically and in some countries have become important percentages of the population. Responding to the need to grant equal treatment to all religions, raised by many WCC member churches, improvements have been made in some national legislations to recognize their rights.

18. Ecumenism has made important contributions to the history of Latin America, particularly in recent times. Churches and ecumenical organizations in the region have played a key role in struggling against dictatorial and authoritarian regimes and defending human rights all over the region. The WCC, through different programmes, and particularly through its Human Rights Resources Office for Latin America, and together with CLAI, has been closely accompanying and supporting the churches and ecumenical, human rights and victims' organizations in their work to combat impunity, achieve peace agreements after civil wars, strengthen democracy and build up reconciliation.

19. The struggle for human dignity by the churches can be traced back to the fervent defence of the Indigenous Peoples by Christians like Fray Bartolomé de las Casas in the 16th century. The struggle for human dignity has been a pillar of Latin American theology ever since. This particular consideration for the poor, the marginalized and the excluded in different societies throughout history has been at the origins of the particular theological approach known as Liberation Theology. Strongly incarnated in the social struggles of the 1960s and 1970s, more recently it has expanded its foci towards the economic, ecological, gender and inter-religious dimensions. Therefore, nurtured in this theological methodology rooted in a deep spiritual experience, Latin American Christianity has become deeply involved in defending, caring for and celebrating life in its multiple manifestations, recognizing God's presence in every life expression and especially in human life. This experience has been a gift of God to the whole Church.

RESOLUTION:

The Ninth Assembly, meeting in Porto Alegre, Brazil, 14-23 February, 2006:

a) *adopts* the statement on Latin America;

b) *commends* the Latin American churches in their work to overcome poverty and injustice, heal the wounds of violence, struggle for life and dignity, grant equal treatment to all religions in national legislations and *asks* them to further develop their work and reflection on issues such as grace, economy, gender, youth, disability, ethnicity, ecology and violence as part of their contribution to the ecumenical movement and in preparation for CLAI's Assembly in 2007;

c) *invites* churches, ecumenical organizations and other civil society groups to have an active participation in the "Decade to Overcome Violence: Churches Seeking Reconciliation and Peace" which focuses this year on Latin America;

d) *appeals* to WCC member churches and staff to emphasize the exchange with Latin American churches and ecumenical organizations and look for new ways of interacting with the churches and peoples of the region;

e) *encourages* Latin American peoples to continue in their struggle to build new societies which respect the dignity of the whole creation and pay special attention to the most vulnerable and excluded, including Indigenous Peoples and African descendants, and to share their visions, concerns and lessons learned with peoples of other regions;

f) *calls* on Latin American governments to strengthen their work towards a more effective integration of the region to face the challenges of the present world; to look for effective policies to overcome poverty, injustice and the degradation of the environment; to strengthen the rule of law and the respect and promotion of human rights and dignity and to continue to look for ways of enhancing democracy in their countries;

g) *urges* the international community, the states and International Financial Institutions to recognize the illegitimacy of the external debt that burdens the region as well as to revise the rationale of free trade agreements in order effectively to respond to the needs of the population and to the concerns expressed recently by the churches in the region regarding the consequences for peasants, workers and communities' rights, the environment and citizen's participation.

VULNERABLE POPULATIONS AT RISK
STATEMENT ON THE RESPONSIBILITY TO PROTECT

INTRODUCTION

1. In January 2001, the Central Committee of the World Council of Churches (WCC) received the document "The protection of endangered populations in situations of armed violence: towards an ecumenical ethical approach". The document, which requested the churches to further study the issue, was also the beginning of a study and consultation process within the WCC, carried out by the Commission of the Churches on International Affairs (CCIA). A deeper reflection on ethical and theological aspects of the Responsibility to Protect is not only of concern to the churches. In a meeting in New York City in 1999, UN General Secretary Kofi Annan asked the then WCC General Secretary, Rev. Dr Konrad Raiser, to contribute to the international debate on "humanitarian intervention" by bringing a theological and ethical perspective on the issue of intervention for humanitarian purposes.

2. The use of force for humanitarian purposes is a controversial issue in most intellectual and political spheres. While some believe that the resort to force must not be avoided when it can alleviate or stop large-scale human rights violations, others can only support intervention by creative, non-violent means. Others, again, give a very high priority to territorial integrity and sovereignty. Churches too have necessarily entered this debate and the current dilemma among the WCC's constituencies has prevailed since the very beginnings of the ecumenical movement. During the 1948 WCC first Assembly in Amsterdam, the Assembly restated the opposing positions:

"a) There are those who hold that, even though entering a war may be a Christian's duty in particular circumstances, modern warfare, with its mass destruction, can never be an act of justice.

In the absence of impartial supra-national institutions, there are those who hold that military action is the ultimate sanction of the rule of law, and that citizens must be distinctly taught that it is their duty to defend the law by force if necessary.

Others, again, refuse military service of all kinds, convinced that an absolute witness against war and for peace is for them the will of God, and they desire that the Church should speak to the same effect."

3. In history, some churches have been among those legitimizing military interventions, leading to disastrous wars. In many cases, the churches have admitted their guilt later on. During the 20th century churches have become more aware of their calling to a ministry of healing and reconciliation, beyond national boundaries. The creation of the WCC can be interpreted as one result of this rediscovery. In the New Testament, Jesus calls us to go beyond loving the neighbour to loving the enemy as well. This is based on the loving character of God, revealed supremely in the death of Jesus Christ for all, absorbing their hostility, and exercising mercy rather than retribution (Rom. 5:10; Luke 6:36). The prohibition against killing is at the heart of Christian ethics (Matt. 5:21-22). But the biblical witness also informs us about an anthropology that takes the human capacity to do evil in the light of the fallen nature of humankind (Gen. 4). The challenge for Christians is to pursue peace in the midst of violence.

4. The member churches of the World Council confess together the primacy of non-violence on the grounds of their belief that every human being is created in the image of God and shares the human nature assumed by Jesus Christ in his incarnation. This resonates with the articles of the Universal Declaration of Human Rights.

The WCC has therefore initiated an ecumenical "Decade to Overcome Violence 2001-2010: Churches Seeking Reconciliation and Peace" parallel to the United Nations "Decade for the Culture of Peace 2001-2010". It is in those who are most vulnerable that Christ becomes visible for us (Matt. 25:40). The responsibility to protect the vulnerable reaches far beyond the boundaries of nations and faith-traditions. It is an ecumenical responsibility, conceiving the world as one household of God, who is the creator of all. The churches honour the strong witness of many individuals who have recognized the responsibility to protect those who are weak, poor and vulnerable, through non-violence, sometimes paying with their lives.

FROM "HUMANITARIAN INTERVENTION" TO THE "RESPONSIBILITY TO PROTECT"

5. The concept of Responsibility to Protect was developed by the International Commission on Intervention and State Sovereignty (ICISS) in its December 2001 report. It shifted the debate from the viewpoint of the interveners to that of the people in need of assistance, thus redefining sovereignty as a duty-bearer status, rather than as an absolute power. This innovative concept focuses on the needs and rights of the civilian population and on the responsibilities of sovereignty, not only on the rights of sovereignty. Hence, the shift from intervention to protection places citizens at the centre of the debate. States can no longer hide behind the pretext of sovereignty to perpetrate human rights violations against their citizens and live in total impunity.

6. The churches are in support of the emerging international norm of the responsibility to protect. This norm holds that national governments clearly bear the primary and sovereign responsibility to provide for the safety of their people. Indeed, the responsibility to protect and serve the welfare of its people is central to a state's sovereignty. When there is failure to carry out that responsibility, whether by neglect, lack of capacity, or direct assaults on the population, the international community has the duty to assist peoples and states, and in extreme situations, to intervene in the internal affairs of the state in the interests and safety of the people.

OUR PRIMARY CONCERN: PREVENTION

7. To be faithful to that responsibility to protect people means above all prevention – prevention of the kinds of catastrophic assaults on individuals and communities that the world has witnessed in Burundi, Cambodia, Rwanda, Sudan, Uganda, the Democratic Republic of Congo, and other instances and locations of human-made

305

crises. WCC studies showed that although churches have different views on the use of force for human protection purposes, they agree on the essential role of preventive efforts to avoid and, if possible, tackle the crisis before it reaches serious stages. Protection becomes necessary when prevention has failed. Hence, churches emphasize the need to concentrate on prevention. While external intervention – by the use of force or non-violently – may seem unavoidable in some situations, churches should nevertheless be engaged in increasing the capacity of the local people to be able to intervene themselves by strengthening structures of the civil society and modern public-private partnerships, in terms of prevention as well as protection. Churches are called to offer their moral authority for mediation between differently powerful actors.

8. The prevention of catastrophic human insecurity requires attention to the root causes of insecurity as well as to more immediate or direct causes of insecurity. Broadly stated, the long-term agenda is to pursue human security and the transformation of life according to the vision of God's kingdom. The key elements of human security are economic development (meeting basic needs), universal education, respect for human rights, good governance, political inclusion and power-sharing, fair trade, control over the instruments of violence (small arms in particular), the rule of law through law-abiding and accountable security institutions, and promoting confidence in public institutions. On the other hand, the more immediate preventive attention to emerging security crises must include specific measures designed to mitigate immediate insecurities and to instill the reliable hope that national institutions and mechanisms, with the support of an attentive international community, will remain committed to averting a crisis of human insecurity.

9. At the national level, governments should undertake self-monitoring to become aware of emerging threats, establish mechanisms for alerting authorities and agencies to such emerging threats, engage civil society and churches in assessing conditions of human security and insecurity, initiate national dialogues, including dialogue with non-state actors, to acknowledge emerging problems and to engage the people in the search for solutions, and develop national action plans.

10. Prevention requires action to address conditions of insecurity as they emerge, before they precipitate crisis, which in turn requires specific prevention capacities such as early warning or identification of emerging threats or conditions of insecurity, and the political will to act before a crisis occurs. To act before a crisis is present requires a special sensitivity to and understanding of the conditions and needs of people, which in turn requires the active cooperation of civil society, and especially faith

306

communities which are rooted in the daily spiritual and physical realities of people. Faith communities are playing a major role in trust-building and truth finding processes in many contexts of crisis, such as truth and reconciliation commissions, trauma-healing centres, providing safe meeting places for adversarial groups, etc.

FORMING THE ECUMENICAL MIND ON THE DILEMMAS OF THE USE OF FORCE

11. It is necessary to distinguish prevention from intervention. From the church and ecumenical perspectives, if intervention occurs, it is because prevention has failed. The responsibility to protect is first and foremost about protecting civilians and preventing any harmful human rights crisis. The international community's responsibility is basically a non-military preventive action through such measures as the deployment of humanitarian relief personnel and special envoys, through capacity-building and the enhancement of sustainable local infrastructure, and the imposition of economic sanctions and embargoes on arms, etc. The international community has a duty to join the pursuit of human security before situations in troubled states degenerate to catastrophic proportions. This is the duty of protection through prevention of assaults on the safety, rights, and well-being of people in their homes and communities and on the well-being of the environment in which they live.

12. In calling on the international community to come to the aid of vulnerable people in extraordinary suffering and peril, the fellowship of churches is not prepared to say that it is never appropriate or never necessary to resort to the use of force for the protection of the vulnerable. This refusal in principle to preclude the use of force is not based on a naïve belief that force can be relied on to solve intractable problems. Rather, it is based on the certain knowledge that the objective must be the welfare of people, especially those in situations of extreme vulnerability and who are utterly abandoned to the whims and prerogatives of their tormentors. It is a tragic reality that civilians, especially women and children, are the primary victims in situations of extreme insecurity and war.

13. The resort to force is first and foremost the result of the failure to prevent what could have been prevented with appropriate foresight and actions, but having failed, and having acknowledged such failure, the world needs to do what it can to limit the burden and peril that is experienced by people as a consequence. This force can be legitimized only to stop the use of armed force in order to reinstate civil means, strictly respecting the proportionality of means. It needs to be controlled by

international law[2] in accordance to the UN Charter and can only be taken into consideration by those who themselves follow international law strictly. This is an imperative condition. The breach of law cannot be accepted even when this, at times, seems to lead – under military aspects – to a disadvantage or to hamper the efficiency of the intervention in the short term. Just as individuals and communities in stable and affluent societies are able in emergencies to call on armed police to come to their aid when they experience unusual or extraordinary threats of violence, churches recognize that people in much more perilous circumstances should have the right to call for and have access to protection.

14. Churches may acknowledge that the resort to force for protection purposes in some circumstances will be an option that cannot guarantee success but that must be tried because the world has failed to find, and continues to be at a loss to find, any other means of coming to the aid of those in desperate situations. It should be noted that some within the churches refuse the use of force in all circumstances. Their form of responsibility is to persist in preventative engagement and, whatever the cost – as a last resort – to risk non-violent intervention during the use of force. Either of these approaches may fail too, but they both need to be respected as expressions of Christian responsibility.

THE LIMITS OF THE USE OF FORCE

15. The churches do not, however, believe in the exercise of lethal force to bring in a new order of peace and safety. By limiting the resort to force quite specifically to immediate protection objectives, the churches insist that the kinds of long-term solutions that are required – that is, the restoration of societies to conditions in which people are for the most part physically safe, in which basic economic, social, and health needs are met, where fundamental rights and freedoms are respected, where the instruments of violence are controlled, and in which the dignity and worth of all people are affirmed – cannot be delivered by force. Indeed, the limiting of legitimate force to protection operations is the recognition that the distresses of deeply troubled societies cannot be quickly alleviated by either military means or diplomacy; and that in the long and painstakingly slow process of rebuilding the conditions for sustainable peace, those that are most vulnerable are entitled to protection from at least the most egregious of threats.

16. The use of force for humanitarian purposes can never be an attempt to find military solutions to social and political problems, to militarily engineer new social

and political realities. Rather, it is intended to mitigate imminent threats and to alleviate immediate suffering while long-term solutions are sought by other means. The use of force for humanitarian purposes must therefore be carried out in the context of a broad spectrum of economic, social, political, and diplomatic efforts to address the direct and long-term conditions that underlie the crisis. In the long run, international police forces should be educated and trained for this particular task, bound to international law. Interventions should be accompanied by strictly separate humanitarian relief efforts and should include the resources and the will to stay with people in peril until essential order and public safety are restored and there is a demonstrated local capacity to continue to build conditions of durable peace.

17. The force that is to be deployed and used for humanitarian purposes must also be distinguished from military war-fighting methods and objectives. The military operation is not a war to defeat a state but an operation to protect populations in peril from being harassed, persecuted or killed. It is more related to just policing – though not necessarily in the level of force required – in the sense that the armed forces are not employed in order to "win" a conflict or defeat a regime. They are there only to protect people in peril and to maintain some level of public safety while other authorities and institutions pursue solutions to underlying problems.

18. It is the case, therefore, that there may be circumstances in which affected churches actively call for protective intervention for humanitarian purposes. These calls will always aim at the international community and pre-suppose a discerning and decision-making process in compliance with the international community, strictly bound to international law. These are likely to be reluctant calls, because churches, like other institutions and individuals, will always know that the current situation of peril could have been, and should have been, avoided. The churches in such circumstances should find it appropriate to recognize their own collective culpability in failing to prevent the crises that have put people in such peril.

RESOLUTION:

The Ninth Assembly, meeting in Porto Alegre, Brazil, 14-23 February 2006:

a) *adopts* the statement on the Responsibility to Protect and expresses thanks to all member churches and individuals involved in the study and consultation process on "The Responsibility to Protect: Ethical and Theological Reflection" and asks the Central Committee to consider further developing guidelines for the member churches, based on the principles in this report;

b) *fosters* prevention as the key tool and concern of the churches, in relation to the Responsibility to Protect. Because churches and other faith communities and their leadership are rooted in the daily spiritual and physical realities of people, they have both a special responsibility and opportunity to participate in the development of national and multilateral protection and war prevention systems. Churches and other faith communities have a particular responsibility to contribute to the early detection of conditions of insecurity, including economic, social and political exclusion. Prevention is the only reliable means of protection, and early detection of a deteriorating security situation requires the constant attention of those who work most closely with, and have the trust of, affected populations;

c) *joins* with other Christians around the world in repenting for our collective failure to live justly and to promote justice. Such a stance in the world is empowered by acknowledging that the Lordship of Christ is higher than any other loyalty and by the work of the Holy Spirit. Critical solidarity with the victims of violence and advocacy against all the oppressive forces must also inform our theological endeavours towards being a more faithful church. The church's ministry with, and accompaniment of, people in need of protection is grounded in a holistic sojourning with humanity throughout all of life, in good times and in bad;

d) *reaffirms* the churches' ministry of reconciliation and healing as an important role in advancing national and political dialogue to unity and trust. A unifying vision of a state is one in which all parts of the population feel they have a stake in the future of the country. Churches should make a particular point of emphasizing the understanding of sovereignty as responsibility. Under the sovereignty of God we understand it to be the duty of humanity to care for one another and all of creation. The sovereignty exercised by human institutions rests on the exercise of the Responsibility to Protect one another and all of creation;

e) *calls* upon the international community and the individual national governments to strengthen their capability in preventive strategies, and violence-reducing intervention skills together with institutions of the civil society, to contribute to and develop further the international law, based on human rights, and to support the development of policing strategies that can address gross human rights violations;

f) *urges* the United Nations Security Council, in situations where prevention has failed and where national governments cannot or will not provide the protection to which people are entitled, to take timely and effective action, in cooperation with regional organizations as appropriate, to protect civilians in extreme peril and foster emergency responses designed to restore sustainable safety and well-being with rigorous respect for the rights, integrity and dignity of the local populations.

g) *further calls upon* the international community and individual national governments to invest much greater resources and training for non-violent intervention and accompaniment of vulnerable peoples;

h) *asks* the Central Committee to consider a study process engaging all member churches and ecumenical organizations in order to develop an extensive ecumenical declaration on peace, firmly rooted in an articulated theology. This should deal with topics such as just peace, the Responsibility to Protect, the role and the legal status of non-state combatants, the conflict of values (for example: territorial integrity and human life). It should be adopted at the conclusion of the Decade to Overcome Violence in 2010.

STATEMENT ON TERRORISM, COUNTER-TERRORISM AND HUMAN RIGHTS

1. "The violence of terrorism – in all its many forms – is abhorrent to all who believe human life is a gift of God and therefore infinitely precious. Every attempt to intimidate others by inflicting indiscriminate death and injury upon them is to be universally condemned. The answer to terrorism, however, cannot be to respond in kind, for this can lead to more violence and more terror. Instead, a concerted effort of all nations is needed to remove any possible justification for such acts."

2. This message, included in the letter of the General Secretary of the WCC to the Secretary-General of the United Nations on October 1, 2001, is reaffirmed by the 9th Assembly of the WCC.

3. In recent times, acts of terror and some aspects of the so-called "war on terror" have introduced new dimensions of violence. In addition, fundamental international laws and norms, including long-established standards of human rights, have come under threat.

4. Terrorists base their actions in absolutist claims. Religion is sometimes used as a pretext for the use of violence as being divinely sanctioned. Assembled as representatives from churches in all corners of the world, we state unequivocally that terror, as indiscriminate acts of violence against unarmed civilians for political or religious aims, can never be justified legally, theologically or ethically.

5. The WCC's 9th Assembly supports the stated goal of the Decade to Overcome Violence to "relinquish any theological justification for violence and to affirm a new spirituality of reconciliation and active non-violence".

6. Acts of terror are criminal acts, and should be addressed by the use of the instruments of the rule of law, both nationally and internationally. These instruments should be strengthened. The internationally accepted norms and standards of human rights and humanitarian law are the result of common efforts and are specifically meant to deal with situations of crisis and threats to individuals and societies. There is a danger that these instruments will be eroded in the response to terror. It is of critical importance to resist this erosion of rights and liberties. The "war on terror" has redefined war and relativized international law and human rights norms and standards. A military response to terror may become indiscriminately destructive and cause fear in affected populations. It may provide legitimacy to a violent approach rather than the criminal justice approach which is appropriate in dealing with cases of terror. The international community should cooperate in addressing terrorism, especially by strengthening the International Criminal Court to respond to acts of terror. Terror can only be overcome by the international community that upholds respect for the dignity of human beings and the rule of law.

7. Churches and all other faith communities are called to respond to the reality of living in a world terrorized by fear. At such a time it is appropriate to point to the rich resources in religion which can guide us to peace and reconciliation. These resources should be utilized when religious communities and religious leaders come together to speak out against all acts of terror and any attempt to legitimize it. They should also take action against any attempt at meeting terror with military means and disrespect for human rights and the rule of law. Religious communities and leaders should be in the forefront of the struggle for a society which is ruled by law and respect for human dignity. Churches have a pivotal role in framing the issues within a culture of dialogue.

RESOLUTION:

The Ninth Assembly, meeting in Porto Alegre, Brazil, 14-23 February 2006:

a) *adopts* the Statement on Terrorism, Counter-Terrorism and Human Rights;

b) *affirms* the role of the churches to seek peace and pursue it. Violence against unarmed and innocent civilians for political or religious aims by states and non-state actors can never be justified legally, theologically or ethically;

c) *requests* UN member states with urgency to agree on a clear definition of Terrorism;

d) *urges* that terrorist acts and threats as well as organizational support for terror be considered as matters of criminal justice. Measures to counter terrorism must be demilitarized and the concept of "war on terror" must be firmly and resolutely challenged by the churches;

e) *appreciates* the theological work done by the churches on the concept of security and calls for its further development;

f) *expresses* the need to accompany and support the churches as they respond prophetically and creatively in a pastoral and prophetic mission to assist those that are caught up in fear;

g) *encourages* interfaith initiatives to mobilize alternate responses to terrorism that do not rely on violence. They should reject all attempts to justify acts of terror as a response to political and social problems and play an active role in the prevention of conflicts by serving as an early warning system and by building a culture of peace for life;

h) *affirms* that all acts to counter terrorism by the state must remain within the framework of the international rule of law, ensuring respect for human rights and humanitarian law. Legislation to counter terrorism should not result in humiliation and violation of the human rights and dignities. It is necessary for the states and the international community to go beyond policing and military cooperation and embrace cooperation in order to address root causes of terrorism.

STATEMENT ON UN REFORM

1. On many previous occasions the governing bodies of the World Council of Churches have affirmed the unique role of the United Nations and the noble ideals embodied in its Charter. The sixtieth anniversary of the UN and the process of reform initiated before the recent summit meeting offer an occasion for this assembly of the World Council to consider the present state of the international order and to call on member churches to renew and strengthen their active support for and engagement with the UN at a critical moment in its history. The churches, together with the wider civil society, carry a responsibility to shape public opinion and to generate the political will for multilateral cooperative action that is needed for the UN to succeed in its mission.

2. Many of the "peoples of the United Nations" continue to cry for justice and peace. We hear this cry especially from peoples living under occupation and oppressive regimes, from victims of war and civil conflict, from the millions of uprooted people, from Indigenous Peoples displaced from ancestral land and from those suffering from the HIV and other pandemics, hunger, the lack of work, clean water and access to land for cultivation. Many have become disappointed in view of the limitations of the capacity of the UN to address their cries. Through droughts, floods, hurricanes and severe climate changes we also hear the cry of the earth that is groaning under the impact of human greed and brutal exploitation of the resources of nature.

3. As Christians we live by the promise and the hope that God hears the cries of the people and will deliver them from their sufferings. When we pray: "God, in your grace, transform the world" we trust that God, through God's life-giving Spirit, continues to offer life in its fullness. As we pray, we must be prepared to act in order to become co-workers with God in transforming ourselves, our communities and the international order and build a culture of life in dignity in just and sustainable communities.

4. When the UN was founded in 1945 it was guided by the vision: to save succeeding generations from the scourge of war, to affirm faith in fundamental human rights, to establish the basic conditions for justice and the rule of law, and to promote social progress and better standards of life in larger freedom. People of faith inspired this vision and it has been the basis for the strong support that the WCC has rendered to the work and the aspirations of the UN and to the principle of multilateralism throughout its 60 years history.

5. After the end of the cold war and the rapid spread of globalization the UN finds itself at a critical juncture. On the one hand, complex global problems require a cooperative and multilateral response. Never before has it been so clear that the challenges of communicable diseases and environmental degradation, of corruption and organized crime, of proliferation of arms and the threat of terrorism cannot be resolved by individual states alone. On the other hand, this very situation has given rise to new fears, to mutual suspicion, and even to acts of indiscriminate violence leading some to withdraw behind barriers of exclusion or to rush to unilateral action believing that it is more effective.

6. The UN is based on the commitment of governments to act together and in solidarity with one another. In spite of weaknesses of the UN and failures of governments to cooperate through its forum it is still the best instrument that we have to

respond to the contemporary challenges. In its 60-year history the UN and its specialized agencies have been able to strengthen the international rule of law, resolve many conflicts (e.g. in Kampuchea, East Timor, Namibia, and Liberia), resettle millions of refugees, raise the level of literacy, support education for all, introduce basic health care, fight poverty and respond to countless emergencies as well as natural and man-made disasters. The adoption of the Millennium Development Goals (MDGs) as well as the commitments for financing development and the recent agreements regarding the cancellation of unpayable and illegitimate debt are indications that this commitment for multilateral action is still alive.

7. The changed global situation, however, obliges the UN and member states to engage in a serious process of reform in order to retain the capacity to respond to the basic mandate of the UN and to the aspirations of the people of the world. The reform process must continue to go beyond the framework of the UN organization and aim at improving global governance based on the principle of multilateralism.

8. One significant achievement of the summit was the acknowledgement that the realization of peace/security, development/social and economic justice and the implementation of human rights are inseparably linked. This should serve as the fundamental framework and policy orientation for the continuing process of reform. In fact, for people on the ground it has always been obvious that there can be no security in a situation of utter deprivation; that economic development at the expense of the recognition of human rights, in particular the rights of the marginalized, women, children, indigenous and differently-abled people does not serve the cause of social justice; and that without basic human security and the satisfaction of human needs the affirmation of human rights loses its meaning.

9. This acknowledgement of the linkage of the three pillars has implications for the ways we conceive of and approach action in the fields of security, development and human rights. We reaffirm the statement by the WCC Assembly at Vancouver (1983): "No nation can pretend to be secure so long as others' legitimate rights to sovereignty and security are neglected or denied. Security can therefore be achieved only as a common enterprise of nations but security is also inseparable from justice. A concept of 'common security' of nations must be reinforced by a concept of 'people's security'. True security for the people demands respect for human rights, including the right to self-determination, as well as social and economic justice for all within every nation, and a political framework that would ensure it" (*Gathered for Life*, p.134). This position was also emphasized again at the previous assembly

at Harare (1998) in the statements on human rights and globalization. "Human rights are the essential basis for a just and durable peace. Failure to respect them often leads to conflict and warfare... There is an urgent need to learn the lessons from the past, and to set up mechanisms of early intervention when danger signals appear" (*Together on the Way*, pp.200f.).

10. The fact that the outcome document of the 2005 UN World Summit recognizes the inseparable linkage of the three pillars of security, development and human rights speaks for determined efforts to strengthen organizational and policy coherence in the UN system across borders and between specialized institutions, interests and constituencies.

11. Compared to expectations raised and perceived needs, the outcome of the UN World Summit in September 2005 was disappointing. Although, in the field of security, important achievements were made with the endorsement of the principle "The Responsibility to Protect" as a normative obligation and the commitment to a more coherent approach to conflict prevention and post-conflict peacebuilding through the establishment of a Peacebuilding Commission, there was no agreement on disarmament and non-proliferation. On terrorism, the summit was not able to agree on a clear international definition making attacks against civilians for political purposes once and for all indefensible, nor to go beyond intelligence, policing and military cooperation to address root causes. The highly politicized proposal for reform and reconstruction of the Security Council also ended in a deadlock.

12. Although, on development, the outcome document of the summit reinforced commitments towards the Millennium Development Goals and goals of full employment and decent work, no new commitments in aid, debt relief or trade were made. In failing to do so the world leaders failed to acknowledge the urgency of action on this area. The WCC was the first organization to propose a target for official development assistance, of two percent of national income. It is vital that member churches in donor countries continue to be strong advocates to their governments and the public of sustaining or increasing aid to the UN target of 0.7 percent of GDP without harmful economic conditions. Combined with more just trade policies and faster and deeper reduction of official debt, it is possible to sustain development and poverty reduction to fulfill the MDGs, and even move beyond these important limited goals.

13. The agreement to double the resources and approve a new action plan for the High Commissioner on Human Rights is an important step. The new Human Rights Council, if given a prominent role in the UN structure and with appropriate

tools, offers a potential to improve the Human Rights Mechanisms. While the Commission on Human Rights played an outstanding role in generating core standards on human rights, it has largely failed in achieving implementation, a failure compounded by the current context of the "War on terror", which has seriously undermined the rule of law internationally and in particular the respect for human rights law. The reluctance by some countries to ratify the Rome Statute of the International Criminal Court is another example of undermining progress of the international rule of law.

14. Non-governmental organizations play an important role at the UN providing crucial information, monitoring decision-making processes, creating opportunities for the voices from the grassroots, often the victims of international policies, to be heard and to overcome attitudes of narrow self-interest and promote the spirit of multilateralism. Churches are called to continue and strengthen their efforts to play a part in this vital role of engaging with the UN and holding it and member states to account for their decisions and policies. The unique role that religions or religious organizations could play in addressing conflict, and working for peace, human rights and ending poverty is not yet fully realized. There is an urgent need for the UN and member states to strengthen the capacity to deal with the growing interaction between religion and politics. There is also an urgent need for the churches and the WCC to strengthen their own capacities to continue and improve their engagements with the UN.

15. The real test for any steps in this reform process will be whether it increases the chances for life in dignity and sustainable communities for the people on the ground. This is the privileged context for the work and witness of the churches. They are entrusted with a message of life and hope that can dispel suspicion and paralyzing fears and set people free to gain courage and confidence in their capacity to transform their lives in community.

RESOLUTION:

The Ninth Assembly, meeting in Porto Alegre, Brazil, 14-23 February 2006:

a) *adopts* the statement on UN Reform, to advance the objective of a more effective United Nations dedicated to the pursuit of global peace with justice;

b) *reaffirms* the dedication of the World Council of Churches and member churches to the principles and purposes of the UN, its charter, and its role in advancing the rule of law and in elaborating norms and standards of state behaviour that serve the safety and well-being of all people. The effectiveness of the UN depends on accountable and inclusive democratic decision-making that does not sideline small, less powerful, and economically deprived members, and the success of UN reform is judged in terms of the capacity of the UN to change the situation of the people on the ground and make a practical positive difference and an improvement to their comprehensive wellbeing. *Reaffirms* furthermore the dedication of the WCC to be present and visible at the UN;

c) *encourages* the churches to urge member states to cooperate actively with the United Nations and to keep faith with their commitments to financing the organization and ensuring that the organization and its agencies are adequately staffed and funded to achieve their mandate.

On Security:

d) *supports* changes to the permanent membership of the UN Security Council that would make it more geographically, politically and culturally representative of today's world, and that would encourage working methods and decision-making processes that enable fair, effective, and timely responses to the needs of vulnerable people and to prevent the outbreak of violent conflict. All current and aspiring members of the UN Security Council should fully comply with the Nuclear Non-Proliferation Treaty;

e) *welcomes* the establishment of the Peacebuilding Commission as a means of developing new and appropriate ways of responding to civil conflict. The Peacebuilding Commission should adopt and endorse peacebuilding principles and practices, which emphasize local ownership in peacebuilding and peacekeeping processes. These should also promote the full participation of women (in accordance with UN Security Council Resolution 1325), the marginalized groups, Indigenous Peoples, differently-abled people and youth. At the same time current disarmament forums and mechanisms must be strengthened and made more effective in advancing the already agreed global objectives of the elimination of nuclear weapons and of controlling conventional arms and arms transfers.

On Development:

f) *underlines* the importance of democratically selected, open and accountable forums for discussion of global economic, social and environmental issues and calls for increasing their significance in comparison with exclusive, unbalanced and secretive forums. The UN Economic and Social Council should be enabled to hold finance ministers, meetings on global macro-economic management, to more actively address environmental issues integrated with social and economic issues and to hold the International Financial Institutions to account. Commitments made by governments in financing for development, towards meeting the Millennium Development Goals, debt cancellation and for sustainable development should be seen as binding and the UN has to be given instruments to ensure their implementation;

g) *encourages* churches to work with member states to make the UN an initiator and a global monitor for management of natural resources and public goods and for strengthening the mechanisms to ensure that transnational corporations are held accountable to global standards.

On Human Rights:

h) *stresses* that reform of the UN human rights architecture must result in an improvement of the capacity of the UN to engage with and make a practical positive difference in the lives of victims of injustice, discrimination and oppression around the world. The system of Special Procedures developed by the Commission on Human Rights, of the UN Human Rights Treaty Bodies as well as of the High Commissioner for Human Rights and her office should be actively supported, and their independence respected and their capacity substantially enhanced;

i) *urges* member states to avoid politicizing the composition of the new Human Rights Council and give it a status within the UN architecture that reflects the central importance of human rights as one of the three pillars of the UN system. Members of the UN Human Rights Council must demonstrate through their policies, actions and domestic and international human rights record a genuine commitment to the promotion and protection of human rights, including the economic, social and cultural rights. Being a UN member state or even a permanent member of the UN Security Council does not by itself meet this criterion[3].

On Civil Society Participation:

j) *asks* all states to ensure the ongoing participation of civil society organizations and faith communities in the work of the UN, at local and international levels, as a means of encouraging transparency and accountability as well as a means of availing itself of essential expertise and information. This should be particularly emphasized with respect to the role of religions and religious organizations in addressing issues of security, human rights, development and the growing interplay between religion and politics.

STATEMENT ON WATER FOR LIFE

1. Water is a symbol of life. The Bible affirms water as the cradle of life, an expression of God's grace in perpetuity for the whole of creation (Gen. 2:5ff.). It is a basic condition for all life on Earth (Gen. 1:2ff.) and is to be preserved and shared for the benefit of all creatures and the wider creation. Water is the source of health and well-being and requires responsible action from us human beings, as partners and priests of Creation (Rom. 8:19ff., Rev. 22). As churches, we are called to participate in the mission of God to bring about a new creation where life in abundance is assured to all (John 10:10; Amos 5:24). It is therefore right to speak out and to act when the life-giving water is pervasively and systematically under threat.

2. Access to fresh water supplies is becoming an urgent matter across the planet. The survival of 1.2 billion people is currently in jeopardy due to lack of adequate water and sanitation. Unequal access to water causes conflicts between and among people, communities, regions and nations. Biodiversity is also threatened by the depletion and pollution of fresh water resources or through impacts of large dams, large-scale mining and hot cultures (irrigation) whose construction often involves the forced displacement of people and disruption of the ecosystem. The integrity and balance of the ecosystem is crucial for the access to water. Forests are an indispensable part in the ecosystem of water and must be protected. The crisis is aggravated by climate change and further deepened by strong economic interests. Water is increasingly treated as a commercial good, subject to market conditions.

3. Scarcity of water is also a growing source of conflict. Agreements concerning international watercourses and river basins need to be more concrete, setting out measures to enforce treaties made and incorporating detailed conflict resolution mechanisms in case disputes erupt.

4. Both locally and internationally there are positive and creative responses to raise the profile of Christian witness to water issues.

5. Churches in Brazil and in Switzerland, for instance, have made a Joint Ecumenical Declaration on Water as a Human Right and a Common Public Good

– by itself an excellent example for ecumenical cooperation. The Ecumenical Patriarch Bartholomew states that water can never be regarded or treated as private property or become the means and end of individual interest. He underlines that indifference towards the vitality of water constitutes both a blasphemy to God the Creator and a crime against humanity. Churches in various countries and their specialized ministries have joined together in the Ecumenical Water Network in working for the provision of fresh water and adequate sanitation and advocating for the right to water. Access to water is indeed a basic human right. The United Nations has called for an International Decade for Action, Water for Life, 2005 to 2015.

6. It is essential for churches and Christian agencies to work together and to seek cooperation with other partners, including other faith traditions and NGOs, and particularly those organizations that work with vulnerable and marginalized populations who hold similar ethical convictions. It is necessary to engage in debate and action on water policies, including dialogue with governments and multilateral or corporate institutions. This is essential to promote the significance of the right to water and to point to alternative ways of living, which are more respectful of ecological processes and more sustainable in the longer term.

RESOLUTION:

The Ninth Assembly, meeting in Porto Alegre, Brazil, 14-23 February 2006:
a) *adopts* the statement on Water for Life and calls on the churches and ecumenical partners to work together with the aim to:
b) *promote* awareness of and take all necessary measures for preservation and protection of water resources against over-consumption and pollution as an integral part of the right to life;
c) *undertake* advocacy efforts for development of legal instruments and mechanisms that guarantee the implementation of the right to water as a fundamental human right at the local, national, regional and international levels;
d) *foster* cooperation of churches and ecumenical partners on water concerns through participation in the Ecumenical Water Network;
e) *support* community-based initiatives whose objectives are to enable local people to exercise responsible control, manage and regulate water resources and prevent the exploitation for commercial purposes;
f) *urge* governments and international aid agencies to give priority to and allocate adequate funds and other resources for programmes designed to provide access to

and make water available to local communities and also promote development of proper sanitation systems and projects, taking into account the needs of people with disabilities to have access to this clean water and sanitation service;

g) *monitor* disputes and agreements related to water resources and river basins to ensure that such agreements contain detailed, concrete and unambiguous provisions for conflict resolution;

h) *contribute* to the International Decade for Action, Water for Life, 2005-2015, by exploring and highlighting the ethical and spiritual dimension of the water crisis.

MINUTE ON THE ELIMINATION OF NUCLEAR ARMS

1. Speaking out of love for the world and in obedience to the God of all life, we raise our voice again with convictions the church has held since nuclear weapons were used six decades ago.

2. In the nuclear age, God who is slow to anger and abounding in mercy has granted humanity many days of grace. Through the troubled years of the cold war and into the present time, it has become clear that, in this as in other ways, God has saved us from ourselves. Although many were and are deceived, God is not mocked (Gal. 6:7). If vengeance in daily life is for God (Rom. 12:19), surely the vengeance of nuclear holocaust[4] is not for human hands. Our place is to labour for life with God.

3. Churches are not alone in upholding the sanctity of life. One shared principle of world religions is greater than all weapons of mass destruction and stronger than any "balance of *terror*": we must do to others what we would have them do to us. Because we do not want nuclear weapons used against us, our nation cannot use nuclear weapons against others. Since Hiroshima and Nagasaki there is uranium within the golden rule.

4. Indeed, governments in the year 2000 made an "unequivocal undertaking" to meet their obligations and eliminate all nuclear weapons under the Nuclear Non-Proliferation Treaty (NPT).

5. Yet instead of progress there is crisis. The basic and compelling bargain at the heart of the treaty is being broken. The five recognized nuclear powers, who pledged "the total elimination of their nuclear arsenals" under the NPT, are now finding new military and political roles for nuclear arms instead. The other 184 states in the treaty pledged never to have nuclear weapons. If the bargain to eliminate nuclear weapons is being broken, they for their part may have an incentive to seek the

weapons too. When states with the biggest conventional arsenals insist for their security on also having nuclear weapons, states with smaller arsenals will feel less secure and do the same. It must be recognized as well that external political and military pressure can provoke countries to pursue nuclear weapons. In short, there is nuclear proliferation now despite the NPT.

6. As more states acquire nuclear arms the risk of nuclear weapons falling into non-state hands increases – just when it is an international imperative to overcome wisely the violence of terrorism. Nuclear arms do not deter non-state agents and nuclear action against them would cause gross slaughter while shattering international law and morality. These are scenarios the parties to the NPT are obligated to prevent.

7. On the question of morality, all people of faith are needed in our day to expose the fallacies of nuclear doctrine. These hold, for example, that weapons of mass destruction are agents of stability; that governments have nuclear arms so they will never use them; and that there is a role in the human affairs of this small planet for a bomb more powerful than all the weapons ever used. With our ageing sisters and brothers who survived atomic bombs in Japan and tests in the Pacific and former Soviet Union, and as people emerging from a century of genocides and global wars, we are bound to confront these follies before it is too late.

8. Churches must prevail upon governments until they recognize the incontrovertible immorality of nuclear weapons.

9. From its birth as a fellowship of Christian churches the WCC has condemned nuclear weapons for their "widespread and indiscriminate destruction" and as "sin against God" in modern war (First WCC Assembly, 1948), recognized early that the only sure defence against nuclear weapons is prohibition, elimination and verification (Second Assembly, 1954) and, *inter alia*, called citizens to "press their governments to ensure national security without resorting to the use of weapons of mass destruction" (Fifth Assembly, 1975).

10. Existing WCC policy urges all states to meet their treaty obligations to reduce and then destroy nuclear arsenals with adequate verification. Our position is that the five original nuclear weapons states (in alphabetical order: China, France, Russia, United Kingdom, United States) must pledge never to be the first to use nuclear weapons, never threaten any use, and remove their weapons from high alert status and from the territory of non-nuclear states. WCC policy calls the three states that have not signed the NPT (India, Israel, Pakistan), the one that has withdrawn (North Korea) and the one threatening to withdraw (Iran), respectively, to join the

treaty as non-nuclear states, to make a fully verifiable return and not to withdraw (WCC Executive Committee Statement on the Nuclear Non-Proliferation Treaty, 19.02.04; WCC Central Committee Statement on Nuclear Disarmament, NATO Policy and the Churches, 05.02.01). These measures have broad support across the international community, yet they remain unrealized.

RESOLUTION:

The Ninth Assembly, meeting in Porto Alegre, Brazil, 14-23 February 2006:

a) *adopts* the minute on the Elimination of Nuclear Arms;

b) *calls* each member church to urge its own government to pursue the unequiv-ocal elimination of nuclear weapons under the terms of the Nuclear Non-Proliferation Treaty. Governments that have decided to abstain from developing nuclear weapons should be affirmed; states that are not signatories of NPT must be pressed to sign the treaty as non-nuclear states;

c) *urges* churches to work to overcome the ignorance and complacency in society concerning the nuclear threat, especially to raise awareness in generations with no memory of what these weapons do;

d) *strongly recommends* that, until the goal of nuclear disarmament is achieved, member churches prevail upon their governments to take collective responsibil-ity for making international nuclear disarmament machinery work including mechanisms to verify compliance, for securing nuclear weapons and weapons-useable material from non-state actors, and for supporting the International Atomic Energy Agency in its critical mission of monitoring fissile material and peaceful uses of nuclear energy;

e) *calls* on member churches and parishes to mobilize their membership to sup-port and strengthen Nuclear Weapons Free Zones, which are established in Latin America and the Caribbean, the South Pacific, Southeast Asia and Africa and are proposed for other inhabited regions of the earth; and *especially com-mends* churches to engage other religions and to advocate for these zones dur-ing the WCC "Decade to Overcome Violence: Churches Seeking Reconciliation and Peace – 2001-2010".

MINUTE ON MUTUAL RESPECT, RESPONSIBILITY AND DIALOGUE WITH PEOPLE OF OTHER FAITHS[5]

1. The international community must work together to nurture global respect for diversity, culture and religion. Religious communities and leaders have a special responsibility to promote tolerance and address ignorance about others. Representatives of 348 churches from 120 countries, gathered in Porto Alegre, Brazil, at the 9th Assembly of the WCC, reaffirm their commitment to respectful dialogue and cooperation between people of different faiths and other convictions. Through dialogue we learn about the faith of the other and better understand their underlying pain and frustration. We see ourselves through the eyes of the other. We can also better perceive the role of religion in national and international politics.

2. In a world where we recognize a growing interaction between religion and politics, many conflicts and tensions carry the imprint of religion. The WCC has always encouraged interfaith dialogue both on the global and the local level. We urge member churches and national councils of churches to create platforms for such dialogues. Dialogue should be accompanied by cooperation where faith communities together can address the rest of civil society and governments on issues of common concern, and particularly when religion, holy places, minority rights and human rights are threatened.

3. Faced with the publication of the cartoons of the Prophet Mohammed of Islam, starting in Denmark in September last year, we recognize it is crucial to strengthen dialogue and cooperation between Christians and Muslims. The publications have caused worldwide controversies. Further publication and the violent reactions to them increase the tension. As people of faith we understand the pain caused by the disregard of something considered precious to faith. We deplore the publications of the cartoons. We also join with the voices of many Muslim leaders in deploring the violent reactions to the publications.

4. Freedom of speech is indeed a fundamental human right, which needs to be guaranteed and protected. It is both a right and a responsibility. It works best when it holds structures of power accountable and confronts misuse of power. By the publication of the cartoons, freedom of speech has been used to cause pain by ridiculing peoples' religion, values and dignity. Doing so, the foundation of this right is being devalued. We remind ourselves of what St Peter wrote: "As servants of God, live as free people, yet do not use your freedom as a pretext for evil – honour everyone" (1 Pet. 2:16-17). Misuse of the right to freedom of speech should be met with non-violent means like critique and expressions of firm disagreement.

325

5. We recognize that there are more than just religious aspects to the present tensions. Failure to find a just and peaceful solution to the Arab-Israeli conflict, reluctance to accept outcomes of free elections, together with the war on Iraq and the war in Afghanistan, add frustration to historical experiences marked by crusades and colonialism. In many parts of the world people identify as being politically and economically excluded, and they often experience that dominant powers and cultures apply double standards in dealing with issues which are important to them. In many countries in the rich and dominant parts of the world, integration policies have failed to welcome new minorities. Instead, they meet racism, stereotyping, xenophobia, and a lack of respect for their religion.

6. The real tension in our world is not between religions and beliefs, but between aggressive, intolerant and manipulative secular and religious ideologies. Such ideologies are used to legitimize the use of violence, the exclusion of minorities and political domination. The main victims of these types of controversies are religious minorities, living in a context of a different majority culture. Nevertheless, we recognize a growing respect and tolerance in all cultures. Many are learning that it is possible to be different, even to disagree and yet remain in calm dialogue and work together for the common good.

7. The recent crisis points to the need for secular states and societies to better understand and respect the role and significance of religion in a multicultural and globalized world, in particular as an essential dimension in human identity. This can help religion and people of faith to be instruments for bridging divisions between cultures and nations and to contribute to solving underlying problems.

RESOLUTION:

The Ninth Assembly, meeting in Porto Alegre, Brazil, 14-23 February 2006:

a) *adopts* the minute on Mutual Respect, Responsibility and Dialogue with People of other Faiths;

b) *asks* member churches and ecumenical partners all over the world to express and demonstrate solidarity to those who are experiencing attacks on their religion and join them in defending the integrity of their faith by non-violent means;

c) *recommends* all member churches, national and regional Councils of Churches to contribute to the creation of platforms for dialogue with people of other faiths or none, and to address immediate as well as underlying social, economic and political reasons for division, including interaction with governments and secular authorities;

d) *urges* member churches and ecumenical partners in contexts where religion interacts with politics in a way which causes division to deepen dialogue with leaders of other faiths, seek common approaches and develop common codes of conduct;

e) *calls* on member churches and ecumenical partners all over the world to continue to address racism, caste, stereotyping and xenophobia in their respective societies and together with people of other faiths to nurture a culture of respect and tolerance;

f) *reaffirms* our commitment to the right to freedom of speech, at the same time as member churches are called to contribute to a needed reflection on how to uphold the need for ethical behaviour and good judgment in using this right.

Notes:

1. Dissent was registered from the delegation of the Serbian Orthodox Church, objecting to the wording of the section.

2. Dissent was registered from John Alfred Steele, delegate from the Anglican Church of Canada, who believes that the strict application of international law should not prevent intervention in extreme situations such as genocide or ongoing widespread killing of civilian populations.

3. Dissent was registered from the delegation of the Russian Orthodox Church regarding the right of UN member states to participate in the Human Rights Council regardless of their political or ideological systems.

4. Dissent was registered from Rev. Helga Rudolf, delegate of the Evangelical Church of the Augsburg Confession in Romania, concerning the theological implications of the expression "nuclear holocaust". She feels that the word "holocaust" is being used without awareness of its original Biblical meaning as a burnt offering to God. She would have preferred to say "nuclear disaster", thus avoiding this misunderstanding and taking responsibility for our use of language.

5. Dissent was registered from:

- Dr Audeh Quawas, delegate of the Greek Orthodox Patriarchate of Jerusalem, who objected to formulations in paragraphs 3 and 5. In paragraph 3, he wished for a statement opposing the assertion of "freedom of speech" as a justification for inflammatory acts by the media, and wished to replace the word "deplore" with "condemn". In paragraph 5, he wished for a stronger statement condemning "collective punishment" in response to the outcome of democratic elections.

- Dr Emmanuel Clapsis, delegate of the Ecumenical Patriarchate, who objected to the failure to include, in paragraph 3, a reference to the disrespect by the media of religious symbols of all living faiths; and

- The Most Rev. Josiah Idowu-Fearon, delegate of the Church of Nigeria, who felt that the word "tolerance" in paragraph 1 needed to be qualified by the adjective "positive".

Messages and addresses received by the Assembly

Message to the Assembly from the National Council of Christian Churches in Brazil (CONIC)

Presented by Bishop Adriel de Souza Maia, President of CONIC

The National Council of Christian Churches in Brazil (CONIC) and the churches of Brazil have great pleasure in welcoming in the name of Jesus Christ all the participants in this Ninth Assembly of the World Council of Churches to this land of Brazil, and in particular to this land of the gauchos.

For the first time since its foundation in 1948 the WCC is holding its Assembly in a Latin American country. It is an honour for Brazilian and Latin American Christians to have this gathering here. It will certainly give new impetus to the ecumenical movement, Christian unity and the advancement of life, here and worldwide.

This gives us great joy. We bless God for you and for the witness to unity and peace that you represent.

The ecumenical movement in Brazil, originating in the shared struggle of Christians of various traditions for justice and freedom, has given rise to many initiatives and organizations that are today working for the full unity of the Church of Jesus Christ.

CONIC was founded in 1982 in this city of Porto Alegre, and was set up following the lines of the ecumenical movement led by the WCC. It was one of the first national councils of churches to have the Roman Catholic Church as one of its founder members. Although not a WCC member church, it works in active collaboration with it. In the course of the years CONIC has acquired a high profile, increasing fellowship and the presence of the churches in public life. Faithful to its mission to "serve the Christian churches in Brazil in strengthening ecumenism and dialogue, in living in Christian fellowship, in defending the integrity of creation, in promoting justice and peace to the glory of God", it has encouraged joint witness and action for a "just, peaceful and humane world, where dignity, human rights and women's rights are respected, hunger no longer exists, there are no weapons, and where the cries of deprived children are replaced by smiles of good health and happiness" (cf. Message of CONIC at its inauguration).

Today a network of ecumenical organizations has relations with CONIC as associated bodies, and many ecumenical groups are recognized as representing it throughout Brazil.

The complex developments behind the religious traditions of Brazil and the history inherited by the Brazilian people have created problems on the ecumenical way and motivated the churches to journey together. At the present time the CONIC member churches are together a witness to our Christian fellowship and are building up new relations between Christians. We do, however, need to expand our areas of dialogue and action.

We in CONIC are now repeating our commitment and our willingness to work in close collaboration with the WCC and to work towards full unity, justice and a culture of peace. We are prepared and open to dialogue with organizations and religious communities committed to the dignity of life.

It is with great satisfaction that CONIC and the Christian churches of Brazil joyfully welcome individuals, churches and organizations to this Ninth Assembly. May the Holy Spirit, who unites us in prayer, in the Word, in sharing and in action, strengthen our bonds of faith, hope and love. May God inspire this Assembly, and make of it an instrument for the transformation of the world.

Messages and addresses received by the Assembly

Message to the Assembly from the Latin American Council of Churches (CLAI)

Presented by Bishop Julio Holguin, President of CLAI

Dear brothers and sisters in Christ,

On behalf of the Latin American churches and the Latin American Council of Churches we welcome you to our region with great pleasure and high expectations. Brothers and sisters, thank you for coming to Latin America. We open our arms and hearts to welcome you with the warmth and joy that are a feature of our peoples and churches, and we invite you in your turn to share in our joy.

You are arriving in Latin America at a time when, alongside the crisis in economic, political and social life – and also in ecumenical and church life – new signs are appearing that are symbolic and indicative of renewal and hope.

In political life, alongside the breakdown of the model of an unrepresentative democracy, signs are appearing of a new participative democracy. In economic life, alongside the model imposed on us which has led to serious inequalities, impoverishment and concentration of power, efforts are appearing to seek more humane and communal ways of conducting economic life, with the aim that the economy should serve people and not people the economy. In cultural life, alongside attempts to impose dominant cultures, both from abroad and at home, there is arising a desire to recognize our diversity and the cries of the indigenous and Afro-Latin American peoples after more than 500 years of domination.

We also do not rule out rejecting models imposed on our ecclesiastical and ecumenical life. While recognizing the value of our church institutions, renewal movements and ways of being church are arising that are different from the models and traditions that have not always been our own. In ecumenical life, traditional and even "routine" ecumenical institutions are being replaced by a new calling that seeks for the unity of the churches based on daily pastoral life.

Together with the theme of the Ninth Assembly "God, in your grace, transform the world", it is our prayer that we be given grace to enable us to discern and encourage these new signs and indications of renewal and hope. May God's grace strengthen us to walk with God in the work of transforming the world, the churches and the oikoumene.

Our only sorrow is that at this Assembly on our continent we are not able to unite around the table of our Lord. We believe that the ecumenical movement should be able to celebrate and worship in the freedom of the Spirit and together share the gift of grace in the eucharist. That gives light and flavour to the ecumenical movement. May the grace of God help us, in a spirit of repentance, to affirm the path to unity, which becomes a celebration of grace in the resurrection of Christ.

May the blessing, mercy and grace of the Triune God abide with us during this Ninth Assembly. Amen.

Messages and addresses received by the Assembly

Message to the Assembly from His All Holiness Ecumenical Patriarch Bartholomew I

Bartholomew, by the grace of God Archbishop of Constantinople, New Rome, and Ecumenical Patriarch,

To the beloved participants of the Ninth Assembly of the World Council of Churches: grace, mercy and peace from our Triune God, Father, Son and Holy Spirit.

From the historic throne of Constantinople we extend cordial wishes to the leadership and the participants of this major inter-ecclesial gathering, marking the beginning of a new era in the history of the ecumenical movement. On the occasion of this auspicious encounter, we greet you with the words of St Paul: "Rejoice in God through our Lord Jesus Christ, through whom we have received reconciliation" (Rom. 5:10-12).

We would also like to express our sadness that, in spite of our desire and commitment, we are unable to be with you at this significant ecumenical event, for reasons independent of our will.

An assembly of the WCC is an exceptional event for the entire ecumenical movement, and for the fellowship of churches constituting the WCC in particular. It is a celebration, an experience of togetherness, an opportunity for a genuine encounter, a moment for common prayer to the almighty God. It is an occasion for a sober assessment of the churches' common journey on their way towards unity. It is an encounter during which delegates from all member churches are called to search for a new vision for the future, and new ways of dialogue, cooperation and interaction. It is an exercise of spiritual discernment in the search for new efforts to redefine and re-appropriate our common commitment on the long path of the search for Christian unity.

We particularly welcome the fact that, for the first time, an assembly of the WCC is taking place in Brazil, on the Latin American continent, at the kind and generous invitation of the Christian churches of this country and this region. It is a region marked by deep pain and suffering but known also for hope and joy grounded in the faith of the people.

In the seven-year period since Harare, our churches have experienced significant developments.

The Special Commission on Orthodox Participation in the WCC, established by the Eighth Assembly, worked hard and raised decisive challenges for our participation in the life of the WCC. For the first time in the history of the WCC, fundamental questions raised by the Orthodox churches were also shared by other member churches. Prayer, ecclesiology, membership, ethical and moral issues, as well as new ways of decision-making were proposed for further reflection and discussion. The Special Commission has presented its report. We have noted with satisfaction the positive reception of this report, particularly by our sister Orthodox churches. We now have to continue our work together for the implementation of its decisions with realism and responsibility, for the benefit of the fellowship of our churches.

The Decade to Overcome Violence was also launched by the Eighth Assembly. Member churches and ecumenical partners were invited to work unceasingly for reconciliation and peace, and for the elimination of all forms of violence, since violence constitutes an offence against God, humanity and creation. At the mid-point of the decade, we realize that a great deal still has to be done, both by the WCC and each one of the member churches.

The need to look afresh at our vision and expectations of the ecumenical movement in the 21st century has become urgent since Harare, and has led to the process of reconfiguration, and a search for realignment of the ecumenical organizations at the service of the imperative of the gospel and human needs. We are following the process with interest and we will gladly contribute to it.

Indeed, in a world where there is still much division, fragmentation, human suffering, poverty, fear of war, injustice and violation of human rights, and where socio-political and economic crises are faced daily, we have high expectations from the ecumenical movement, and particularly from this Ninth Assembly of the WCC.

The Ecumenical Patriarchate is committed to the WCC and the ecumenical movement as a whole. It will continue to offer its witness and to share the richness of its theological and ecclesial tradition in the search for unity among Christian churches, in all efforts towards reconciliation and peace, in all attempts to serve the manifold human needs, and in the protection of creation which is a gift of God entrusted to humanity.

It is our fervent prayer that the Holy Spirit will guide the deliberations at the Assembly and will bestow on all participants in this gathering wisdom, discernment and courage.

"May the grace of the Lord Jesus Christ, and the love of God, and the fellowship of the Holy Spirit be with you all" (2 Cor. 13:14).

At the Ecumenical Patriarchate, Phanar, February 2nd, 2006
Feast of the Presentation of Our Lord to the Temple

Your fervent supplicant before God,
+ Bartholomew,
Archbishop of Constantinople and Ecumenical Patriarch

MESSAGES AND ADDRESSES RECEIVED BY THE ASSEMBLY

MESSAGE TO THE ASSEMBLY FROM THE MOST REVEREND ROWAN WILLIAMS
ARCHBISHOP OF CANTERBURY

335

It gives me great pleasure to send you my warmest greetings as you begin the Ninth Assembly of the World Council of Churches. I look forward to joining you in Porto Alegre later this week and in the meantime I will be praying with you as you meet, using the words of the Assembly theme, "God, in your grace, transform the world".

As we pray these words together, we keep in mind not just the world that is to be transformed but the work of this Assembly, the churches we each represent and indeed the future role of the World Council of Churches. In doing so, our underlying desire is surely for the combined witness of our churches to have its full impact; that it will keep pace, in this fast-changing and often perplexing world, with what it means to be an effective sign and instrument of God's transforming grace. I very much welcome the participation of young people at this Assembly to help maintain this kind of focus on the unfolding needs of the future and not just the patterns of the past. Yet if we truly believe that the churches to which we belong are so deeply implicated in God's transforming purposes, we dare not be complacent, especially when we come together to assess our shared priorities. In the face of so much disorder in our so-called world order, we cannot allow ourselves to be overwhelmed or distracted, however conscious we are of our own fractured condition as churches. As those who carry the name of Christ, we must instead draw strength and clarity of purpose from our utter dependence on the One whom we know to be "full of grace and truth". In Christ too, we can find renewed impetus in our painstaking quest for theological convergence, in the knowledge that this also will be used by God, in his grace, to transform the world, opening up, as it does, new possibilities for common mission as divisions are healed and we deepen our fellowship together.

With such confidence in Christ then, in the words of the Petrine epistles, may "grace and peace be yours in abundance" at this Assembly, for the sake of God's world and for His glory.

MESSAGES AND ADDRESSES RECEIVED BY THE ASSEMBLY

MESSAGE TO THE ASSEMBLY FROM HIS HOLINESS ABUNE PAULOS
PATRIARCH OF ETHIOPIA

In the name of the Father, the Son, the Holy Spirit, One God, Amen.
Holy Fathers, the leadership of the WCC, invited guests, ladies and gentlemen.

It is a unique privilege to have been accorded the honour to send a message to this august Assembly. It had been my desire that by God's grace I might have been at the Assembly so that I could enjoy the fellowship and the transformative process of this historic event. Due to circumstances beyond the limit of my working calendar, it was not possible to be with you. Although I am absent and unable to be with you, I was encouraged by the plan, preparation, conduct and venue of the Assembly to send you my humble message of congratulations and prayers.

The central theme of my message is a verse from St Luke's gospel, chapter 4:18, which reads as follows: "The spirit of the Lord is upon me, because he hath anointed me to preach the gospel to the poor, he hath sent me to heal the broken-hearted, to preach deliverance to the captives and recovering of sight to the blind, to set at liberty they that are bruised."

When we reflect on the above, there are a number of issues to be deducted from each phrase.

The interpretation of each phrase clearly shows the reality of the conditions of people during biblical times. But the Lord must have reason to use this for us so that, also today, we are open to the poor, the broken-hearted, the captives and the blind.

If we focus on Africa, the level and scale of marginalization has deepened to the extent that national and international efforts to reduce poverty and improve the conditions of the people have not brought about significant changes in the lives of our people.

The challenge in Africa is a search for a new paradigm and approaches to policies, programmes and strategies appropriate to the continent.

The unfolding human tragedy, its impact on human development, and its consequences on politics, are indeed too ghastly to contemplate. Whereas the challenge, simply stated, underpins the need to connect to the energies of youth, our people have been discouraged from mobilizing themselves for local actions and for their own development, finding themselves in positions of unequal power and making it very tempting for many in politics to dictate conditions and terms of relationships to them. As a result, the overwhelming majority of our citizens are preoccupied by the need for sheer survival.

The African dilemma is therefore the struggle between many contradictions: the struggle between free will versus dominance, inclusion and participation versus marginalization, education versus ignorance and livelihood, security versus famines, hunger and poverty. It is also a struggle between the necessary enabling environment for conducting responsible human development and human security versus hypocrisy and arrogance on the part of the protagonists of international development. Africa has launched many initiatives in an effort to tackle such formidable development challenges facing the continent.

Finally, as a founding member of the WCC, the Ethiopian Orthodox Tewahedo Church places on record its appreciation of the worthy deeds of the World Council of Churches since its inception in 1948. In particular our church recognizes the deep commitment and dedication of the critical and remarkable contributions to enhance the initiatives of national churches on a partnership basis, aimed at capaci-tating the poor and the powerless.

We pray that the Assembly shall attain this Christian mission.
God, in your grace, transform Africa.
God, in your grace, transform our society.
May God bless you all.

MESSAGES AND ADDRESSES RECEIVED BY THE ASSEMBLY

MESSAGE TO THE ASSEMBLY FROM POPE BENEDICT XVI

DELIVERED BY WALTER CARDINAL KASPER PRESIDENT OF THE PONTIFICAL COUNCIL FOR PROMOTING CHRISTIAN UNITY

I am pleased to greet all of you who are gathered for the Ninth Assembly of the World Council of Churches being held in Porto Alegre to reflect on the theme: *God, in your grace, transform the world.* In a special way I greet the General Secretary, Dr Samuel Kobia, Archbishop Dadeus Grings, the Bishops of the Catholic Church in Brazil and all those who have worked for the realization of this important event. To all of you I express my heartfelt good wishes in the words of Saint Paul to the Romans: "Grace to you and peace from God our Father and the Lord Jesus Christ" (Rom. 1:7).

Mindful of our shared baptismal faith in the Triune God, the Catholic Church and the World Council of Churches seek ways to cooperate ever more effectively in the task of witnessing to God's divine love. After forty years of fruitful collaboration, we look forward to continuing this journey of hope and promise, as we intensify our endeavours towards reaching that day when Christians are united in proclaiming the gospel message of salvation to all. As we together make this journey, we must be open to the signs of divine providence and the inspiration of the Holy Spirit, for we know that "the holy objective of reconciling all Christians in the unity of the one and the only Church of Christ transcends human powers and gifts" (*Unitatis Redintegratio*, 24). Our trust therefore is solely in the prayer of Christ himself: "Holy Father, keep them in thy name, which thou hast given me, that they may be one, even as we are one" (John 17:11).

During this Assembly thousands of Christians join in this same prayer for unity. As we ask *God, in his grace, to transform the world*, we pray that he will bless our ecumenical dialogue with the progress we so ardently desire.

Assuring you of my spiritual closeness and reaffirming the Catholic Church's intention to continue a solid partnership with the World Council of Churches in its important contribution to the ecumenical movement, I invoke God's abundant blessings of peace and joy upon all of you.

From the Vatican, 25 January 2006, Feast of the Conversion of Saint Paul

Messages and addresses received by the Assembly

Statement of the World Evangelical Alliance to the Assembly

Delivered by Geoffrey Tunnicliffe WEA International Director

The World Evangelical Alliance deeply appreciates the offer from the World Council of Churches to observe the proceedings at the Ninth Assembly in Porto Alegre, Brazil. As a parallel network representing almost 400 million evangelical Christians around the world, our community identifies with many of the themes raised at this Assembly.

In particular, the focus on the scandal of global poverty, HIV and AIDS, injustice and violence against children at risk, are deep-felt concerns within our community.

In responding to these critical issues, the World Evangelical Alliance two years ago launched the Micah Challenge, a global Christian campaign that seeks to raise a prophetic and powerful voice with the poor. With 18 national campaigns currently functioning and an additional 20 campaigns being launched this year, the Micah Challenge has two primary aims. First of all we want to deepen Christian engagement with the poor. Secondly, we want to influence leaders of rich and poor nations to fulfill their public promise to achieve the Millennium Development Goals, and so halve absolute global poverty by 2015.

As evangelical Christians, the foundation for our engagement with these issues comes from a deep commitment to integral mission.

"Integral mission or holistic transformation is the proclamation and demonstration of the gospel. It is not simply that evangelism and social involvement are to be done alongside each other. Rather, in integral mission our proclamation has social consequences as we call people to love and repentance in all areas of life. And our social involvement has evangelistic consequences as we bear witness to the transforming grace of Jesus Christ. If we ignore the world, we betray the word of God which sends us out to serve the world. If we ignore the word of God we have nothing to bring to the world. Justice and justification by faith, worship and political action, the spiritual and the material, personal conversion and structural change belong together. As in the life of Jesus, being, doing and saying are at the heart of our integral task." [From the Micah Declaration on Integral Mission, 2001]

Here in Porto Alegre evangelicals are found in many of the church streams represented at the Assembly. There are Pentecostal, Baptist, Anglican, Reformed and other Christians who also identify themselves with the evangelical movement. It is our hope that they will have a positive influence on the outcomes of the Assembly.

In a world filled with pain, hate and struggle, we strongly affirm that the only solution is found in God's transforming grace.

MESSAGES AND ADDRESSES RECEIVED BY THE ASSEMBLY

MESSAGE TO THE ASSEMBLY FROM THE WORLD YWCA AND WORLD ALLIANCE OF YMCAS

DELIVERED BY LOURDES SAAD OLIVERA

My name is Lourdes Saad Olivera and I come from Argentina, where I am a member of a local association of the YWCA of Argentina. I just returned home from a year's internship in Geneva with the World YWCA.

I am happy and honoured to bring greetings to this 9th Assembly on behalf of two organizations, the World YWCA and the World Alliance of YMCAs. Both of these organizations have been in existence for over 150 years and both were instrumental to the formation of the World Council of Churches and continue to participate in the ecumenical movement in various ways. Both have participated strongly in the "Reconfiguration" discussions, in the formation and leadership of the Ecumenical Advocacy Alliance, and also continue to serve on various World Council Committees and Working Groups. Our movements also share with the World Council of Churches relationships with the same ecumenical donor agencies. We hope to bring whatever we learn from this Assembly to the World Alliance of YMCAs' Assembly which will take place in Durban, South Africa from July 9-16, 2006 and the World YWCA Assembly to take place in Nairobi, Kenya, July 1-12, 2007.

The YWCA and the YMCA believe in the leadership of young people. We therefore congratulate the World Council of Churches for giving this Assembly a specific emphasis on young people. We urge all those present in this Assembly to make financial resources available for youth work. The future of the ecumenical movement requires investment in the development of young leadership now. You cannot wait for tomorrow.

As a young woman I would like to make a special plea for the inclusion of young women in decision-making and in programmes. I specifically would like to appeal that churches consider enabling young women to overcome obstacles that stand in our way for utilizing our gifts for the benefit of the church and society.

The YWCA and YMCA wish you a successful Assembly, fruitful deliberations, discussions, and exchanges. May the grace of God enable us to transform our world!

Thank you.

MESSAGES AND ADDRESSES RECEIVED BY THE ASSEMBLY

MESSAGE TO THE ASSEMBLY FROM KOFI A. ANNAN

SECRETARY-GENERAL OF THE UNITED NATIONS

You meet at a crucial time for our United Nations. We have just celebrated our 60th anniversary, yet this is a time not only to look back on the six decades behind us. It is also a time to prepare for what lies ahead. We have tried to unite behind a common vision: to ensure that the UN is equipped to deal with the challenges of the 21st century.

To do that, we must recognize that the world today is very different from that of our founders. Our mission is still to serve the cause of peace, advance development, and defend the dignity of every human being. But we must adapt to new realities. This is so, whether we are fighting poverty, disease and environmental degradation, or working to strengthen democracy; whether we are advancing human rights and the rule of law, or combating terrorism; whether we are building peace, or making the United Nations more effective and more accountable to the peoples it exists to serve.

At a time when some would seek to divide the human family by exploiting differences among peoples, the United Nations needs more than ever the support of men and women of faith like you. That is why I am pleased to extend my best wishes to this Ninth Assembly of the World Council of Churches. As you pray for the United Nations, I hope you will pray that whatever the challenges and crises that confront us, we may make this indispensable instrument as effective as it can be. Pray that world leaders find the wisdom and the will to use this tool to its full capacity. Pray for peace in the family of nations.

Messages and addresses received by the Assembly

Message to the Assembly from Juan Somavia

Director-General of the International Labour Organization

Delivered by Dominique Peccoud S.J., special advisor to the Director-General

Dear friends,

Please allow me to address you in these familiar terms, in view of the solid and long-standing relations between the World Council of Churches (WCC) and the International Labour Organization (ILO).

Even before the Second World War, the ILO enjoyed close ties with those who were preparing the birth of the WCC. As you are well aware, they wished to give all Christian churches, gathered within a single institution, greater visibility and weight in social and political discussions and action to guide world development towards greater justice and peace.

As time has passed, these relations have continued to strengthen.

Shortly after my arrival at the ILO, former WCC general secretary Konrad Raiser and I very quickly understood that we were pursuing the same objective: how could we, together, respond more effectively to the calls of the poorest and most vulnerable in the world?

If we take the time to listen to them, we can see that, over and above emergency relief, what they are seeking and calling for is work: work which associates them with the creation of our world; work which gives just access to its resources; work which respects and ensures respect for their human dignity as men and women with sufficient income to bring up their children in dignity; or, in short, "decent work".

Several of the subjects that you are covering are directly related to the ILO's concerns.

The first is violence, and particularly "Youth overcoming violence". If youth is to contribute its full capacities to this cause, it has to be properly educated. Yet today too many children are compelled too early in their lives to earn their livelihood or that of their families in mines, domestic work outside their own homes and in many other activities. All their innate creativity is thus condemned to remain unfulfilled. Worse still, vulnerable and exposed, they are at risk of being the first to be affected by the violence which so often coexists with deep-rooted poverty.

The ILO's most important cooperation programme is concerned with the eradication of child labour. Moreover, at the Millennium Summit, the Heads of State emphasized the need to find decent and productive work for young people. In this context, the ILO has been called upon to take the lead in a Youth Employment Network, in close cooperation with the Secretariat of the United Nations and the World Bank. Already, 19 countries have committed themselves at the highest level to implementing a national action plan on youth employment.

A second theme that you are addressing is economic justice, in relation to which you affirm that "A world without poverty is possible". In 2003, my report to the International Labour Conference set out the same convictions under the title "Working out of poverty". The ILO has since engaged in many efforts at the global, regional and national levels to show how whole communities can escape from poverty through decent work. At the United Nations Summit held in September 2005 in New York, the Heads of State recognized and called for the expansion of these efforts in their final statement, emphasizing the link between the sustainable reduction of poverty and the creation of decent work.

One joint activity by our two institutions was directed by Samuel Kobia, general secretary of the World Council of Churches, and relates perfectly to the third theme of your Assembly on religious plurality. We undertook an in-depth examination of the

ILO's Decent Work Agenda from the viewpoint of all the major philosophical and spiritual traditions underlying the principal cultures in an attempt to give meaning to genuinely humane development for each and every person within our common humanity. We established a very diversified inter-cultural group of women and men from the world over, which engaged in highly productive exchanges over a period of one year. The convergence of views, enriched by the specificities of the various traditions, is set out in a joint work published by the ILO and the World Council of Churches: "Philosophical and spiritual perspectives on decent work". This work emphasizes the importance of developing, above and beyond face-to-face and sometimes confrontational inter-denominational dialogue, collaborative side-by-side dialogue in which everyone joins together in trying to respond to a pressing topical issue. This type of discussion gives rise to vigorous consensus, which is clarified and enriched by the differences added by each participant in response to practical issues.

Once again, in our common advance, we can see the extent to which the major concerns of the WCC meet those of the ILO. That is why we accepted with great pleasure your invitation to be present in Porto Alegre. I would have most willingly attended in person, had my obligations in relation to the Maritime Conference not required my presence in Geneva. But I felt it important that Dominique Peccoud should represent our organization during the whole of your Assembly and a CD-ROM has been produced for all participants containing a number of documents on the three subjects of your debates.

Our struggle to attain greater social justice which gives practical recognition to the dignity of each individual is as legitimate as it is difficult. Our collaboration has been productive for both our organizations. Together, we can hope to achieve objectives which it would be impossible to attain separately. The ILO today needs your support in its combat to create more job opportunities that are synonymous with human dignity. In response to your prayer "God, in your grace, transform the world", there can be no doubt that the first gift that He is ready to accord us is that of working together. Just as you can count on the availability of the ILO, I count on you to support our organization's action for decent work.

Thank you.

MESSAGES AND ADDRESSES RECEIVED BY THE ASSEMBLY

MESSAGE TO THE ASSEMBLY FROM ARCHBISHOP DESMOND TUTU

TRANSFORM YOUR WORLD – THE SEARCH FOR UNITY

What a great privilege and honour to have been asked to address this wonderful august Assembly gathered from all the corners of the globe and consisting of all sorts and conditions of women, men and youth – tall, short, white, black, old, yellow, clever and maybe not so clever (no, you're all clever), beautiful and otherwise, rich, poor – a splendid kaleidoscope, a foretaste, a foreshadowing, a glorious foreshadowing of what will be. Thank you for asking me.

Sometimes they say, "Oh, he is well-known." A few years ago I was in San Francisco when a lady came up to greet me very warmly. "Hello, Archbishop Mandela" – sort of getting two for the price of one!

Dear friends, I come from South Africa. It is nearly twelve years now since we became free. We scored a spectacular victory over the ghastly awfulness of apartheid. But that victory would have been totally impossible without the support of the international community. The WCC and its constituent members were prominent and wonderfully committed parts of that community. You were marvellous in the support you gave to us. You established the Programme to Combat Racism (PCR) which, yes, was controversial but was quite critical in saying our cause was just and noble and that those who as a last resort had opted for the armed struggle were not terrorists but freedom fighters. Nelson Mandela was no terrorist even if that is what a British Prime Minister said he was. And you were absolutely correct, for when that so-called terrorist walked out of gaol he amazed the world with his magnanimity, his readiness to forgive, to reject retribution and revenge and to walk the path of forgiveness and reconciliation. Today that former so-called terrorist has become the world's most revered statesperson, a colossus, an icon of forgiveness and reconciliation and South Africa has improbably become a beacon of hope for all those lands torn by strife, emerging from oppression and having to deal with a violent past. The world's former pariah, a repulsive caterpillar, has become a gorgeous butterfly. And you had a very substantial part in that metamorphosis. Thank you.

I personally owe a very great deal to the WCC and was helped to grow as a person and widened my experience of the world through my term on the TEF[1] as Assistant Director for Africa. I learned then about the subversive nature of the scriptures and the infinite worth of each individual person. The WCC was my mentor preparing me for my ministry and witness as the General Secretary of the South African Council of Churches and after. I would not have been what I became without this TEF experience and I thank you for preparing me for that ministry.

How wonderfully you supported us through those dark days. All of you, our friends in the UK, the US, Switzerland, Sweden, Denmark, Norway, Finland, Germany, the Netherlands, New Zealand, Australia, you were fantastic, especially when we were being harassed and investigated by the Eloff Commission. I picked up the phone and called our friends, You. And you came to testify on our behalf. The apartheid government was hoisted with its own petard, far from discrediting us they gave us greater credibility and the world gave us the Nobel Peace Prize in 1984. It was not my prize. It was our prize and you shared in it. Thank you.

I have given this catalogue because it is important to remember we overcame apartheid through the crucial help of the united world church. Apartheid shares the defining characteristic of sin, its divisiveness. Sin in its essence divides, separates, alienates. Adam and Eve hide from God, they were alienated from the rest of creation, and they quarrel and blame each other, and each has become a fragmented personality with a divided heart... *for the good I would do I do not and the evil I would not do, I do.* You, the WCC, demonstrated God's concern for unity, for harmony, for togetherness, for friendship, for peace and you must celebrate that, you must celebrate the success you notched up in defeating apartheid, for you were inspired not by a political ideology but by biblical and theological imperatives.

Apartheid continued so long in part because the church was divided. Some Christians, many Christians, tried to provide scriptural justification for it. See how a divided church has exacerbated the conflict in Northern Ireland.

God intended us to live in harmony with God, with one another, with the rest of God's creation – that is the beginning of the story in the Garden of Eden. God's dream was shattered by sin. The alienation just got worse, reaching a kind of climax in the scattering of the peoples in the story of the Tower of Babel when human community became impossible because humans could no longer communicate in a common language. But God did not wipe the slate clean and say, "Good riddance to bad rubbish".

No, God set in motion the process by which God intended to recover the primordial harmony and unity of all things. This was the God project par excellence, beginning with the call of Abraham and the other patriarchs and matriarchs, continuing with the people of Israel, culminating with the coming of Christ, the Son of God for, as Ephesians declares: "God has made known to us his secret purpose in accordance with the plan which he determined beforehand in Christ to be put into effect when the time was ripe, namely that the universe, everything in heaven and earth, might be brought into unity in Christ", and so, at the birth of the Church of this Christ, there was a reversal of what had happened at the Tower of Babel. There the people were scattered and set apart from one another, here at Pentecost they were drawn together from every nation under heaven. There they could not understand one another, here they could hear the good news each in their own language.

This church was/is the embodiment of this Jesus Christ, described as he who is our peace coming into a polarized and fragmented and stratified world, the one who broke all barriers between peoples, barriers represented by the middle wall of partition in the Jewish temple that had separated the holy people of God from the gentiles. In this Christ all were holy, none were profane, all are now seen to be God's people. Galatians declares categorically: "There is no such thing as Jew or Greek, slave or free, male or female, for all are now one person in Christ Jesus." Ethnic, political, socio-economic, gender barriers have been transcended. Not surprisingly, for this Jesus, speaking of his coming glorification on the cross declares: "I, if I be lifted up, will draw all to me." Not some, all.

I reckon the most revolutionary words Jesus uttered were those he spoke to Mary Magdelene in the Garden: "Go and tell my brothers that I am ascending to my

Father and your Father, to my God and your God." He called these men, such abject cowards, one who had betrayed him, another who denied him not once but three times, and who had all abandoned him. He did not say, "those so-and-sos" but breathtakingly, "My brothers".

Jesus it appears was quite serious when he said that God was our father, that we belonged all to one family, because in this family all, not some, are insiders. No one is an outsider – I, if I be lifted up will draw all – black and white, yellow and red, rich and poor, educated and not educated, beautiful and not so beautiful, Christian, Muslim, Buddhist, Hindu, atheist, all belong, all are held in a divine embrace that will not let us go – all, for God has no enemies, least of all my enemies are not God's enemies. Bush, Bin Laden, all belong, gay, lesbian, so-called straight, all belong and are loved, are precious.

In a family, the ethic of family prevails – from each according to their ability to each according to their need. Dear friends, if we are family, how can we spend such obscene amounts on budgets of death and destruction when we know that a small fraction of these would ensure that God's children everywhere, our sisters and brothers, would have enough food to eat, clear water to drink and would have acceptable and affordable health care, decent homes, a good education?

We will not, we cannot win a war against terror as long as there are conditions of poverty and squalor, ignorance and disease, that make God's children, members of our family, desperate.

You recall that old film, "The Defiant Ones", in which two convicts, one white, one black, escape. They are manacled together. They fall down a ditch with slippery sides. The one struggles up the slope and nearly makes it to the top but he can't get out for he is still manacled to his fellow convict at the bottom, and slithers back. The only way they can make it is together, up, up, up and out.

We too can make it only together – we can be safe only together. We can be prosperous only together. We can survive only together. We can be human only together.

A united church is not an optional extra. A united church is indispensable for the salvation of God's world, when we will see the fulfillment of the vision of St John the Divine:

After that I looked and saw a vast throng, which no one could count, from all races and tribes, nations and languages, standing before the throne and the Lamb. They were robed in white and had palm branches in their hands, and they shouted aloud: "Victory to our God who sits on the throne, and to the Lamb!" And all the angels who stood around the throne and around the elders and the four living creatures prostrated themselves before the throne and worshipped God, crying: "Amen! Praise and glory and wisdom, thanksgiving and honour, power and might, be to our God for ever! Amen." Revelation 7:9-12.

Copyright Desmond Tutu. Used with permission.

Note:
1. Theological Education Fund

Messages and addresses received by the Assembly

Message to the Assembly from Luiz Inácio Lula da Silva
President of the Republic of Brazil

His Holiness Aram I, Moderator of the World Council of Churches,

Mrs Dilma Rousseff, Presidential Chief of Staff,

Mr Miguel Rossetto, Minister for Agricultural Development,

My dear partner Marisa Letícia Lula da Silva,

Rev. Dr Samuel Kobia, General Secretary of the World Council of Churches,

Ministers Adão Pretto, Beto Albuquerque, Henrique Fontana, Marco Maia, Maria do Rosário, Orlando Desconsi, Pastor Reinaldo, Paulo Pimenta, Tarcísco Zimmermann, Professor Joaquim Clotet, Vice-Chancellor of the Pontifical Catholic University of Rio Grande do Sul,

My friends, former ministers in my government, Tarso Genro, Olívio Dutra and Benedita da Silva,

Members of the World Council of Churches,

Participants in the 9th Assembly of the World Council of Churches,

Members of the press,

Friends,

As guests you have probably noticed that democracy is alive and well outside the hall here. For a country that experienced 23 years under an authoritarian regime there is no more pleasurable sound than the sound of people shouting – whether it is for or against does not matter. What matters is that they are shouting.

Brazil is very proud to welcome this 9th Assembly of the WCC which began last Tuesday.

This is an important event and it provides us not only with an excellent opportunity for intense dialogue, but also the opportunity for me to present on behalf of our government a summary of what we have done in these past three years to transform the reality of Brazil.

Much that unites us today in the form of values, principles and effective practical action began in the very difficult times in the past. When we were struggling, for example, some decades ago, for democracy in our country, we found in the World Council of Churches not only moral and spiritual support but also active practical solidarity and support which enabled us to continue confidently in these struggles.

Those were years of hard struggle in defence of freedom and human dignity. There are many examples that I could give to testify to our gratitude towards the Council, but I will limit myself to just one which symbolizes all the others. It was the WCC which welcomed between 1970 and 1980 one of the most respected Brazilians in the field of education world-wide. He had been persecuted and compelled to leave our country, our much missed companion Paulo Freire. Working as a consultant at the headquarters of the WCC in Geneva he was able to develop important projects of education for freedom in Europe, Asia, America, the Pacific, and above all in Portuguese-speaking African countries. The democracy and freedom achieved by the Brazilian people owe much to the participation and solidarity of the churches.

In this Assembly the values which give dignity to human existence continue more vigorously than ever. The commitment of the WCC in the global struggle against hunger and poverty, for example, has immense significance for furthering this cause, in which we Brazilians are very proud to participate.

In 2004 together with my colleagues from France, Chile and Spain, I organized a high level meeting to promote international action against hunger and poverty. Sixty heads of state and heads of government and more than 100 delegations, during the UN General Assembly, gave a positive response to this initiative, which is now also supported by Germany and Algeria, who have joined the initial group. Since then we have proposed innovative mechanisms for international financing of funds to combat hunger and poverty, and we are discussing within the Community of Nations the best way in which to implement them.

We know that firm positions and concrete actions on the part of states are indispensable for us to reach the hoped-for results. But participation by national and international civil society has been and is essential for us to move forward on this path. And I wish to highlight here the important role that the WCC has in combating hunger and poverty throughout the world; this means that we are continuing today as closely as we did in the past, in the quest for social justice, struggling for freedom, democracy and human dignity. All of us here believe that spiritual strength is indispensable in order to foster indefatigable individual and collective militancy, in solidarity, for the common good. Minds, hearts and willing hands that share values of love and respect for others are certainly essential for building a kingdom of justice in this world of inequalities.

My dear friends, these are the values and principles that we have sought to put into practice since our entry into government. And these actions of ours have, thanks to God, contributed in these three years to change, greatly, the lives of millions of Brazilians. All our efforts have been towards promoting development and reducing social inequality in our country.

It is necessary, however, to make clear that many of our government's actions and initiatives have their origin in the mobilization that has taken place in our society, its aims and its demands.

Today, more than 8,700,000 families – 77 percent of the population living beneath the poverty line – receive Family Allowance, the main tool in the Zero Hunger programme, in exchange for keeping their children at school and regularly looking after their health.

With the income from the Family Allowance, around 40 million people, previously almost forgotten by the authorities, are able to have three meals a day and look forward to their future like other people do.

We are combining wide-reaching emergency programmes with structural changes that are increasingly enabling a rise in new opportunities for employment and income-generation for millions of Brazilians.

The government's commitment to promoting agricultural reform, for example, is already showing significant results. In 36 months we have registered 245 thousand families and brought infrastructure and technical assistance to the vast majority of them.

For many of you, it might be difficult to imagine that millions of families in this country still live without access to electricity. In fact, there used to be approximately 12 million, 12 million people in Brazil who did not have access to electricity. But today, fortunately, through the Light for All programme, more than 2,200,000 of those people, mainly in rural areas, including some of the remaining *quilombos*, now

have electricity for the first time in their lives. And by 2008, according to our established timetable, we hope there will be nobody living in Brazil without electricity.

Another example I would like to highlight is being done in conjunction with civil
society in the region of the country that suffers most from drought, the semi-arid
part of north-eastern Brazil. One hundred and thirteen thousand tanks to collect
and store rainwater have been built, enabling families to live with dignity, despite
the age-old problem of drought.

In the field of education, we are making access more democratic, giving opportunities to study to those who have never had them and improving the quality of teaching
in our country. We are also creating effective public policies to reduce racial inequality.

Today, there is an admissions quota policy for federal universities for young people of African or indigenous origin. The quotas are also part of the University for
All, or ProUni, programme, a groundbreaking programme we have created which
has already given 203,000 student grants to low-income students in private higher
education institutions. That number is equal to over one and a half times the number of annual places in public universities in Brazil. Having quality education in
Brazil is no longer a privilege of the few, which is a real revolution for the democra-
tization of education and a future of opportunity.

I would like to tell the participants of this 9th Assembly that the National
Congress of Brazil has recently approved a fundamental law for Brazil, the National
Basic Education Fund, which will enable the Brazilian government, from 2008, to
invest an extra 4,300 million reals in education to take care of children from birth
until secondary school, giving children from poor families an opportunity to have
basic primary education and be as prepared as other sectors of society who can pay
to privately educate their children.

We are raising from eight to nine the number of years of school attendance in basic
education, and the State is taking responsibility for doing three fundamental things
in education. Three fundamental things: first, the process of university reform that
should be passed this year in Brazil, to give autonomy to Brazilian universities.
Second, university expansion. To give you an idea, this government is creating four
new federal universities, we are transforming five universities into new federal universities and we are expanding 32 federal universities – which would normally be in
the capital – into the interior of the country, to give an opportunity for children in
small and medium-sized cities to study without having to go to the capital, often
without any money or anywhere to live.

Even more importantly, in Brazil, the federal government had given up responsibility for technical education. The National Congress had passed a law stipulating that there could only be a new technical college if the city or state took responsibility for running it. We have made the decision, through my colleague Minister Tarso Genro, who is here with us, and his successor Fernando Haddad, for the federal government to take responsibility for technical education in Brazil. This year we are building 32 new technical colleges, of which we will be inaugurating 25 before June.

Obviously one of the achievements we are most proud of, and which shows the social reach of the changes we have made in our country, is the creation of almost four million new jobs with social security workbooks, formal jobs, in only 36 months, not including informal jobs.

In Brazil we are creating the best credit policy for workers in the history of any South American country. Credit with interest at half the normal interest rate, so that workers can pay over 24 or 36 months, out of their salary. This has enabled, in 17 months, 31 billion reals to be put onto the Brazilian market as credit for Brazilian workers. It has also enabled jobs to be created and people's lives to be improved.

This new situation in Brazil has already been reflected in the National Household Sample Survey, done by the Brazilian Institute of Geography and Statistics (IBGE), whose data show that, between 2003 and 2004, three million Brazilians were brought out of a condition of absolute misery, moved above the poverty line and were able to reach a new level of citizenship.

This is an important point. As President of the Republic, over the past 36 months, I have participated in 17 national conferences: on stateless workers, on health, on disability, and to discuss education. Seventeen national conferences in which some of the things we were doing were a result of that participation by the people and that exercise of democracy which, often, is easy to talk about but very difficult to put into practice.

I would like to go beyond publicly recognizing the effective contribution of the World Council of Churches to social action in Brazil. I would like to call on the WCC to continue working with us to build an ever more just and united society.

Friends, in many cases, it is the nationwide and grassroots presence of religious institutions that have enabled the state to provide social security benefits to the population through agreements and partnerships. Both by raising the awareness of the people and through organizing the gathering of data for social purposes, or even through financing government programmes, religious institutions have played an irreplaceable role in this process of transformation in Brazil. And we are confident that this cooperation will become closer and closer.

In the search for a world of peace, Christian ecumenism, as represented by this Council, is an example. I am certain that such ecumenism should continue to be promoted and widened.

Fortunately the Brazilian people in the course of their history have developed a feature of which we are very proud: religious freedom and tolerance, despite the many prejudices that we have inherited from the past. We are a multiracial and multifaith country. Our secular state, through its constitution, guarantees that everyone can follow their own faith, according to their conscience.

A recent example strengthened religious freedom in our country in a practical way. Our new Brazilian Civil Code, as regards the legal status of churches and religious institutions, by clearly defining rights and responsibilities, has simplified the administrative procedures for their establishment. Thus we have guaranteed to all religions, and especially to the many evangelical and Pentecostal denominations, the legal framework within which they can function. In parallel to this, our government has intensified its dialogue with society and produced public education policies in an effort to promote greater healthy mutual respect between all religions as they live alongside one another.

I would like to thank the World Council of Churches for having chosen for its 9th Assembly, Brazil and our beloved city of Porto Alegre – birthplace of the World Social Forum – a city that embodies the ideals and diversity of contemporary civil society.

Here, sharing ideas, taking decisions together, exchanging experiences and strengthening one another spiritually, we are also – and this is what is most important – continuing the sacred task of keeping alive the flame of fraternity and solidarity between all peoples in the world.

Many thanks.

MESSAGES AND ADDRESSES RECEIVED BY THE ASSEMBLY

A LETTER TO THE ASSEMBLY FROM THE US CONFERENCE OF WCC MEMBER CHURCHES

Grace to you and peace from God the Holy Trinity: Father, Son and Holy Spirit. As leaders from the World Council of Churches' member communions in the United States we greet the delegates to the Ninth Assembly with joy and gratitude for your partnership in the gospel in the years since we were last in Harare. During those years you have been constant in your love for us. We remember in particular the ways you embraced us with compassion in the days following the terrorist attacks on September 11, 2001, and in the aftermath of Hurricane Katrina just months ago. Your pastoral words, your gifts, and your prayers sustained us, reminding us that we were not alone but were joined in the Body of Christ to a community of deep encouragement and consolation. Even now you have welcomed us at this Assembly with rich hospitality. Know that we are profoundly grateful.

Yet we acknowledge as well that we are citizens of a nation that has done much in these years to endanger the human family and to abuse the creation. Following the terrorist attacks you sent "living letters" inviting us into a deeper solidarity with those who suffer daily from violence around the world. But our country responded by seeking to reclaim a privileged and secure place in the world, raining down terror on the truly vulnerable among our global neighbours. Our leaders turned a deaf ear to the voices of church leaders throughout our nation and the world, entering into imperial projects that seek to dominate and control for the sake of our own national interests. Nations have been demonized and God has been enlisted in national agendas that are nothing short of idolatrous. We lament with special anguish the war in Iraq, launched in deception and violating global norms of justice and human rights. We mourn all who have died or been injured in this war; we acknowledge with shame abuses carried out in our name; we confess that we have failed to raise a prophetic voice loud enough and persistent enough to deter our leaders from this path of preemptive war. Lord, have mercy.

The rivers, oceans, lakes, rainforests, and wetlands that sustain us, even the air we breathe, continue to be violated, and global warming goes unchecked while we allow God's creation to veer towards destruction. Yet our own country refuses to acknowledge its complicity and rejects multilateral agreements aimed at reversing disastrous trends. We consume without replenishing; we grasp finite resources as if they are private possessions; our uncontrolled appetites devour more and more of the earth's gifts. We confess that we have failed to raise a prophetic voice loud enough and persistent enough to call our nation to global responsibility for the creation, that we ourselves are complicit in a culture of consumption that diminishes the earth. Christ, have mercy.

The vast majority of the peoples of the earth live in crushing poverty. The starvation, the HIV/AIDS pandemic, the treatable diseases that go untreated indict us, revealing the grim features of global economic injustice we have too often failed to acknowledge or confront. Our nation enjoys enormous wealth, yet we cling to our possessions rather than share. We have failed to embody the covenant of life to which our God calls us; hurricane Katrina revealed to the world those left behind in our own nation by the rupture of our social contract. As a nation we have refused to confront the racism that exists in our own communities and the racism that infects our policies around the world. We confess that we have failed to raise a prophetic voice loud enough and persistent enough to call our nation to seek just economic structures so that sharing by all will mean scarcity for none. In the face of the earth's poverty, our wealth condemns us. Lord, have mercy.

Sisters and brothers in the ecumenical community, we come to you in this Assembly grateful for hospitality we don't deserve, for companionship we haven't earned, for an embrace we don't merit. In the hope that is promised in Christ and thankful for people of faith in our own country who have sustained our yearning for peace, we come to you seeking to be partners in the search for unity and justice. From a place seduced by the lure of empire we come to you in penitence, eager for grace, grace sufficient to transform spirits grown weary from the violence, degradation, and poverty our nation has sown, grace sufficient to transform spirits grown heavy with guilt, grace sufficient to transform the world. Lord, have mercy. Christ, have mercy. Lord, have mercy. Amen.

MESSAGES AND ADDRESSES RECEIVED BY THE ASSEMBLY

STATEMENT ON YOUTH CONTRIBUTION

PREPARED BY THE YOUTH CONTRIBUTION COMMITTEE

Extract from the report of the Policy Reference Committee:

"In light of the meeting of the Moderator and the General Secretary with young adult delegates to the Ninth Assembly, and the Statement on Youth Contribution delivered to the Assembly, the Assembly directs the Central Committee to create a representative body of young adults who would coordinate the various roles of young adults connected to the WCC and facilitate communication between them. Such a body would create space for a meaningful participation of young adults in the life and decision-making of the WCC, and would be able to hold the WCC accountable to its goals regarding young adults."

The text presented to the Assembly in relation to the Policy Reference Committee report, outlining the concerns of young people and the proposals to strengthen their participation, follows:

In the spirit of the Ninth Assembly as a "youth assembly", the youth gathered here, through a Committee created with an attempt to be as representative as possible, present the following summary of youth consensus in regard to their contributions to the WCC and the global ecumenical movement.

It is of grave concern to the youth present at this assembly that the WCC may not be able to meet the stated goal of 25 percent youth members on the Central Committee. Hence, we are strongly recommending that member churches of the WCC assume their responsibility in the development and promotion of youth leadership, in this manner, encouraging and supporting youth to form part of the different committees. We are aware of the many difficulties presented by this goal but we are seeking constructive ways to make effective contributions through the building of bridges between the youth concerns and the work of the WCC. We believe that possibilities for youth contribution to all programme areas of the WCC would be furthered by the creation of a structure such as the following:

SPECIAL BODY TO FACILITATE YOUTH CONTRIBUTION TO THE WCC
Purpose
The creation of a permanent body of young people would coordinate the various roles of young people within the WCC and facilitate communication between them. Such a body would **create space** for youth leadership in the WCC as it reconfigures; and would be able to hold the WCC **accountable** to its goals regarding young people. This body should meet prior to every central committee meeting.

Recommended Objectives
1. Promote leadership of young people in the global ecumenical movement.
2. Serve as a consultative body that can give voice to youth concerns.
3. Encourage "**youth mainstreaming**" throughout the life of the WCC.
4. Support and inform the work of the WCC youth desk and central committees.
5. Strengthen youth contributions to all programme areas.
6. Serve as a network between local ecumenical youth and the youth leadership in the WCC.
7. Equip youth leadership with ecumenical formation on topics of general inter est in the ecumenical movement.
8. Facilitate the communication process between the grass-root, national and global levels.
9. Liaison between member churches and the WCC on youth concerns.

Composition
A process would need to be created to determine the size of this body, the appropriate members, and how they would be selected.

Messages and addresses received by the Assembly

Transformation from within

Indigenous voices and the life of the church: a statement to the Ninth Assembly

Indigenous Peoples, men and women, are the voice of the land, the voice of the water, the voice of the air. We are the hope of the future. Indeed our hope is renewed to be meeting in what is now called South America where Indigenous Peoples are reasserting their identity and making their voices heard. We now have members of Indigenous communities taking their seats even as heads of state for the first time since the beginning of colonialism 500 years ago. This gives us cause for celebration.

On the other hand, as caretakers of the earth our mother, we Indigenous Peoples have observed and experienced the degradation of creation. We have experienced the highest levels of environmental racism. Despite pretences, all of humankind lives in absolute reliance upon nature. Because Indigenous communities live in intimate relation with the land and seas, we are the first peoples affected by the destruction of the creation. We know, however, that what happens to the least of these will also affect all.

We, the representatives of Indigenous nations attending the Indigenous Pre-Assembly, have noted that the churches of Brazil, a land with more than 740 thousand Indigenous inhabitants formed into 215 separate Indigenous nations and speaking 180 distinct languages, have no Indigenous delegates to this assembly.

Brazil is not the only country, but it highlights the problem of inclusion of Indigenous Peoples within the churches and the nations of the world. Words have been said but little action has followed.

Transformation is something that Indigenous Peoples are going through every day. We feel it is time for the mainstream to begin to make space in its own structures so as to listen more closely to, and learn from, the voices of Indigenous Peoples.

We applaud the conscientious inclusion of women and youth in the work of the WCC structures. We call for the same intentionality for the inclusion of Indigenous Peoples. Specifically, we call on this Assembly to establish a baseline of Indigenous participation for inclusion on committees as part of the balance in representation and delegations. Therefore we propose that the goal for Indigenous representation be set at 8 percent, in the same way as there are goals for specific percentages of participation for women and youth.

We, the Indigenous Peoples, have fought for many years to have space in the WCC offices in Geneva and now we feel we have been placed to one side. The Indigenous desk was moved to Bolivia in 2003. We are convinced that moving the desk out of Geneva sends the wrong message to already marginalized peoples. More importantly, it significantly cripples the effectiveness of the international coordination of Indigenous work. Decentralization is fine in theory, but we need to have a permanent presence where the decision-making is taking place. Moving the desk back to Geneva would allow for direct input into WCC programmes that affect Indigenous Peoples.

Our rich cultures and our invaluable lands are being slowly eroded by the onslaught of Western mono-culture and by economic globalization through neo-liberalism. Our languages are the key to our understanding of our world and our place in it. They are the vehicle for transmitting our original values and cultures to future generations. However, our languages are quickly disappearing and soon we too may be assimilated unless the current course is dramatically changed.

The churches have historically played a role in the suppression of Indigenous languages. It is time for the churches now to put an equivalent amount of effort into the reclaiming, preserving and enhancing of our languages. Our churches, too, peddle culture in the pretence of being the Word of God. We, as Indigenous Peoples, are fighting to ward off these attacks on our identity, but need the support of our fellow Christian brothers and sisters. Because our languages are disappearing at the rate of one language every two weeks (according to UNESCO) we must act together swiftly to reverse the silencing of our original voices. Churches can play a big role in helping our communities to revitalize our languages, reinvigorate our values and perpetuate our cultures. In support of, and in continuation with, the recent Statement on Human Rights and Languages of Indigenous Peoples from the WCC Central Committee in 2005, we call upon the church to help us effect positive change.

The stealing of our land, as well as the destruction of our homelands and forests, has left us where we are today. The world owes a lot to Indigenous Peoples, as does the church. Increasingly the world is closing its doors to meetings of Indigenous Peoples. Events for Indigenous Peoples to meet locally, regionally, and internationally to celebrate their stories, both negative and especially positive, are becoming fewer. The church can support such gatherings and thus strengthen the Indigenous Peoples' global networking. It could sponsor an international church event or series of gatherings during the next seven years for Indigenous Peoples to celebrate their stories and plan a better tomorrow for our youth and children.

In conclusion, we call on the Assembly and its member churches to:

- place the Indigenous Peoples' programme desk back in Geneva and strengthen the effectiveness of the work of the programme;
- give Indigenous Peoples their rightful place by setting allocated seats for us in the Central Committee and its sub-committees, as well as a minimum of 8 percent representation in delegations to general assemblies;
- promote a United Nations International Year of Indigenous Languages, and a WCC Decade of Indigenous Languages; and
- consider ways in which churches can respond to this world-wide crisis in Indigenous languages by making practical contributions towards saving, promoting and funding Indigenous languages, by calling attention to the critical issue of language loss and loss of identity and working towards remedies both in their local areas and at international levels.

Messages and addresses received by the Assembly

Ecumenical Disability Advocates Network (EDAN) Pre-Assembly Statement

The EDAN network meeting in its first ever pre-assembly convocation of 10th-13th February 2006, Porto Alegre, Brazil, issues this statement:

- Recalling with pride the concern and initial work of the World Council of Churches on disability from as early as 1971;
- Recognizing that different strategies of addressing disability concerns have been used over time in the Council;
- Appreciating the evidence of God's grace in the 8th WCC Assembly when 10 invited advisors with a range of disabilities formed the EDAN network;
- Recording with gratitude the readiness with which WCC leadership adopted the initiative as a viable new approach of working;
- Noting the support that the work of the network has enjoyed from the Council and its various programme teams;
- Recognizing that the church is a constituent part of a world which has set up walls of exclusion;
- Further recognizing that most people with disabilities still find themselves isolated behind walls of shame and fear, walls of ignorance and prejudice, walls of anger, walls of rigid dogma and cultural misunderstanding;
- Appreciating that this situation contradicts the church's calling to be one inclusive body, a model for a transformed world;

• Recognizing that the process of sensitization and conscientization calls EDAN to redouble its efforts to this end:

EDAN reaffirms its commitment to advocate for the inclusion, participation and active involvement of persons with disabilities in all the spiritual, social, development and structural life of the church and society;

And further commits itself to continue building networks in all the WCC regions in consultation with churches, national and regional ecumenical partners, governments and other organizations interested in the promotion of the disability issues;

EDAN impresses upon its constituents that persons with disabilities share the responsibility to be agents of change, acknowledging the strength from the grace of God.

EDAN calls upon the 9th WCC Assembly meeting at Porto Alegre in 2006 to:

1) Reaffirm its commitment to disability issues and to ensure that in its agenda and mission, disability issues are treated as a cross-cutting concern in all WCC programmes.

2) Urge its constituent member churches to recognize that responding to and fully including people with disabilities is not an option for the churches of Christ. It is the church's defining characteristic.

3) And further urge them to "widen their tents" to provide space for all, ensuring that persons with disabilities are included not just as passive observers.

4) Use its influence to challenge governments, bilateral and multilateral world structures on the need for enabling legislations and policies, inclusive programmes and services, and the recognition of marginalization of persons with disabilities as an issue of human rights and justice.

For all these concerns, EDAN prays with the Assembly "God, in your grace, transform the world" so that it can be a better place for all.

Messages and addresses received by the Assembly

Message to the Assembly from HRH Prince El Hassan bin Talal of Jordan

moderator of the World Conference of Religions for Peace

Reverend Dr Samuel Kobia, honourable delegates, ladies and gentlemen,

It is appropriate that I deliver my message of peace from Mount Nebo. In the Church of St Georges at Khirbat al-Mukhayyat on Mount Nebo, an inscription with the first evidence of Arabic script in the mosaics of Jordan was found with the same message: *bisalameh* meaning "in peace". I had the privilege of accompanying his holiness Pope John Paul on his visit to the Holy Land, to this very site.

I thank you for inviting me to address this Ninth Assembly of the World Council of Churches. I regret that I cannot be with you in person. Sadly I had already accepted an invitation to be in Brazil in the second half of March to deliver the 2006 Aula Magna at the Candido Mendes University in Rio de Janeiro. However, in my capacity as the moderator of the World Conference of Religions for Peace, I would like to pay my respects to you, the servants of your respective communities and to say, as a servant of the servants, that to participate in a special forum dedicated to reconciliation and understanding and indeed good governance of our shared resources – human, spiritual, aesthetic – is an extremely important recognition of shared universal consciousness and shared humanitarian values.

No doubt the term "ecumenical" will be used numerous times over the course of the next few days. It is my humble opinion that it is a word that should be used in two senses; there should not only be a concern for promoting the unity of church-es, but also the unity of religions, and indeed in that context, the unity of values.

In an address at Lambeth Palace some years ago, I had the opportunity, under the rubric of "Face to Face to meet and to greet", to remind the participants that Muslims and Christians believe in God, who created the world to whom they owe their lives. Muslims, Christians and Jews believe in one God. The ethical and moral codes of our faiths centre on justice, equality, freedom, charity and faith in God. We believe, as in the monotheistic faiths, that the "other" represents the core problem between our respective faiths: "problem" in the sense of challenge; how do we comprehend each other? How do we develop understanding? The religious groupings tend not to ask themselves why it is that the "other" thinks of us the way that he or she does.

I would like to quote from Abdullah Al-Mamun Al-Suhrawardi's compilation of the sayings of the Prophet Muhammad. The Suhrawardi Sufi lineage is that of my wife who was born in Calcutta and having just come from India myself, I would like to start by quoting the preface by Mahatma Gandhi. As you will see ladies and gen-tlemen, pluralism for my family is not a theoretical or academic exercise, but reali-ty; we do believe in and respect and love the "other". Gandhi says, "I am a believer in all the great religions of the world. There will be no lasting peace in the world unless we learn not merely to tolerate, but to respect, the other faiths as our own. A reverence of the different sayings of the teachers of mankind is a step in the right direction of such mutual respect."

On the subject of neighbourliness, I would like to say that in this troubled world of misunderstanding of the "other" and the rise of what I call the hatred industry, it is worth remembering the sayings of the Prophet and I quote, "Do you love your creator? Love your fellow beings first. The best person in God's sight is the best among his friends and the best of neighbours near God is the best person in his own neighbourhood."

In developing a Code of Conduct for understanding between faiths, over 25 years of promoting the noble art of conversation, I would like to make the following sug-gestions: the need to emphasize the association between theology and practicality, to begin with our commonalities, to take into account the Enlightenment tradition, to embrace the principle of "no coercion", but most of all to uphold the right to pro-claim one's own religion. Of course in terms of youth, I would like to address the importance of reconsidering the content of education, of ensuring a free flow of information, of being courageous in looking afresh at firstly our own, and secondly each other's texts, heritage, and history. Can we ladies and gentlemen, distinguished delegates, develop a framework, a civilized framework for disagreement? Can we accept that certitude divides, that diversity unifies, that accepting responsibility for words and actions at all levels is the template by which we celebrate and promote the respect for the other? Can we recognize the political and economic dimensions of interfaith dialogue?

I recall working with Cardinal Evaristo Arentz of Sao Paulo on the subject of street children, and I think that issues relating to the dispossessed and the poor of the world are issues that need to be discussed, placing emphasis on *anthropolicy*, on policies where people are at the centre of our thoughts and our deeds.

In referring to the work of the World Council of Churches, I would pay tribute to Christian teaching. "Peace is a divine and incomprehensible gift that touches the soul, heart and mind of the individual believer. Once it reigns in the heart, it changes human behaviour, ultimately eliminating greed and selfishness." Yet I would like to point out in legal terms that though we have a law of war, we have not yet developed a law of peace. I have called, along with 26 nations, starting in 1988, in the General Assembly of the United Nations, for a Humanitarian Order. I am delighted that the Committee of the Red Cross has produced customary, international humanitarian law, possibly a building block towards a law of peace. But I would like to suggest that today we are not interested in: "What causes wars, and what causes fighting among you?" and I am quoting from the Bible of King James, "Is it not your passions…? You desire and do not have; so you kill."

I hope that this Assembly can address issues of haves and have-nots, can legitimate the aspirations of human beings within the context of a code of ethics and a code of conduct. I would like to suggest that working for a law of peace is more admirable than continuing to work against the aberrations and the ugliness that exist in the context of racial discrimination, xenophobia, "Semiticophobia", Islamophobia – issues that we have discussed in the context of several international meetings. Yet today polarities between monopolizers of the truth, privatizers of religion, privatizers of war, seem to distance us from one of the main messages of Christianity, and indeed of the community of faiths.

The message that peaceful coexistence among peoples should be paramount is made clear in several references in the gospel of Matthew, presented as the actual words of God in the person of Jesus Christ. During the Sermon on the Mount, Jesus instructed his followers with words such as these: "Blessed are the meek for they shall inherit the earth." I come to the conclusion, working as I do with commissions on governance and recommendations made to the United Nations for refocusing the mission of multilateralism, of us all, of humanity, that issues such as 600 million children below the poverty line in the context of West and South Asia alone are not given adequate attention. Our West Asian region requires over 35 million job opportunities in the next 10 years. Not providing these opportunities is handing the meek, if I may say so, to the machinations and the manipulations of extremist organizations that recognize in populace terms the importance of the disenfranchised, that recognize that the disenfranchised can be recruited by heightening their awareness of the negative conditions of their lives to a point of militancy and violence. And I would like to suggest that the time has come for the silenced majority to be motivated in the context of promoting the public good, regional commons and global commons. The importance of peace for the individual is emphasized in the Torah for example. Psalm 34 advises that the way to a long life and happiness is to "Strive for peace with all your heart." I would also add that in terms of the Noachide Laws, the importance for society of peace prevailing is implicit. These laws include prohibitions against theft and murder, and the exhortation to "set up courts and bring offenders to justice".

I would like to draw your attention to the times we live in, times of crisis. In times of crisis, as in war, the Torah urges leaders to act mercifully and to make a final effort to avoid conflict: "When approaching a town to attack it, first offer them peace".

Where does this place our call for a Law of Peace? Where does it place the Swedish proposal for fundamental rights of humanity? The Canadian and Norwegian proposals for Human Security? Our call, in the context of the Commission for Human Rights, for a Racial Equality Index?

Sometimes I must confess my frustration at feeling that one can speak of a world order in terms of technology, in terms of investment, in terms of security, but where is soft and human security in this scheme of things?

One of my most recent efforts in trying to communicate what I believe to be the true message of Islam is a conversation with a Jewish Italian friend, Alain Elkann. We produced together a book *To Be A Muslim*. He has had similar conversations with Rabbi Rene Sirat and with representatives of the Holy See. I am aware of similar conversations between Buddhists and Hindus. And I wonder whether a round table conversation could not be held to emphasize once again the importance of producing an analytical concordance of human values that we share to develop a partnership in our common humanity!

Islam places a high value on social harmony; even its name, which signifies submission to the will of God, is derived from the Arabic word for "peace", *salaam.* When Muslims meet, they greet each other with the words *salaam 'alaykum*, "peace be upon you". The God of Islam is *rabb al-'alamin*, the "God of the worlds", and not only the God of the Muslims. The home of peace to which we aspire is referred to in the Qur'an when we speak of the hereafter in verse 10: "And the angels shall enter unto them from every gate [saying]: "Peace be unto you for that you have persevered in patience! Excellent indeed is the final home!"

Thus the element of enduring harmony, the element of patience in the face of adversity is so important if we are to speak of revisiting a code of conduct and a code of behaviour based on our shared morality.

We Muslims regard Abraham as the father of the believers and the first Muslim. We regard the call of the Abrahamic code as a call for harmony between the monotheistic faiths. But Muslims who abhor controversy and confrontation have, unfortunately, been forced into a situation of confrontation over issues of today's wealth, questions of oil and energy, questions of real estate. You recall that the Versailles Conference at the end of World War I was a conference that repartitioned our world. World War II ended with Yalta and the creation of the United Nations and the creation of the Bretton Woods institutions.

Is it not time that we consider that what has often been referred to as the "Cold War" is not a cold war at all, but a proxy war? Is it not time that multilateralism was ethically revived by a new conference which brings a greater alliance between academics, between men of faith, between men and women who are prepared to put their actions where their words are in calling for a new, multinational peace corps?

I would like to see a new international initiative that emphasizes the importance of calling for a law of peace, a charter which can promulgate minority rights, emphasize the rights of protected peoples within complex religions and within cultural autonomies. I would like to see an approach which, in short, brings this troubled region a step further away from the impending Balkanization, ethnic and sectarian in-fighting, and rather offers a concept of humanitarian pluralism.

So I ask you, is the essence of our beliefs not the same? To draw once more from the Bible, is it not time that we overcome our own story of Babel to create a new, common language that includes *salaam, shalom,* and *peace?* We have 167 satellite frequencies in our part of the world that seem to me to be producing "info-tain-ment" and "info-terror", but where is the "info-humanity"?

We shall be hosting in Jordan the World Congress of Middle East Studies in June of this year. I hope that it will not only be a gathering of scholars congratulating each other on their respective scholarship, but also a meeting where natural alliances develop between scholarship, the media, civil society and governments. We need those script writers to address the subject of harmony yesterday.

I thank Professor Khalidi from Jerusalem for his study *The Muslim Jesus* which traces an intense reverence and devotion and love for Jesus that has characterized Islamic thought for more than a thousand years. I would like to emphasize to you the importance of the "encuentro" between the Mediterra, the Mediterranean, the Terra Media, the Iberian Peninsula and Latin America. I think that this encounter which I hope to address in a production on television in the near future in the con-text of paying tribute to my monodies, to Ibn Khaldun, to Avi Rose and Avi Cenna, can bring together our shared cultural roots and perceptions.

Despite our ever-increasing inter-connectedness, communities around the globe remain ill-informed about each other. As I see it, a clear knowledge of the other is essential; trust and mutual security can only be built on a clearly non-violent moral-ity combined with a personal certainty that basic agreements are shared with one another.

Dialogue between adherents of the faiths must involve engagement at the level of people; and the role of dialogue and conversation in peace-making within and between countries and communities is not really about religions talking to one another, it is about the adherents of religions, the 3,000 people involved in this con-ference, for example, talking to one another. I think you will agree that discussion at this level will breed the kind of understanding necessary to affect the attitudes of generations to come.

I would like to thank you for giving me this opportunity to suggest a few practi-cal thoughts, I hope, in the direction of a partnership in our common humanity. We need to act yesterday if our silent, or silenced majority, is to express its voice in mak-ing the 21st century a century of peace for all peoples.

Thank you ladies and gentlemen.

MESSAGES AND ADDRESSES RECEIVED BY THE ASSEMBLY

MESSAGE TO THE ASSEMBLY FROM AHMAD HASYIM MUZADI

GENERAL CHAIRMAN OF THE NAHDLATUL ULAMA BOARD OF DIRECTORS (PBNU) AND MUSLIM GUEST AT THE ASSEMBLY

As a part of the Indonesian delegation, as the General Chairman of the Nahdlatul Ulama Board of Directors, I have come to this honourable WCC Ninth Assembly bringing a message of peace and friendship to all the religious communities of the world, particularly to all the Christians who are gathered here. Islam is a religion of peace because the word Islam itself means peace. Hence, we proclaim that there is no violence, cruelty, chaos and viciousness on behalf of religion, including Islam.

We have to fight together to cleanse religion from all inappropriateness that can cause the world to suffer, including violence and terror, which are issues that can make the people in the world live in suffering.

Violence, extremes and new terrorism have universally spread within the past six to seven years. If religion becomes the basis of violence and terrorism, then this should have occurred centuries ago. Why is it occurring now when it had not done so in the past? Indeed there must be some non-religious causes behind all this that have influenced religious communities and been included in their religion.

There are several factors that must be considered in order to analyze the sources of violence and conflicts within the communities, among others:

1. Exclusivism and extreme factors

In all religious communities, there are often small groups of followers who are very secluded and unwilling to adapt to their environment. This can create exclusiveness and extremes that are susceptible to conflicts in the community. In fact, religion should be universal and must relate to the local cultures and traditions; it must adapt and acculturate as long as it does not violate the religious norms. Therefore there should be inter-religious, traditional and cultural synergy. If there is no synergy in that relationship then it can create sources of internal as well as external religious conflicts.

2. Religious misunderstandings

The factor of religious misunderstanding can also lead to the emergence of religious conflicts; by delivering it to the community in the wrong way, it can create social barriers which can actually be avoided by giving a clear understanding of religion and its application in the community.

3. Poverty and ignorance in the community

In a community of poverty and ignorance, it is generally easier to be involved in the use of violence, irrespective of their religious beliefs.

4. The Inter-religious communication factor

Inter-religious communication should be proportionally and democratically placed. Differences have existed ever since the creation of man. In our religion (Islam) it is prohibited to force someone to convert to Islam; if done by force then it is not genuine. Therefore conversion is not merely a will but also it is through a calling process that comes from a sincere desire to follow Islam. From one religion to another there are similarities and differences. All religions believe in God, but who their God is, is what makes the difference. Every religion has its own ritual practices towards God, practised in different forms and order. Each religion wishes for a peaceful and united community with dignity, but how we achieve this is done using various strategies. In terms of humanity, all religions favour justice, honesty, cooperation, etc. Therefore, the differences should not be equalized, whereas the similarities should not be differentiated.

5. Relations between religion and state

The relationship between religion and state should be placed so as to complement each other and so that there are no clashes between state power and religious values. In countries that are historically and factually mono-religious (with only one religion), there is the possibility of formulating religion into the governance. But in a pluralistic country, what is absorbed into the governance and system of the state should simply be the religious values formulated democratically. Since the true values of one religion become a point of encounter with the true values of other religions, it should be formulated differently. If those true values are adequately packaged, then the state should be able to protect all the religions, as the true values become the moral basis of the country.

The positive norms of a religion are practised by its followers with sufficient tolerance towards others and within the framework of a civil society and not a nation-state. This framework is implemented in Indonesia, so that Indonesia, where the majority of the population is Muslim, is based on the ideology of Pancasila (the five principles). The enforcement of religious formulation into the state of a pluralistic community can indeed induce constraints and conflicts.

377

6. Political, economic and sovereign injustice

Conflicts between nations that trigger attacks towards other nations would surely face resistance from those countries. If a citizen is a follower of a certain religion, it is likely that he will use his religious symbols to resist, although such attacks are not necessarily religiously motivated; quite possibly they are politically, economically or even hegemonically motivated. In this regard, religion is involved not due to the religious factor itself, but more due to issues of injustice and sovereignty.

Relating to the factors mentioned above, I feel that there are several things that can be initiated by religious communities, individually or in collaboration, as follows:

1. Clarification and enlightenment of misunderstandings and misusing of religion.
2. Convincing the small exclusive groups to be more open to interact with other traditions and environments.
3. A need for more intensive efforts to systematically eradicate poverty and increase the equality and quality of education, including the need to provide a cross subsidy between wealthy countries and poor countries.
4. A need to increase the intensity of communication and strengthen unity among religious communities in order to avoid inter-religious conflicts, so that there

will be more awareness towards issues that are non-religious that can become an excess to a religion or can be made a part of a religion.

5. Together there is a need to create a government that can protect all religions.

6. Together the elite religious communities need to initiate serious constructive steps to prevent possibilities of invasion of one country by another.

7. To eliminate an attitude and awareness leading towards islamophobia so that non-Muslims can see and understand the problems related to the Muslim communities more clearly and far from disadvantaging prejudices.

8. To avoid all forms of provocation, particularly those of religious disrespect, such as the case of disrespect of the Al-Quran in Guantanamo and the caricature of the Prophet Mohamed in Denmark recently, for these will only trigger extremism and radicalism on the part of extreme Islamic groups.

9. Issues on Papua.

MESSAGES AND ADDRESSES RECEIVED BY THE ASSEMBLY

MESSAGE TO THE ASSEMBLY FROM ANANTANAND RAMBACHAN

PROFESSOR OF RELIGION AT SAINT OLAF COLLEGE, MINNESOTA, USA

On behalf of the guests of other faiths, I want to express our heartfelt joy and gratitude for the honour of being with you and participating in this important event in the life of the World Council of Churches. Your choice, once again, to have people with different religious commitments and worldviews listening and contributing to your deliberations, is a strong testimony of your value for the multi-religious character of our world, our interrelated lives and our need for each other. Our traditions speak not only of individual human destiny and fulfillment but, even more importantly, proclaim a joyful vision of existence that is characterized by love, justice, peace, prosperity and freedom from violence and oppression. Any religion that dedicates itself to the pursuit of this vision must reach across boundaries and join hands with people of other faiths in confronting and overcoming the causes of human suffering. This is a necessary, though not easy task, requiring humility, wisdom and patient love. We do not have a choice between acting separately and acting together. Our hopes for just and peaceful communities will be realized together or not at all. Your invitation and our response unite us in this understanding.

Our need for each other is today nowhere more evident than in the challenge of overcoming violence. In paradoxically contrasting ways, violence unites our traditions. It unites us in condemnation and responsibility for the fact that, at one time or another, in one place or another, our traditions have legitimized violence through active support or silence and indifference. Those of us who are often quick to claim exemption from complicity with violence narrowly identify violence with warfare. We ignore the violence that is structurally embedded in our communities by the unjust ordering of our economic and political life and by oppression on the basis of race, gender, caste, ethnicity and social status. For centuries of religiously sanctioned dehumanization and oppression of the Dalits, we Hindus must own responsibility and work towards its overcoming. We must begin with a critical examination of the assumptions of our tradition that make this caste-based discrimination and violence against the Dalits possible.

If violence unites us in responsibility and guilt, it also unites us in the conviction that our traditions are not defined by the way of violence, but by a shared hope for and commitment to peace, justice and compassion. It is these non-negotiable values that define the essence of our traditions and that we must actualize through inter-religious cooperation. Our traditions are rich in teachings and examples for this task. Ahimsa or non-violence is the supreme ethical expression of Hindu religious insight, but must today be enlarged in interpretation and application to overcome violence in all of its diverse forms. Interior peace must not detach us from the world, but liberate us to commit ourselves to the actualization of peace in our communities.

As a Hindu pilgrim who, for twenty-five years, has been travelling the inter-religious path of challenge and enrichment with precious friends from the World Council of Churches, especially through its pioneering programme on inter-religious relations and dialogue, I find the inspiration for my small steps in the nature of God who my tradition asks me to recognize and embrace in every face. The love of God is inseparable from the love of every being and this love is meaningfully expressed only through relationships that affirm the equal worth and dignity of all. It is this love that energizes us for the work of transforming our world.

The transformation of our world through justice and peace will be the fruit of a divine-human partnership, beautifully described in a couplet from the Ramayana, one of Hinduism's favourite sacred texts.

> *Rama sindhu ghana sajjana dhira*
> *Chandana taru hari santa samira*
> *God is the ocean; God's servants are the rain-clouds*
> *God is the sandal tree; God's servants are the winds*

380

The ocean is the source of all life-giving water, but it is the clouds that transform the earth by bringing water to our fields, rivers and lakes. The fragrance of the sandal tree is beautiful, but the wind is required to convey and spread it everywhere. In a similar way, the grace of God transforms our world only when it finds expression in lives of loving compassion.

Today, our human partnership with God cannot be limited to any one religious community. Our ability to make manifest the reality of God in our world requires us to learn about and from each other. It demands that we labour together inter-religiously so that our world reflects the nourishing and fragrant beauty of God.

MESSAGES AND ADDRESSES RECEIVED BY THE ASSEMBLY

MESSAGE TO THE ASSEMBLY FROM DEBORAH WEISSMAN

A JEWISH GUEST AT THE ASSEMBLY

Shalom from Jerusalem.

It is indeed an honour for me to be greeting this most impressive assemblage, as a Jew and as an Israeli. I have the privilege of serving on the Executive of the Inter-religious Coordinating Council in Israel, which is also the Israeli chapter of the World Conference of Religions for Peace.

I have attended many other WCC functions over the past 18 years, but this is the largest, most diverse and exciting.

What a thrill and a privilege to be living in a time when people of many different traditions can work together as partners in the quest for peace, justice, human rights, an end to racism and oppression. I am grateful to the WCC for having given me this opportunity to be part of your deliberations. Very soon, I will have to leave the conference for a day, in order to be able to celebrate the Sabbath, the *Shabbat*, with the local Jewish community. Coincidentally, tomorrow's weekly Torah Portion is "*Yitro*", or "Jethro", from the Book of Exodus, chapters 18 through 20. Jethro, Moses' father-in-law and intimate advisor, was a Midianite priest. This kind of ancient interfaith cooperation was foreshadowed earlier in Exodus by the life-saving deeds of the midwives and Pharaoh's daughter.

Unfortunately, because I will not be here tomorrow, I will not be able to participate in the very important session on "Overcoming Violence". This is a crucial challenge for all of us but particularly for my region of the world, the troubled and volatile Middle East. The common wisdom is that religion is a factor that fans the flames of hatred and violence. But for many of us, religion can also be a positive factor, promoting peaceful dialogue. As we have seen in the WCC's interfaith initiative called "Thinking Together", under the leadership of Hans Ucko, our religious cultures may indeed contain potentially problematic texts and traditions, but they also contain tools for alternative interpretations of those texts, as well as spiritual and cultural resources for developing a more positive approach to the Other. For example, we in the Inter-religious Coordinating Council in Israel have, for the past three years, sponsored a dialogue among rabbis, imams and priests called *Kedem*, a Hebrew acronym for "Voices of Religious Reconciliation". Those voices sometimes seem to be drowned out by the extremists in all of our communities, but they do exist and must be supported and strengthened.

You have, in the theme chosen for your assembly, called upon God, in His grace, to transform the world. I would like to conclude with a Jewish contribution to this discussion. When human beings discover cures for diseases, develop medicine, science, technology, preserve our environment, we are partners with God in Creation. When we study and interpret sacred texts, write new commentaries, apply the insights of those texts to changing situations, we are partners with God in Revelation. And when we engage in *Tikkun Olam*, literally "mending" or "fixing" or perhaps transforming the world, through our striving for peace, justice, human life and dignity, we are partners with God in Redemption. For Jews, the opportunity for contemplating these challenges, resolving to undertake them and anticipating what a transformed world might be like, is the Sabbath. I will leave you with the traditional Jewish greeting of Sabbath peace, "*Shabbat Shalom*".

Messages and addresses received by the Assembly

Message to the Assembly from Katsunori Yamanoi

Chairman of the Board of Directors of Rissho Kosei-kai and Buddhist guest at the Assembly

Greetings everyone, my name is Katsunori Yamanoi and I am the Chairman of the Board of Directors of Rissho Kosei-kai. On behalf of Rissho Kosei-kai, I would like to express my profound gratitude for this opportunity to participate in the Ninth WCC Assembly. I would also like to express my deep respect for the WCC, which has made a great contribution to harmony among different churches and inter-religious dialogue for more than half a century.

Rissho Kosei-kai has sent representatives to every WCC Assembly since the Sixth Assembly was convened in Vancouver, Canada. And since 1985, Rissho Kosei-kai has continued dialogue with the WCC through its liaison office in Geneva, Switzerland. Rissho Kosei-kai is also the parent organization of the Niwano Peace Foundation, which in 1986 awarded the Fourth Niwano Peace Prize to Dr Philip A. Potter, the former WCC General Secretary. Long before then, in 1969, Nikkyo Niwano, founder of Rissho Kosei-kai, met with then WCC General Secretary Eugene Carson Blake at WCC headquarters in Switzerland. Their exchange of ideas formed a bond transcending their differences of faith.

Rissho Kosei-kai is a lay Buddhist organization aiming to live life according to the True Dharma revealed by Shakyamuni. We continue to grow spiritually confirming and reconfirming the essence of what Shakyamuni wanted to convey to us.

This year, Rissho Kosei-kai will reach a turning point as we observe the 100th anniversary of the birth of Founder Nikkyo Niwano. In life, Founder Niwano's goal was the realization of peace through inter-religious dialogue and cooperation, and so he worked tirelessly to establish and develop WCRP, the World Conference of Religions for Peace. The basis of his work was the "One Vehicle" spirit, that is: "Since by nature all human beings are riding together on the same vehicle, we should be broad-minded, respect one another, and cooperate with each other." Today, as I participate in this Ninth Assembly, I once again realize that the world all of you in the WCC are striving towards is the same for me as a Buddhist.

The WCC has proclaimed the first decade of the twenty-first century to be "The Decade to Overcome Violence". Truly, this is a timely appeal. At present, war and acts of terrorism continue unabated in our world. People's hearts are swelling with suspicion, antagonism, and misunderstanding. We religious people cannot afford to overlook this.

Shakyamuni showed us the True Way when he said, "Truly, malice cannot be extinguished with malice. Only through compassion can it be extinguished." And Dr Martin Luther King said that, "Returning violence with violence increases violence, and only makes a dark, starless night that much darker. Darkness cannot be chased away with darkness. Only light can do that. Hatred is not dispelled by hatred. Only love can do that." Compassion and love are all we can rely upon to overcome violence.

I understand that the world of compassion, the world of love for which we strive, cannot be realized in a day and a night. Nevertheless, I believe that if religious leaders can have sincere dialogue and cooperate with each other, then step by step society, and the world, will have peace. This belief is etched in my heart, and my hope is that from now on, I will strive in that direction, hand in hand with all the members of the WCC.

By the way, in August of this year, the Eighth Assembly of WCRP will be convened in Kyoto, Japan. The host of this Assembly is Nichiko Niwano, President of Rissho Kosei-kai. This will be WCRP's first Assembly of the twenty-first century, and I sincerely hope, from the bottom of my heart, that many members of the WCC will be able to cooperate with and participate in the Assembly so that it will be even more productive.

I would like to conclude my address today with my earnest prayer that the results of this Ninth WCC Assembly will become a chapter of brightly shining hope in world history and be an inspiration showing humanity how to live.

Thank you very much.

MESSAGES AND ADDRESSES RECEIVED BY THE ASSEMBLY

MESSAGE TO THE ASSEMBLY FROM A BRAZILIAN INTER-RELIGIOUS GROUP

PRESENTED BY JORGE DELLAMORA MELLO

Dear brothers and sisters, members from different Christian confessions gathered together at the 9th WCC Assembly,

Belonging to different religions, faith traditions and inter-religious initiatives, we express our joy in congregating with brothers and sisters from the WCC and its Christian denominations, in a spirit of faith, love and hope, as experienced in the multiple forms it has taken throughout the history of humanity. Our voices will join together in a plural and united hymn of thanksgiving to the God of all names, times and places, for this great moment of meeting and fraternity.

We rejoice with all our hearts at the openness revealed by the WCC regarding the importance of inter-religious dialogue, in particular at this time in human history full of conflicts and challenges. We respond to this reality with all our faith and hope. Fully aware of our limits, we are comforted by the certainty that history is the only thing preventing true dialogue from overcoming the distances that have grown between us. We wish to be part of the spirit and fraternity which is so vigorously manifested by the participants of this Assembly.

We live in a part of the world which has a history of suffering and intolerance against non-Christian religious expressions. The colonization of our continent was disrespectful of other traditions, in particular those of Africans and indigenous peoples. Today, the context is changing through the search for dialogue, reciprocal forgiveness and the hope that all forms of intolerance will be overcome. There are signs encouraging us to strive for a culture of peace, in obedience to the God in all His forms, who desires dignity for all, especially in this continent with such a diversity of beautiful faces!

We must jointly ask for forgiveness for the harm caused to so many people throughout the world, victims of the religious intolerance and the quest for power for pseudo-religious reasons. With humble hearts we need to build genuine reconciliation, taking as a reference our multiform God, whom we must serve with all our hearts. On behalf of our creeds we are ready to dialogue and to build the bridges that are necessary to confront the great problems that afflict humankind. Peace and justice need to leave the world of ideas and become reality in our lives!

We hope that the WCC Assembly will become a moment of inspiration and renewal of the commitment to a humanity which is closer to the Creator of all beings.

APPENDICES

APPENDIX I
ASSEMBLY TIMETABLE

God, in Your Grace, Transform...

Time	the World		the Earth	our Societies	our Lives	our Churches				our Witness	
	Tuesday 14 February	Wednesday 15 February	Thursday 16 February	Friday 17 February	Saturday 18 February	Sunday 19 February	Monday 20 February	Tuesday 21 February	Wednesday 22 February	Thursday 23 February	
08:30 / 09:00		Prayer	Prayer	Prayer	Prayer	WORSHIP with Host Churches	Prayer	Prayer	Prayer	Prayer	
09:15 / 10:30	Orientation Plenary	Bible Study	Bible Study	Bible Study	Bible Study		Bible Study	Bible Study	Bible Study	Decision Plenary Reports	
10:30	Break	Break	Break	Break	Break		Break	Break	Break	Break	
11:00 / 12:30	From Harare to Porto Alegre	Business: Constitution Procedures Committees	Ecumenical Conversations	Ecumenical Conversations	Ecumenical Conversations		Plenary: Church Unity	Plenary: God, in Your Grace	Decision Plenary Reports	Decision Plenary Reports	
12:30 / 15:00	Lunch daily between 12:00 and 15:00			Mutirão and Committee Meetings							
15:00 / 16:30	Opening Plenary	Plenary: Moderator's Report	Plenary: Economic Justice	Plenary: Christian Identity & Religious Plurality	Plenary: Overcoming Violence	Plenary: Latin America (16:30)	Decision Plenary Elections	Decision Plenary Reports	Decision Plenary Reports	Decision Plenary Reports	
16:30	Break	Break	Break	Break	Break		Break	Break	Break	Break	
17:00 / 18:15	Opening Prayers (18:00)	Plenary: General Secretary's Report	Business: Constitution Membership Nominations	Regional Meetings	Confessional Meetings	Dinner and Celebration with Latin American Churches	Decision Plenary Reports	Decision Plenary Reports	Decision Plenary Reports	Closing Prayers	
18:45 / 19:15		Prayer	Prayer	Prayer	Prayer		Prayer	Prayer	Prayer	Central Committee Meeting	
19:30		Dinner	Dinner	Dinner	Dinner		Dinner	Dinner	Dinner	Dinner	

APPENDIX II
ASSEMBLY DELEGATES AND PARTICIPANTS

DELEGATES OF MEMBER CHURCHES

Aasa-Marklund, Ms Inger, fl, Svenska Kyrkan (Sweden)

Abd Alahad, Archbishop Matti Youssef, mo, Syrian Orthodox Patriarchate of Antioch and All the East (Argentina)

Abeng, Mrs Justina Yuo Dze, fl, Presbyterian Church in Cameroon (Cameroon)

Abu El-Assal, Bishop Riah, mo, Episcopal Church in Jerusalem and the Middle East (Palestine/Israel)

Aboagye-Mensah, Most Rev. Robert, mo, Methodist Church Ghana (Ghana)

Abounu, Mrs Mary, fl, Methodist Church Nigeria (Nigeria)

Abraham, Mr Varkey, ml, Mar Thoma Syrian Church of Malabar (United States of America)

Abrahams, Bishop Ivan Manuel, mo, Methodist Church of Southern Africa (South Africa)

Abramides, Lic. Elias Crisostomo, ml, Ecumenical Patriarchate of Constantinople (Argentina)

Abramov, Rev. Alexander, mo, Russian Orthodox Church (United States of America)

Abuom, Dr Agnes, fl, Anglican Church of Kenya (Kenya)

Adadikam, Rev. Matheus, mo, Gereja Kristen Injili Di Tanah Papua (GKITP) (Indonesia)

Adinyira, Justice Sophia O.A., fl, Church of the Province of West Africa (Ghana)

Adriano Francisco, Mrs Esperança, fl, Missao Evangélica Pentecostal Angola (Angola)

Aisi-Eliesa (Malangton), Ms Martha, fl, Evangelical Lutheran Church of Papua New Guinea (Papua New Guinea)

391

Aitlahti, Rev. Kaisa Karina, yfo, Evangelical Lutheran Church of Finland (Finland)

Akamisoko, Venerable Duke, mo, Church of Nigeria (Anglican Communion) (Nigeria)

Akinola, Mr Olusegun Emmanuel, yml, Church of Nigeria (Anglican Communion) (Nigeria)

Aleksanyan, Miss Gayane, yfl, Armenian Apostolic Church (Holy See of Etchmiadzin) (Armenia)

Alemezian, Bishop Nareg, mo, Armenian Apostolic Church (Holy See of Cilicia) (Lebanon)

Alexander, Rev. James Lagos, mo, Africa Inland Church Sudan (Sudan)

Alfeev, Bishop Dr Hilarion, mo, Russian Orthodox Church (Austria)

Altmann, Rev. Dr Walter, mo, Igreja Evangélica de Confissão Luterana no Brasil (Brazil)

Amanho épouse Daipo, Mme Djoman Odetté, fl, Eglise Harriste (Côte d'Ivoire)

Ambrosius of Helsinki, H.E. Metropolitan, mo, Suomen ortodoksinen Kirkko (Finland)

Anderson, Mr Derek, yml, African Methodist Episcopal Church (United States of America)

Aneyé, Mme Jeannette Akissi, fl, Eglise protestante méthodiste Unie de Côte d'Ivoire (Côte d'Ivoire)

Angaelos, H.G. Bishop, mo, Coptic Orthodox Church (United Kingdom)

Angleberger, Rev. Dr Judy, fo, Presbyterian Church (USA) (United States of America)

Antonyan, Miss Lilit, yfl, Armenian Apostolic Church (Holy See of Etchmiadzin) (Armenia)

Apostu, Mr Andrei Dan, ml, Orthodox Church of the Czech Lands and Slovakia (Czech Republic)

Aprem, Most Rev. Dr Mooken, mo, Holy Apostolic Catholic Assyrian Church of the East (India)

Aram I, H.H., mo, Armenian Apostolic Church (Holy See of Cilicia) (Lebanon)

Arongo, Rt Rev. Emmanuel Anyindana, mo, Church of the Province of West Africa (Ghana)

Asana, Rev. Dr Festus A., mo, Presbyterian Church in Cameroon (Cameroon)

The list of delegates and participants represents persons registered for the assembly in Porto Alegre and may include persons who were not able to attend. Participants registered through the Mutirão programme are not listed here. The titles used are those requested by the participants themselves. The name of the country in parenthesis indicates the participant's country of residence. The abbreviations following the name of the participants indicate: y=youth; m=male; f=female; o=ordained; l=layperson.

Ashaye, Mr Samuel, yml, Church of the Lord (Aladura) Worldwide (Nigeria)

Asiimwe, Mr Onesimus, ml, Church of the Province of Uganda (Uganda)

Athanasios of Achaia, H.G. Bishop, mo, Church of Greece (Belgium)

Attarian, Father Dimitrios, mo, Greek Orthodox Patriarchate of Antioch and All the East (Brazil)

Aumua, Rev. Dr Chester, mo, United Methodist Church (United States of America)

Aven, Ms Katie, fl, Canadian Yearly Meeting of the Religious Society of Friends (Canada)

Avis, Rev. Dr Paul, mo, Church of England (United Kingdom)

Awow, Rev. Stephen Oyol, mo, Presbyterian Church of the Sudan (Sudan)

Aykazian, Bishop Vicken, mo, Armenian Apostolic Church (Holy See of Etchmiadzin) (United States of America)

Azariah, Bishop Samuel Robert, mo, Church of Pakistan (Pakistan)

Azariah, Mr Victor, ml, Presbyterian Church of Pakistan (Pakistan)

Badejo, Rev. Mrs Olubunmi Adedoyini, fo, Church of the Lord (Aladura) Worldwide (Nigeria)

Bae, Ms Yu-Mi, yfl, Presbyterian Church in the Republic of Korea (Korea, Republic of)

Bakala Koumouno, Mme Louise, fl, Eglise évangélique du Congo (Congo, Republic of)

Baliozian, H.E. Archbishop Aghan, mo, Armenian Apostolic Church (Holy See of Etchmiadzin) (Australia)

Baljian, Ms Nayiri, yfl, Armenian Apostolic Church (Holy See of Cilicia) (United States of America)

Balog, Rev. Ms Margit, fl, Magyarországi Református Egyház (Hungary)

Bambe Cishiku, Madame Annie, fl, Eglise de Jésus Christ sur la Terre par son Envoyé spécial Simon Kimbangu (Congo, Democratic Republic of)

Baonizafimanana, Mme Jeannette, fl, Eglise luthérienne malgache (Madagascar)

Baral, Mme Sabina, yfl, Chiesa Evangelica Valdese (Italy)

Barloso, Bishop Benjamin, mo, United Church of Christ in the Philippines (Philippines)

Barton, Rev. Paul, mo, United Methodist Church (United States of America)

Basher, Ms Alya, fl, Syrian Orthodox Patriarchate of Antioch and All the East (United States of America)

Bayrakdarian-Kabakian, Dr Nora, fl, Armenian Apostolic Church (Holy See of Cilicia) (Lebanon)

Bebey, Rev. Pasteur André Franck, mo, Eglise baptiste camerounaise (Cameroon)

Beetge, Bishop David Albert, mo, Church of the Province of Southern Africa (South Africa)

Beneteri, Ms Terauango, yfl, Kiribati Protestant Church (Kiribati)

Bent Omeir, Rev. Steadman, mo, Iglesia Morava en Nicaragua (Nicaragua)

Bento, M. Guilliot, yml, Eglise méthodiste du Togo (Togo)

Bernard, Ms Justice Désirée, fl, Church in the Province of the West Indies (Trinidad and Tobago)

Best, Dr Marion Stephani, fl, United Church of Canada (Canada)

Bezikian, Mr Alecco, ml, Armenian Apostolic Church (Holy See of Cilicia) (Italy)

Bhajan, Miss Evelyn, yfl, Church of Pakistan (Pakistan)

Biere, Frau Christina, yfl, Evangelische Kirche in Deutschland (Germany)

Bigari, Mrs Josephine, fl, Eglise épiscopale du Burundi (Burundi)

Bilokur, Archpriest Oleksandr, mo, Russian Orthodox Church (Ukraine)

Birabi, Dr Bridget, fl, Church of Nigeria (Anglican Communion) (Nigeria)

Bishoy, H.E. Metropolitan, mo, Coptic Orthodox Church (Egypt)

Björnsdottir, Ms Steinunn A., fl, Evangelical Lutheran Church of Iceland (Iceland)

Boediman, Rev. Marthen, mo, Gereja Masehi Injili di Halmahera (GMIH) (Indonesia)

Bogiannou, Rev. Deacon Triantafyllos Aimilianos, ymo, Ecumenical Patriarchate of Constantinople (Belgium)

Boru, Bishop William Waqo, mo, Anglican Church of Kenya (Kenya)

Bosch, Rev. Leandro Oscar, ymo, Ecumenical Patriarchate of Constantinople (Italy)

Bosien, Pfarrerin Heike, fo, Evangelische Kirche in Deutschland (Germany)

Boukis, Rev. Dimitrios, mo, Greek Evangelical Church (Greece)

Boulevard, Rev. Abram, mo, Gereja Masehi Injili Sangihe Talaud (GMIST) (Indonesia)

Brackmann, Sra Ana Maria, fl, Igreja Evangélica de Confissão Luterana no Brasil (Brazil)

Breukink, Rev. Alexandra, fo, Eglise de la Confession d'Augsbourg d'Alsace et de Lorraine (France)

Brooks, Mrs Maria del Carmen, fl, Episcopal Church in the USA (United States of America)

Brown, Rev. Colin, mo, United Free Church of Scotland (United Kingdom)

Buama, Rt Rev. Dr Livingstone, mo, Evangelical Presbyterian Church, Ghana (Ghana)

Buana Patiku, Mr Yunus, yml, Gereja Toraja (GT) (Indonesia)

Bubik, Mag. Michael, ml, Evangelischen Kirche A.u.H.B in Österreich (Austria)

Bubnov, Mr Pavel, yml, Russian Orthodox Church (Belarus)

Burdina, Ms Tatyana, fl, Russian Orthodox Church (Uzbekistan)

Butler, Rt Rev. Thomas Frederick, mo, Church of England (United Kingdom)

Caetano, Rev. José Domingos, mo, Missao Evangélica Pentecostal Angola (Angola)

Camnerin, Rev. Sofia Ann, fo, Svenska Missionskyrkan (Sweden)

Cao, Rev. (Ms) Shengjie, fo, China Christian Council (China)

Carter, Rev. Jeffrey, mo, Church of the Brethren (United States of America)

Celestine, Miss Nerissa, yfl, Church in the Province of the West Indies (Grenada)

Chackummoottil, Prof. Dr Kuruvilla Alexander, ml, Malankara Orthodox Syrian Church (India)

Chain, Dr Anna May, fl, Myanmar Baptist Convention (Myanmar)

Chaplin, Archpriest Vsevolod, mo, Russian Orthodox Church (Russian Federation)

Chapman, Ms Clare J., fl, United Methodist Church (United States of America)

Cheibas, Archpriest Vadim, ymo, Russian Orthodox Church (Moldova)

Chen, Mrs Meilin, fl, China Christian Council (China)

Cheng, Rev. Dr Yang-En, mo, Presbyterian Church in Taiwan (Taiwan)

Cherian, Rev. Dr. Paul, ymo, Malankara Orthodox Syrian Church (United States of America)

Chernov, Mr Vasily V., yml, Russian Orthodox Church (Russian Federation)

Chhangte, Rev. Rothangliani, fo, American Baptist Churches in the USA (United States of America)

Chiang, Mr Lung-Huang, yml, Presbyterian Church in Taiwan (Taiwan)

Chipesse, Rev. Augusto, mo, Igreja Evangélica Congregacional em Angola (Angola)

Chomutiri, Rev. Enos, mo, Reformed Church in Zimbabwe (Zimbabwe)

Chowdhury, Dr S. M., mo, Bangladesh Baptist Church Sangha (Bangladesh)

Christensen, Rev. Joergen, mo, Evangelical Lutheran Church in Denmark (Denmark)

Cies'lar, Bischof Jan, mo, Slezská církev evangelická a.v. (Czech Republic)

Clapsis, Rev. Dr Emmanuel, mo, Ecumenical Patriarchate of Constantinople (United States of America)

Clarke, Mrs Hera Rere, fl, Anglican Church in Aotearoa, New Zealand and Polynesia (New Zealand-Aotearoa)

Clelland, Mr Paul, ml, Church of Scotland (United Kingdom)

Collange, Prof. Jean-François, mo, Eglise de la Confession d'Augsbourg d'Alsace et de Lorraine (France)

Condrea, His Eminence Corin Nicolae, mo, Romanian Orthodox Church (United States of America)

Coorilos, Metropolitan Geevarghese Mar, mo, Malankara Orthodox Syrian Church (India)

Cowan, Rev. Collin Isaiah, mo, United Church in Jamaica and the Cayman Islands (Jamaica)

Cox, Ms Anthea, fl, The Methodist Church of Great Britain (United Kingdom)

Craver, Ms Rebecca Diane, yfl, Moravian Church in America (United States of America)

Critchfield, Ms Sara, yfl, Christian Church (Disciples of Christ) (United States of America)

Cruz, Rev. Adahyr, mo, Igreja Metodista do Brasil (Brazil)

Cubreacov, Mr Vlad, ml, Romanian Orthodox Church (Romania)

Daniel, Bishop, mo, Coptic Orthodox Church (Australia)

Daniel Gemechis, Mr Lalissa, yml, Ethiopian Evangelical Church Mekane Yesus (Ethiopia)

Daughrity, Rev. Dr Dyron, mo, Christian Church (Disciples of Christ) in Canada (Canada)

Davey, Ms Elspeth, fl, Scottish Episcopal Church (United Kingdom)

David, Bishop Godofredo, mo, Iglesia Filipina Independiente (Philippines)

Dávila-Luciano, Ms Vanesa, yfl, Presbyterian Church (USA) (United States of America)

Day, Rev. R. Randy, mo, United Methodist Church (United States of America)

De La Cruz, Ms Claudia, yfl, United Church of Christ (United States of America)

Delikostantis, Professor Dr Konstantinos, ml, Ecumenical Patriarchate of Constantinople (Greece)

Devejian, Mrs Paula, fl, Armenian Apostolic Church (Holy See of Etchmiadzin) (Armenia)

Devletian, Mrs Lucia, fl, Armenian Apostolic Church (Holy See of Cilicia) (Venezuela)

Dibeela, Rev. Dr Moiseraele Prince, mo, United Congregational Church of Southern Africa (South Africa)

Dimas, Rev. Fr George, mo, Greek Orthodox Patriarchate of Antioch and All the East (Lebanon)

Dimetros, Ambassador Yoftahe, ml, Eritrean Orthodox Tewahdo Church (Eritrea)

Dimtsu, Dr Gebre Georgis, mo, Ethiopian Orthodox Tewahedo Church (United Kingdom)

Dina Ndomanuele, Pasteur Emmanuel, mo, Eglise de Jésus Christ sur la Terre par son Envoyé spécial Simon Kimbangu (Congo, Democratic Republic of)

Dirokpa Balufuga, Most Rev. Dr Fidèle, mo, ECC - Communauté anglicane au Congo (Congo, Democratic Republic of)

Dobrijevic, H.G. Bishop Irinej, mo, Serbian Orthodox Church (Serbia and Montenegro)

Dogbo, Pastor Abolé, mo, Eglise Harriste (Côte d'Ivoire)

Doghramajian, Bishop Khoren, mo, Armenian Apostolic Church (Holy See of Cilicia) (Greece)

Doloksaribu, Bishop Dr H., mo, Gereja Methodist Indonesia (GMI) (Indonesia)

Dossou, Pasteur Simon K., mo, Eglise protestante méthodiste du Bénin (Benin)

Dragas, Very Rev. Prof. Dr George, mo, Greek Orthodox Patriarchate of Jerusalem (United States of America)

Duarte, Pastor Carlos, mo, Iglesia Evangélica del Rio de la Plata (Argentina)

Dube, Rev. Fraser Bongani, mo, Moravian Church in South Africa (South Africa)

Dube, Bishop Litsietsi Maqethuka, mo, Evangelical Lutheran Church in Zimbabwe (Zimbabwe)

Dyck, Bishop Sally, fo, United Methodist Church (United States of America)

Dyvasirvadam, Rt Rev. Dr Govada, mo, Church of South India (India)

El Baiady, Rev. Dr Safwat Nagieb Ghobrial, mo, Evangelical Presbyterian Church of Egypt Synod of the Nile (Egypt)

El-Anba-Bishoy, Bishop Suriel, mo, Coptic Orthodox Church (United States of America)

394

Eliki Ikete, Rév. Engetele, fo, ECC - Communauté des Disciples du Christ (Congo, Democratic Republic of)

Eliseev, Fr Andrey, mo, Russian Orthodox Church (Belgium)

Elu, Ms MacRose Togiab, fl, Anglican Church of Australia (Australia)

Endalkachew, Rev. Dr Mikre Sellassie G. Ammanuel, mo, Ethiopian Orthodox Tewahedo Church (Ethiopia)

Enns, Rev. Dr Fernando, mo, Vereinigung der Deutschen Mennonitengemeinden (Germany)

Epting, Rt Rev. C. Christopher, mo, Episcopal Church in the USA (United States of America)

Erdélyi, Bischof Dr Géza, mo, Reformed Christian Church in Slovakia (Slovakia)

Esber, Fr Dr Elias, mo, Greek Orthodox Patriarchate of Antioch and All the East (Germany)

Espinoza Jiménez, Pastor Luis Guillermo, mo, Misión Iglesia Pentecostal (Chile)

Eugène, Rév. Gédéon, mo, Convention Baptiste d'Haiti (Haiti)

Evans, Mr Siôn Ifan, yml, Union of Welsh Independents (United Kingdom)

Evans, Ms Wendy, yfl, United Church of Canada (Canada)

Falani, Rev. Tofinga Vaevalu, mo, Ekalesia Kelisiano Tuvalu E. (Tuvalu)

Feoktistov, Archpriest Pavel, mo, Russian Orthodox Church (Brazil)

Ferreira, Srta Regina da Silva, yfl, Igreja Evangélica de Confissão Luterana no Brasil (Brazil)

Fimbo, Rév. Ganvunze Dieudonne, mo, ECC - Communauté mennonite au Congo (Congo, Democratic Republic of)

Fisher, Canon Rita Elizabeth, fl, Church of England (United Kingdom)

Fitzpatrick, Ms Tara, fl, United Methodist Church (United States of America)

Fodac, Ms Florina, fl, Romanian Orthodox Church (Romania)

Formilleza, Mrs Prima S., fl, Convention of Philippine Baptist Churches (Philippines)

Frimpong-Manso, Rt Rev. Dr Yaw, mo, Presbyterian Church of Ghana (Ghana)

Fritz, Rev. Drs Ilona, fo, Protestantse Kerk in Nederland (Netherlands)

Gabutu, Bishop Oika, mo, United Church in Papua New Guinea (Papua New Guinea)

Gadegaard, Dean Anders, mo, Evangelical Lutheran Church in Denmark (Denmark)

Galitis, Prof. George, ml, Church of Greece (Greece)

Galstanyan, His Grace Bishop Bagrat (Vazgen), mo, Armenian Apostolic Church (Holy See of Etchmiadzin) (Canada)

Gáncs, Mrs Márta Péterné, fl, Lutherische Kirche in Ungarn (Hungary)

Gáncs, Bishop Peter, mo, Lutherische Kirche in Ungarn (Hungary)

Gao, Rev. Ying, fo, China Christian Council (China)

García Rodríguez, Lic. Adalid, ml, Convención Bautista de Nicaragua (Nicaragua)

Gardner, Rev. Dr Paul, mo, Moravian Church in Jamaica (Jamaica)

Garlington, Ms Tee, fl, International Evangelical Church (United States of America)

Gathanju, Mr David, ml, Presbyterian Church of East Africa (Kenya)

Gazer, Dr Hacik Rafi, ml, Armenian Apostolic Church (Holy See of Etchmiadzin) (Germany)

Gebre Kristos, H.G. Abune Abba Ewostateos, mo, Ethiopian Orthodox Tewahedo Church (Ethiopia)

Genjian, Ms Izabel, yfl, Armenian Apostolic Church (Holy See of Etchmiadzin) (Brazil)

Gennadios of Sassima, Metropolitan Prof. Dr, mo, Ecumenical Patriarchate of Constantinople (Turkey)

Genre, Rev. Giovanni Pietro, mo, Chiesa Evangelica Valdese (Italy)

George, Rev. Dr Kondothra M., mo, Malankara Orthodox Syrian Church (India)

Getanel, Father Abbamelaku, mo, Ethiopian Orthodox Tewahedo Church (Ethiopia)

Getcha, Archimandrite Dr Job, mo, Ecumenical Patriarchate of Constantinople (France)

Ghaly, Rev. Father Yacob Naim, mo, Coptic Orthodox Church (United States of America)

Ghantous, Mr Hadi, yml, National Evangelical Synod of Syria and Lebanon (Lebanon)

Ghibanu, Mr Ionut Adrian, yml, Romanian Orthodox Church (Romania)

Gibson, Rev. Mark, mo, Te Hahi Weteriana O Aotearoa (New Zealand-Aotearoa)

Girsang, Mrs Jenny Rio Rita, fl, Gereja Kristen Protestan Simalungun (GKPS) (Indonesia)

Glynn-Mackoul, Ms Anne, fl, Greek Orthodox Patriarchate of Antioch and All the East (United States of America)

Gobena Molte, Rev. Iteffa, mo, Ethiopian Evangelical Church Mekane Yesus (Ethiopia)

Gómez Ríos, Rev. Guadalupe Antonio, mo, Convención Bautista de Nicaragua (Nicaragua)

Goodbourn, Dr David Robin, ml, Baptist Union of Great Britain (United Kingdom)

Goto, Ms Jennifer Irvine, yfl, United Methodist Church (United States of America)

Goundiaev, Father Mikhail, mo, Russian Orthodox Church (Switzerland)

Griffin, Jr., Dr Arlee, ml, American Baptist Churches in the USA (United States of America)

Gudmundsdottir, Mrs Karolina Hulda, fl, Evangelical Lutheran Church of Iceland (Iceland)

Guerra Quezada, Pastora Rosa Ester, fo, Iglesia Pentecostal de Chile (Chile)

Gundersen, Mr Harald, yml, Church of Norway (Norway)

Guvsám, Ms Kirsti, yfl, Church of Norway (Norway)

Gwama, Mr Filibus Kumba, mo, Church of the Brethren in Nigeria (Nigeria)

Gyakye-Amoateng, Rev. Yaw, mo, Evangelical Lutheran Church of Ghana (Ghana)

Habashy Youssef, Mrs Nahed F., fl, Coptic Orthodox Church (Egypt)

Haddad, Mr Alaa, ml, Greek Orthodox Patriarchate of Antioch and All the East (Syria)

Hagos, H.E. Archbishop Dioskoros, mo, Eritrean Orthodox Tewahdo Church (Eritrea)

Hakh, Rev. Dr Samuel Benyamin, mo, Gereja Protestan di Indonesia (GPI) (Indonesia)

Hamblin, Rev. Roslyn, fo, Moravian Church, Eastern West Indies Province (Antigua and Barbuda)

Hanchinmani, Mr John, ml, Methodist Church in India (India)

Hanna, Father Augustinos, mo, Coptic Orthodox Church (United States of America)

Hanna Al-Kass, Miss Faten, fl, Syrian Orthodox Patriarchate of Antioch and All the East (Syria)

Hanson, Bishop Mark S., mo, Evangelical Lutheran Church in America (United States of America)

Harmelink, Rev. Herman, mo, International Council of Community Churches (United States of America)

Harris, Ms Jillian, fl, Anglican Church of Canada (Canada)

Harte, Ms Sarah, yfl, Episcopal Church in the USA (United States of America)

Heetderks, Rev. Jan-Gerd, mo, Protestantse Kerk in Nederland (Netherlands)

Heidel, Herr Klaus, ml, Evangelische Kirche in Deutschland (Germany)

Hein, Bischof Dr Martin Hermann, mo, Evangelische Kirche in Deutschland (Germany)

Heitz, Ms Monika Josefine Maria, fl, Altkatholische Kirche Österreichs (Austria)

Henderson, Rev. Gregor, mo, Uniting Church in Australia (Australia)

Hendery, The Rev. Noel Arthur, mo, Anglican Church in Aotearoa, New Zealand and Polynesia (New Zealand-Aotearoa)

Hendriks-Ririmasse, Rev. Dr Margaretha M., fo, Presbyterian Protestant Church in the Moluccas (Indonesia)

Heuvelink, Ms Jantine, yfl, Protestantse Kerk in Nederland (Netherlands)

Hodgson Rios, Sr Ashley Wesley, ml, Iglesia Morava en Nicaragua (Nicaragua)

Holder, The Rt Rev. Dr John Walder Dunlop, mo, Church in the Province of the West Indies (Barbados)

Holstenkamp, Herr Lars, yml, Evangelische Kirche in Deutschland (Germany)

Houweling, Rev. Wies, fo, Protestantse Kerk in Nederland (Netherlands)

Hovorun, Priest Serhiy, mo, Russian Orthodox Church (Russian Federation)

Hudson-Wilkin, Rev. Rose Josephine, fo, Church of England (United Kingdom)

Huggins, Bishop Philip, mo, Anglican Church of Australia (Australia)

Hutabarat-Lebang, Rev. Henriette, fo, Gereja Toraja (GT) (Indonesia)

Hutchison, Most Rev. Andrew, mo, Anglican Church of Canada (Canada)

Huttunen, Rev. Fr Heikki, mo, Suomen ortodoksinen Kirkko (Finland)

Idowu-Fearon, Most Rev. Dr Josiah Atkins, mo, Church of Nigeria (Anglican Communion) (Nigeria)

Ieuti, Rev. Teeruro, mo, Kiribati Protestant Church (Kiribati)

Igbari, Ven. Dr John Olusola, mo, Church of Nigeria (Anglican Communion) (Nigeria)

Ignatios of Dimitrias, Metropolitan, mo, Church of Greece (Greece)

Ignatyev, Priest Oleg, mo, Russian Orthodox Church (Kazakhstan)

Ignjatije, H.G. Dr, mo, Serbian Orthodox Church (Serbia and Montenegro)

Iitula, Pastor Simon Panduleni, mo, Evangelical Lutheran Church in Namibia (Namibia)

Ingram, Rev. William, mo, Presbyterian Church in Canada (Canada)

Ioannis of Thermopylae, Bishop, mo, Church of Greece (Greece)

Issa, Mr Theodore B.T., ml, Syrian Orthodox Patriarchate of Antioch and All the East (Australia)

Itty, Prof. Adiyanil Varghese, mo, Mar Thoma Syrian Church of Malabar (India)

Jacob, Mrs Elizabeth, yfl, Mar Thoma Syrian Church of Malabar (United Arab Emirates)

Jagucki, Bischof Janusz, mo, Kosciol Ewangelicko-Augsburgski w Polsce (Poland)

Jakobsone, Ms Anita, fl, Evangelical Lutheran Church of Latvia (Latvia)

Jaworski, Bischof Zdzislaw, mo, Staro-Katolicki Kosciol Mariawitow w Polsce (Poland)

Jebelean, Pfr Ioan Livius, mo, Kosciola Polskokatolickiego w RP (Switzerland)

Jekwa, Mrs Novayi Vitta, fl, Uniting Presbyterian Church in Southern Africa (South Africa)

Jemison, Dr Major Lewis, mo, Progressive National Baptist Convention, Inc. (United States of America)

Jeremiasz of Wroclaw, Archbishop Jan, mo, Polski Autokefaliczny Kosciol Prawoslawny (Poland)

Jones, Rev. Kathy, fo, Church in Wales (United Kingdom)

Jones, The Rev. Dr Robert Scott, mo, National Baptist Convention USA, Inc. (United States of America)

Joseph, Prof. Roy, ml, Mar Thoma Syrian Church of Malabar (Singapore)

Joseph, Rev. William Premkumar Ebenezer, mo, Methodist Church Sri Lanka (Sri Lanka)

Joseph of Cochin, H.E. Archbishop Mar Gregorios, mo, Syrian Orthodox Patriarchate of Antioch and All the East (India)

Jovanovic, Mrs Olivera, fl, Serbian Orthodox Church (Bosnia and Herzegovina)

Judkins, Mrs Mary, fl, Church of England (United Kingdom)

Jung, Ms Hae-Sun, fl, Korean Methodist Church (Korea, Republic of)

Kabwe, Mgr. Evêque Ka-Leza, mo, ECC - Communauté épiscopale baptiste en Afrique (Congo, Democratic Republic of)

Kabwika Tshituka, Mlle Donatienne, yfl, Eglise du Christ - Lumière du Saint Esprit (Congo, Democratic Republic of)

Kakkouras, Dr Georgios, ml, Church of Cyprus (Cyprus)

Kakpo, Pasteur Yawo Senyeebia, mo, Eglise évangélique presbytérienne du Togo (Togo)

Kalimba, Bishop Jered, mo, Province de l'Eglise Episcopale au Rwanda (Rwanda)

Kallas Malek, Mrs Muna, fl, Greek Orthodox Patriarchate of Antioch and All the East (Syria)

Kalongo, Rev. Prof. Teddy, mo, United Church of Zambia (Zambia)

Kaloyirou, Ms Chrystalla, fl, Church of Cyprus (Cyprus)

Kamba Kasongo, Rev. Micheline, fo, ECC - Communauté presbytérienne de Kinshasa (Congo, Democratic Republic of)

Kameeta, Bishop Dr Zephania, mo, Evangelical Lutheran Church in the Republic of Namibia (Namibia)

Kandema, Mrs Julie, fl, Eglise presbytérienne au Rwanda (Rwanda)

Kapa, Rev. Za Hlei, mo, Methodist Church, Upper Myanmar (Myanmar)

Kaplan, Ms Ayda, fl, Syrian Orthodox Patriarchate of Antioch and All the East (Belgium)

Karagdag, Ms Carmencita, fl, Iglesia Filipina Independiente (Philippines)

Karayiannis of Trimithus, H.G. Bishop Dr Vasilios, mo, Church of Cyprus (Cyprus)

Karim, Archbishop Mor Cyril Aphrem, mo, Syrian Orthodox Patriarchate of Antioch and All the East (United States of America)

Karkala-Zorba, Mag. Aikaterini, fl, Church of Greece (Greece)

Karthäuser, Frau Sylvia, yfl, Evangelische Kirche in Deutschland (Germany)

Kasidokosta, Ms Pinelopi Anna, yfl, Ecumenical Patriarchate of Constantinople (Greece)

Kässmann, Landesbischöfin Dr Margot, fo, Evangelische Kirche in Deutschland (Germany)

Kathindi, Very Rev. Nangula E., fo, Church of the Province of Southern Africa (Namibia)

Kayuwa Tshibumbu wa Kapinga, Patriarche Moïse, mo, Eglise du Christ - Lumière du Saint Esprit (Congo, Democratic Republic of)

Kellellu, Ms Vinata, yfl, Church of North India (India)

Kembo, Rév. Emmanuel Dindonga, mo, ECC - Communauté baptiste du Congo Ouest (Congo, Democratic Republic of)

Kern, Mr Alexander, ml, Religious Society of Friends: Friends General Conference (United States of America)

Kesting, Rev. Sheilagh Margaret, fo, Church of Scotland (United Kingdom)

Kgatla, Prof. Selaelo Thias, mo, Uniting Reformed Church in Southern Africa (South Africa)

Kilpin, Ms Juliet, fo, Baptist Union of Great Britain (United Kingdom)

Kim, Rev. Kyung In, fo, Presbyterian Church of Korea (Korea, Republic of)

Kimani, Rt Rev. Dr Julius Karanja, mo, African Christian Church and Schools (Kenya)

Kimhachandra, Rev. Dr Sint, mo, Church of Christ in Thailand (Thailand)

Kinfe Michuel, Archbishop Melke Tsedek, mo, Ethiopian Orthodox Tewahedo Church (Ethiopia)

Kirkpatrick, Rev. Dr Clifton, mo, Presbyterian Church (USA) (United States of America)

Kishkovsky, Very Rev. Leonid, mo, Orthodox Church in America (United States of America)

Kisku, Ms Sanchita, yfl, United Evangelical Lutheran Church in India (India)

Kitsinian, Ms Vanna, yfl, Armenian Apostolic Church (Holy See of Cilicia) (United States of America)

Kjolaas, Bishop Per Oskar, mo, Church of Norway (Norway)

Kolovopoulou, Dr Marina, fl, Church of Greece (Greece)

Koppe, Bischof Dr Rolf, mo, Evangelische Kirche in Deutschland (Germany)

Kronshage, Frau Christa, fl, Evangelische Kirche in Deutschland (Germany)

Krüger, Oberkirchenrätin Marita Karin, fo, Evangelische Kirche in Deutschland (Germany)

Krystof, His Eminence, mo, Orthodox Church of the Czech Lands and Slovakia (Czech Republic)

Kuch, Dr Priscilla Joseph, fl, Episcopal Church of the Sudan (Sudan)

Kumir, Rt Rev. Ezekiel Kondo, mo, Episcopal Church of the Sudan (Sudan)

Kurien, Rev. Dr Jacob, mo, Malankara Orthodox Syrian Church (India)

Kyafa, Mrs Pati, fl, Reformed Church of Christ in Nigeria (Nigeria)

Lachman, Rev. Ferdinand, mo, Moravian Church in Suriname (Suriname)

Laengner, Frau Ruth, yfl, Evangelische Kirche in Deutschland (Germany)

Laham, Mr Samer, ml, Greek Orthodox Patriarchate of Antioch and All the East (Syria)

Lam, Rev. Holger, mo, Baptistkirken i Danmark (Denmark)

Lambert, Mr Saw, ml, Church of the Province of Myanmar (Myanmar)

Lambriniadis, Very Rev. Dr Elpidophoros Yani, mo, Ecumenical Patriarchate of Constantinople (Turkey)

Lansdowne, Ms Carmen, yfl, United Church of Canada (Canada)

Larentzakis, Mag. Emanuela, fl, Ecumenical Patriarchate of Constantinople (Greece)

Lavatai, Mr Sanele Faasua, ml, Methodist Church of Samoa (Samoa)

Lazaro, Bishop Nathanael, mo, Evangelical Methodist Church in the Philippines (Philippines)

Lee, Prof. Dr Samuel, ml, Presbyterian Church of Korea (Korea, Republic of)

Lee, Rev. Dr Yo-Han, mo, Korean Methodist Church (Korea, Republic of)

Leegte, Rev. Henk, mo, Mennonite Church in the Netherlands (Netherlands)

Legesse, Dr Nigussu, fl, Ethiopian Orthodox Tewahedo Church (Ethiopia)

Lengelsen, Dr Monika, fl, Evangelische Kirche in Deutschland (Germany)

Leuluaiali'i, Rev. Siatua, mo, Methodist Church of Samoa (Samoa)

Liagre, Dr Guy, mo, Eglise protestante unie de Belgique (Belgium)

Lightner Fuller, Dr Ann, fo, African Methodist Episcopal Church (United States of America)

Lin Cheng, Mrs Ming-Min, fl, Presbyterian Church in Taiwan (Taiwan)

Liuvaie, Rev. Falkland Gary Fereti, mo, Ekalesia Niue (Niue)

Lohre, Ms Kathryn, yfl, Evangelical Lutheran Church in America (United States of America)

Lolowang, Rev. Decky, mo, Gereja Masehi Injili di Minahasa (GMIM) (Indonesia)

Love, Dr Janice, fl, United Methodist Church (United States of America)

Lutui, Mrs Melenaite Katea, fl, Free Wesleyan Church of Tonga (Methodist Church in Tonga) (Tonga)

Lwali, Ms Rachel Juliana Mathew, fl, Moravian Church in Tanzania (Tanzania)

M'Impwii, Bishop Stephen Kanyaru, ymo, Methodist Church in Kenya (Kenya)

Madhiba, Rev. Simon, mo, Methodist Church in Zimbabwe (Zimbabwe)

Maghina, Mr Emmanuel, yml, Evangelical Lutheran Church in Tanzania (Tanzania)

Majoe, Rev. Liphoko, mo, Methodist Church of Southern Africa (South Africa)

Majule, Mrs Neema Geoffrey Peter, fl, Anglican Church of Tanzania (Tanzania)

Makabori, Ms Paula, fl, Gereja Kristen Injili Di Tanah Papua (GKITP) (Indonesia)

Makarios of Kenya and Irinoupolis, H.E. Archbishop, mo, Greek Orthodox Patriarchate of Alexandria and All Africa (Kenya)

Makisanti, Rev. (Ms) Liesje Vonny Emma, fo, Gereja Protestan di Indonesia (GPI) (Indonesia)

Malelak-de Haan, Dra Sophia, fl, Gereja Masehi Injili di Timor (GMIT) (Indonesia)

Malungo, Pasteur António Pedro, mo, Igreja Evangélica Reformada de Angola (Angola)

Mandowen, Mr Welly Esau, ml, Gereja Kristen Injili Di Tanah Papua (GKITP) (Indonesia)

Mandröm, Ms Lina, yfl, Svenska Kyrkan (Sweden)

Mans, Ms Isabell, yfl, Vereinigung der Deutschen Mennonitengemeinden (Germany)

Mansour, H.E. Damascinos, mo, Greek Orthodox Patriarchate of Antioch and All the East (Brazil)

Mansour, Father Fayez, mo, Greek Orthodox Patriarchate of Antioch and All the East (Germany)

Manukyan, Rev. Fr Hovakim (Vardges), ymo, Armenian Apostolic Church (Holy See of Etchmiadzin) (Armenia)

Mar Philoxenos, Bishop Dr Isaac, mo, Mar Thoma Syrian Church of Malabar (India)

Maraea, Rev. Taaroanui, mo, Eglise Protestante Maòhi (French Polynesia)

Mardirossian, Father Housig, ymo, Armenian Apostolic Church (Holy See of Cilicia) (Lebanon)

Markos, Bishop Antonious, mo, Coptic Orthodox Church (South Africa)

Marpaung, Bishop Sabam Parulian, mo, Gereja Kristen Protestan Angkola (GKPA) (Indonesia)

Marquand, Rt Rev. Garry, mo, Presbyterian Church of Aotearoa New Zealand (New Zealand-Aotearoa)

Martin, Rev. Chandran Paul, mo, United Evangelical Lutheran Church in India (India)

Martin, Rev. OKR Michael, mo, Evangelische Kirche in Deutschland (Germany)

Martzelos, Prof. Georgios, ml, Church of Greece (Greece)

Masandu, Rev. Sopirid, mo, Protestant Church in Sabah (Malaysia)

Masango, Rev. Dr Maake J. S., mo, Uniting Presbyterian Church in Southern Africa (South Africa)

Masih, Mrs Prabhjot Prim Rose, fl, Church of North India (India)

Maske, Pastora Neli, fo, Iglesia Evangélica Luterana en Chile (Chile)

Mathew, Ms Neena, yfl, Mar Thoma Syrian Church of Malabar (South Africa)

Mathew Kaniyanthra, Dr Ms Susy, fl, Malankara Orthodox Syrian Church (India)

Matonga, Rev. Forbes, mo, United Methodist Church (Zimbabwe)

Mayela Tshimungu, Rev. Josué, mo, ECC - Communauté presbytérienne de Kinshasa (Congo, Democratic Republic of)

Mbise, Mrs Loerose Thomas, fl, Evangelical Lutheran Church in Tanzania (Tanzania)

McAteer, Rev. Canon Bruce James, mo, Anglican Church of Australia (Australia)

McCullough Dauway, Ms Lois, fl, United Methodist Church (United States of America)

McGeoch, Mr Graham Gerald, yml, Church of Scotland (Brazil)

McKenzie, Rev. Jeffrey, mo, Jamaica Baptist Union (Jamaica)

Mdegella, Bishop Dr Owdenburg Moses, mo, Evangelical Lutheran Church in Tanzania (Tanzania)

Megerditchian, Rev. Serop, mo, Union of the Armenian Evangelical Churches in the Near East (Syria)

Mekel, Ms Peggy Adeline, yfl, Gereja Masehi Injili di Minahasa (GMIM) (Indonesia)

Melikyan, Rev. Father Vahram (Mikayel), mo, Armenian Apostolic Church (Holy See of Etchmiadzin) (Armenia)

Menessy, Rev. Miklos-Bela, mo, Reformierte Kirche in Rumänien (Romania)

Mesco, Rev. Alejandro, mo, Iglesia Anglicana del Cono Sur de América (Peru)

Mfitumukiza, Rév. André, mo, Association des Eglises Baptistes au Rwanda (Rwanda)

Mfochive, Rév. Dr Joseph, mo, Eglise évangélique du Cameroun (Cameroon)

Mhogolo, Bishop Godfrey Mdimi, mo, Anglican Church of Tanzania (Tanzania)

Michau, Madame Marie-Christine, fl, Eglise évangélique luthérienne de France (France)

Mikhail, Mr Bishoy M., yml, Coptic Orthodox Church (United States of America)

Millamena, Ms Hope, yfl, Iglesia Filipina Independiente (Philippines)

Misenga, Mme Ngoy Mukuna Monique, fl, ECC - Communauté presbytérienne de Kinshasa (Congo, Democratic Republic of)

Mlynkova, Ms Kristyna, yfl, Czechoslovak Hussite Church (Czech Republic)

Mokhahlane, Rev. John Rapelang, mo, Lesotho Evangelical Church (Lesotho)

Mone, Rev. Dr Alifaleti, mo, Free Wesleyan Church of Tonga (Methodist Church in Tonga) (Tonga)

Morris, Rev. Dr Heather, fo, Methodist Church in Ireland (United Kingdom)

Mosoiu, Prof. Rev. Dr Nicolae Viorel, mo, Romanian Orthodox Church (Romania)

Motec, Rev. Hynna, mo, Evangelical Lutheran Church of Papua New Guinea (Papua New Guinea)

Motlhagodi, Ms Anna, fl, Evangelical Lutheran Church in Southern Africa (Botswana)

Moukheiber, Ms Lina, fl, Greek Orthodox Patriarchate of Antioch and All the East (Lebanon)

Mounier, M. Jocelyn Jean-Louis, ml, Eglise de la Confession d'Augsbourg d'Alsace et de Lorraine (France)

Mourad, Rev. Georges, mo, National Evangelical Synod of Syria and Lebanon (Lebanon)

Mputu, Rév. Clement, mo, ECC - Communauté des Disciples du Christ (Congo, Democratic Republic of)

Muanda Mikiama, Rev. Fidèle, mo, ECC - Communauté évangélique (Congo, Republic of)

Muchogu, Ms Hellen, fl, Presbyterian Church of East Africa (Kenya)

Mukuba-Kasule, Mrs Sarah, fl, Church of the Province of Uganda (Uganda)

Mukundi, Rev. Dr Joseph Mulumba M., mo, ECC - Communauté presbytérienne (Congo, Democratic Republic of)

Mularczyk Zdanuk, Ms Magda, yfl, Polski Autokefaliczny Kosciol Prawoslawny (Poland)

Müller, Ms Christine Angelika, yfl, Evangelische Kirche in Deutschland (Germany)

Müller, Superintendentin Luise, fo, Evangelischen Kirche A.u.H.B in Österreich (Austria)

Mulrain, Rev. Dr George MacDonald, mo, Methodist Church in the Caribbean and the Americas (Antigua and Barbuda)

Munezero, Mr Siméon Aime, yml, Eglise presbytérienne au Rwanda (Rwanda)

Muriyankal, H.E. Archbishop Thomas Kurivilla, mo, Syrian Orthodox Patriarchate of Antioch and All the East (India)

Musa, Rev. Adamu Manasseh, mo, Reformed Church of Christ in Nigeria (Nigeria)

Musemakweli, Rev. Dr Elisée, mo, Eglise presbytérienne au Rwanda (Rwanda)

Musuamba Bilenga, Mme Francisca, fl, ECC - Communauté presbytérienne (Congo, Democratic Republic of)

Mutoro, Jane, yfl, Religious Society of Friends: Friends United Meeting (Kenya)

Mwale, Rev. Moses Lukas, mo, Reformed Church in Zambia (Zambia)

Mwangi, Rev. Grace Nyambura, yfo, Anglican Church of Kenya (Kenya)

Mwendar, Mrs Selina, fl, Methodist Church in Kenya (Kenya)

Mwenisongole, Rev. Tuntufye, mo, Moravian Church in Tanzania (Tanzania)

Nabieu, Rev. Francis Samuel, mo, Methodist Church Sierra Leone (Sierra Leone)

Nafilo, Rev. Rui Garcia, mo, Igreja Evangélica Baptista em Angola (Angola)

Nagel, Ms Jennifer, fl, Evangelical Lutheran Church in America (United States of America)

Namwembe, Ms Jane Despina, fl, Greek Orthodox Patriarchate of Alexandria and All Africa (Uganda)

Napitupulu, Rev. Dr Bonar, mo, Huria Kristen Batak Protestan (HKBP) (Indonesia)

Nascimento Cunha, Dra Magali, fl, Igreja Metodista do Brasil (Brazil)

Nassis, Deacon Chrysostomos, mo, Ecumenical Patriarchate of Constantinople (Greece)

Naulapwa, Ms Bridget, fl, United Church of Zambia (Zambia)

Naylor, Mrs Yvonne, fl, Church of Ireland (Ireland)

Nazaryan, Dr Karen, ml, Armenian Apostolic Church (Holy See of Etchmiadzin) (Armenia)

Ndraha, Mrs Debora, fl, Gereja-Gereja Kristen Jawa (GKJ) (Indonesia)

Ndudzo, Mr Itayi, yml, Methodist Church in Zimbabwe (Zimbabwe)

Nelyubova, Mrs Margarita, fl, Russian Orthodox Church (Russian Federation)

Ngewu, Rev. Lubabalo Livingstone, mo, Church of the Province of Southern Africa (South Africa)

Nguvumali, Rev. Conrad Ernest, mo, Moravian Church in Tanzania (Tanzania)

Nickel, Frau Katharina, fl, Katholisches Bistum der Alt-Katholiken in Deutschland (Germany)

Nicol, The Very Rev. Ajayi Eleborra, mo, Church of the Province of West Africa (Sierra Leone)

Nifon, Archbishop Dr, mo, Romanian Orthodox Church (Romania)

Nistea, Mr Iulian, yml, Romanian Orthodox Church (France)

Nitzsche, Frau Angela, fl, Evangelische Kirche in Deutschland (Germany)

Nkebi-Luamba, Pasteur Brigittes, fo, Eglise de Jésus Christ sur la Terre par son Envoyé spécial Simon Kimbangu (Congo, Democratic Republic of)

Nkhuwa, Mrs Faidess, fl, Reformed Church in Zambia (Zambia)

Norman, The Rev. Andrew, mo, Church of England (United Kingdom)

Norman, Mr Arthur, ml, Evangelical Lutheran Church in America (United States of America)

Nortan, Sister Ingrid, fl, Moravian Church in Suriname (Suriname)

N'Souami, Rév. Dr Patrice, mo, Eglise évangélique du Congo (Congo, Republic of)

Ntahoturi, The Most Rev. Bernard, mo, Eglise épiscopale du Burundi (Burundi)

Nuzum, Rev. Daniel R., mo, Church of Ireland (Ireland)

Nyangi Kasa-Vubu, Rév. Gabrielle, fo, ECC - Communauté baptiste du Congo Ouest (Congo, Democratic Republic of)

Nyirampirwa, Mme Alivera, fl, Association des Eglises Baptistes au Rwanda (Rwanda)

Obah, Miss Elizabeth, fl, Presbyterian Church of Ghana (Ghana)

Oden, Bishop William B., mo, United Methodist Church (United States of America)

Odoi, Ms Gladys Afarchoe, fl, Methodist Church, Ghana (Ghana)

Oedoy, Rev. Prapatriotis Hofman, mo, Gereja Kalimantan Evangelis (GKE) (Indonesia)

Ofori, Mr Edward Nana Adansi, ml, Presbyterian Church of Ghana (Ghana)

Ogara, Dr William O., ml, Anglican Church of Kenya (Kenya)

Olagboye, Mr Benjamin, yml, Eglise protestante méthodiste Unie de Côte d'Ivoire (Côte d'Ivoire)

Omiya, Rev. Dr Hiroshi, mo, United Church of Christ in Japan (Japan)

Onadotun Onanuga, Most Rev. Abraham, mo, African Church (Nigeria)

Opincariu, Mr Marius, yml, Romanian Orthodox Church (United States of America)

Ositelu, Archbishop Dr Rufus, mo, Church of the Lord (Aladura) Worldwide (Nigeria)

Osterlind, Ms Eva Marie, yfl, Evangelical Lutheran Church in Denmark (Denmark)

Overton, Rev. Peter Arthur, mo, Churches of Christ in Australia (Australia)

Oyekola, Ms Iyabo, yfl, Church of the Lord (Aladura) Worldwide (Nigeria)

Paik, Ms Agathi, yfl, Ecumenical Patriarchate of Constantinople (Korea, Republic of)

Palopää, Mr David, yml, Svenska Kyrkan (Sweden)

Papadhopuli, Mr Jorgo, ml, Kisha Orthodhokse Autoqefale e Shqipërisë (Albania)

Papadopoulos, Mrs Georgia, yfl, Ecumenical Patriarchate of Constantinople (Australia)

Papanicolaou, Archimandrite Gabriel, ymo, Church of Greece (Greece)

Park, Rev. Dr Jong-Wha, mo, Presbyterian Church in the Republic of Korea (Korea, Republic of)

Park, Prof. Dr Seong-Won, mo, Presbyterian Church of Korea (Korea, Republic of)

Parker, Dr Evelyn, fl, Christian Methodist Episcopal Church (United States of America)

Patnaningsih, Rev. Sri Agus, fo, Gereja Kristen Indonesia (GKI) (Indonesia)

Patuleanu, Rev. Prof. Dr Constantin, mo, Romanian Orthodox Church (Romania)

Peña, Mr Charles, ml, Evangelical Lutheran Church in America (United States of America)

Peranginangin, Dr Minda, fo, Gereja Batak Karo Protestan (GBKP) (Indonesia)

Perangin-angin, Rev. Dr Jadiaman, mo, Gereja Batak Karo Protestan (GBKP) (Indonesia)

Perelini, Dr Otele, mo, Congregational Christian Church in Samoa (Samoa)

Perisic, Archpriest Vladan, mo, Serbian Orthodox Church (Serbia and Montenegro)

Peristeris, Archbishop Aristarchos, mo, Greek Orthodox Patriarchate of Jerusalem (Palestine/Israel)

Peters, Mr Humphrey Sarfraz, ml, Church of Pakistan (Pakistan)

Petersen, Bishop Sofie, fo, Evangelical Lutheran Church in Denmark (Greenland)

Petrossian, H.G. Bishop Dr Yeznik (Samvel), mo, Armenian Apostolic Church (Holy See of Etchmiadzin) (Armenia)

Peura, Bishop Simo, mo, Evangelical Lutheran Church of Finland (Finland)

Phidas, Mr Vlassios, ml, Church of Greece (Greece)

Pickens, Rev. Dr Larry, mo, United Methodist Church (United States of America)

Pico, Mr Jason Charles, yml, Iglesia Filipina Independiente (Philippines)

Pillay, Rev. Dr Jerry, mo, Uniting Presbyterian Church in Southern Africa (South Africa)

Pitts, Rev. Dr Tyrone, mo, Progressive National Baptist Convention, Inc. (United States of America)

Plaisier, Dr Bastiaan, mo, Protestantse Kerk in Nederland (Netherlands)

Poh, Mrs Emilienne, fl, Union des Eglises baptistes du Cameroun (Cameroon)

Poortman, Mrs Simone, fl, Protestantse Kerk in Nederland (Netherlands)

Poulos, Rev. Elenie, fo, Uniting Church in Australia (Australia)

Powell, Rev. Gareth John, mo, The Methodist Church of Great Britain (United Kingdom)

Powell, Rev. Dr Staccato, mo, African Methodist Episcopal Zion Church (United States of America)

Prabhakara Rao, Miss Tabitha Gnana Priya, yfl, Church of South India (India)

Pradhan, Rev. Enos Das, mo, Church of North India (India)

Praesoody, Ms Barbara, fl, Church of Ceylon (Sri Lanka)

Preston, Ms Alison Jane, yfl, Anglican Church of Australia (Australia)

Priana, Rev. I. Made, mo, Gereja Kristen Protestan di Bali (GKPB) (Indonesia)

Proshyan, Rev. Mkrtich (Hayk), ymo, Armenian Apostolic Church (Holy See of Etchmiadzin) (Armenia)

Prostrednik, Pastor Ondrej, mo, Evangelical Church of the Augsburg Confession in Slovakia (Slovakia)

Puii, Ms Lal Din, fl, Methodist Church, Upper Myanmar (Myanmar)

Purba, Rev. Martin Rumandja, mo, Gereja Kristen Protestan Simalungun (GKPS) (Indonesia)

Purwadisastra, Rev. Dr Semuel Obadya, mo, Gereja Kristen Indonesia (GKI) (Indonesia)

Quawas, Dr Audeh, ml, Greek Orthodox Patriarchate of Jerusalem (Jordan)

Rakoto, Dr Endor Modeste, mo, Eglise luthérienne malgache (Madagascar)

Rakotomandimby, Mme Blandine, fl, Church of the Province of the Indian Ocean (Madagascar)

Ralph, Ms Jessica, yfl, National Baptist Convention USA, Inc. (United States of America)

Rama, Ms Razel del Rosario, yfl, Ecumenical Patriarchate of Constantinople (Hong Kong)

Ranoh, Rev. Dr Ayub, mo, Gereja Masehi Injili di Timor (GMIT) (Indonesia)

Rasendrahasina, Rév. Lala, mo, Eglise de Jésus-Christ à Madagascar (Madagascar)

Razanadrakoto, Mme Suzette Vaolimanga, fl, Eglise de Jésus-Christ à Madagascar (Madagascar)

Redie, Dr Agedew Redie, ml, Ethiopian Orthodox Tewahedo Church (Ethiopia)

Reichel, Pfr Christoph, mo, Moravian Church (Germany)

Rein, Pfr Harald, mo, Christkatholische Kirche der Schweiz (Switzerland)

Renta, Rev. Nishihara, mo, Nippon Sei Ko Kai (Japan)

Rentel, The Rev. Dr Alexander, mo, Orthodox Church in America (United States of America)

Ribeiro, Revda Margarida Fátima Souza, fo, Igreja Metodista do Brasil (Brazil)

Richmond, Mr Benjamin, ml, Religious Society of Friends: Friends United Meeting (United States of America)

Ritchie, Obispa Nelida, fo, Iglesia Evangélica Metodista Argentina (Argentina)

Rodoussakis, Metropolitan Cornelius Emmanuel, mo, Greek Orthodox Patriarchate of Jerusalem (Palestine/Israel)

Rodrigo, Rev. Dushantha Lakshman, mo, Church of Ceylon (Sri Lanka)

Roham, H.E. Metropolitan Mor Eustathius Matta, mo, Syrian Orthodox Patriarchate of Antioch and All the East (Syria)

Rovere, Sr Pablo Daniel, ml, Iglesia Evangélica Metodista Argentina (Argentina)

Row, Mr Anthony, ml, Methodist Church in Malaysia (Malaysia)

Rozitis, Erzbischof Elmars E., mo, Evangelisch-Lutherische Kirche Lettlands im Ausland (Germany)

Rudolf, Rev. Helga Ingrid, fo, Evangelical Church of the Augsburg Confession in Romania (Romania)

Ruhulessin, Rev. Dr John Chr., mo, Gereja Protestan Maluku (GPM) (Indonesia)

Ruiters, Ms Erne, fl, Evangelical Lutheran Church in the Republic of Namibia (Namibia)

Rukimbira, Mr Maurice Klebert, ml, Province de l'Eglise Episcopale au Rwanda (Rwanda)

Rytkönen, Mr Aaro Paavo Samuli, yml, Evangelical Lutheran Church of Finland (Finland)

Sagar, Bishop Taranath S., mo, Methodist Church in India (India)

Sakaly, H.G. Bishop Niphon, mo, Greek Orthodox Patriarchate of Antioch and All the East (Russian Federation)

Saliba, H.E. Metropolitan Mar Theophilus George, mo, Syrian Orthodox Patriarchate of Antioch and All the East (Lebanon)

Salumäe, The Very Rev. Tiit, mo, Eesti Evangeelne Luterlik Kirik (Estonia)

Sambira, Rev. Marthen Jacob, mo, Gereja Protestan di Sulawesi Tenggara (GEPSULTRA) (Indonesia)

Sanchez, Mrs Christine Danielle, yfl, United Methodist Church (United States of America)

Sandu, Rev. Dr Dan, mo, Romanian Orthodox Church (Romania)

Santiago, Rev. Job A., mo, Convention of Philippine Baptist Churches (Philippines)

Sarkissian, Archbishop Sebouh, mo, Armenian Apostolic Church (Holy See of Cilicia) (Iran)

Sathiamurthy, Ms Pauline, fl, Church of South India (India)

Sawirios Malke Mourad, H.E. Archbishop Mor Severius, mo, Syrian Orthodox Patriarchate of Antioch and All the East (Palestine/Israel)

Sawyer, Dr Robert, mo, Moravian Church in America (United States of America)

Schmidt, Kirchenpräsident Jann, mo, Evangelische Kirche in Deutschland (Germany)

Schoon-Tanis, Rev. Gretchen, yfo, Reformed Church in America (United States of America)

Schultz, Bishop Raymond L., mo, Evangelical Lutheran Church in Canada (Canada)

Schürer-Behrmann, Rev. Frank, mo, Evangelische Kirche in Deutschland (Germany)

Scouteris, Professor Dr Constantine, mo, Church of Greece (Greece)

Seloana, Mrs Dineo Talitha, fl, Uniting Reformed Church in Southern Africa (South Africa)

Senturias, Dr Erlinda, fl, United Church of Christ in the Philippines (Philippines)

Shanazari, Rev. Hendrik, mo, Synod of the Evangelical Church of Iran (Iran)

Shanks, Rev. Dr Norman, mo, Church of Scotland (United Kingdom)

Shaw, Dr William J., mo, National Baptist Convention USA, Inc. (United States of America)

Shegena Gobena, Dr Muluemebet Shegena, fl, Ethiopian Orthodox Tewahedo Church (Ethiopia)

Shenouda, Rev. Father Antonious Thabet, mo, Coptic Orthodox Church (United Kingdom)

Sherer, Bishop Ann, fo, United Methodist Church (United States of America)

Shikongo, Mrs Katriina-Kuna Idhidhimika, fl, Evangelical Lutheran Church in Namibia (Namibia)

Shin, Rev. Seung Min, mo, Presbyterian Church in the Republic of Korea (Korea, Republic of)

Shune, Mr Paulos, ml, Ethiopian Evangelical Church Mekane Yesus (Ethiopia)

Sibiya, Bishop Louis, mo, Evangelical Lutheran Church in Southern Africa (South Africa)

Siegien, Ms Anna, yfl, Polski Autokefaliczny Kosciol Prawoslawny (Poland)

Sigilipoe, Rev. Drijandi L., mo, Gereja Kristen Jawi Wetan (GKJW) (Indonesia)

Sigurdson, Rev. Janet, fo, United Church of Canada (Canada)

Silalahi, Mrs Roswita, fl, Huria Kristen Batak Protestan (HKBP) (Indonesia)

Silantiev, Dr Roman, yml, Russian Orthodox Church (Russian Federation)

Simamora, Rev. Maurids, mo, Gereja Kristen Protestan Indonesia (GKPI) (Indonesia)

Simanjuntak, Rev. Rudolf, mo, Huria Kristen Indonesia (HKI) (Indonesia)

Simarmata, Rev. Willem, mo, Huria Kristen Batak Protestan (HKBP) (Indonesia)

Sinaga, Rev. Dr Deonal, mo, Huria Kristen Batak Protestan (HKBP) (Indonesia)

Sixt-Gateuille, Mme Claire, yfl, Eglise Réformée de France (France)

Sköldh Jonsson, Rev. Ulla, fo, United Methodist Church (Sweden)

So, Rev. Eric, mo, Hong Kong Council of the Church of Christ in China (China)

Soliba, Most Rev. Ignacio C., mo, Episcopal Church in the Philippines (Philippines)

Spencer, Rev. Glenna, fo, Methodist Church in the Caribbean and the Americas (Guyana)

Speranskaya, Ms Elena, fl, Russian Orthodox Church (Russian Federation)

Stabb, Ms Heidi Rebecca, yfl, Uniting Church in Australia (Australia)

Starcova, Ms Iveta, yfl, Orthodox Church of the Czech Lands and Slovakia (Slovakia)

Statcenko, Father Sergey, mo, Russian Orthodox Church (Uzbekistan)

Steele, Rev.Canon John Alfred, mo, Anglican Church of Canada (Canada)

Stefanowski, Rev. Pawel Wlodzimierz, mo, Polski Autokefaliczny Kosciol Prawoslawny (Poland)

Stephen, Bishop Michael Kehinde, mo, Methodist Church Nigeria (Nigeria)

Stokes, Mrs Perfecta D. Pelagio, fl, Episcopal Church in the Philippines (Philippines)

Storheim, Bishop Seraphim, mo, Orthodox Church in America (Canada)

Stückelberger, Rev. Prof. Dr Christoph, mo, Schweizerischer Evangelischer Kirchenbund (Switzerland)

Sudarmo, Rev. Johanes Bedjo, mo, Gereja-Gereja Kristen Jawa (GKJ) (Indonesia)

Sukhu, Rev. Rawle, mo, Presbyterian Church in Trinidad and Tobago (Trinidad and Tobago)

Sunny, Mr Pattasaril Oommen, ml, Mar Thoma Syrian Church of Malabar (India)

Supit, Rev. Dr Albert Obethnego, mo, Gereja Masehi Injili di Minahasa (GMIM) (Indonesia)

Takatsu Winnischofer, Ms Christina, fl, Igreja Episcopal Anglicana do Brasil (Brazil)

Tamasha, Mlle Ruth Ntagulwa, fl, ECC - Communauté anglicane au Congo
(Congo, Democratic Republic of)

Tarr, Rev. Zoltán, mo, Magyarországi Református Egyház (Hungary)

Tashjian, Mr Robert Zareh, ml, Armenian Apostolic Church (Holy See of Etchmiadzin) (Egypt)

Tawfik, Dr Wedad A., fl, Coptic Orthodox Church (Egypt)

Teodoridis, Ms Anna, yfl, Ecumenical Patriarchate of Constantinople (Turkey)

Tering, Dr Wivina, fl, United Church of Christ in the Philippines (Philippines)

Thai, Mrs Alphoncinah 'Matseko, fl, Lesotho Evangelical Church (Lesotho)

Theocharis, Mr Dimosthenis, yml, Church of Greece (Greece)

Thomas, Rev. John, mo, United Church of Christ (United States of America)

Thomas, Ms Sibyl, fl, Malankara Orthodox Syrian Church (United States of America)

Thomas, Ms Theodora, yfl, Methodist Church Nigeria (Nigeria)

Thompson, Ms Carolyn, fl, United Church of Christ (United States of America)

Thomsen, Ms Inger, yfl, Evangelical Lutheran Church in Denmark (Denmark)

Thor, Rev. Sjöfn, yfo, Evangelical Lutheran Church of Iceland (Iceland)

Thornell, Rev. Dr Kwasi, mo, Episcopal Church in the USA (United States of America)

Thornton, Rev. Jill Margaret, fo, United Reformed Church (United Kingdom)

Tialavea, Rev. Samuel T., mo, Congregational Christian Church in American Samoa (American Samoa)

Tiki-Koum (Soppo), Mme Madeleine Sara, fl, Eglise évangélique du Cameroun (Cameroon)

Timofticiuc, Ms Elena, fl, Romanian Orthodox Church (Romania)

Tisell, Rev. Daniel, mo, Svenska Kyrkan (Sweden)

Tita, Rev. Dr Michael, mo, Romanian Orthodox Church (Romania)

Tolstova, Ms Veera, fl, Russian Orthodox Church (Russian Federation)

Torppa, Mrs Mirkka, fl, Evangelical Lutheran Church of Finland (Finland)

Tron Urban, Pastora Carola Ruth, yfo, Iglesia Evangélica Valdense del Rio de la Plata (Uruguay)

Tsegay, Rev. Samuel, mo, Eritrean Orthodox Tewahdo Church (Eritrea)

Tshawane, Rev. Dr Ngamilorho Joseph, mo, Evangelical Presbyterian Church in South Africa (South Africa)

Tu Lum, Rev. K. D., mo, Myanmar Baptist Convention (Myanmar)

Tudorie, Mr Ionut, ml, Romanian Orthodox Church (Romania)

Turinayo, Miss Jackline, yfl, Church of the Province of Uganda (Uganda)

Tyler, Mrs Arlene, fl, Progressive National Baptist Convention, Inc. (United States of America)

Uka, Rev. Prof. Emele Mba, mo, Presbyterian Church of Nigeria (Nigeria)

Ulanday, Mr Jonathan, ml, United Methodist Church (Philippines)

Usung, Mrs Helen Ubon, fl, Presbyterian Church of Nigeria (Nigeria)

Usung, Right Rev. Ubon Bassey, mo, Presbyterian Church of Nigeria (Nigeria)

Utia, Mr Piniki, ml, Cook Islands Christian Church (Cook Islands)

Vad Nilsen, Rev. Ingrid, fo, Church of Norway (Norway)

Van Leeuwen, Prof. Dr Theodoor Marius, mo, Remonstrantse Broederschap (Netherlands)

Vanags, Erzbischof Janis, mo, Evangelical Lutheran Church of Latvia (Latvia)

Varea, Miss Geraldine, yfl, Methodist Church in Fiji and Rotuma (Fiji)

Vasilejic, H.G. Bishop Maxim, mo, Serbian Orthodox Church (Bosnia and Herzegovina)

Vasko, Ms Outi, yfo, Suomen ortodoksinen Kirkko (Finland)

Vasyutin, Rev. Alexander, mo, Russian Orthodox Church (Russian Federation)

Vercammen, Archbishop Joris, mo, International Old Catholic Bishops Conference (Netherlands)

Vince, Ms Ruth, fl, Evangelical Lutheran Church in Canada (Canada)

Vladimirou, Metropolitan Georgios, mo, Greek Orthodox Patriarchate of Alexandria and All Africa (Zimbabwe)

Vyzhanov, Father Igor, mo, Russian Orthodox Church (Russian Federation)

Wade, Rev. Dr Cheryl H., fo, American Baptist Churches in the USA (United States of America)

Walker-Smith, Rev. Dr Angelique, fo, National Baptist Convention USA, Inc. (United States of America)

Waqairatu, Rev. Tuikilakila Kolilevu, mo, Methodist Church in Fiji (Fiji)

Wartenberg-Potter, Bischöfin Bärbel, fo, Evangelische Kirche in Deutschland (Germany)

Watkins, Rev. Dr Sharon, fo, Christian Church (Disciples of Christ) (United States of America)

Weber, Bishop Dr Friedrich, mo, Evangelische Kirche in Deutschland (Germany)

Wehbe, Mrs Maha, fl, Greek Orthodox Patriarchate of Antioch and All the East (Lebanon)

Wejryd, Bishop Anders, mo, Svenska Kyrkan (Sweden)

Welsh, Dr Robert, mo, Christian Church (Disciples of Christ) (United States of America)

Wen, Mr Ge, yml, China Christian Council (China)

Wete, Pasteur Hnoija Jean, mo, Eglise évangélique en Nouvelle-Calédonie et aux Iles Loyauté (New Caledonia)

Williams, Rev. Dr Adrian Pugh, mo, Presbyterian Church of Wales (United Kingdom)

Williams, Mr Jay, yml, United Methodist Church (United States of America)

Winbush, Rev. Robina, fo, Presbyterian Church (USA) (United States of America)

Wipf, Pfr Thomas, mo, Schweizerischer Evangelischer Kirchenbund (Switzerland)

Yamada, Ms Motoe, yfl, United Methodist Church (United States of America)

Yannoulatos, Archbishop Anastasios, mo, Kisha Orthodhokse Autoqefale e Shqipërisë (Albania)

Yeboah, Ms Anita Emelia, yfl, Methodist Church, Ghana (Ghana)

Yewangoe, Rev. Dr Andreas, mo, Gereja Kristen Sumba (GKS) (Indonesia)

Yohannes, Mr Seifesellassie, ml, Ethiopian Orthodox Tewahedo Church (Ethiopia)

Youannes, H.G. Bishop, mo, Coptic Orthodox Church (Egypt)

Young, Bishop McKinley, mo, African Methodist Episcopal Church (United States of America)

Youssef, H.G. Bishop, mo, Coptic Orthodox Church (United States of America)

Yowakim, Bishop Paul, mo, Coptic Orthodox Church (Kenya)

Zahirsky, Mrs Valerie, fl, Orthodox Church in America (United States of America)

Zaki, Rev. Emile, mo, Evangelical Presbyterian Church of Egypt Synod of the Nile (Egypt)

Zapolskaya, Ms Anna, yfl, Russian Orthodox Church (Russian Federation)

Zarsky, Rev. Radim, mo, Ceskobratrská církev evangelická (Czech Republic)

Zazaza, Rev. Simon, mo, United Congregational Church of Southern Africa (South Africa)

Zecharias, H.G. Abune, mo, Ethiopian Orthodox Tewahedo Church (Ethiopia)

Zettergren, Rev. Lars Göran, mo, Svenska Missionskyrkan (Sweden)

Zeyi Ndingambote, Pasteur Simon, mo, Eglise de Jésus Christ sur la Terre par son Envoyé spécial Simon Kimbangu (Congo, Democratic Republic of)

Zinsou-Lawson, Rév. Martine G.N., fo, Eglise méthodiste du Togo (Togo)

Zorn, Rév. Jean-François, mo, Eglise Réformée de France (France)

Representatives of associate member churches

Aravena Bravo, Obispo Neftali, mo, Iglesia Metodista de Chile (Chile)

Baroi, Rt Rev. Michael Savaranjan, mo, Church of Bangladesh (Bangladesh)

Benitez, Pastor Miguel Angel, mo, Iglesia de Dios (Argentina)

Bolioli Murdoch, Presidente Oscar Luis, mo, Iglesia Metodista en el Uruguay (Uruguay)

Bravo Caballero, Obispo Jorge, mo, Iglesia Metodista del Peru (Peru)

Catunta Nacho, Lic. Rodolfo Fredy, ml, Iglesia Evangélica Luterana Boliviana (Bolivia)

Dorado Porras, Sra Alina, yfl, Iglesia Metodista en el Uruguay (Uruguay)

Ela Eyang, Pastor Juan Ebang, mo, Iglesia Reformada Presbiteriana de Guinea Ecuatorial (Equatorial Guinea)

García Bachmann, Rev. Dr Mercedes Laura, fo, Iglesia Evangélica Luterana Unida (Argentina)

Gasparini, Sra Sandra Viviana, fl, Iglesia Cristiana Biblica (Argentina)

Kahuku, Bishop Zakaria, mo, Kenya Evangelical Lutheran Church (Kenya)

Kinda, Pasteur Sombepouire Lazare, mo, Association des Églises Evangéliques Réformées du Burkina Faso (Burkina Faso)

Lopez-Lozano, Obispo Carlos, mo, Iglesia Episcopal Reformada de España (Spain)

Macchi, Pastor Luis Reinaldo, mo, Iglesia Evangélica de los Discipulos de Cristo (Argentina)

Magomere, Archbishop Nathan, mo, African Church of the Holy Spirit (Kenya)

Mana Saguiga, Pasteur Emmanuel, mo, Eglise protestante africaine (Cameroon)

Matsinhe, M. Paulo Vasco, ml, Igreja Presbiteriana de Moçambique (Mozambique)

Mejia Camargo, Pastor Milton, mo, Iglesia Presbiteriana de Colombia (Colombia)

Mello, Rev. Josué da Silva, mo, Igreja Presbiteriana Unida do Brasil (Brazil)

Mendez Rodriguez, Rev. Dr Hector Jose, mo, Iglesia Presbiteriana-Reformada en Cuba (Cuba)

Park, Rev. Dr Sookil, mo, Korean Christian Church in Japan (Japan)

Pereira Díaz, Obispo Ricardo, mo, Iglesia Metodista en Cuba (Cuba)

Petrecca, Pastor Hector Osvaldo, mo, Iglesia Cristiana Biblica (Argentina)

Pina-Cabral, Rev. José Jorge, mo, Igreja Lusitana Catolica (Portugal)

Poma Apaza, Obispo Carlos, mo, Iglesia Evangélica Metodista en Bolivia (Bolivia)

Rapisarda, Rev. Salvatore, mo, Evangelical Baptist Union of Italy (Italy)

Rivas Hernández, Lic. Manuel Enrique, ml, Asociación Bautista de El Salvador (El Salvador)

Soares, Bishop Andrés, mo, Igreja Evangélica Unida "Comunhão Anglicana em Angola" (Angola)

Valente, Mr David, ml, Igreja Evangélica Presbiteriana de Portugal (Portugal)

Vera Méndez, Obispo Juan Antonio, mo, Iglesia Metodista de Puerto Rico (Puerto Rico)

Advisors to the delegations

Adams, Rev. Dr Charles G., mo, Progressive National Baptist Convention, Inc. (United States of America)

Allan, Dr Gail, fl, United Church of Canada (Canada)

Amunazo Katanda, Mme Naomi, fl, ECC - Communauté anglicane au Congo (Congo, Democratic Republic of)

Assis da Silva, Rev. Francisco de, mo, Igreja Episcopal Anglicana do Brasil (Brazil)

Auken Nielson, Mrs Kirsten Margrete, fl, Evangelical Lutheran Church in Denmark (Denmark)

Ayete Nyampong, Rev. Dr Samuel, mo, Presbyterian Church of Ghana (Ghana)

Baji, Bishop Dr Philip Dunstan, mo, Anglican Church of Tanzania (Tanzania)

Barnett-Cowan, Canon Dr Alyson, fo, Anglican Church of Canada (Canada)

Biakliana, Rev. K., mo, Methodist Church, Upper Myanmar (Myanmar)

Black, Very Rev. Cynthia L., fo, Episcopal Church in the USA (United States of America)

Bock, Mr Carlos Gilberto, ml, Igreja Evangélica de Confissão Luterana no Brasil (Brazil)

Buys, Rev. Jameson Dawn, mo, Uniting Reformed Church in Southern Africa (South Africa)

Charilaou, Mr Ioannis, ml, Church of Cyprus (Cyprus)

Cho, Rev. Sung Ki, mo, Presbyterian Church of Korea (Korea, Republic of)

Corvalan-Vasquez, Dr Oscar Enrique, ml, Iglesia Pentecostal de Chile (Chile)

Crouzet, Pasteur Didier, mo, Eglise Réformée de France (France)

Cunningham, Bishop Ronald, mo, Christian Methodist Episcopal Church (United States of America) *de Chickera*, The Rt Rev. Duleep Kamil, mo, Church of Ceylon (Sri Lanka)

Digby, Rev. Nathan, mo, Christian Church (Disciples of Christ) (United States of America)

Dina, Prophetess Dr Titi, fl, Church of the Lord (Aladura) Worldwide (Nigeria)

Djema, Rév. Mathieu Fridolin, ml, Eglise évangélique du Congo (Congo, Republic of)

Dockhorn de Sievers, Pastora Irene, fl, Iglesia Evangélica Luterana Boliviana (Bolivia)

Doom, Mr John Taroanui, ml, Eglise Protestante Maòhi (French Polynesia)

Freier, Bishop Philip, mo, Anglican Church of Australia (Australia)

Fromm, Rev. Douglas, mo, Reformed Church in America (United States of America)

Fubara-Manuel, Rev. Dr Benebo, mo, Presbyterian Church of Nigeria (Nigeria)

Gerny, Bishop Hans, mo, Christkatholische Kirche der Schweiz (Switzerland)

Gitonga, Rev. Josphat Munyoro, mo, African Christian Church and Schools (Kenya)

Gohar, Mr Insar, ml, Church of Pakistan (Pakistan)

Gomis, Mme Ebla Bernadette, fl, Eglise Harriste (Côte d'Ivoire)

Grace, Ms Eden, fl, Religious Society of Friends: Friends United Meeting (Kenya)

Györky, Rev. Szilvia, fo, Reformed Christian Church in Slovakia (Slovakia)

Heller, Rev. Dr Dagmar, fo, Evangelische Kirche in Deutschland (Germany)

Istephanous, Rev. Dr Andrea Zaki, mo, Evangelical Presbyterian Church of Egypt Synod of the Nile (Egypt)

Johnson, Rev. Paul N., mo, Evangelical Lutheran Church in Canada (Canada)

Kan, Rev. Baoping, mo, China Christian Council (China)

Kim, Rev. Dr Kwan Lyun, mo, Korean Methodist Church (Korea, Republic of)

Kongi, Bishop John, mo, Africa Inland Church - Sudan (Sudan)

Lee, Rev. Randall R., mo, Evangelical Lutheran Church in America (United States of America)

Luczak, Mr Bartosz Przemyslaw, yml, Staro-Katolicki Kosciol Mariawitow w Polsce (Poland)

Lukman, Dr Tiandi, fl, Gereja Methodist Indonesia (GMI) (Indonesia)

Lumenta, Rev. Dr Dirk Johan, mo, Gereja Protestan di Indonesia (GPI) (Indonesia)

Mangoyo, Pasteur Joseph, mo, Eglise de Jésus Christ sur la Terre par son Envoyé spécial Simon Kimbangu (Congo, Republic of)

McCloud, Jr., Bishop E. Earl, mo, African Methodist Episcopal Church (United States of America)

McClure, Rev. Dr Marian, fo, Presbyterian Church (USA) (United States of America)

Meyendorff, Dr Paul, ml, Orthodox Church in America (United States of America)

Moraes, Rev. Stanley da Silva, mo, Igreja Metodista do Brasil (Brazil)

Ngoy Wa Banza, Evêque Marie-Thérèse, fo, ECC - Communauté épiscopale baptiste en Afrique (Congo, Democratic Republic of)

Noffsinger, Mr Stanley, ml, Church of the Brethren (United States of America)

Nokise, Rev. Dr Feleterika, mo, Presbyterian Church of Aotearoa New Zealand (Fiji)

Ortiz Vidal, Dr Víctor R., ml, Iglesia Metodista de Puerto Rico (Puerto Rico)

Ott-Bächler, Pasteur Isabelle, fo, Schweizerischer Evangelischer Kirchenbund (Switzerland)

Parginos, Archimandrite Peter, mo, Greek Orthodox Patriarchate of Alexandria and All Africa (South Africa)

Paxson, Dr Thomas, ml, Religious Society of Friends: Friends General Conference (United States of America)

Pradeep Samuel, Rev. Dr Elia, mo, Methodist Church in India (India)

Röselaers, Mr Joost Hubert, yml, Remonstrantse Broederschap (Netherlands)

Schvindt, Rev. Juan Abelardo, mo, Iglesia Evangélica del Rio de la Plata (Argentina)

Selinder, Rev. Per-Magnus, mo, Svenska Missionskyrkan (Sweden)

Souza Miranda, Rev. Manoel, ml, Igreja Presbiteriana Unida do Brasil (Brazil)

Sparkes, The Rev. Graham Russel, mo, Baptist Union of Great Britain (United Kingdom)

Sugandhar, Bishop Badda Peter, mo, Church of South India (India)

Tamaweol, Rev. Roy Dekky, mo, Gereja Masehi Injili di Minahasa (GMIM) (Indonesia)

Theophilus, Bishop Dr Zacharias Mar, mo, Mar Thoma Syrian Church of Malabar (India)

Tveit, Rev. Dr Olav Fykse, mo, Church of Norway (Norway)

Ueda, Rev. Hiroko, fo, United Church of Christ in Japan (Japan)

Vaccaro, Pastor Jorge Julio, ml, Iglesia de Dios (Argentina)

Vellem, Rev. Vuyani, mo, Uniting Presbyterian Church in Southern Africa (South Africa)

Vogelaar, Dr Hubert, ml, Eglise protestante unie de Belgique (Netherlands)

Vreden, Mr Franklin Eduard, ml, Moravian Church in Suriname (Suriname)

Woods, Rev. Philip James, mo, United Reformed Church (United Kingdom)

Yabaki, Rev. Akuila Dreudreu, mo, Methodist Church in Fiji (Fiji)

Yoon, Rev. Kil-Soo, mo, Presbyterian Church in the Republic of Korea (Korea, Republic of)

Yule, Rev. Dr Sandy, mo, Uniting Church in Australia (Australia)

Presidents of the WCC
(present at the Assembly and not attending as delegates)

Kang, Dr Moon-Kyu, ml, Presbyterian Church in the Republic of Korea (Korea, Republic of)

Pagura, Obispo Federico José Natalio, mo, Iglesia Evangélica Metodista Argentina (Argentina)

Powell Jackson, Rev. Dr Bernice, fo, United Church of Christ (United States of America)

Renz, Bischof Dr Eberhardt, mo, EKD – Evangelische Landeskirche in Württemberg (Germany)

Members of the retiring Central Committee of the WCC (present at the Assembly and not attending as delegates)

Ambrosios of Kalavryta and Aigealia, H.E. Metropolitan, mo, Church of Greece (Greece)

Bakkevig, Rev. Canon Dr Trond, mo, Church of Norway (Norway)

Etchegoyen, Obispo Aldo Manuel, mo, Iglesia Evangélica Metodista Argentina (Argentina)

Finlay, Canon Alice Jean, fl, Anglican Church of Canada (Canada)

Kinnunen, Rev. Mari, fo, Evangelical Lutheran Church of Finland (Finland)

Muchopa, Mr Naboth M., ml, The Methodist Church of Great Britain (United Kingdom)

Pantupong, Mrs Woranut, fl, Church of Christ in Thailand (Thailand)

Souza, Rev. Inamar Corrêa de, fo, Igreja Episcopal Anglicana do Brasil (Brazil)

Tharawanich, Mrs Woraporn, fl, Church of Christ in Thailand (Thailand)

Delegated Representatives of WCC associate councils
and other ecumenical organizations

Alvim, Dr Gustavo Jacques Dias, ml, World Methodist Council (Brazil)

Anders, Rev. Christoph, mo, Evangelisches Missionswerk in Deutschland (Germany)

Anderson, Rev. Dr Lesley, mo, Caribbean Conference of Churches (Jamaica)

Bakker, Rev. Drs Hermina Johanna (Ineke), fo, Council of Churches in the Netherlands (Netherlands)

Barnett, Bishop Thomas J., mo, Council of Churches in Sierra Leone (Sierra Leone)

Batista Guerra, Rev. Israel, mo, Consejo Latinoamericano de Iglesias (Ecuador)

Bensen, Dr Kenneth, mo, Habitat for Humanity International (United States of America)

Bond, Commissioner Linda Christene Diane, fo, Salvation Army (Canada)

Borgegård, Ms Gunnel, fo, International Council of Christians and Jews (Sweden)

Brune, Mr Peter, ml, Life and Peace Institute (Sweden)

Bruning, Mr Johannes, ml, Interchurch Organization for Development Cooperation (Netherlands)

Bula, Ms Omega, fl, United Church of Canada – Justice, Global and Ecumenical Relations (Canada)

Byu, Dr Esther, fl, Fellowship of the Least Coin (Thailand)

Cameron, Rev. Gregory Kenneth, mo, Anglican Consultative Council (United Kingdom)

Carlsen, Rev. (Ms) Liv Berit, fo, Norwegian Church Aid (Norway)

Cook, Rev. Gary, mo, Presbyterian Church (USA) - Worldwide Ministries (United States of America)

Dandala, Bishop H. Mvume, mo, All Africa Conference of Churches (Kenya)

Daudé, Pasteur Gill, mo, Fédération Protestante de France (France)

Daulay, Dr Richard, ml, Communion of Churches in Indonesia (PGI) (Indonesia)

Díaz Vandorsee, Mr Mauricio, ml, World Alliance of YMCAs (Brazil)

Dirdak, Rev. Paul, ml, United Methodist Church - General Board of Global Ministries (United States of America)

Edgar, Dr Robert W., mo, National Council of the Churches of Christ in the USA (United States of America)

Edström, Rev. Jan Rafael, mo, Finnish Ecumenical Council (Finland)

Fast, Rev. Sven-Bernhard, mo, Christian Council of Sweden (Sweden)

Fraser, Ms Margaret R., fl, Friends World Committee for Consultation (United States of America)

Füllkrug-Weitzel, Pfarrerin Cornelia, fo, Diakonisches Werk der EKD (Germany)

Galloway, Rev. Kathryn Johnston, fo, Iona Community (United Kingdom)

Gmünder, Herr Reto, mo, Brot für Alle (Switzerland)

Gonzáles Zorrilla, Pastora Rhode, fo, Consejo de Iglesias de Cuba (Cuba)

Grape, Ms Margareta, fl, International Mission and Diakona, Church of Sweden (Sweden)

Graz, Dr John, mo, General Conference of Seventh-day Adventists (United States of America)

Groth, Rev. Reiner, mo, United Evangelical Mission (Germany)

Gull, Mr Tor G., ml, Oikocredit (Netherlands)

Hamilton, Rev. Dr Karen, fo, Canadian Council of Churches (Canada)

Heisey, Dr Nancy R., fl, Mennonite World Conference (United States of America)

Henderson, Rev. John, mo, National Council of Churches in Australia (Australia)

Hewitt, Rev. Dr Roderick, mo, Council for World Mission (Jamaica)

Holguin Khoury, Obispo Julio Cesar, mo, Consejo Latinoamericano de Iglesias (Dominican Republic)

Johnston, Rev. Andrew, mo, Presbyterian World Service and Development (Canada)

Kanerva, Mr Timo Mikko, ml, Global Fellowship of Christian Youth (Finland)

Kearon, Rev. Canon Kenneth, mo, Anglican Consultative Council (United Kingdom)

Khid-arn, Dr Prawate, ml, Christian Conference of Asia (Hong Kong)

Kolia, Rev. Fepai Fiu, mo, Samoa Council of Churches (Samoa)

Lara, Dr Antonio, ml, United Bible Societies (United States of America)

Lartey, Mr Benjamin Dorme, ml, Liberian Council of Churches (Liberia)

Livingston, Rev. Michael, mo, National Council of the Churches of Christ in the USA (United States of America)

Lotz, Dr Denton, ml, Baptist World Alliance (United States of America)

Maia, Bishop Adriel de Souza, mo, Conselho Nacional de Igrejas Cristãs do Brasil - CONIC (Brazil)

Malpica Padilla, The Rev. Rafael, mo, Evangelical Lutheran Church in America - Global Mission (United States of America)

Mateus, Dr Odair Pedroso, mo, World Alliance of Reformed Churches (Switzerland)

McCullough, Rev. John L., mo, Church World Service (United States of America)

Milloy, Rev. A. Miller, mo, United Bible Societies (United Kingdom)

Modiega, Mr David Joshua, ml, Botswana Council of Churches (Botswana)

Molin, Rev. Dr Lennart, mo, Svenska Missionskyrkan (Sweden)

Montacute, Mr Paul, ml, Baptist World Alliance (United States of America)

Mtaita, Rev. Dr Leonard Amos, mo, Christian Council of Tanzania (Tanzania)

Mukarji, Dr Daleep, ml, Christian Aid (United Kingdom)

Nauta, Ms Rommie, fl, Kerkinactie (Netherlands)

Naylor, Rev. Dr Randolph, mo, World Association for Christian Communication (United Kingdom)

Ndhlovu, Rev. Japhet, mo, Christian Council of Zambia (Zambia)

Nguimbi, Rev. Luís, mo, Council of Christian Churches in Angola (Angola)

Nicolaisen, Ms Lene Suh, yfl, National Council of Churches in Denmark (Denmark)

Noko, Rev. Dr Ishmael, mo, Lutheran World Federation (Switzerland)

Nyomi, Rev. Dr Setri, mo, World Alliance of Reformed Churches (Switzerland)

Okorie, Rev. Ike, mo, Christian Council of Nigeria (Nigeria)

Oppegaard, Rev. Sven, mo, Lutheran World Federation (Switzerland)

Palu, Rev. Valamotu, fo, Pacific Conference of Churches (Fiji)

Peiris, Rev. Dr Pedurupeirisge Jayasiri Thidas, mo, National Christian Council of Sri Lanka (Sri Lanka)

Pentikainen, Mr Antti, ml, FinnChurchAid (Finland)

Penttinen, Rev. Pirjo-Liisa Kaarina, fo, World Young Women's Christian Association (Finland)

Pétremand, Mme Françoise, fl, International Fellowship of Reconciliation (Switzerland)

Phiri, Pastor Canaan, mo, Malawi Council of Churches (Malawi)

Pohjolainen, Deaconess Terttu Kyllikki, fo, World Federation of Diaconal Associations (Finland)

Price, Canon Janice Amanda, fo, Churches' Commission on Mission (United Kingdom)

Queiroz, Ms Antônio Celso, mo, Conselho Nacional de Igrejas Cristãs do Brasil - CONIC (Brazil)

Quintero Perez, Mr Manuel Abundio, ml, Frontier Internships in Mission (Switzerland)

Reddie, Mr Richerd Stuart, ml, Churches Together in England (United Kingdom)

Rey, Pasteur Alain Charles, mo, Communauté évangélique d'action apostolique (France)

Rhys Evans, Mr Siôn, yml, CYTUN: Churches Together in Wales (United Kingdom)

Rosenthal, Lic. Nicolás, ml, Federación Argentina de Iglesias Evangélicas (Argentina)

Rudolph, Rev. Barbara, fo, Arbeitsgemeinschaft Christlicher Kirchen in Deutschland (Germany)

Rumsey, Ms Suzanne Elizabeth, fl, Primate's World Relief & Development Fund - Anglican Church of Canada (Canada)

Rwaje, Bishop Onesphore, mo, Conseil Protestant du Rwanda (Rwanda)

Saad Oliviera, Ms Lourdes, yfl, World Young Womens' Christian Association (Switzerland)

Sahu, Bishop Dr Dhirendra Kumar, mo, National Council of Churches in India (India)

Saleh, Mr Guirguis, ml, Middle East Council of Churches (Lebanon)

Sanders, Ms Susan M., fl, United Church of Christ - Wider Church Ministries (United States of America)

Sanderson, Rev. Lindsey Heather, fo, Action of Churches Together in Scotland (United Kingdom)

Scott, Ms Janet, ml, Friends World Committee for Consultation (United Kingdom)

Shastri, Rev. Dr Hermen, mo, Council of Churches of Malaysia (Malaysia)

Simiyu, Mr Oliver Kisaka, ml, National Council of Churches of Kenya (Kenya)

Solomon, Mr Lambert Chirtranjan Devadasen, ml, Ecumenical Coalition on Third World Tourism (Hong Kong)

Sommerfeldt, Rev. Atle, mo, Norwegian Church Aid (Norway)

Soo, The Rt Rev. Dr Yee Po Thomas, mo, Hong Kong Christian Council (China)

Soto Vélez, Pastor Héctor, mo, Consejo de Iglesias de Puerto Rico (Puerto Rico)

Steen, Rev. Ørnulf, mo, Christian Council of Norway (Norway)

Steuernagel, Dr Valdir Raul, mo, World Vision International (Brazil)

Strydom, Rev. Philip Ancoat, mo, Council of Churches in Namibia (Namibia)

Stubkjaer, Rev. Henrik, mo, DanChurchAid (Denmark)

Sturve, Mr Göran, mo, Svenska Missionsradet (Sweden)

Tammo, Rev. Joosep, mo, Estonian Council of Churches (Estonia)

Tsele, Dr Molefe, mo, South African Council of Churches (South Africa)

Tunnicliffe, Rev. Geoffrey, mo, World Evangelical Alliance (Canada)

van der Water, Rev. Dr Desmond Peter, mo, Council for World Mission (United Kingdom)

van Drimmelen, Mr Robert Wilhelmus Fredrik, ml, Association of WCC-related Development Organisations in Europe (Belgium)

van Houten, Rev. Richard L., mo, Reformed Ecumenical Council (United States of America)

van Laar, Rev. Drs Wout, mo, Netherlands Missionary Council (Netherlands)

Vanhaverbeke, Ms Sylvia Lisk, fl, World Day of Prayer - International Committee (Canada)

Vargas, Rev. David, mo, Christian Church (Disciples of Christ) (United States of America)

Vea, Rev. Simote, mo, Tonga National Council of Churches (Tonga)

Villumstad, Mr Stein, ml, World Conference of Religions for Peace (United States of America)

Von Bonin, Dr Konrad, ml, Evangelischer Entwicklungsdienst (Germany)

Wallace, Mr Michael, ml, World Student Christian Federation (Switzerland)

Williams, The Ven. Colin, mo, Conference of European Churches (Switzerland)

Yamamoto, Rev. Toshimasa, mo, National Christian Council in Japan (Japan)

Zachraj, Mrs Aleksandra, yfl, Ecumenical Youth Council in Europe (Poland)

Delegated Observers

Aguado, Ms María Aranzazu, fl, Roman Catholic Church (Switzerland)

Albornoz Guevara, Rev. Pasteur Juana Rosa, fo, Iglesia Misión Apostólica (Chile)

Back, Dr Joan Patricia, fl, Roman Catholic Church (Italy)

Bezerra da Costa, Pastor José Wellington, mo, Convenção Geral das Assembléias de Deus no Brasil (Brazil)

Byamungu, Dr Gosbert, mo, Roman Catholic Church (Switzerland)

Castillo, Rev. Ramon, ml, Unión Evangélica Pentecostal Venezolana (Venezuela)

Conti, Archbishop Mario, mo, Roman Catholic Church (United Kingdom)

Edghill, Bishop Juan A., mo, Guyana Council of Churches (Guyana)

Emberti Gialloreti, Dr Leonardo, ml, Roman Catholic Church (Italy)

Farrell, Bishop Brian, mo, Roman Catholic Church (Vatican City)

Giordano, Rev. Msgr Aldo, mo, Roman Catholic Church (Switzerland)

Gonzalez de Castejon, Sister Maria Victoria, fl, Roman Catholic Church (Italy)

Grings, Archbishop Dadeus, mo, Roman Catholic Church (Brazil)

Guerrero Fariño, Pastor Freddy Pompilio, mo, Iglesia del Nazareno y Fundación Latinoamericano de Estudios de Teologia (Ecuador)

Lapoorta, Dr Japie, ml, Apostolic Faith Mission in South Africa (South Africa)

Lovett, Dr Leonard, ml, Church of God in Christ, Inc. (United States of America)

Lovett, Mrs Marie Phyllis, fl, Church of God in Christ, Inc. (United States of America)

Lugo Morales, Rev. Gamaliel, mo, Comisión Evangélica Pentecostal Latinoamericana (CEPLAL) (Venezuela)

Marchiori, Most Rev. João Oneres, mo, Roman Catholic Church (Brazil)

Mendoza Vega, Obispo Richar Rene, mo, Iglesia de Dios, Misión Mundial (Ecuador)

Michel, Rev. Thomas, mo, Roman Catholic Church (Italy)

Munono Muyembe, Mgr Bernard, mo, Roman Catholic Church (Vatican City)

Mutiso-Mbinda, Msgr John, mo, Roman Catholic Church (Italy)

Ntumy, Dr Michael Kwabena, ml, The Church of Pentecost (Ghana)

Nunes, Pastor Ivan, mo, Igreja Evangélica Pentecostal o Brasil para Cristo (Brazil)

Ortiz Ortiz, Pastor Rafael, mo, Cuerpo de Pastores de Quito (Ecuador)

Pereira, Rev. Assir, mo, Igreja Presbiteriana Independente do Brasil (Brazil)

Radano, Monsignor John A., mo, Roman Catholic Church (Vatican City)

Sayah, Archbishop Paul Nabil, mo, Roman Catholic Church (Palestine/Israel)

Sklba, Bishop Richard, mo, Roman Catholic Church (United States of America)

Suico, Rev. Dr Joseph, mo, Asian Pentecostal Society (Philippines)

Trabucco, Rev. Pietro, mo, Roman Catholic Church (Italy)

Usma Gomez, Rev. Msgr Juan, mo, Roman Catholic Church (Vatican City)

Winterle, Rev. Dr Carlos Walter, mo, Igreja Evangélica Luterana do Brasil - IELB (Brazil)

Observers

Adhikari, Mr Joyanta, ml, National Council of Churches, Bangladesh (Bangladesh)

Amoa, Mr Baffour Dokyi, ml, Fellowship of Christian Councils and Churches in West Africa (FEC-CIWA) (Ghana)

Andréas, Rev. Marianne, fo, Swedish Free Church Council (Sweden)

Andriatsiratahina, Rev. Dr Roger, mo, Fedération des Eglises protestantes à Madagascar (Madagascar)

Askola, Rev. Irja, fo, Evangelical Lutheran Church of Finland (Finland)

Biebinger, Pf. Dr Frank, mo, Evangelische Kirche in Deutschland (Germany)

Bore, Mr Thor Bjarne, ml, Norwegian Church Aid (Norway)

Bouman, Mr Dick, ml, Kerkinactie (Netherlands)

Browne, Rev. Dr William C., mo, Presbyterian Church (USA) (United States of America)

Busch, Pfarrerin Christine, fo, EKD – Evangelische Kirche im Rheinland (Germany)

Cantell, Rev. Dr Risto Jaakko Juhani, mo, Evangelical Lutheran Church of Finland (Finland)

Castillo Gutierrez, Hon. Eduardo, ml, Iglesia Metodista de Mexico (Mexico)

Chang, Ms Chung-Chih, yfl, Christian Conference of Asia (Hong Kong)

Chikasa, Mr Abraham Chungu, ml, Christian Council of Zambia (Zambia)

Chirappurath, Mr George John, ml, Mar Thoma Syrian Church of Malabar (Bahrain)

Cipriani, Father Gabriele, mo, Conselho Nacional de Igrejas Cristãs do Brasil - CONIC (Brazil)

Clarke, Rev. Dr Knolly, mo, Caribbean Conference of Churches (Trinidad and Tobago)

Cortés Marchena, Dr Benjamín, mo, Communidad Cristiana Mesoamericana (Nicaragua)

Coulter, Mr Thomas, ml, Uniting Presbyterian Church in Southern Africa (South Africa)

D'Aloisio, Mr Christophe, yml, SYNDESMOS - The World Fellowship of Orthodox Youth (Belgium)

Damon, Rev. Malcolm, mo, Fellowship of Councils of Churches in Southern Africa (FOCCISA) (South Africa)

Dedji, Rév. Dr Valentin, mo, Eglise protestante méthodiste du Bénin (United Kingdom)

Deegbe, Rev. Dr Frederick Primrose, mo, Christian Council of Ghana (Ghana)

Denecke, Oberkirchenrat Norbert, mo, Lutheran World Federation (Germany)

Drayton, Rev. Dr Rodney Dean, mo, Uniting Church in Australia (Australia)

Earle, Mr John Michael, ml, Irish Council of Churches (United Kingdom)

Ebner-Golder, Rev. Dr Roswitha, fo, Ecumenical Forum of European Christian Women (Switzerland)

Edwards, Rev. Trevor, mo, Jamaica Baptist Union (Jamaica)

Fee, Rev. Richard W., mo, Presbyterian World Service and Development (Canada)

Francis, Commissioner William W., mo, Salvation Army (United Kingdom)

Friedner, General Secretary Lars, ml, Svenska Kyrkan (Sweden)

Friedrich, Rev. Dr Nestor Paulo, mo, Igreja Evangélica de Confissão Luterana no Brasil (Brazil)

Gerber, Dr Jacobus Johannes, mo, Dutch Reformed Church in South Africa (South Africa)

Getman, Mr Thomas, ml, World Vision International (Switzerland)

Granado, Mr Gerard, ml, Caribbean Conference of Churches (Trinidad and Tobago)

Granberg-Michaelson, Rev. Wesley, mo, Reformed Church in America (United States of America)

Groen, Prof. Dr Basilius Jacobus, fl, Pro Oriente (Austria)

Guy, Sister Anne-Emmanuelle, fl, Communauté de Grandchamp (Switzerland)

Halldorf, Mr Joel Samuel, yml, Swedish Free Church Council (Sweden)

Hartke, Ms Linda, fl, Ecumenical Advocacy Alliance (Switzerland)

Heitmann, Pfarrerin Anne, fo, EKD – Evangelische Landeskirche in Baden (Germany)

Hilborn, Rev. Dr David, mo, World Evangelical Alliance (United Kingdom)

Hitzler, Oberkirchenrat Dr Eberhard, mo, Evangelische Kirche in Deutschland (Germany)

Hollins, Rev. Beverley Jayne, fo, Association of Interchurch Families (United Kingdom)

Hsu, Rev. Dr King-Vi Eugene, mo, General Conference of Seventh-day Adventists (United States of America)

Janssen, Pastor Jan, mo, Deutscher Evangelischer Kirchentag (Germany)

Johnson, Rev. Dr Lydia, fl, Presbyterian Church of Aotearoa New Zealand (New Zealand-Aotearoa)

Joy, Mrs Elizabeth Thavamani, fl, Council for World Mission (United Kingdom)

Kanyoro, Mr Muhungi, ml, Ecumenical Church Loan Fund (Switzerland)

Karamoy, Mrs Meiske Soedjadi, fl, Gereja Protestan di Indonesia (GPI) (Indonesia)

Kelly, Ms Alison, fl, Christian Aid (United Kingdom)

Keum, Rev. Dr Jooseop, mo, Council for World Mission (United Kingdom)

Kim, Mr In Soo, yml, Korean Methodist Church (Korea, Republic of)

Koroma, Mr Alimamy Philip, ml, Council of Churches in Sierra Leone (Sierra Leone)

Küenzlen, Pfarrer Heiner, mo, EKD – Evangelische Landeskirche in Württemberg (Germany)

Kwabi, Rev. Albert Bitatsi, mo, Christian Council of Ghana (Ghana)

Laudermill, Jr., Rev. Sylvester, mo, African Methodist Episcopal Church (United States of America)

Lenz, Herrn Wolfgang, ml, Ecumenical Association of Academies and Laity Centres in Europe (Germany)

Lim, Rev. Heung-Ki, mo, National Council of Churches in Korea (Korea, Republic of)

Loeser, Brother Alois, ml, Taizé Community (France)

Long, Ms Callie, fl, Action by Churches Together (Switzerland)

Lund, Ms Helene, fl, Church of Norway (Norway)

Lundgren, Rev. Christofer, mo, Svenska Kyrkan (Sweden)

Marchinkowski, Rev. George, mo, Uniting Presbyterian Church in Southern Africa (South Africa)

Marshall, Ms Katherine, fl, World Faiths Development Dialogue (United States of America)

Marteleur Agrell, Ms Britt Louise, fl, Svenska Kyrkan (Sweden)

Mbillah, Rev. Dr Johnson Apenad, mo, PROCMURA/SRICA (Kenya)

Mokhosi, Rev. 'Mapeete, fo, Christian Council of Lesotho (Lesotho)

Moritz, Mr Torsten, ml, Churches' Commission for Migrants in Europe (Belgium)

Mundakkalazhikathu, Dr Yohannan Abraham, ml, United Religions Initiative (India)

Nathaniel, Rev. Leslie Satianathan, mo, Church of South India (Germany)

Nielsen, Rev. Villy Moelgaard, mo, Evangelical Lutheran Church in Denmark (Denmark)

Nyabera, Mr Fredrick, ml, Fellowship of Christian Councils & Churches in the Great Lakes & the Horn of Africa (Kenya)

Ohligschläger, Pfr Peter, mo, EKD – Evangelische Kirche von Westfalen (Germany)

Oikonomou, Dr Dimitri, ml, Alliance of Religions and Conservation (United Kingdom)

Oliveira, Archbishop Orlando Santos de, mo, Igreja Episcopal Anglicana do Brasil (Brazil)

Ozigi, Most Senior Apostle James Abiodun, mo, Council of African and Caribbean Churches UK (United Kingdom)

Paik, Rev. Dr Do-Woong, ymo, National Council of Churches in Korea (Korea, Republic of)

Parks, Ms Suzanne, fl, Anglican Consultative Council (United Kingdom)

Pavlovic, Rev. Dr Peter, mo, Conference of European Churches (Belgium)

Pawlikowski, Rev. Dr John Thaddeus, mo, International Council of Christians and Jews (United States of America)

Peccoud, Curé Dominique, mo, International Labour Organisation (Switzerland)

Petty, Mr George, ml, Ecumenical Church Loan Fund (Switzerland)

Pratt, Rev. Timothy, mo, Global Fellowship of Christian Youth (New Zealand-Aotearoa)

Puig Soler, Mr Luis Rafael, ml, Initiatives of Change International (Brazil)

Ramos Corona, Pastor Isaias, mo, Iglesia Metodista de Mexico (Mexico)

Riggs, Rev. Jennifer, fo, Church World Service (United States of America)

Rokaya, Dr Kali Bahadur, ml, Nepal Christian Council (Nepal)

Roring, Mr Royke, ml, Gereja Masehi Injili di Minahasa (GMIM) (Indonesia)

Schindehütte, Rev. Martin, ml, Evangelische Kirche in Deutschland (Germany)

Schneider, Brother Richard, ml, Taizé Community (France)

Short, Rev. Dr Peter, mo, United Church of Canada (Canada)

Sievers, Pfr Luis Henrique, mo, Evangelische Kirche von Kurhessen-Waldeck (Germany)

Skriewe, Frau Kathrin, fl, Evangelische Kirche in Deutschland (Germany)

Songulashvili, Bishop Malkhaz, mo, Baptist World Alliance (Georgia)

Studer, Frau Lilian, fl, Schweizerischer Evangelischer Kirchenbund (Switzerland)

Swamidawson, The Rt Rev. Dr Jeyapaul David, mo, National Council of Churches in India (India)

Tapia, Rev. Dr Elizabeth S., fo, United Methodist Church in the Philippines (United States of America)

Tokbi, Mr Anderson, ml, National Council of Churches in India (India)

Tyler, Dr Timothy E., ml, African Methodist Episcopal Church (United States of America)

Ucko, Ms Agneta, fl, Global Network of Religions for Children (Switzerland)

Uwadi, Archbishop Rogers Onuabughichi, mo, Christian Council of Nigeria (Nigeria)

Veliko, Rev. Lydia, fo, United Church of Christ (United States of America)

Weiss, Dr Hans-Martin, mo, EKD – Evangelisch-Lutherische Kirche in Bayern (Germany)

Williams, Rev. Dr Andrew, mo, Council for World Mission (United Kingdom)

Wilson, Rev. Elder Nancy, fo, Universal Fellowship of Metropolitan Community Churches (United States of America)

Wirth, Pfr Martin, mo, EKD – Evangelisch-Lutherische Kirche in Bayern (Germany)

Wullur-Waleleng, Mrs Emma, fl, Gereja Protestan di Indonesia (GPI) (Indonesia)

Guests

Alegría de Pagura, Sra Rita Margarita, fl, Iglesia Evangélica Metodista Argentina (Argentina)

Ariarajah, Dr S. Wesley, Drew University (United States of America)

Bischoff, Ms Uta, fl, Evangelische Kirche in Deutschland (Germany)

Castro Pombo, Pastor Emilio Enrique, mo, Evangelical Methodist Church in Uruguay (Switzerland)

Cerviño, Sr Raúl Enrique, ml (Argentina)

Cournou Heredia, Sr Víctor, ml (Argentina)

De Gaay Fortman, Prof. Bastiaan, yml, Protestantse Kerk in Nederland (Netherlands)

Dometian, H.E. Metropolitan, mo, Bulgarian Orthodox Church (Bulgaria)

Grant, Ms Nekira, fl, The Riverside Church (United States of America)

Haire, Rev. Prof. Ian James Mitchell, mo, National Council of Churches in Australia (Australia)

Huber, Bischof Prof. Dr Wolfgang, mo, Evangelische Kirche in Deutschland (Germany)

Huber-Kaldrack, Frau Kara Bringfriede, fl, Evangelische Kirche in Deutschland (Germany)

Jordan, Ms Rhonda, yfl, The Riverside Church (United States of America)

Kang, Rev. Yong Sop, mo, Central Committee of Korean Christian Federation (Korea, Democratic People's Republic)

Kasper, H.E. Walter Cardinal, mo, Roman Catholic Church (Vatican City)

Kim, Mr Yong Chol, ml, Central Committee of Korean Christian Federation (Korea, Democratic People's Republic)

Kobia, Mrs Ruth, fl, Methodist Church in Kenya (Switzerland)

Koshy, Dr Ninan, ml, Church of South India (India)

Kovachev Petrov, His Eminence Metropolitan Kyril, mo, Bulgarian Orthodox Church (Bulgaria)

Kyrill of Smolensk, H.E. Metropolitan, mo, Russian Orthodox Church (Russian Federation)

Mar Iranaeus, Metropolitan Joseph, mo, Mar Thoma Syrian Church of Malabar (India)

Míguez Bonino, Pastor Dr José, mo, Iglesia Evangélica Metodista Argentina (Argentina)

Miller, Minister Melvin, yml, The Riverside Church (United States of America)

Miranda, Pastor Marcos, mo (Brazil)

Nababan, Mrs Alida Lientje, fl, Huria Kristen Batak Protestan (HKBP) (Indonesia)

Nababan, Dr Soritua Albert Ernst, mo, Huria Kristen Batak Protestan (HKBP) (Indonesia)

Nilsen, Mr Ulf, ml, Church of Norway (Norway)

Otunnu, Mr Olara A., ml, President, LBL Foundation for Children (United States of America)

Park, Dr Kyung-Seo, ml, North East Asia Peace Institute (NEAPI) (Korea, Republic of)

Park (Oh), Ms Young-Ok, fl, North East Asia Peace Institute (NEAPI) (Korea, Republic of)

Perez Esquivel, Sr Adolfo Maria, ml, Fundacion Servico Paz y Justicia (Argentina)

Potter, Rev. Dr Philip A., mo, Methodist Church in the Caribbean and the Americas (Germany)

Quinteros, Sr Roberto Daniel, ml (Argentina)

Raiser, Dr Elisabeth, fl, Evangelische Kirche in Deutschland (Germany)

Raiser, Rev. Dr Konrad, mo, Evangelische Kirche in Deutschland (Germany)

Rantakari, Mrs Arja Birgitta, fl, Evangelical Lutheran Church of Finland (Finland)

Rantakari, Ambassador Markus Ilari, ml, Evangelical Lutheran Church of Finland (Finland)

Ri, Mr Jong Ro, ml, Central Committee of Korean Christian Federation
    (Korea, Democratic People's Republic)

Seoka, Rt Rev. Dr Johannes Thomas, mo, Church of the Province of Southern Africa (South Africa)

Silva, Pastor Orlando, mo (Brazil)

Tevi, Mrs Lorine, fl, Methodist Church in Fiji (Fiji)

Tudorov-Sabev, Prof. Todor, mo, Bulgarian National Christian Committee (Switzerland)

Tutu, Most Rev. Desmond M., mo, Church of the Province of Southern Africa (South Africa)

Vazquez, Sra Alicia, fl, Gobierno de la Ciudad de Buenos Aires (Argentina)

Williams, H.G. The Most Rev. Dr Rowan, mo, Church of England (United Kingdom)

Guests of other faiths

Aram, Dr Kezevino, Hindu (India)

Borges, Sra Laurinda, Indigenous (Guarani) (Brazil)

Cicek, Mr Orhan, Australian Intercultural Society (Australia)

Coen, Sister Monja, Buddhist (Brazil)

Fatah, Mr Abdul, (Indonesia)

Gross, Dr Rita, Buddhist (Vajrayana) (United States of America)

Huanacuni Mamani, Sr Fernando, Centro de Estudios de Cosmovision SARIRI (Bolivia)

Hussein Saleh, Sr Armando, Muslim (Brazil)

Muzadi, Dr Ahmad Hasyim, Nahdat al-Ulama (Indonesia)

Naik, Mr Deepak, Hindu (United Kingdom)

Omar, Imam A. Rashied, Muslim (United States of America)

Pedersen, Dr Kusumita P., Interfaith (United States of America)

Pereira Franco, Sr Divaldo, Karetist (Brazil)

Rambachan, Prof. Anantanand, Hindu (United States of America)

Schulthess F., Ms Beatriz, Retorno a la Tierra (Indigenous) (Costa Rica)

Sobel, Rabbi Henry Isaac, Jewish (Brazil)

Szczytnicki Broutman, Sr Elías Claudio, World Conference of Religions for Peace (Peru)

Trindade Serra, Dr Ordep José, Candomblé (Brazil)

Wattal, Ms Ameeta Mulla, Hindu (India)

Weissman, Dr Deborah, Jewish (Israel)

Ya'akub, Mrs Thawra Yousif, Muslim (Iraq)

Yamanoi, Rev. Katsunori, Rissho Kosei-Kai (Japan)

Advisors

Åkesson, Mr Christer, ml, Svenska Kyrkan (Sweden)

Aleinik, Ms Volha, yfl, SYNDESMOS - The World Fellowship of Orthodox Youth (Greece)

Amoah, Dr Elizabeth, fl, Methodist Church of Ghana (Ghana)

Araujo, Ms Veronica, fl, Focolare Movement (Italy)

Berinyuu, Rev. Dr Abraham A., mo, Ecumenical Disability Advocates Network (Ghana)

Bottoms, Rev. Ruth Anne, fo, Baptist Union of Great Britain (United Kingdom)

Cardoso Pereira, Rev. Nancy, fo, Igreja Metodista do Brasil (Brazil)

Cela Heffel, Lic. Victorio David, yml, Consejo Latinoamericano de Iglesias (Argentina)

Cowans, Rev. Dr Gordon Earl, mo, Ecumenical Disability Advocates Network (Jamaica)

Deicha, Prof. Dr Sophie, fl, St Sergius Theological Institute (France)

Fernandez, Rev. Noel Osvaldo, mo, Ecumenical Disability Advocates Network (Cuba)

Fritzson, Rev. Dr Arne, mo, Ecumenical Disability Advocates Network (Sweden)

Garcia, Ms Liza Lei, fl, United Church of Christ in the Philippines (Philippines)

Grounds, Dr Richard A., ml, United Methodist Church (United States of America)

Hungnes, Ms Tale, yfl, Changemakers (Norway)

Jonson, Bishop Dr Jonas, mo, Svenska Kyrkan (Sweden)

Joseph, Rev. Dr Ipe, mo, Mar Thoma Syrian Church of Malabar (India)

Kang, Prof. Namsoon, fl, World Conference of Associations of Theological Institutions (Korea, Republic of)

Kanyoro, Dr Musimbi, fo, World Young Women's Christian Association (Switzerland)

Katsuno, Ms Lynda Susan, fl, Ecumenical Disability Advocates Network (Canada)

Kattan, Prof. Dr Assaad Elias, ml, Greek Orthodox Patriarchate of Antioch and All the East (Germany)

Kengne Djeutane, Ms Georgine, fl, World Student Christian Federation (Kenya)

Kiplagat, Ambassador Bethuel, ml, Anglican Church of Kenya (Kenya)

Koinante, Ms Jennifer, fl, Indigenous Peoples (Yaaku Masai) (Kenya)

Lee, Ms Ye Ja, fl, Ecumenical Disability Advocates Network (Korea, Republic of)

Marainen, Mr Johannes, ml, Sámi Council Church of Sweden (Sweden)

Morales de León, Sra Catarina Elena, fl, Fraternidad de Presbiteriales Mayas (Guatemala)

Müller, Mr Daniel, ml, Ecumenical Youth Council in Europe (Belgium)

Mundine, Mr Graeme, ml, National Council of Churches in Australia (Australia)

Newland-Martin, Mrs Sarah, fl, Ecumenical Disability Advocates Network (Jamaica)

Njobvu, Ms Idah, fl, Reformed Church in Zambia (Zambia)

Njoroge, Mr John Ngige, yml, Greek Orthodox Patriarchate of Alexandria and All Africa (Greece)

Oduyoye, Dr Mercy Amba, fl, Methodist Church, Ghana (Ghana)

Peers, Archbishop Michael Geoffrey, mo, Anglican Church of Canada (Canada)

Phiri, Dr Isabel Apawo, fl, Uniting Presbyterian Church of Southern Africa (South Africa)

Regule, Ms Teva, fl, St Nina's Quarterly (United States of America)

Robbins, Rev. Dr Bruce W., mo, United Methodist Church (United States of America)

Ross Quiroga, Ms Gracia Violeta, yfl, International Community of Women Living with HIV/AIDS (Bolivia)

Saracco, Dr Jose Norberto, mo, Iglesia Evangélica Buenas Nuevas (Argentina)

Scampini, Father Jorge A., mo, Roman Catholic Church (Argentina)
Sepúlveda, Pastor Juan Esteban, mo, Misión Iglesia Pentecostal (Chile)
Sheerattan-Bisnauth, Rev. Patricia, fo, World Alliance of Reformed Churches (Switzerland)
Tabing-Reyes, Ms Corazon, fl, Christian Conference of Asia (Hong Kong)
Tamez, Dra Elsa, fl, Universidad Biblica Latino-Americana (Costa Rica)
Tandon, Prof. Yashpal, ml, South Centre, (Switzerland)
Tanner, Dr Mary, fl, Church of England (United Kingdom)

National host committee
Andrade, Bispo Maurício, mo, Igreja Episcopal Anglicana do Brasil (Brazil)
Bernhard, Rev. Rui, mo Igreja Evangélica de Confissão Luterana no Brasil (Brazil)
Bock, Rev. Dr Carlos Gilberto, mo, Igreja Evangélica de Confissão Luterana no Brasil (Brazil)
Galvão, Sr Antonio Dimas, ml, CESE - Coordenadoria Ecumênica de Serviço (Brazil)
Grecco Teixeira, Rev. Luiz Caetano, mo, CLAI Brasil (Brazil)
Marchiori, Most Rev. João Oneres, mo, Roman Catholic Church (Brazil)
Pereira Padilha, Sr Anivaldo, ml, KOINONIA - Presença Ecumênica e Serviço (Brazil)
Petrecca, Pastor Hector Osvaldo, mo, Consejo Latinoamericano de Iglesias (Argentina)
Santos, Rev. Leontino Farias dos, mo, Igreja Presbiteriana Independente do Brasil (Brazil)
Schmidt, Rev. Ervino, mo, Conselho Nacional de Igrejas Cristãs do Brasil - CONIC (Brazil)

Local host committee
Bernhard, Rev. Rui, mo, Igreja Evangélica de Confissão Luterana no Brasil (Brazil)
Bock, Mr Carlos Gilberto, ml, Igreja Evangélica de Confissão Luterana no Brasil (Brazil)
de Assis da Silva, Rev. Francisco, mo, Centro Ecumênico de Evangelização, Capacitação e Assessoria -
    CECA (Brazil)
Duarte de Duarte, Sra Rosina, fl, Igreja Evangélica de Confissão Luterana no Brasil (Brazil)
Lima, Mr Valdir Aparecido, ml, Igreja Católica Apostólica Romana (Brazil)
Mota, Rev. (Ms) Sônia Gomes, fo, Igreja Presbiteriana Unida do Brasil (Brazil)
Neuenfeld, Dra. Elaine, fl, CEBI - Centro de Estudos Bíblicos (Brazil)
Normann Ew, Rev. Liziane, fo, Igreja Metodista do Brasil (Brazil)
Pereira da Silva, Srta Solange, fl, Igreja Episcopal Anglicana do Brasil (Brazil)
Schneider, Dr Marcelo, mo, Igreja Evangélica de Confissão Luterana no Brasil (Brazil)
Sell, Ms Marcia, fl, Roman Catholic Church (Brazil)
Stoffel, Father José Carlos, mo, Conselho Nacional de Igrejas Cristãs do Brasil - CONIC (Brazil)
Takatsu Winnischofer, Ms Christina, fl, Igreja Episcopal Anglicana do Brasil (Brazil)

Stewards
Agragel, Ms Nadhji, yfl, Iglesia Episcopal de Panamá (Panama)
Ananyan, Father Shahe, ymo, Armenian Apostolic Church (Holy See of Etchmiadzin) (Armenia)
Andriamahazo, Ms Ravaka Olivia, yfl, Eglise de Jésus-Christ à Madagascar (Madagascar)
Barbosa Junior, Mr Etelney, mly, Igreja Presbiteriana Unida do Brasil (Brazil)
Bayisabe, Mr Edmond, yml, Eglise épiscopale du Burundi (Burundi)
Bedran, Ms Alina, yfl, Greek Orthodox Patriarchate of Antioch and All the East (Argentina)
Bellei Moreira, Mr Eduardo, yml, Igreja Metodista do Brasil (Brazil)

Blackwood, Rev. Lara Beth, yfo, Christian Church (Disciples of Christ) (United States of America)

Blocksome, Ms Rebecca, yfl, American Baptist Churches in the USA (Hungary)

Brazauskas, Mr Justas, yml, Lithuanian Evangelical Reformed Church (Lithuania)

Brust, Ms Priscila Goergen, yfl, Igreja Evangélica de Confissão Luterana no Brasil (Brazil)

Caraig, Mr Ronald Paz, yml, Iglesia Unida Ekyumenikal (Philippines)

Cerqueira Lazier, Mr Tiago, yml, Igreja Metodista do Brasil (Brazil)

Charbonnier, Mr Michel, yml, Chiesa Evangelica Valdese (Italy)

Child, Ms Kerry Lyn, yfl, United Church of Canada (Canada)

Cho, Mr Won Hee, yml, Presbyterian Church of Korea (Korea, Republic of)

Coleman, Ms Patience Oryouweneh, yfl, Episcopal Church of Liberia (Liberia)

Collins, Mr Mark Alistair, yml, Moravian Church in South Africa (South Africa)

Collymore, Mr Dave, yml, Jamaica Baptist Union (Jamaica)

Cossa, Ms Zelda Cristina, yfl, Igreja Evangélica Luterana em Moçambique (Mozambique)

Cruz da Cruz, Ms Ana Rita, yfl, Igreja Episcopal Anglicana do Brasil (Brazil)

Cuadra López, Mr Josué Benjamín, yml, Convención Bautista de Nicaragua (Nicaragua)

Cudjoe, Mr Lawrence Young, yml, Greek Orthodox Patriarchate of Alexandria and All Africa (Ghana)

Demir, Ms Eleni Irini, yfl, Ecumenical Patriarchate of Constantinople (Turkey)

Djamboulian, Mr Hrayr, yml, Armenian Apostolic Church (Holy See of Cilicia) (Lebanon)

Escobar Hernández, Ms Claudia, yfl, Convención Bautista de Nicaragua (Nicaragua)

Espinosa Palmer, Ms Yarany Yireh, yfl, Iglesia Episcopal de Panamá (Panama)

Faulhafer, Ms Sara, yfl, Evangelical Lutheran Church in Canada (Canada)

Fedor, Ms Monika Csilla, yfl, Roman Catholic Church (Hungary)

Fernandes Ribeiro Maia, Mr Filipe, yml, Igreja Metodista do Brasil (Brazil)

Flores, Mr Morse, yml, Kalinga Tradition (Costa Rica)

Fokas, Ms Adamadia, yfl, Ecumenical Patriarchate of Constantinople (United States of America)

Fong, Mr Timothy Raju, yml, Anglican Church in Aotearoa, New Zealand and Polynesia (Fiji)

Fornos Gomes, Mr Rodolfo, yml, Igreja Episcopal Anglicana do Brasil (Brazil)

Fusimalohi, Mrs Luisa Anne, yfl, Anglican Church in Aotearoa, New Zealand and Polynesia (New Zealand-Aotearoa)

Gergis, Ms Sophia Shokry, yfl, Evangelical Presbyterian Church of Egypt Synod of the Nile (Egypt)

Gibson, Rev. Jermaine Tousaint, ymo, Moravian Church in Jamaica (Jamaica)

Gikandi, Ms Dawn Karungari, yfl, Presbyterian Church of East Africa (Kenya)

Gill, Ms Anam, yfl, Presbyterian Church of Pakistan (Pakistan)

Ginting, Ms Sri Ulina, yfl, Karo Batak Protestant Church (GKBP) (Indonesia)

Gomes, Ms Lílian, yfl, Igreja Episcopal Anglicana do Brasil (Brazil)

Gomes Alves, Ms Cárin Marisa, yfl, Igreja Evangélica Presbiteriana Portugal (Portugal)

Gomes Correa, Mr Isaque, yml, Igreja Católica Apostólica Romana (Brazil)

Gomes da Silva Prazeres, Ms Giselle, yfl, Igreja Episcopal Anglicana do Brasil (Brazil)

González Juárez, Ms Suriana Gaddy, yfl, Comunidad Evangélica Indígena Amoxcalli (Mexico)

Grant, Ms Krystal, yfl, United Methodist Church (United States of America)

Grounds, Ms Renée, yfl, United Methodist Church (United States of America)

Györi, Rev. Matilda, yfo, Reformed Christian Church in Slovakia (Slovakia)

Haarbeck, Mr Christopher Joachim, yml, EKD-Evangelische Landeskirche in Baden (Germany)

Hala'api'api, Ms Sepiuta, yfl, Anglican Church in Aotearoa, New Zealand and Polynesia (Fiji)

Hauger, Mr Tyler, yml, Evangelical Lutheran Church in America (United States of America)

Hodgson Rios, Mr Garneth Luther, yml, Iglesia Morava en Nicaragua (Nicaragua)

Hosken dos Santos, Ms Luma, yfl, Igreja Metodista do Brasil (Brazil)

Hovland, Ms Kristine Hofseth, yfl, Church of Norway (Norway)

Jacky, Mr Jean Paul Victor, yml, Roman Catholic Church (Senegal)

Jeffrey, Ms Karryl Michelle P., yfl, Caribbean Conference of Churches - Roman Catholic Church (Trinidad and Tobago)

John, Ms Hemalatha, yfl, Church of South India (India)

Junni, Mr Jussi, yml, Evangelical Lutheran Church of Finland (Finland)

Kamarzarian, Ms Evline, yfl, Synod of the Evangelical Church of Iran (Iran)

Kang, Mr Thomas Hyeono, yml, Igreja Evangélica de Confissão Luterana no Brasil (Brazil)

Kareliusson, Mr Kjell Gustaf Mattias, yml, Svenska Kyrkan (Sweden)

Kasapoglu, Mr Corc, yml, Ecumenical Patriarchate of Constantinople (Greece)

Kent, Ms Aimee, yfl, Uniting Church in Australia (Australia)

Kercyku, Ms Monda, yfl, Kisha Orthodhokse Autoqefale e Shqipërisë (Albania)

Khalaf, Ms Mary, yfl, National Evangelial Synod of Syria and Lebanon (Syria)

Khosrovian, Ms Narine, yfl, Armenian Apostolic Church (Holy See of Cilicia) (Iran)

Kilisimasi Maopa, Ms Ngana, yfl, The Free Wesleyan Church of Tonga (Tonga)

Kirmiz, Ms Irene, yfl, Network of Christian Organizations in Bethlehem (Palestine)

Kitab, Ms Nancy, yfl, Episcopal Church of the Sudan (Sudan)

Klukach, Ms Natasha Alexis, yfl, Anglican Church of Canada (Canada)

Kreher, Ms Stefanie Mirjam, yfl, Iglesia Evangélica del Rio de la Plata (Argentina)

Kuseka, Mr Prince Bekizenzo, yml, Methodist Church in Zimbabwe (Zimbabwe)

Lee, Ms Sae Leum, yfl, Korean Methodist Church (Korea, Republic of)

Lewis, Ms Leandra, yfl, Church in the Province of the West Indies (Antigua and Barbuda)

Lin, Ms Naw Lar Pwe Paw, yfl, Myanmar Baptist Convention (Myanmar)

Locher, Mr Daniel, yml, Reformierte Kirchen Bern-Jura-Solothurn (Switzerland)

Lopez Sanchez, Mr Henry Rolando, yml, Iglesia Episcopal de Honduras (Honduras)

Lopez Vazquez, Mr Marcos Abner, yml, Iglesia Presbiteriana (Mexico)

Luamanuvae, Mr Junior Seilala, yml, Congregational Christian Church in Samoa (Samoa)

Luist, Ms Marjana, yfl, United Methodist Church (Estonia)

Machado, Ms Ana Lúcia de Almeida, yfl, Igreja Episcopal Anglicana do Brasil (Brazil)

Mackovic, Mr Dejan, yml, Serbian Orthodox Church (Bosnia and Herzegovina)

Madona, Ms Tirza, yfl, Gereja Protestan di Sulawesi Tenggara (GEPSULTRA) (Indonesia)

Magala, Mr Enoch, yml, Greek Orthodox Patriarchate of Alexandria and All Africa (Uganda)

Magda, Mr Gabriel Ciprian, yml, Romanian Orthodox Church (Romania)

Mahling, Ms Jadwiga, yfl, EKD – Evangelisch-Lutherische Landeskirche Sachsens (Germany)

Malecdan, Ms Mae Maureen, yfl, Episcopal Church in the Philippines (Philippines)

Martin Chandran, Ms Daphne Shakuntala, yfl, United Evangelical Lutheran Church in India (India)

Martins da Silva, Mr Richarlls, yml, Igreja Metodista do Brasil (Brazil)

Maturana de la Cruz, Mr Selwins Daniel, yml, Iglesia Presbiteriana de Colombia (Colombia)

Mbise, Ms Joan Thomas, yfl, Evangelical Lutheran Church in Tanzania (Tanzania)

McMahon, Mr James Rossman, yml, Episcopal Church in the USA (United Kingdom)

Miguez Barolin, Ms Ana Rut, yfl, Iglesia Metodista en el Uruguay (Uruguay)

Moilwa, Ms Botshelo, yfl, Botswana Council of Churches (Botswana)

Muthuka, Ms Clara Minoo, yfl, Baptist Church of Kenya (Kenya)

Nascimento, Ms Nena Hadsell do, yfl, Presbyterian Church (USA) (Brazil)

Nazarko, Ms Urszula Julia, yfl, Polski Autokefaliczny Kosciol Prawoslawny (Poland)

Ngotty Essebe, Ms Ruth-Aimée Chanceline, yfl, Presbyterian Church in Cameroon (Cameroon)

Nicholls, Ms Meghan Kathleen, yfl, Anglican Church of Canada (Canada)

Nkhoma, Mr Friday, yml, United Church of Zambia (Zambia)

Nota, Mr Kaierua, yml, Kiribati Protestant Church (Kiribati)

Ogbonnaya, Mr Umachi Samuel, yml, Presbyterian Church of Nigeria (Nigeria)

Ortiz, Ms Marina Dolores, yfl, Iglesia Bautista (El Salvador)

Paraskeva-Gkizi, Ms Elisavet, yfl, Church of Greece (Greece)

Pathrose, Mr Ferdinand, yml, Malankara Orthodox Syrian Church (India)

Petcoff, Ms Deborah Ana, yfl, Iglesia Evangélica Metodista Argentina (Argentina)

Peyroux, Ms TeRito, yfl, Methodist Church of New Zealand (New Zealand-Aotearoa)

Pontes de Campos, Ms Marcella, yfl, Igreja Presbiteriana Unida do Brasil (Brazil)

Porcelana, Ms Brenda Noelia, yfl, Iglesia Cristiana Biblica (Argentina)

Qalobulamaiwasawasa, Mr Mikaele Maria, yml, Roman Catholic Church (Fiji)

Ramzy Maurice, Mr Michael, yml, Coptic Orthodox Church (Egypt)

Ranker, Mr Raymond, yml, Evangelical Lutheran Church in America (United States of America)

Renck, Mr Henrique Brusius, yml, Igreja Evangélica de Confissão Luterana no Brasil (Brazil)

Rorbaek, Mr Thorsten, yml, Evangelical Lutheran Church in Denmark (Denmark)

Ruaro Zachow, Ms Juliana, yfl, Igreja Evangélica de Confissão Luterana no Brasil (Brazil)

Salib, Ms Magy, yfl, Coptic Orthodox Church (Egypt)

Schmidt, Mr Tiago Pablo, yml, Igreja Evangélica de Confissão Luterana no Brasil (Brazil)

Seal, Mr Allan, yml, United Church of Canada (Canada)

Sewnarine, Ms Ilene, yfl, Igreja Episcopal Anglicana do Brasil (Brazil)

Shahin, Mr Jeries, yml, Syrian Orthodox Patriarchate of Antioch and All the East (Jordan)

Shastri, Ms Miriam Shanti, yfl, Deutsch-sprächige Evangelische Gemeinde Malaysia (Malaysia)

Smith, Mr Horatio, yml, Church in the Province of the West Indies (Bahamas)

Smith Perez, Ms Jaquelin Patricia, yfl, Iglesia Presbiteriana de Colombia (Colombia)

Sokhin, Mr Vladislav, yml, Russian Orthodox Church (Russian Federation)

Soto Rodríguez, Ms Zelma, yfl, Iglesia Metodista de Puerto Rico (Puerto Rico)

Suyala, Ms Waraporn, yfl, Church of Christ in Thailand (Thailand)

Teixeira de Loyola, Mr Erico, yml, Igreja Evangélica de Confissão Luterana no Brasil (Brazil)

Thomas, Ms Ealu Merium, yfl, Mar Thoma Syrian Church of Malabar (India)

Tiim, Ms Riiteta, yfl, Kiribati Protestant Church (Kiribati)

Tiko, Mr Tomasi, yml, Methodist Church in Fiji (Fiji)

Udgirkar, Mr Vishwas Ramu, yml, Methodist Church in India (India)

Vasilevich, Ms Natallia, yfl, Russian Orthodox Church (Belarus)

Visotchi, Mr Pavel, yml, Romanian Orthodox Church (Moldova)

Welty, Ms Emily, yfl, Presbyterian Church (USA) (United States of America)

Wermeling, Ms Erika, yfl, Svenska Missionskyrkan (Sweden)

Wu, Mr Bing, yml, China Christian Council (China)

Yopaang, Ms Rila Mandela Moï, yfl, Eglise évangélique luthérienne de France (France)
Zhang, Ms Lili, yfl, China Christian Council (China)

WCC staff

Aoukich-Sägesser, Ms Christine, yfl (Switzerland)
Asfaw, Ms Semegnish, yfl (Ethiopia)
Bazin, Mr Jean-Nicolas, ml (Switzerland)
Belopopsky, Mr Alexander, ml (United Kingdom)
Best, Rev. Dr Thomas F., mo (United States of America)
Bonato, Mr Gustavo Alberto, yml (Brazil)
Braunschweiger, Ms Nan, fl (United Kingdom)
Bropleh, Dr Laurence Konmla, mo (Liberia)
Bruschweiler, Ms Miriam Patricia, fl (Peru)
Charles, Ms Anjeline Okola, fl (Kenya)
Chervet, Mrs Veena, fl (Sri Lanka)
Chial, Mr Douglas L., ml (United States of America)
Christ-Taha, Mrs Catherine, fl (Switzerland)
Constant, Ms Brigitte, fl (Germany)
Conti, Ms Tiziana, yfl (Switzerland)
Deardorff, Ms Sarah, yfl (United States of America)
DeWinter, Rev. Deborah, fo (United States of America)
Djomo Ngomedje, Ms Adèle, yfl (Cameroon)
Dykes, Mrs Elaine, fl (United Kingdom)
Eggli, Ms Silvia, fl (Argentina)
Ergas, Mrs Simone, fl (Switzerland)
Faure, Mrs Francisca, fl (Switzerland)
Feliciano, Ms Gloria I., fl (United States of America)
Ferris, Dr Elizabeth, fl (United States of America)
Ford, Mrs Linda, fl (United Kingdom)
Frerichs, Mr Jonathan, ml (United States of America)
George, Dr Mathews, ml (India)
Gerber, Rev. Hansulrich, mo (Switzerland)
Gill, Rev. Theodore, mo (United States of America)
Gnanadason, Dr Aruna, fl (India)
Grdzelidze, Dr Tamara, fl (Georgia)
Ham, Rev. Dr Carlos, mo (Cuba)
Hardon, Mr Michiel, ml (Netherlands)
Hegetschweiler, M. Luc, ml (Switzerland)
Heijs, Dr Hans, ml (Netherlands)
Heiniger, Mr Marc-Henri, yml (Switzerland)
Hennessy, Ms Caroline, fl (United States of America)
Hercigonja, Mr Darko, ml (Croatia)
Inoubli, Mrs Catherine, fl (France)
Jacques, Ms Geneviève, fl (France)

John, Mr Clement, ml (Pakistan)
John, Mrs Violet, fl (Pakistan)
Kabue, Mr Samuel Njuguna, ml (Kenya)
Karamaga, Rev. Dr André, mo (Rwanda)
Kassis, Mr Rifat Odeh, ml (Palestine)
Kaulics, Ms Iren Barbara, yfl (Hungary)
Kerber, Dr Guillermo, ml (Uruguay)
Kifle, Mr Melaku, ml (Ethiopia)
Kobia, Rev. Dr Samuel, mo (Kenya)
Kurian, Dr Manoj, ml (Malaysia)
Lee, Ms Susan, yfl (Canada)
Léger, Ms Denyse, fl (Canada)
Lemopoulos, Mr Georges, ml (Turkey)
López Vázquez, Mr José, yml (Mexico)
Lupai, Ms Lona Wilson, fl (Sudan)
Manchala, Rev. Dr Deenabandhu, mo (India)
Mann, Dr Christoph Erich, ml (Germany)
Matthey, Rev. Jacques, mo (Switzerland)
Maxson, Ms Natalie Kim, yfl (Canada)
Michel, Mr Juan Carlos, ml (Argentina)
Milosevic, Mrs Yvette Ann, fl (United Kingdom)
Monteiro, Mrs Simei, fl (Brazil)
Mshana, Dr Rogate, ml (Tanzania)
Mustafa, Mr Zejnulla, ml (Kosovo)
Nazarko, Mr Lukasz, yml (Poland)
Nicole Strandell, Ms Johanna, yfl (Sweden)
Nightingale, Ms Katherine, yfl (United Kingdom)
Njoroge, Rev. Dr Nyambura, fo (Kenya)
Nseir, Mr Michel, ml (Lebanon)
Oxley, Rev. Simon, mo (United Kingdom)
Palma, Ms Marta, fl (Chile)
Peiponen, Rev. Matti Paavo, mo (Finland)
Pirri-Simonian, Mrs Teny, fl (Lebanon)
Poma, Bishop Eugenio, mo (Bolivia)
Pomezny, Ms Alexandra, fl (Switzerland)
Provost, Mr Yannick, ml (France)
Qayyum, Ms Naveen, yfl (Pakistan)
Reidy Prost, Ms Miriam, fl (Australia)
Remos, Mr Benjamin, yml (United States of America)
Robra, Rev. Dr Martin W.H., mo (Germany)
Ross, Ms Dawn, fl (Canada)
Sandoval Merritt, Ms Laura Catalina, fl (Mexico)
Sauca, Fr Dr Ioan, mo (Romania)
Scarff, Mr Gerard Lloyd, ml (United Kingdom)

425

Schmid, Ms Hannelore, fl (Germany)
Schopfer, Rev. Olivier, mo (Switzerland)
Schüller, Ms Marilia, fl (Brazil)
Storch, Rev. Kersten, fo (Germany)
Stranz, Rev. Jane, fo (United Kingdom)
Talapusi, Ms Faautu, yfl (Samoa)
Tautari, Ms Tara, fl (New Zealand)
Taylor, Dr John Bernard, ml (United Kingdom)
Temu, Dr William, ml (Tanzania)
Tevi, Mr Fe'iloakitau Kaho, ml (Fiji)
Ucko, Rev Dr Hans, mo (Sweden)
Udodesku, Rev. Sabine, fo (Germany)
Vanel, Mrs Charlotte, fl (Mexico)
van Heemstra, Dr Maria Ingeneta, fl (Switzerland)
Vercauteren, Mr Damien, ml (Switzerland)
Visinand, Ms Libby, fl (Switzerland)
Visinand, Ms Yasmina, fl (Switzerland)
Von Arx, Ms Denise, fl (Ireland)
Wasyluk, Mr Aleksander, yml (Poland)
Wehrle, Ms Luzia, fl (Switzerland)
Weiderud, Mr Peter, ml (Sweden)
Wieser, Mr Daniel, ml (Switzerland)
Williams, Mr Peter, ml (Denmark)
Yoder, Mr Kent, yml (United States of America)
Yonker, Mr Thomas, yml (United States of America)
Zarraga Tschaikowskij, Ms Tania, fl (Russia)
Zierl, Ms Ursula, fl (Germany)

Co-opted staff

Abdul-Mohan, Rev. Joy Evelyn, fo (Trinidad and Tobago)
Acuña, Sra Paula Isabel, yfl (Argentina)
Affonson Neves, Ms Beatriz, fl (Brazil)
Apii, Mr Daniel, ml (Cook Islands)
Barbosa, Mrs Zenaide, fl (Brazil)
Becker, Ms Bettina, fl (Brazil)
Benes, Ms Nadja, yfl (Switzerland)
Booth, Rev. Dr Rodney, mo (Canada)
Braun Endo, Ms Ana Claudia, fl (Brazil)
Buchweitz, Ms Susanne, fl (Brazil)
Buss, Rev. Théo, mo (Nicaragua)
Caille, Ms Linda, yfl (France)
Clements, Rev. Dr Keith, mo (United Kingdom)
Coates, Rev. Tony, mo (United Kingdom)
Conway, Dr David Martin, mo (United Kingdom)

Crismo, Ms Phebe Gamata, fl (Philippines)
Degenhardt, Rev. Friedrich, mo (Germany)
Delmonte, Ms M. C. Elisabeth, fl (Uruguay)
Elnecave, Ms Regina Helena, fl (Brazil)
Emmanuel, Rev. Sonny, mo (Indonesia)
Fauzi, Ms Silke, fl (Germany)
Favaro, Pastor Daniel, mo (Argentina)
Ferguson, Rev. Christopher, mo (Canada)
Fertis, Ms Christina, fl (Switzerland)
Ginglas-Poulet, Mrs Roswitha, fl (France)
Giozza, Mr Wilney, ml (Brazil)
Goodwin, Rev. Douglas, mo (Canada)
Guirado, Mr Marcos, ml (Brazil)
Hasenack, Pastor Johannes Friedrich, mo (Brazil)
Havea, Rev. Dr Jione, mo (Australia)
Hawkey, Mr Sean, ml (United Kingdom)
Hawn, Rev. Dr Charles Michael, mo (United States of America)
Henry-Crowe, Rev. Susan, fo (United States of America)
Heuser, Ms Christina, fl (Brazil)
Hofmann, Mr Hedy, ml (Brazil)
Hollas, Pastor Armin Andreas, mo (Brazil)
Illenseer, Sr Louis Marcelo, ml (Brazil)
Isernhagen, Sra Edda, fl (Brazil)
Junker, Dr Tércio, mo (Brazil)
Kasselouri, Dr Eleni, fl (Greece)
Kawak, Father Jean, mo (Syria)
Kessler, Rev. Dr Diane C., fo (United States of America)
Kliewer, Dr Gerd Uwe, ml (Brazil)
Knutsen, Rev. Freddy, mo (Norway)
Kollander, Ms Kerstin, fl (Sweden)
Kuss, Rev. Cibele, fo (Brazil)
Laugesen, Mr Anders, ml (Denmark)
Lobulu, Mrs Elizabeth, fl (Tanzania)
Lockward, Mr Jorge, ml (United States of America)
Lucke, Rev. Hartmut, mo (Switzerland)
Machabert, Rev. Gérald, ymo (France)
Mandagi, Ms Hanneke C., fl (Indonesia)
McCullum, Dr Hugh, ml (Canada)
Mesones, Sr Horacio, ml (Argentina)
Míguez, Dr Néstor Oscar, mo (Argentina)
Neuroth, Mr Michael, yml (United States of America)
Negro, Rev. Luca, mo (Switzerland)
Obrer, Ms Doris, fl (Brazil)
Pater, Ms Margaret A., fl (Germany)

Paz, Mr José Aurélio, ml (Cuba)

Peres Leite, Reverendo Dessórdi, mo (Brazil)

Puippe, Mr Jean Charles, ml (Switzerland)

Raulo, Ms Sylvia, fl (Finland)

Reasoner, Mr Donald, ml (Brazil)

Rivera-Pagán, Dr Luis, ml (Puerto Rico)

Sabanes Plou, Ms Dafne, fl (Argentina)

Salazar Sanzana, Dra Elizabeth del Carmen, fl (Chile)

Sánchez, Mr Marcos Miguel Angel, ml (Chile)

Sander, Mr Luis, ml (Brazil)

Sbeghen, Mrs Renate, fl (Switzerland)

Schechtel, Sra Valeria Sofia, fl (Argentina)

Schinke, Mr Sigurd, ml (Brazil)

Schlupp, Mr Walter, ml (Brazil)

Schwantes, Professor Dr Milton, mo (Brazil)

Seubert, Mr Bruno, ml (Brazil)

Shikiya, Sr Humberto Martin, ml (Argentina)

Silveira, Ms Angela, fl (Brazil)

Simeone, Rev. Inés, fo (Uruguay)

Sintado, Rev. Carlos Alberto, mo (Spain)

Sintado, Mrs Myriam Marcela, fl (Switzerland)

Soares, Ms Veronica, fl. (Switzerland)

Sovik, Ms Liv Rebecca, fl (Brazil)

Stimson, Ms Eva, fl (United States of America)

Struempfel, Ms Annegreth, yfl (Germany)

Strüssmann, Mrs Caroline, yfl (Brazil)

Tabart, Dr Jill, fl (Australia)

Tamez Luna, Pastor Carlos Cesar, mo (Honduras)

Tatu, Ms Evelyne, fl (Switzerland)

Tosat Delaraye, Mrs Pilar, fl (Switzerland)

Ueti Barasioli, Prof. Paulo Cesar, ml (Brazil)

Van Beek, Mr Huibert, ml (Switzerland)

Van den Heuvel, Mrs Sylviane, fl (Switzerland)

Wanless, Mr David M., ml (South Africa)

Webb, Mr Stephen, ml (Australia)

West, Prof. Gerald, ml (South Africa)

Wiltschek, Rev. Walt, mo (United States of America)

Woods, Mr Mark, ml (United Kingdom)

Wyatt Favaro, Sra Nelida Silvia, fl (Argentina)

Yablonsky, Ms Lisa, yfl (United States of America)

APPENDIX III
ASSEMBLY COMMITTEE LEADERSHIP AND MEMBERSHIP
BUSINESS COMMITTEE

Aram I, Catholicos, mo, Armenian Apostolic Church (Holy See of Cilicia) (Lebanon), Moderator

Abrahams, Bishop Ivan Manuel, mo, Methodist Church of Southern Africa (South Africa)

Abuom, Dr Agnes, fl, Anglican Church of Kenya (Kenya)

Adinyira, Mrs Sophia Ophilia Adjeibea, fl, Church of the Province of West Africa (Ghana)

Altmann, Rev. Dr Walter, mo, Igreja Evangélica de Confissão Luterana no Brasil (Brazil)

Athanasios of Achaia, H.G. Bishop, mo, Church of Greece (Belgium)

Best, Dr Marion Stephani, fl, United Church of Canada (Canada)

Clarke, Mrs Hera Rere, fl, Anglican Church in Aotearoa, New Zealand and Polynesia (New Zealand-Aotearoa)

Evans, Ms Wendy, yfl, United Church of Canada (Canada)

Fisher, Canon Rita Elizabeth, fl, Church of England (United Kingdom)

Gadegaard, Dean Anders, mo, Evangelical Lutheran Church in Denmark (Denmark)

Gennadios of Sassima, H.E. Metropolitan Prof. Dr, mo, Ecumenical Patriarchate of Constantinople (Turkey)

George, Rev. Dr Kondothra M., mo, Malankara Orthodox Syrian Church (India)

Kang, Dr Moon Kyu, ml, Presbyterian Church in the Republic of Korea (Korea, Republic of)

Kobia, Rev. Dr Samuel, mo, World Council of Churches (Switzerland)

Koppe, Bischof Dr Rolf, mo, Evangelische Kirche in Deutschland (Germany)

Laham, Mr Samer, ml, Greek Orthodox Patriarchate of Antioch and All the East (Syria)

Nilsen, Rev. Ingrid Vad, fo, Church of Norway (Norway)

Pagura, Obispo Federico José Natalio, mo, Iglesia Evangélica Metodista Argentina (Argentina)

Petrossian, H.G. Bishop Dr Yeznik (Samvel), mo, Armenian Apostolic Church (Holy See of Etchmiadzin) (Armenia)

Powell Jackson, Rev. Dr Bernice, fo, United Church of Christ (United States of America)

Renz, Bischof Dr Eberhardt, mo, Evangelische Landeskirche in Württemberg (Germany)

Rytkönen, Mr Aaro Paavo Samuli, yml, Evangelical Lutheran Church of Finland (Finland)

Shanks, Rev. Dr Norman, mo, Church of Scotland (United Kingdom)

Spencer, Rev. Glenna, fo, Methodist Church in the Caribbean and the Americas (Guyana)

Yamada, Ms Motoe, yfl, United Methodist Church (United States of America)

NOMINATIONS COMMITTEE

Powell Jackson, Rev. Dr Bernice, fo, United Church of Christ (United States of America), Moderator

Hutabarat-Lebang, Rev. Henriette, fo, Gereja Toraja (GT) (Indonesia), Rapporteur

Chowdhury, Dr S.M., mo, Bangladesh Baptist Church Sangha (Bangladesh)

Frimpong-Manso, Rt Rev. Dr Yaw, mo, Presbyterian Church of Ghana (Ghana)

Kallas Malek, Mrs Muna, fl, Greek Orthodox Patriarchate of Antioch and All the East (Syria)

Kim, Rev. Dr Kyung In, fo, Presbyterian Church of Korea (Korea, Republic of)

Lachman, Rev. Ferdinand, mo, Moravian Church in Suriname (Suriname)

The list contains the names of member church delegates and associate member church representatives serving on Assembly committees. The list does not contain the names of persons serving Assembly committees as advisors. The titles used are those requested by the participants themselves. The name of the country in parenthesis indicates the participant's country of residence. The abbreviations following the name of the participants indicate: y=youth; m=male; f=female; o=ordained; l=layperson.

Lambriniadis, Very Rev. Archimandrite Yani, mo, Ecumenical Patriarchate of Constantinople (Turkey)

Lutui, Mrs Melenaite Katea, fl, Free Wesleyan Church of Tonga (Methodist Church in Tonga) (Tonga)

Nazaryan, Dr Karen, ml, Armenian Apostolic Church (Holy See of Etchmiadzin) (Armenia)

Prostrednik, Pastor Ondrej, mo, Evangelical Church of the Augsburg Confession in Slovakia (Slovakia)

Ritchie, Obispa Nelida, fo, Iglesia Evangélica Metodista Argentina (Argentina)

Sarkissian, Archbishop Sebouh, mo, Armenian Apostolic Church (Holy See of Cilicia) (Iran)

Schmidt, Kirchenpräsident Jann, mo, Evangelische Kirche in Deutschland (Germany)

Speranskaya, Ms Elena, fl, Russian Orthodox Church (Russian Federation)

Tawfik, Dr Wedad A., fl, Coptic Orthodox Church (Egypt)

Thor, Rev. Sjöfn, yfo, Evangelical Lutheran Church of Iceland (Iceland)

Turinayo, Miss Jackline, yfl, Church of the Province of Uganda (Uganda)

Williams, Mr Jay, yml, United Methodist Church (United States of America)

Zazaza, Rev. Simon, mo, United Congregational Church of Southern Africa (South Africa)

MESSAGE COMMITTEE

Evans, Ms Wendy, yfl, United Church of Canada (Canada), Moderator

Bolioli Murdoch, Presidente Oscar Luis, mo, Iglesia Metodista en el Uruguay (Uruguay), Rapporteur

Aykazian, Bishop Vicken, mo, Armenian Apostolic Church (Holy See of Etchmiadzin) (United States of America)

Kaloyirou, Ms Chrystalla, fl, Church of Cyprus (Cyprus)

Kesting, Rev. Sheilagh Margaret, fo, Church of Scotland (United Kingdom)

Kishkovsky, Very Rev. Leonid, mo, Orthodox Church in America (United States of America)

Leuti, Rev. Teeruro, mo, Kiribati Christian Church (Kiribati)

McKenzie, Rev. Jeffrey, mo, Jamaica Baptist Union, (Jamaica)

Mhogolo, Bishop Godfrey Mdimi, mo, Anglican Church of Tanzania (Tanzania)

Nascimento Cunha, Dra Magali, fl, Igreja Metodista do Brasil (Brazil)

Oyekola, Ms Lyabo, yfl, Church of the Lord (Aladura) Worldwide (Nigeria)

Petersen, Bishop Sophie, fo, Evangelical Lutheran Church in Denmark (Greenland)

Pico, Mr Jason Charles, yml, Iglesia Filipina Independiente (Philippines)

Sathiamurthy, Ms Pauline, fl, Church of South India (India)

Walker-Smith, Rev. Dr Angelique, fo, National Baptist Convention USA, Inc. (United States of America)

FINANCE COMMITTEE

Gadegaard, Dean Anders, mo, Evangelical Lutheran Church in Denmark (Denmark), Moderator

Tering, Dr Wivina, fl, United Church of Christ in the Philippines (Philippines), Rapporteur

Anderson, Mr Derek, yml, African Methodist Episcopal Church (United States of America)

Bent Omeir, Pastor Steadman, mo, Iglesia Morava en Nicaragua (Nicaragua)

Constantinos, Dr Berhé T., ml, Ethiopian Orthodox Tewahedo Church (Ethiopia)

Daughrity, Rev. Dr Dyron, mo, Christian Church (Disciples of Christ) in Canada (Canada)

Epting, Rt Rev. C. Christopher, mo, Episcopal Church in the USA (United States of America)

Guvsám, Ms Kirsti, yfl, Church of Norway (Norway)

Kasidokosta, Ms Pinelopi Anna, yfl, Ecumenical Patriarchate of Constantinople (Greece)

Lee, Prof. Dr Samuel, ml, Presbyterian Church of Korea (Korea, Republic of)

Lengelsen, Dr Monika, fl, Evangelische Kirche in Deutschland, (Germany)

Liuvaie, Rev. Falkland Gary Fereti, mo, Ekalesia Niue (Niue)

Misenga, Mme Ngoy Mukuna Monique, fl, ECC - Communauté presbytérienne de Kinshasa (Congo, Democratic Republic of)

Namwembe, Ms Jane Despina, fl, Greek Orthodox Patriarchate of Alexandria and All Africa (Uganda)

Poortman, Mrs Simone, fl, Protestantse Kerk in Nederland (Netherlands)

Spencer, Rev. Glenna, fo, Methodist Church in the Caribbean and the Americas (Guyana)

Wade, Rev. Dr Cheryl H., fo, American Baptist Churches in the USA (United States of America)

PROGRAMME GUIDELINES COMMITTEE

Altmann, Rev. Dr Walter, mo, Igreja Evangélica de Confissão Luterana no Brasil (Brazil), Moderator

Welsh, Dr Robert, mo, Christian Church (Disciples of Christ) (United States of America), Rapporteur

Aasa-Marklund, Ms Inger, fl, Svenska Kyrkan (Sweden)

Celestine, Miss Nerissa, yfl, Church in the Province of the West Indies (Grenada)

Clapsis, Rev. Dr Emmanuel, mo, Ecumenical Patriarchate of Constantinople (United States of America)

Elu, Ms MacRose Togiab, fl, Anglican Church of Australia (Australia)

Ghantous, Mr Hadi, yml, National Evangelical Synod of Syria and Lebanon (Lebanon)

Harris, Ms Jillian, fl, Anglican Church of Canada (Canada)

Hein, Bischof Dr Martin Hermann, mo, Evangelische Kirche in Deutschland (Germany)

Hodgson Rios, Sr Ashley Wesley, ml, Iglesia Morava en Nicaragua (Nicaragua)

Kim, Rev. Kyung In, fo, Presbyterian Church of Korea (Korea, Republic of)

Martin, Rev. Chandran Paul, mo, United Evangelical Lutheran Church in India (India)

Mbise, Mrs Loerose Thomas, fl, Evangelical Lutheran Church in Tanzania (Tanzania)

McCullough Dauway, Ms Lois, fo, United Methodist Church (United States of America)

Mekel, Ms Peggy Adeline, yfl, Gereja Masehi Injili di Minahasa (GMIM) (Indonesia)

Muriyankal, H.E. Archbishop Thomas Kurivilla, mo, Syrian Orthodox Patriarchate of Antioch and All the East (India)

Nelyubova, Mrs Margarita, fl, Russian Orthodox Church (Russian Federation)

Ntahoturi, Rt Rev. Bernard, mo, Eglise épiscopale du Burundi (Burundi)

Osterlind, Ms Eva Marie, yfl, Evangelical Lutheran Church in Denmark (Denmark)

Redie, Dr Agedew, ml, Ethiopian Orthodox Tewahedo Church (Ethiopia)

Scouteris, Professor Dr Constantine, mo, Church of Greece (Greece)

Siegien, Ms Anna, yfl, Polski Autokefaliczny Kosciol Prawoslawny (Poland)

Stephen, Bishop Michael Kehinde, mo, Methodist Church Nigeria (Nigeria)

Stückelberger, Rev. Prof. Dr Christoph, mo, Schweizerischer Evangelischer Kirchenbund (Switzerland)

Tiki-Koum (Soppo), Mme Madeleine Sara, fl, Eglise évangélique du Cameroun (Cameroon)

Waqairatu, Rev. Tuikilakila Kolilevu, mo, Methodist Church in Fiji (Fiji)

Winbush, Rev. Robina, fo, Presbyterian Church (USA) (United States of America)

POLICY REFERENCE COMMITTEE

George, Rev. Dr Kondothra M., mo, Malankara Orthodox Syrian Church (India), Moderator

Glynn-Mackoul, Ms Anne, fl, Greek Orthodox Patriarchate of Antioch and All the East (United States of America), Rapporteur

Ashaye, Mr Samuel, yml, Church of the Lord (Aladura) Worldwide (Nigeria)

Aven, Ms Katie, fl, Canadian Yearly Meeting of the Religious Society of Friends (Canada)

Beetge, Bishop David Albert, mo, Church of the Province of Southern Africa (South Africa)

Bhajjan, Miss Evelyn, yfl, Church of Pakistan (Pakistan)

Brackmann, Sra Ana Maria, fl, Igreja Evangélica de Confissão Luterana no Brasil (Brazil)

Chen, Mrs Meilin, fl, China Christian Council (China)

Chhangte, Rev. Rothangliani, fo, American Baptist Churches in the USA (United States of America)

Clarke, Mrs Hera Rere, fl, Anglican Church in Aotearoa, New Zealand and Polynesia (New Zealand-Aotearoa)

Delikostantis, Professor Dr Konstantinos, ml, Ecumenical Patriarchate of Constantinople (Greece)

Goundiaev, Father Mikhail, mo, Russian Orthodox Church (Switzerland)

Granberg-Michaelson, Rev. Wesley, mo, Reformed Church in America (United States of America)

Guerra Quezada, Pastora Rosa Ester, yfo, Iglesia Pentecostal de Chile (Chile)

Habashy Youssef, Mrs Nahed F., fl, Coptic Orthodox Church (Egypt)

Kirkpatrick, Rev. Dr Clifton, mo, Presbyterian Church (USA) (United States of America)

Maraea, Rev. Taaroanui, mo, Eglise Protestante Maòhi (French Polynesia)

Mikre Sellasie, Rev. Dr G. Ammanuel, mo, Ethiopian Orthodox Tewahedo Church (Ethiopia)

Musemakweli, Pasteur Elisée, mo, Eglise presbytérienne au Rwanda (Rwanda)

Nilsen, Rev. Ingrid Vad, fo, Church of Norway (Norway)

Papanicolaou, Archimandrite Gabriel, ymo, Church of Greece (Greece)

Plaisier, Dr Bastiaan, mo, Protestantse Kerk in Nederland (Netherlands)

Schürer-Behrmann, Rev. Frank, mo, Evangelische Kirche in Deutschland (Germany)

Starcova, Ms Yveta, yfl, Orthodox Church of the Czech Lands and Slovakia (Slovakia)

Sukhu, Rev. Rawle, mo, Presbyterian Church in Trinidad and Tobago (Trinidad and Tobago)

Tita, Rev. Dr Michael, mo, Romanian Orthodox Church (Romania)

Yeboah, Ms Anita Emelia, yfl, Methodist Church, Ghana (Ghana)

PUBLIC ISSUES COMMITTEE

Abuom, Dr Agnes, fl, Anglican Church of Kenya (Kenya), Moderator

Butler, Rt Rev. Thomas Frederick, mo, Church of England (United Kingdom), Rapporteur

Angleberger, Rev. Judy, fo, Presbyterian Church (USA) (United States of America)

Bayrakdarian-Kabakian, Dr Nora, fl, Armenian Apostolic Church (Holy See of Cilicia) (Lebanon)

Bernard, Ms Justice Désirée, fl, Church in the Province of the West Indies (Trinidad and Tobago)

Bosien, Pfarrerin Heike, fo, Evangelische Kirche in Deutschland (Germany)

Chaplin, Archpriest Vsevolod, mo, Russian Orthodox Church (Russian Federation)

Critchfield, Ms Sara, yfl, Christian Church (Disciples of Christ) (United States of America)

Enns, Rev. Dr Fernando, mo, Vereinigung der Deutschen Mennonitengemeinden, (Germany)

Formilleza, Mrs Prima S., fl, Convention of Philippine Baptist Churches (Philippines)

Henderson, Rev. Gregor, mo, Uniting Church in Australia (Australia)

Joseph, Rev. William Premkumar Ebenezer, mo, Methodist Church Sri Lanka (Sri Lanka)

Kameeta, Bishop Zephania, mo, Evangelical Lutheran Church in the Republic of Namibia (Namibia)

Karim, Archbishop Mor Cyril Aphrem, mo, Syrian Orthodox Patriarchate of Antioch and All the East (United States of America)

Lansdowne, Ms Carmen Rae, yfl, United Church of Canada (Canada)

Mandowen, Mr Welly Esau, ml, Gereja Kristen Injili Di Tanah Papua (GKITP) (Indonesia)

Mejia Camargo, Pastor Milton, mo, Iglesia Presbiteriana de Colombia (Colombia)

Moukheiber, Ms Lina S., fl, Greek Orthodox Patriarchate of Antioch and All the East (Lebanon)

Nifon, Archbishop Dr, mo, Romanian Orthodox Church (Romania)

Olagboye, Mr Benjamin, yml, Eglise protestante méthodiste Unie de Côte d'Ivoire (Côte d'Ivoire)

Perelini, Rev. Dr Otele, mo, Congregational Christian Church in Samoa (Samoa)

Shegena Gobena, Dr Muluemebet, fl, Ethiopian Orthodox Tewahedo Church (Ethiopia)

Silva Ferreira, Srta Regina da, yfl, Igreja Evangélica de Confissão Luterana no Brasil (Brazil)

Vasko, Ms Outi, yfl, Suomen ortodoksinen Kirkko (Finland)

WORSHIP COMMITTEE

Gennadios of Sassima, H.E. Metropolitan Prof. Dr, mo, Ecumenical Patriarchate of Constantinople (Turkey), Moderator

Henry-Crowe, Rev. Susan, fo, United Methodist Church (United States of America), Rapporteur

Apii, Mr Daniel, ml, Cook Islands Christian Church (Cook Islands)

Aboagye-Mensah, Most Rev. Dr Robert, mo, Methodist Church Ghana (Ghana)

Chernov, Mr Vasily V., yml, Russian Orthodox Church (Russian Federation)

Crismo, Ms Phebe Gamata, fl, Ecumenical Bishop's Initiative for Children and Families (Philippines)

Kawak, Fr Jean, mo, Syrian Orthodox Patriarchate of Antioch and All the East (Syria)

Kuss, Rev. Cibele, fo, Igreja Evangélica de Confissão Luterana no Brasil (Brazil)

Appendix IV
Presidents, Officers and Central Committee members elected in Porto Alegre

Presidium

Anastasios of Tirana, Durrës and All Albania, H.B. Archbishop, Orthodox Autocephalous Church of Albania, mo

Doom, Mr John, Maòhi Protestant Church [French Polynesia], ml

Dossou, Pasteur Simon K., Protestant Methodist Church of Benin, mo

Nababan, Dr Soritua Albert Ernst, Protestant Christian Batak Church (HKBP) [Indonesia], ml

Ortega Suárez, Rev. Dr Ofelia, Presbyterian-Reformed Church in Cuba, fo

Paulos, H.H. Abune, Ethiopian Orthodox Tewahedo Church, mo

Powell Jackson, Rev. Dr Bernice, United Church of Christ [United States of America], fo

Tanner, Dr Mary, Church of England, fl

Officers

Altmann, Rev. Dr Walter, Evangelical Church of the Lutheran Confession in Brazil, mo

Gennadios of Sassima, Metropolitan Prof. Dr, Ecumenical Patriarchate [Turkey], mo

Hendriks-Ririmasse, Rev. Dr Margaretha M., Protestant Church in the Moluccas (GPM) [Indonesia], fo

Kobia, Rev. Dr Samuel, Methodist Church in Kenya [Switzerland], mo

Members

*Aasa-Marklund, Ms Inger, Church of Sweden, fl

Aboagye-Mensah, Most Rev. Dr Robert, Methodist Church Ghana, mo

*Abrahams, Bishop Ivan Manuel, Methodist Church of Southern Africa [South Africa], mo

*Abuom, Dr Agnes, Anglican Church of Kenya, fl

Adinyira, Mrs Sophia Ophilia Adjeibea, Church of the Province of West Africa [Ghana], fl

Alemezian, Bishop Nareg, Armenian Apostolic Church (Holy See of Cilicia) [Lebanon], mo

Alexander, Rev. James Lagos, Africa Inland Church Sudan, mo

*Alfeev, Bishop Dr Hilarion, Russian Orthodox Church, mo

Aneyé, Mme Akissi Jeannette, United Methodist Church [Côte d'Ivoire], fl

Angleberger, Rev. Judy, Presbyterian Church (USA), fo

Asana, Rev. Dr Festus Ambe, Presbyterian Church in Cameroon, mo

Asiimwe, Mr Onesimus, Church of the Province of Uganda, ml

*Aykazian, Bishop Vicken, Armenian Apostolic Church (Holy See of Etchmiadzin) [United States of America], mo

*Azariah, Bishop Samuel Robert, Church of Pakistan, mo

Bayrakdarian-Kabakian, Dr Nora, Armenian Apostolic Church (Holy See of Cilicia) [Lebanon], fl

Beneteri, Ms Terauango, Kiribati Protestant Church, fly

Biere, Frau Christina, Evangelical Church in Germany, fly

On the list of Presidents, Officers and Central Committee members elected in Porto Alegre, the name of the country in square brackets indicates the country of residence where it is not obvious from or different to the name of the church. The abbreviations following at the end of each line indicate: y=youth; m=male; f=female; o=ordained; l=layperson. An asterisk (*) before Central Committee member's name indicates that he or she is a member of the Executive Committee.

Bishoy, H.E. Metropolitan, Coptic Orthodox Church [Egypt], mo
Bosien, Pfarrerin Heike, Evangelical Church in Germany, fo
Butler, Rt Rev. Thomas Frederick, Church of England, mo
Camerin, Rev. Sofia Ann, Mission Covenant Church of Sweden, fo
Celestine, Miss Nerissa, Church in the Province of the West Indies [Grenada], fly
Chan, Dr Anna May, Myanmar Baptist Convention, fl
Chaplin, Archpriest Vsevolod, Russian Orthodox Church, mo
Chen, Mrs Meilin, China Christian Council, fl
Chhangte, Rev. Rothangliani, American Baptist Churches in the USA, fo
Clarke, Mrs Hera Rere, Anglican Church in Aotearoa, New Zealand and Polynesia, fl
Devejian, Mrs Paula, Armenian Apostolic Church (Holy See of Etchmiadzin), fl
Dibeela, Rev. Dr Moiseraele Prince, United Congregational Church of Southern Africa [South Africa], mo
Dimas, Rev. Fr George, Greek Orthodox Patriarchate of Antioch and All the East [Lebanon], mo
Dobrijevic, Rev. Hieromonk Irinej, Serbian Orthodox Church [Australia], mo
Duarte, Pastor Carlos, Evangelical Church of the River Plate [Argentina], mo
Dyck, Bishop Sally, United Methodist Church [United States of America], fo
Dyvasirvadam, Rt Rev. Dr Govada, Church of South India, mo
El Baiady, Rev. Dr Safwat Nagieb Ghobrial, Evangelical Presbyterian Church Egypt, mo
Enns, Rev. Dr Fernando, Mennonite Church in Germany, mo
Falani, Rev. Tofinga Vaevalu, Congregational Christian Church of Tuvalu, mo
Gadegaard, Dean Anders, Evangelical Lutheran Church in Denmark, mo
Gáncs, Bishop Peter, Lutheran Church in Hungary, mo
Gao, Rev. Ying, China Christian Council, fo
Gardner, Rev. Dr Paul, Moravian Church in Jamaica, mo
George, Rev. Dr Kondothra M., Malankara Orthodox Syrian Church [India], mo
Getcha, Archimandrite Dr Job, Ecumenical Patriarchate [Turkey], mo
Girsang, Mrs Jenny Rio Rita, Simalungun Protestant Christian Church (GKPS) [Indonesia], fl
Glynn-Mackoul, Ms Anne, Greek Orthodox Patriarchate of Antioch and All the East [United States of America], fl
Gobena Molte, Rev. Iteffa, Ethiopian Evangelical Church Mekane Yesus, mo
Goodbourn, Dr David Robin, Baptist Union of Great Britain, ml
Goundiaev, Father Mikhail, Russian Orthodox [Switzerland], mo
Harte, Ms Sarah, Episcopal Church in the USA, fly
Hein, Bischof Dr Martin Hermann, Evangelical Church in Germany, mo
Henderson, Rev. Gregor, Uniting Church in Australia, mo
Houweling, Rev. Wies, Protestant Church in the Netherlands, fo
Huttunen, Rev. Fr Heikki (Tuomas), Orthodox Church of Finland, mo
Idowu-Fearon, Rt Rev. Dr Josiah Atkins, Church of Nigeria (Anglican Communion), mo
Ingram, Rev. William, Presbyterian Church in Canada, mo
Ioannis of Thermopylae, Bishop, Church of Greece, mo
Jakobsone, Ms Anita, Evangelical Lutheran Church of Latvia, fl
Jones, Rev. Kathy, Church in Wales, fo
Joseph, Rev. W.P. Ebenezer, Methodist Church, Sri Lanka, mo
Jung, Ms Hae-Sun, Korean Methodist Church, fl
Kamba Kasongo, Rev. Micheline, Church of Christ in Congo - Presbyterian Community of Kinshasa [Democratic Republic of Congo], fo

Karagdag, Mrs Carmencita, Philippine Independent Church, fl
*Karayiannis of Trimithus, H.G. Bishop Dr Vasilios, Church of Cyprus, mo
Kathindi, Very Rev. Nangula E., Church of the Province of Southern Africa [South Africa], fo
Kimhachandra, Rev. Dr Sint, Church of Christ in Thailand, mo
Kinda, Pasteur Sombepouire Lazare, Association of Evangelical Reformed Churches of Burkina Faso, mo
Kishkovsky, Very Rev. Leonid, Orthodox Church in America, mo
Kisku, Ms Sanchita, United Evangelical Lutheran Church in India, fly
*Koppe, Bischof Dr Rolf, Evangelical Church in Germany, mo
Kyafa, Mrs Pati, Reformed Church of Christ in Nigeria, fl
*Lansdowne, Ms Carmen Rae, United Church of Canada, fly
*Larentzakis, Mag. Emanuela, Ecumenical Patriarchate [Greece], fl
Lavatai, Rev. Sanele Faasua, Methodist Church of Samoa, mo
Legesse, Dr Nigussu, Ethiopian Orthodox Tewahedo Church, ml
Lin Cheng, Mrs Ming-Min, Presbyterian Church in Taiwan, fl
Lohre, Ms Kathryn, Evangelical Lutheran Church in America, fly
Lopez-Lozano, Obispo Carlos, Spanish Reformed Episcopal Church, mo
Makarios of Kenya and Irinoupolis, H.E. Archbishop, Greek Orthodox Patriarchate of Alexandria and All Africa [Kenya], mo
*Malungo, Pasteur António Pedro, Evangelical Reformed Church of Angola, mo
Mansour, Metropolitan Damascinos, Greek Orthodox Patriarchate of Antioch and All the East [Brazil], mo
Mar Philoxenos, Bishop Isaac, Mar Thoma Syrian Church of Malabar [India], mo
Martzelos, Prof. Georgios, Church of Greece, ml
Masih, Mrs Prabhjot Prim Rose, Church of North India, fl
McCullough Dauway, Ms Lois, United Methodist Church [United States of America], fl
*McGeoch, Mr Graham Gerald, Church of Scotland, mly
Mdegella, Bishop Dr Owdenburg Moses, Evangelical Lutheran Church in Tanzania, mo
Mekel, Ms Peggy Adeline, Christian Evangelical Church in Minahasa (GMIM) [Indonesia], fly
Michau, Mme Marie-Christine, Evangelical Lutheran Church of France, fl
Mlynkova, Ms Kristyna, Czechoslovak Hussite Church, fly
Morris, Rev. Dr Heather, Methodist Church in Ireland, fo
Musemakweli, Rev. Dr Elisée, Presbyterian Church in Rwanda, mo
Mutoro, Jane, Religious Society of Friends: Friends United Meeting [Kenya], foy
Nascimento Cunha, Dra Magali, Methodist Church in Brazil, fl
Naulapwa, Ms Bridget, United Church of Zambia, fly
Ndudzo, Mr Itayi, Methodist Church in Zimbabwe, mly
Nelyubova, Mrs Margarita, Russian Orthodox Church, fl
*Nifon of Targoviste, Archbishop, Romanian Orthodox Church, mo
Nilsen, Rev. Ingrid Vad, Church of Norway, fo
Nishihara, Rev. Renta, Anglican Church in Japan, mo
Ntahoturi, Rt Rev. Bernard, Province of the Anglican Church of Burundi, mo
*Oyekola, Ms Iyabo, Church of the Lord (Aladura) Worldwide [Nigeria], fly
Papadhopuli, Mr Jorgo, Orthodox Autocephalous Church of Albania, ml
Park, Prof. Dr Seong-Won, Presbyterian Church of Korea, mo
Parker, Dr Evelyn, Christian Methodist Episcopal Church [United States of America], fl
Peña, Mr Charles, Evangelical Lutheran Church in America, ml
Peranginangin, Dr Minda, Karo Batak Protestant Church (GBKP) [Indonesia], fo

Perisic, Archpriest Vladan, Serbian Orthodox Church [Serbia and Montenegro], mo

Peristeris, Archbishop Aristarchos, Greek Orthodox Patriarchate of Jerusalem [Palestine/Israel], mo

Petersen, Bishop Sofie Bodil Louise Lisbeth, Evangelical Lutheran Church in Denmark [Greenland], fo

Petrecca, Pastor Hector Osvaldo, Christian Biblical Church [Argentina], mo

Peura, Bishop Simoo, Evangelical Lutheran Church of Finland, mo

* *Pickens*, Rev. Dr Larry, United Methodist Church [United States of America], mo

* *Pitts*, Rev. Dr Tyrone, Progressive National Baptist Convention, Inc. [United States of America], mo

Poma Apaza, Obispo Carlos, Evangelical Methodist Church in Bolivia, mo

Preston, Ms Alison Jane, Anglican Church of Australia, fly

Priana, Rev. I. Made, Protestant Christian Church in Bali (GKPB), mo

Quawas, Dr Audeh, Greek Orthodox Patriarchate of Jerusalem [Jordan], ml

Razanadrakoto, Mme Suzette Vaolimanga, Church of Jesus Christ in Madagascar, fl

Roham, H.E. Metropolitan Mor Eustathius Matta, Syrian Orthodox Patriarchate of Antioch and All the East [Syria], mo

Row, Mr Anthony, Methodist Church in Malaysia, ml

Rytkönen, Mr Aaro Paavo Samuli, Evangelical Lutheran Church of Finland, mly

Sagar, Bishop Taranath S., Methodist Church in India, mo

Schoon-Tanis, Rev. Gretchen, Reformed Church in America, foy

Schürer-Behrmann, Rev. Frank, Evangelical Church in Germany, mo

Spencer, Rev. Glenna, Methodist Church in the Caribbean and the Americas [Antigua and Barbuda], fo

Starcová, Ms Iveta, Orthodox Church of the Czech Lands and Slovakia [Czech Republic], fly

Steele, Rev. Canon John Alfred, Anglican Church of Canada, mo

Stefanowski, Rev. Pawel Wlodzimierz, Polish Autocephalous Orthodox Church in Poland, mo

Stückelberger, Rev. Prof. Dr Christoph, Federation of Swiss Protestant Churches, mo

Teodoridis, Ms Anna, Ecumenical Patriarchate [Turkey], fly

Thomas, Rev. John, United Church of Christ [United States of America], mo

Thornton, Rev. Jill Margaret, United Reformed Church [United Kingdom], fo

Tita, Rev. Dr Michael, Romanian Orthodox Church, mo

Usung, Mrs Helen Ubon, Presbyterian Church of Nigeria, fl

Varea, Miss Geraldine, Methodist Church in Fiji and Rotuma, fly

* *Vasko*, Ms Outi, Orthodox Church of Finland, fly

Vercammen, Archbishop Joris, Old-Catholic Church of the Netherlands, mo

Vyzhanov, Father Igor, Russian Orthodox Church, mo

Watkins, Rev. Dr Sharon, Christian Church (Disciples of Christ) in the United States, fo

Wete, Pasteur Hnoija Jean, Evangelical Church in New Caledonia and the Loyalty Isles, mo

Winbush, Rev. Robina, Presbyterian Church (USA), fo

Yamada, Ms Motoe, United Methodist Church [United States of America], fly

Yewangoe, Rev. Dr Andreas, Christian Church of Sumba (GKS) [Indonesia], mo

Youannes, H.G. Bishop, Coptic Orthodox Church [Egypt], mo

Young, Bishop McKinley, African Methodist Episcopal Church [United States of America], mo

Zecharias, H.G. Abune, Ethiopian Orthodox Tewahedo Church, mo

Zeyi Ndingambote, Pasteur Simon, Church of Jesus Christ on Earth by His Special Envoy Simon Kimbangu [Democratic Republic of Congo], mo

APPENDIX V

MEMBER CHURCHES AND ASSOCIATE COUNCILS

Names and locations of churches are given according to information available to the WCC at the time of the Assembly. The name of the country appears in square brackets where it is not obvious from the name of the church. Geographical references are provided only where they are necessary to identify the church or when they indicate the location of headquarters of churches with regional or world membership. The mention of a country in this list does not imply any political judgment on the part of the WCC. In the list, a single asterisk (*) indicates that the church, at the time of the Assembly, was an associate member church of the WCC. A double asterisk (**) indicates a national council of churches associated with the WCC.

AFRICA

Africa Inland Church – Sudan
African Christian Church and Schools [Kenya]
African Church of the Holy Spirit [Kenya]*
African Israel Nineveh Church [Kenya]
African Protestant Church [Cameroon]*
Anglican Church of Kenya
Anglican Church of Tanzania
Association of Baptist Churches in Rwanda
Association of Evangelical Reformed Churches of Burkina Faso*
Botswana Christian Council**
Christian Council of Churches in Madagascar**
Christian Council of Ghana**
Christian Council of Nigeria**
Christian Council of Tanzania**
Christian Council of Zambia**
Church of Christ – Harrist Mission (Harrist Church) [Ivory Coast]
Church of Christ – Light of the Holy Spirit [Congo]
Church of Christ in Congo – Anglican Community of Congo [Democratic Republic of Congo]
Church of Christ in Congo – Baptist Community of Congo [Democratic Republic of Congo]
Church of Christ in Congo – Community of Disciples of Christ in Congo [Democratic Republic of Congo]
Church of Christ in Congo – Evangelical Community of Congo [Democratic Republic of Congo]
Church of Christ in Congo – Mennonite Community in Congo [Democratic Republic of Congo]
Church of Christ in Congo – Presbyterian Community of Congo [Democratic Republic of Congo]
Church of Christ in Congo – Presbyterian Community of Kinshasa [Democratic Republic of Congo]
Church of Christ in Congo – Protestant Baptist Church in Africa/Episcopal Baptist Community in Africa [Democratic Republic of Congo]
Church of Jesus Christ in Madagascar
Church of Jesus Christ on Earth by His Special Envoy Simon Kimbangu [Democratic Republic of Congo]
Church of the Brethren in Nigeria
Church of the Lord (Aladura) Worldwide [Nigeria]
Church of Nigeria (Anglican Communion)
Church of the Province of Central Africa [Malawi]
Church of the Province of Southern Africa [South Africa]

Church of the Province of the Indian Ocean [Madagascar]
Church of the Province of West Africa [Ghana]
Church of Uganda
Council of African Instituted Churches [South Africa]
Council of Christian Churches in Angola**
Council of Churches in Namibia**
Council of Churches in Sierra Leone**
Council of Protestant Churches in Cameroon**
Council of Protestant Churches of Equatorial Guinea**
Council of Swaziland Churches**
Ecumenical Council of Christian Churches of Congo [Republic of Congo]**
Episcopal Church of the Sudan
Eritrean Orthodox Tewahedo Church
Ethiopian Evangelical Church Mekane Yesus
Ethiopian Orthodox Tewahedo Church
Evangelical Baptist Church in Angola
Evangelical Church of Cameroon
Evangelical Church of Gabon
Evangelical Church of the Congo [Republic of Congo]
Evangelical Congregational Church in Angola
Evangelical Lutheran Church in Congo [Zambia]
Evangelical Lutheran Church in Namibia
Evangelical Lutheran Church in Southern Africa [South Africa]
Evangelical Lutheran Church in Tanzania
Evangelical Lutheran Church in the Republic of Namibia
Evangelical Lutheran Church in Zimbabwe
Evangelical Lutheran Church of Ghana
Evangelical Pentecostal Mission of Angola
Evangelical Presbyterian Church in South Africa
Evangelical Presbyterian Church of Togo
Evangelical Presbyterian Church, Ghana
Evangelical Reformed Church of Angola
Gambia Christian Council**
Kenya Evangelical Lutheran Church*
Lesotho Evangelical Church
Liberian Council of Churches**
Lutheran Church in Liberia
Malagasy Lutheran Church [Madagascar]
Malawi Council of Churches**
Methodist Church Ghana
Methodist Church in Kenya
Methodist Church in Zimbabwe
Methodist Church Nigeria
Methodist Church of Southern Africa [South Africa]
Methodist Church of Togo
Methodist Church Sierra Leone
Moravian Church in Southern Africa [South Africa]
Moravian Church in Tanzania

439

National Council of Churches of Burundi**
Native Baptist Church of Cameroon
Nigerian Baptist Convention
Presbyterian Church in Cameroon
Presbyterian Church in Rwanda
Presbyterian Church of Africa [South Africa]
Presbyterian Church of Cameroon
Presbyterian Church of East Africa [Kenya]
Presbyterian Church of Ghana
Presbyterian Church of Liberia*
Presbyterian Church of Mozambique*
Presbyterian Church of Nigeria
Presbyterian Church of the Sudan
Protestant Church of Algeria*
Protestant Council of Rwanda**
Protestant Methodist Church of Benin
Province of the Anglican Church of Burundi
Province of the Episcopal Church in Rwanda
Reformed Church in Zambia
Reformed Church in Zimbabwe
Reformed Church of Christ in Nigeria
Reformed Presbyterian Church of Equatorial Guinea*

South African Council of Churches**
Sudan Council of Churches**
The African Church [Nigeria]
Uganda Joint Christian Council**
Union of Baptist Churches of Cameroon
United Church of Christ in Zimbabwe
United Church of Zambia
United Congregational Church of Southern Africa [South Africa]
United Methodist Church of Côte d'Ivoire
United Evangelical Church "Anglican Communion in Angola"*
Uniting Presbyterian Church in Southern Africa [South Africa]
Uniting Reformed Church in Southern Africa [South Africa]
Zimbabwe Council of Churches**

Asia

Anglican Church in Aotearoa, New Zealand and Polynesia
Anglican Church in Japan
Anglican Church of Australia
Anglican Church of Korea
Associated Churches of Christ in New Zealand
Bangladesh Baptist Church Sangha
Baptist Union of New Zealand
Batak Christian Community Church (GPKB) [Indonesia]*
Bengal-Orissa-Bihar Baptist Convention [India]*
China Christian Council
Christian Church in East Timor

Christian Church of Central Sulawesi (GKST) [Indonesia]
Christian Church of Sumba (GKS) [Indonesia]
Christian Evangelical Church in Minahasa (GMIM) [Indonesia]
Christian Evangelical Church in Sangihe Talaud (GMIST) [Indonesia]
Christian Protestant Angkola Church (GKPA) [Indonesia]
Christian Protestant Church in Indonesia (GKPI)
Church of Bangladesh*
Church of Ceylon
Church of Christ in Thailand
Church of North India
Church of Pakistan
Church of South India
Church of the Province of Myanmar
Churches of Christ in Australia
Communion of Churches in Indonesia**
Convention of Philippine Baptist Churches
Council of Churches of Malaysia**
East Java Christian Church (GKJW) [Indonesia]
Episcopal Church in the Philippines
Evangelical Christian Church in Halmahera (GMIH) [Indonesia]
Evangelical Christian Church in Irian Jaya (GKITP) [Indonesia]
Evangelical Methodist Church in the Philippines
Hong Kong Christian Council [China]**
Hong Kong Council of the Church of Christ in China
Indonesian Christian Church (GKI)
Indonesian Christian Church (HKI)
Javanese Christian Churches (GKJ) [Indonesia]
Kalimantan Evangelical Church (GKE) [Indonesia]
Karo Batak Protestant Church (GBKP) [Indonesia]
Korean Christian Church in Japan*
Korean Methodist Church
Malankara Orthodox Syrian Church [India]
Maori Council of Churches [Aotearoa-New Zealand]**
Mar Thoma Syrian Church of Malabar [India]
Mara Evangelical Church [Myanmar]*
Methodist Church in India
Methodist Church in Indonesia
Methodist Church in Malaysia
Methodist Church in Singapore*
Methodist Church of New Zealand
Methodist Church, Sri Lanka
Methodist Church, Upper Myanmar
Myanmar Baptist Convention
Myanmar Council of Churches**
National Christian Council in Japan**
National Christian Council of Sri Lanka**
National Council of Churches in Australia**
National Council of Churches in India**

National Council of Churches in Korea**
National Council of Churches in the Philippines**
National Council of Churches of Singapore**
Nias Protestant Christian Church (BNKP) [Indonesia]
Orthodox Church in Japan
Pasundan Christian Church (GKP) [Indonesia]
Philippine Independent Church
Presbyterian Church in Taiwan
Presbyterian Church in the Republic of Korea
Presbyterian Church of Aotearoa New Zealand
Presbyterian Church of Korea
Presbyterian Church of Pakistan
Protestant Christian Batak Church (HKBP) [Indonesia]
Protestant Christian Church in Bali (GKPB) [Indonesia]*
Protestant Church in Indonesia (GPI)
Protestant Church in Sabah [Malaysia]
Protestant Church in South-East Sulawesi (GEPSULTRA) [Indonesia]
Protestant Church in the Moluccas (GPM) [Indonesia]
Protestant Church of Timor Lorosa'e [Timor Lorosa'e]
Protestant Church in Western Indonesia (GPIB)
Protestant Evangelical Church in Timor (GMIT) [Indonesia]
Samavesam of Telugu Baptist Churches [India]
Simalungun Protestant Christian Church (GKPS) [Indonesia]
Toraja Church (GT) [Indonesia]
United Church of Christ in Japan
United Church of Christ in the Philippines
United Evangelical Lutheran Churches in India
Uniting Church in Australia

Caribbean

Baptist Convention of Haiti
Church in the Province of the West Indies [Bahamas]
Council of Churches of Cuba**
Council of Churches of Porto Rico**
Jamaica Baptist Union
Jamaica Council of Churches**
Methodist Church in Cuba*
Methodist Church in the Caribbean and the Americas [Antigua]
Methodist Church in Porto Rico*
Moravian Church in Jamaica
Moravian Church in Suriname
Moravian Church, Eastern West Indies Province [Antigua]
Presbyterian Church in Trinidad & Tobago
Presbyterian-Reformed Church in Cuba*
Saint Vincent and the Grenadines Christian Council**
United Church in Jamaica and the Cayman Islands
United Protestant Church [Netherlands Antilles]*

EUROPE

Action of Churches Together in Scotland**
Armenian Apostolic Church
Baptist Union of Denmark
Baptist Union of Great Britain
Baptist Union of Hungary
Catholic Diocese of the Old–Catholics in Germany
Christian Council of Norway**
Christian Council of Sweden**
Church in Wales
Church of England
Church of Greece
Church of Ireland
Church of Norway
Church of Scotland
Church of Sweden
Church of the Augsburg Confession of Alsace and Lorraine [France]
Churches Together in Britain and Ireland**
Churches Together in England**
Council of Christian Churches in Germany**
Council of Christian Churches in Switzerland**
Council of Churches in the Netherlands**
CYTUN – Churches Together in Wales**
Czechoslovak Hussite Church [Czech Republic]
Ecumenical Council of Churches in Austria**
Ecumenical Council of Churches in Hungary**
Ecumenical Council of Churches in Serbia and Montenegro**
Ecumenical Council of Churches in the Czech Republic**
Ecumenical Council of Churches in the Slovak Republic**
Ecumenical Patriarchate [Turkey]
Estonian Evangelical Lutheran Church
Evangelical Baptist Union of Italy*
Evangelical Church in Germany
– Bremen Evangelical Church
– Church of Lippe
– Evangelical Church in Baden
– Evangelical Church in Berlin-Brandenburg-Silesian Oberlausitz
– Evangelical Church in Hesse and Nassau
– Evangelical Church in Württemberg
– Evangelical Church in Rhineland
– Evangelical Church of Anhalt
– Evangelical Church of Kurhessen Waldeck
– Evangelical Church of the Palatinate
– Evangelical Church of the Province of Saxony
– Evangelical Church of the Silesian Oberlausitz
– Evangelical Church of Westphalia
– Evangelical Lutheran Church in Bavaria
– Evangelical Lutheran Church in Brunswick

– Evangelical Lutheran Church in Oldenburg
– Evangelical Lutheran Church in Thuringia
– Evangelical Lutheran Church in Württemberg
– Evangelical Lutheran Church of Hanover
– Evangelical Lutheran Church of Mecklenburg
– Evangelical Lutheran Church of Saxony
– Evangelical Lutheran Church of Schaumburg-Lippe
– Evangelical Reformed Church in North-West Germany
– North-Elbian Evangelical Lutheran Church
– Pomeranian Evangelical Church
Evangelical Church of Czech Brethren [Czech Republic]
Evangelical Church of the Augsburg and Helvetic Confessions in Austria
Evangelical Church of the Augsburg Confession in Poland
Evangelical Church of the Augsburg Confession in Romania
Evangelical Church of the Augsburg Confession in Slovakia
Evangelical Lutheran Church in Denmark
Evangelical Lutheran Church of Finland
Evangelical Lutheran Church of France
Evangelical Lutheran Church of Iceland
Evangelical Lutheran Church of Latvia
Evangelical-Lutheran Church in Romania
Evangelical Methodist Church of Italy
Evangelical Presbyterian Church of Portugal*
Federation of Swiss Protestant Churches
French Protestant Federation**
Finnish Ecumenical Council**
Greek Evangelical Church
Latvian Evangelical Lutheran Church Abroad [Germany]
Lusitanian Church of Portugal*
Lutheran Church in Hungary
Mennonite Church in Germany
Mennonite Church in the Netherlands
Methodist Church [United Kingdom]
Methodist Church in Ireland
Mission Covenant Church of Sweden
Moravian Church British Province and EFBU [Germany]
National Council of Churches in Denmark**
Old-Catholic Church of Austria
Old-Catholic Church of Switzerland
Old-Catholic Church of the Netherlands
Old-Catholic Mariavite Church in Poland
Orthodox Autocephalous Church of Albania
Orthodox Church of Finland
Orthodox Church of the Czech Lands and Slovakia [Czech Republic]
Polish Autocephalous Orthodox Church in Poland
Polish Catholic Church in Poland
Polish Ecumenical Council**
Presbyterian Church of Wales

Protestant Church in the Netherlands
Reformed Christian Church in Serbia and Montenegro
Reformed Christian Church in Slovakia [Slovak Republic]
Reformed Church in Hungary
Reformed Church in Romania
Reformed Church of Alsace and Lorraine [France]
Reformed Church of France
Remonstrant Brotherhood [Netherlands]
Romanian Orthodox Church
Russian Orthodox Church
Scottish Episcopal Church
Serbian Orthodox Church [Serbia and Montenegro]
Silesian Evangelical Church of the Augsburg Confession in the Czech Republic
Slovak Evangelical Church of the Augsburg Confession in Serbia and Montenegro
Spanish Evangelical Church*
Spanish Reformed Episcopal Church*
Union of Welsh Independents
United Free Church of Scotland
United Protestant Church of Belgium
United Reformed Church [United Kingdom]
Waldensian Church [Italy]

LATIN AMERICA

Anglican Church of the Southern Cone of America [Argentina]
Association The Church of God [Argentina]*
Baptist Association of El Salvador
Baptist Convention of Nicaragua
Bolivian Evangelical Lutheran Church*
Christian Biblical Church [Argentina]*
Christian Reformed Church of Brazil
Episcopal Anglican Church of Brazil
Evangelical Church of the Disciples of Christ in Argentina*
Evangelical Church of Lutheran Confession in Brazil
Evangelical Church of the River Plate [Argentina]
Evangelical Lutheran Church in Chile
Evangelical Methodist Church in Bolivia*
Evangelical Methodist Church Argentina
Free Pentecostal Missions Church of Chile
Methodist Church in Brazil
Methodist Church in Mexico
Methodist Church in Uruguay*
Methodist Church of Chile*
Methodist Church of Peru*
Moravian Church in Nicaragua
National Council of Christian Churches in Brazil**
Pentecostal Church of Chile
Pentecostal Mission Church [Chile]
Presbyterian Church of Colombia*

Salvadorean Lutheran Synod*
United Evangelical Lutheran Church [Argentina]*
United Presbyterian Church of Brazil*

MIDDLE EAST

Armenian Apostolic Church (Holy See of Cilicia) [Lebanon]
Church of Cyprus
Coptic Orthodox Church [Egypt]
Episcopal Church in Jerusalem and the Middle East [Israel/Palestine]
Evangelical Presbyterian Church of Egypt
Greek Orthodox Patriarchate of Alexandria and All Africa [Egypt]
Greek Orthodox Patriarchate of Antioch and All the East [Syria]
Greek Orthodox Patriarchate of Jerusalem [Israel/Palestine]
National Evangelical Synod of Syria and Lebanon [Lebanon]
Synod of the Evangelical Church of Iran
Syrian Orthodox Patriarchate of Antioch and All the East
Union of the Armenian Evangelical Churches in the Near East [Lebanon]

NORTH AMERICA

African Methodist Episcopal Church [United States of American]
African Methodist Episcopal Zion Church [United States of American]
American Baptist Churches in the USA
Anglican Church of Canada
Canadian Council of Churches**
Canadian Yearly Meeting of the Religious Society of Friends
Christian Church (Disciples of Christ) in Canada
Christian Church (Disciples of Christ) in the United States of America
Christian Methodist Episcopal Church [United States of America]
Church of the Brethren [United States of America]
Episcopal Church in the USA
Estonian Evangelical Lutheran Church Abroad [Canada]
Evangelical Lutheran Church in America
Evangelical Lutheran Church in Canada
Holy Apostolic Catholic Assyrian Church of the East [United States of America]
Hungarian Reformed Church in America
International Council of Community Churches [United States of America]
International Evangelical Church [United States of America]
Moravian Church in America
National Baptist Convention of America, Inc.
National Baptist Convention USA, Inc.
National Council of the Churches of Christ in the USA**
Orthodox Church in America
Polish National Catholic Church [United States of America]
Presbyterian Church (USA)
Presbyterian Church in Canada
Progressive National Baptist Convention, Inc. [United States of America]
Reformed Church in America
Religious Society of Friends – Friends General Conference [United States of America]

Religious Society of Friends – Friends United Meeting [United States of America]
United Church of Canada
United Church of Christ [United States of America]
United Methodist Church [United States of America]

PACIFIC

Church of the Province of Melanesia [Solomon Islands]
Congregational Christian Church in American Samoa
Congregational Christian Church in Samoa
Congregational Christian Church of Niue
Congregational Christian Church of Tuvalu
Cook Islands Christian Church
Evangelical Church in New Caledonia and the Loyalty Isles
Evangelical Lutheran Church of Papua New Guinea
Free Wesleyan Church of Tonga
Kiribati Protestant Church
Maòhi Protestant Church [French Polynesia]
Methodist Church in Fiji and Rotuna
Methodist Church in Samoa
National Council of Churches in American Samoa**
Papua New Guinea Council of Churches**
Presbyterian Church of Vanuatu

APPENDIX VI
CONSTITUTION AND RULES OF THE WORLD COUNCIL OF CHURCHES
(as amended by the 9th Assembly, Porto Alegre, Brazil, February 2006)

CONSTITUTION

I. BASIS

The World Council of Churches is a fellowship of churches which confess the Lord Jesus Christ as God and Saviour according to the scriptures and therefore seek to fulfil together their common calling to the glory of the one God, Father, Son and Holy Spirit.

II. MEMBERSHIP

Churches shall be eligible for membership in the fellowship of the World Council of Churches who express their agreement with the basis upon which the Council is founded and satisfy such criteria for membership as the assembly or central committee may prescribe. The central committee shall consider applications for membership in accordance with Rule I.

III. PURPOSES AND FUNCTIONS

The World Council of Churches is constituted by the churches to serve the one ecumenical movement. It incorporates the work of the world movements for Faith and Order and Life and Work, the International Missionary Council, and the World Council of Christian Education.

The primary purpose of the fellowship of churches in the World Council of Churches is to call one another to visible unity in one faith and in one eucharistic fellowship, expressed in worship and common life in Christ, through witness and service to the world, and to advance towards that unity in order that the world may believe.

In seeking koinonia in faith and life, witness and service, the churches through the Council will:
- promote the prayerful search for forgiveness and reconciliation in a spirit of mutual accountability, the development of deeper relationships through theological dialogue, and the sharing of human, spiritual and material resources with one another;
- facilitate common witness in each place and in all places, and support each other in their work for mission and evangelism;
- express their commitment to diakonia in serving human need, breaking down barriers between people, promoting one human family in justice and peace, and upholding the integrity of creation, so that all may experience the fullness of life;
- nurture the growth of an ecumenical consciousness through processes of education and a vision of life in community rooted in each particular cultural context;
- assist each other in their relationships to and with people of other faith communities;
- foster renewal and growth in unity, worship, mission and service.

In order to strengthen the one ecumenical movement, the Council will:
- nurture relations with and among churches, especially within but also beyond its membership;
- establish and maintain relations with national councils, regional conferences of churches, organizations of Christian world communions and other ecumenical bodies;
- support ecumenical initiatives at regional, national and local levels;
- facilitate the creation of networks among ecumenical organizations;
- work towards maintaining the coherence of the one ecumenical movement in its diverse manifestations.

IV. AUTHORITY

The World Council shall offer counsel and provide opportunity for united action in matters of common interest.

It may take action on behalf of constituent churches only in such matters as one or more of them may commit to it and only on behalf of such churches.

The World Council shall not legislate for the churches; nor shall it act for them in any manner except as indicated above or as may hereafter be specified by the constituent churches.

V. ORGANIZATION

The World Council shall discharge its functions through an assembly, a central committee, an executive committee, and other subordinate bodies as may be established.

449

1. *The assembly*
   a) The assembly shall be the supreme legislative body governing the World Council and shall ordinarily meet at seven-year intervals
   b) The assembly shall be composed of official representatives of the member churches, known as delegates, elected by the member churches.
   c) The assembly shall have the following functions:
      1) to elect the president or presidents of the World Council;
      2) to elect not more than 145 members of the central committee from among the delegates which the member churches have elected to the assembly;
      3) to elect not more than 5 members from among the representatives elected to the assembly by churches which do not fulfil the criteria of size and have not been granted membership for exceptional reasons;
      4) to determine the overall policies of the World Council and to review programmes undertaken to implement policies previously adopted;
      5) to delegate to the central committee specific functions, except to amend this constitution and to allocate the membership of the central committee granted by this constitution to the assembly exclusively.

2. *The central committee*
   a) The central committee shall be responsible for implementing the policies adopted by the assembly and shall exercise the functions of the assembly itself delegated to it by the assembly between its meetings, except its power to amend this constitution and to allocate or alter the allocation of the membership of central committee.
   b) The central committee shall be composed of the president or presidents of the World Council of Churches and not more than 150 members.

1) Not more than 145 members shall be elected by the assembly from among the delegates the member churches have elected to the assembly. Such members shall be distributed among the member churches by the assembly giving due regard to the size of the churches and confessions represented in the Council, the number of churches of each confession which are members of the Council, reasonable geographical and cultural balance, and adequate representation of the major interests of the Council.

2) Not more than 5 members shall be elected by the assembly from among the representatives elected to the assembly by churches which do not fulfil the criteria of size and have not been granted membership for exceptional reasons.

3) A vacancy in the membership of the central committee, occurring between meetings of the assembly, shall be filled by the central committee itself after consultation with the church of which the person previously occupying the position was a member.

c) The central committee shall have, in addition to the general powers set out in (a) above, the following powers:

1) to elect its moderator and vice-moderator or vice-moderators from among the members of the central committee;

2) to elect the executive committee from among the members of the central committee;

3) to elect committees, commissions, and boards;

4) within the policies adopted by the assembly, and on the recommendation of the programme committee, to initiate and terminate programmes and activities and to set priorities for the work of the Council;

5) to adopt the budget of the World Council and secure its financial support;

6) to elect the general secretary and to elect or appoint or to make provision for the election or appointment of all members of the staff of the World Council;

7) to plan for the meetings of the assembly, making provision for the conduct of its business, for worship and study, and for common Christian commitment. The central committee shall determine the number of delegates to the assembly and allocate them among the member churches giving due regard to the size of the churches and confessions represented in the Council; the number of churches of each confession which are members of the Council; reasonable geographical and cultural balance; the desired distribution among church officials, parish ministers and lay persons; among men, women and young people; and participation by persons whose special knowledge and experience will be needed;

8) to delegate specific functions to the executive committee or to other bodies or persons.

3. *Rules*

The assembly or the central committee may adopt and amend rules not inconsistent with this constitution for the conduct of the business of the World Council.

4. *By-laws*

The assembly or the central committee may adopt and amend by-laws not inconsistent with this constitution for the functioning of its committees, boards, working groups and commissions.

5. *Quorum*

A quorum for the conduct of any business by the assembly or the central committee shall be one-half of its membership.

VI. OTHER ECUMENICAL CHRISTIAN ORGANIZATIONS

1. Such world confessional bodies and such international ecumenical organizations as may be designated by the central committee may be invited to send representatives to the assembly and to the central

committee, in such numbers as the central committee shall determine; however, these representatives shall not have the right to participate when decisions are taken.

2. Such national councils and regional conferences of churches, other Christian councils and missionary councils as may be designated by the central committee may be invited to send representatives to the assembly and to the central committee, in such numbers as the central committee shall determine; however, these representatives shall not have the right to participate when decisions are taken.

VII. Amendments

The constitution may be amended by a two-thirds vote of the delegates to the assembly present and voting, provided that the proposed amendment shall have been reviewed by the central committee, and notice of it sent to the member churches not less than six months before the meeting of the assembly. The central committee itself, as well as the member churches, shall have the right to propose such amendment.

Rules

I. Membership in the fellowship of the World Council of Churches

The World Council of Churches is comprised of churches which have constituted the Council or which have been admitted into membership and which continue to belong to the fellowship of the World Council of Churches. The term "church" as used in this article could also include an association, convention or federation of autonomous churches. A group of churches within a country or region, or within the same confession, may choose to participate in the World Council of Churches as one member. Churches within the same country or region or within the same confession may apply jointly to belong to the fellowship of the Council, in order to respond to their common calling, to strengthen their joint participation and/or to satisfy the requirement of minimum size rule (I.3.b.3). Such groupings of churches are encouraged by the World Council of Churches; each individual church within the grouping must satisfy the criteria for membership in the fellowship of the World Council of Churches, except the requirements of size. A church seeking affiliation with a grouping of autonomous churches which is a member of the World Council of Churches must agree with the basis and fulfil the criteria for membership.

The general secretary shall maintain the official lists of member churches that have been accepted to belong to the fellowship of the World Council of Churches, noting any special arrangement accepted by the assembly or central committee. Separate lists shall be maintained of member churches belonging to the fellowship of the WCC that do or do not participate in decision-making.

1. *Application*
A church that wishes to join the World Council of Churches shall apply in writing to the general secretary.

2. *Processing*
The general secretary shall submit all such applications through the executive committee to the central committee together with such information as he or she considers necessary to enable the central committee to make a decision on the application.

3. *Criteria*

Churches applying to join the World Council of Churches ("applicant churches") are required first to express agreement with the basis on which the Council is founded and confirm their commitment to the purposes and functions of the Council as defined in articles I and III of the constitution. The basis states: "The World Council of Churches is a fellowship of churches which confess the Lord Jesus Christ as God and Saviour according to the scriptures and therefore seek to fulfil together their common calling to the glory of the one God, Father, Son and Holy Spirit."

Applicant churches should give an account of how their faith and witness relate to these norms and practices:

a) Theological

1) In its life and witness, the church professes faith in the triune God according to the scriptures, and as this faith is reflected in the Nicene-Constantinopolitan Creed.

2) The church maintains a ministry of proclaiming the gospel and celebrating the sacraments as understood by its doctrines.

3) The church baptizes in the name of the one God, "Father, Son and Holy Spirit" and acknowledges the need to move towards the recognition of the baptism of other churches.

4) The church recognizes the presence and activity of Christ and the Holy Spirit outside its own boundaries and prays for the gift of God's wisdom to all in the awareness that other member churches also believe in the Holy Trinity and the saving grace of God.

5) The church recognizes in the other member churches of the WCC elements of the true church, even if it does not regard them "as churches in the true and full sense of the word" (Toronto statement).

b) Organizational

1) The church must produce evidence of sustained autonomous life and organization.

2) The church must be able to take the decision to apply for formal membership in the WCC and continue to belong to the fellowship of the WCC without obtaining the permission of any other body or person.

3) An applicant church must ordinarily have at least fifty thousand members. The central committee, for exceptional reasons, may dispense with this requirement and accept a church that does not fulfil the criteria of size.

4) An applicant church with more than 10,000 members but less than 50,000 members that has not been granted membership for exceptional reasons under rule I.3.b.3, but is otherwise eligible for membership, can be admitted as a member subject to the following conditions: (a) it shall not have the right to participate in decision-making in the assembly, and (b) it may participate with other churches in selecting five representatives to the central committee in accordance with rule IV.4.b.3. Such church shall be considered as a member church belonging to the fellowship of the WCC in all other respects.

5) Churches must recognize the essential interdependence of the member churches belonging to the fellowship of the WCC, particularly those of the same confession, and should make every effort to practise constructive ecumenical relations with other churches within their country or region. This will normally mean that the church is a member of the national council of churches or similar body and of the regional/sub-regional ecumenical organization.

4. *Consultation*

Before admitting a church to membership in the fellowship of the World Council of Churches, the appropriate world confessional body or bodies and national council or regional ecumenical organization shall be consulted.

5. *Decision on acceptance*
The Central Committee shall consider applications for membership according to the consensus model of decision making. The application shall be accepted for a specified interim period of participation in the work of the World Council of Churches and for interaction with the local fellowship of member churches. The member churches of the World Council of Churches shall be consulted during the interim period. The Central Committee shall assess whether a consensus of member churches has developed in favour of the application, in which event the applicant church shall be considered a new member church. If there is no consensus, the Central Committee shall deem the application rejected.

6. *Resignation*
A church which desires to resign its membership in the fellowship of the Council can do so at any time. A church which has resigned but desires to rejoin the Council must again apply for membership.

II. RESPONSIBILITIES OF MEMBERSHIP

Membership in the World Council of Churches signifies faithfulness to the basis of the Council, fellowship in the Council, participation in the life and work of the Council and commitment to the ecumenical movement as integral to the mission of the church. Churches which are members of the World Council of Churches are expected to:

1) appoint delegates to the assembly, the major policy-making body of the Council, and participate in council with other member churches in shaping the ecumenical vision and the ecumenical agenda;

2) inform the World Council of their primary concerns, priorities, activities and constructive criticisms as they may relate to its programmes as well as any matters which they feel need expression of ecumenical solidarity or which merit the attention of the Council and/or churches around the world;

3) communicate the meaning of ecumenical commitment, to foster and encourage ecumenical relations and action at all levels of their church life and to pursue ecumenical fellowship locally, nationally, regionally and internationally;

4) interpret both the broader ecumenical movement and the World Council of Churches, its nature, purpose and programmes throughout their membership as a normal part of their own reporting to their constituency;

5) encourage participation in World Council programmes, activities and meetings, including:
a) proposing persons who could make a particular contribution to and/or participate in the Council's various committees, meetings and consultations, programmes, publications and staff;
b) establishing links between their own programme offices and the appropriate World Council programme offices; and
c) submitting materials for and promoting World Council communications resources: books, periodicals and other publications;

6) respond to decisions of the central committee which call for study, action or other follow-up by the member churches as well as respond to requests on matters referred by the central or executive committee or the general secretary for prayer, advice, information or opinion;

7) make an annual contribution to the general budget of the Council: the amount of the contribution shall be agreed upon in consultation between the church and the Council and shall be regularly reviewed;

8) participate, in ways commensurate with their resources and in consultation with the Council, in assuming responsibility for the costs of the Council's programmes and for expenses related to travel and accommodation of their representatives to Council events.

The implications of not fulfilling such obligations shall be such as the central committee shall decide.

III. Churches in association with the World Council of Churches

A church that agrees with the basis of the Council may request in writing to be received as a church in association with the World Council of Churches, stating its reasons for requesting this mode of relating with the Council. If the reasons are approved by the central committee, such a church may be accepted to be in association with the World Council of Churches.

Churches in association with the World Council of Churches:

1) can send representative(s) to the assembly and the central committee who can speak with permission of the chair, but have no right to participate in formal decision-making, whether by consensus or by vote;

2) can be invited to participate in the work of the commissions, advisory groups and other consultative bodies of the Council as consultants or advisers;

3) have the possibility of participating in the work of the WCC as described, but will not be identified with decisions taken or statements issued by the Council;

4) shall make an annual contribution to the general budget of the Council; the amount of the contribution shall be agreed upon in consultation between the church and the Council and shall be regularly reviewed; no financial support will ordinarily be made available from the Council to such churches to facilitate their participation.

The general secretary shall maintain a list of churches in association with the Council.

IV. The assembly

1. *Composition of the assembly*

a) *Persons with the right to speak and the responsibility to participate in decision-making*

The assembly shall be composed of official representatives of the member churches, known as delegates, elected by the member churches, with the right to speak and with the responsibility to participate in decision-making.

1) The central committee shall determine the number of delegates to the assembly well in advance of its meeting.

2) The central committee shall determine the percentage of the delegates, not less than 85 percent, who shall be both nominated and elected by the member churches. Each member church shall be entitled to a minimum of one delegate. The central committee shall allocate the other delegates in this group among the member churches giving due regard to the size of the churches and confessions represented in the World Council of Churches, the number of churches of each confession which are members of the Council, and reasonable geographical and cultural balance. The central committee shall recommend the proper distribution within delegations among church officials, parish ministers and lay persons; and among men, women, young people and Indigenous peoples. The central committee may make provision for the election by the member churches of alternate delegates who shall serve only in place of such delegates who are unable to attend meetings of the assembly.

3) The remaining delegates, not more than 15 percent, shall be elected by certain member churches upon nomination of the central committee as follows:

1. If the moderator or any vice-moderator of the central committee is not elected a delegate within the provisions of paragraph 2 above, the central committee shall nominate such officer to the member church of which such officer is a member. Paragraphs 5 and 6 below apply to such nominees.

2. The central committee shall determine the categories of additional delegates necessary to achieve balance in respect of:

    a) the varied sizes of churches and confessions;

    b) the historical significance, future potential or geographical location and cultural background of particular churches, as well as the special importance of united churches;

    c) the presence of persons whose special knowledge and experience will be necessary to the assembly;

    d) proportions of women, youth, lay persons and local pastors;

    e) participation of Indigenous peoples.

3. The central committee shall invite the member churches to propose the names of persons in the categories so determined whom the churches would be willing to elect, if nominated by the central committee.

4. From the list so compiled, the central committee shall propose the nomination of particular individuals to their respective member church.

5. If that member church elects the said nominee, he or she shall become an additional delegate of that member church.

6. The member churches shall not elect alternate delegates for such delegates.

Member churches are encouraged to consult regionally in the selection of the delegates described in paragraphs 2 and 3 above, provided that every delegate is elected by the church of which he or she is a member in accordance with its own procedures.

b) *Persons with the right to speak but not to participate in decision-making*

In addition to the delegates, who alone have the right to vote, the following categories of persons may attend meetings of the assembly with the right to speak:

1) *Presidents and officers:* Any president or presidents of the Council or moderator or vice-moderator or vice-moderators of the central committee who have not been elected delegates by their churches.

2) *Members of the retiring central committee:* Any members of the retiring central committee who have not been elected delegates by their churches.

3) *Representatives of churches which do not fulfil the criteria of size and have not been granted membership for exceptional reasons:* Each one of these churches may elect one representative.

4) *Advisers:* The central committee may invite a small number of persons who have a special contribution to make to the deliberations of the assembly or who have participated in the activities of the World Council. Before an invitation is extended to an adviser who is a member of a member church, that church shall be consulted.

5) *Delegated representatives:* The central committee may invite persons officially designated as delegated representatives by organizations with which the World Council maintains relationship.

6) *Delegated observers:* The central committee may invite persons officially designated as delegated observers by non-member churches.

c) *Persons without the right to speak or to participate in decision-making*

The central committee may invite to attend the meetings of the assembly without the right to speak or to participate in decision-making:

1) *Observers*: Persons identified with organizations with which the World Council maintains relationship which are not represented by delegated representatives or with non-member churches which are not represented by delegated observers.

2) *Guests*: Persons named individually.

2. *Presiding officers and committees*

a) At the first decision session of the assembly the central committee shall present its proposals for the moderatorship of the assembly and for the membership of the business committee of the assembly and make any other proposals, including the appointment of other committees, their membership and functions, for the conduct of the business of the assembly as it sees fit.

b) At the first or second decision session, additional nominations for membership of any committee may be made in writing by any six concurring delegates.

c) Election shall be by ballot unless the assembly shall otherwise determine.

3. *Agenda*

The agenda of the assembly shall be proposed by the central committee to the first decision session of the assembly. A delegate may propose changes to the agenda in accordance with rule XX.6.c. New business or any change may be proposed by the business committee under rule IV.5.b.2.

4. *Nominations committee of the assembly*

a) At an early decision session of the assembly, the assembly shall elect a nominations committee, on which there shall be appropriate confessional, cultural and geographical representation of the membership of the assembly and representation of the major interests of the World Council.

b) The nominations committee in consultation with the officers of the World Council and the executive committee shall make nominations for the following:

1) the president or presidents of the World Council;

2) not more than 145 members of the central committee from among the delegates which the member churches have elected to the assembly;

3) not more than 5 members of the central committee from among the representatives elected to the assembly by the churches which do not fulfil the criteria of size and have not been granted membership for exceptional reasons.

c) In making nominations, the nominations committee shall have regard to the following principles:

1) the personal qualifications of the individual for the task for which he or she is to be nominated;

2) fair and adequate confessional representation;

3) fair and adequate geographical and cultural representation;

4) fair and adequate representation of the major interests of the World Council.

The nominations committee shall satisfy itself as to the general acceptability of the nominations to the churches to which the nominees belong.

Not more than seven persons from any one member church shall be nominated as members of the central committee.

The nominations committee shall secure adequate representation of lay persons – men, women and young people – so far as the composition of the assembly makes this possible.

d) The nominations committee shall present its nominations to the assembly. Additional nominations may be made by any six delegates concurring in writing, provided that each such nominee shall be proposed in opposition to a particular nominee of the nominations committee.

e) Election shall be by ballot unless the assembly shall otherwise determine.

5. *Business committee of the assembly*

a)   The business committee of the assembly shall consist of the moderator and vice-moderator or vice-moderators of the central committee, the general secretary, the presidents of the Council, the co-moderators of the permanent committee on consensus and collaboration participating as a delegate, the moderator or a member of the assembly planning committee participating as a delegate, the moderators of hearings and committees who may appoint substitutes and ten delegates who are not members of the outgoing central committee, who shall be elected in accordance with rule IV.2. If a co-moderator of the permanent committee and/or the moderator of the assembly planning committee is not a delegate, he/she shall be invited as an adviser to the assembly and its business committee with the right to speak but not to participate in decision-making.

b)   The business committee shall:

1)   coordinate the day-to-day business of the assembly and may make proposals for rearrangement, modification, addition, deletion or substitution of items included on the agenda. Any such proposal shall be presented to the assembly at the earliest convenient time by a member of the business committee with reasons for the proposed change. After opportunity for discussion on the proposal, the moderator shall put the following question to the assembly: Shall the assembly approve the proposal of the business committee? The assembly shall decide the question by consensus or voting procedures. If decided according to voting procedures, then any proposed change must receive a two-thirds (2/3) majority of those present to be adopted;

2)   consider any item of business or change in the agenda proposed to the business committee by a delegate under rule XX.6.c;

3)   determine whether the assembly sits in general, hearing or decision session as defined in rule XX.2;

4)   receive information from and review the reports of other committees in order to consider how best the assembly can act on them.

6. *Other committees of the assembly*

a)   Any other committee of the assembly shall consist of such members and shall have such powers and duties as are proposed by the central committee at the first decision session or by the business committee after its election and accepted by the assembly.

b)   Any such committee shall, unless the assembly otherwise directs, inform the business committee about its work and shall make its report or recommendations to the assembly.

V. PRESIDENTS

1. The assembly shall elect the president or presidents of the World Council of Churches; the number of presidents elected shall, however, not exceed eight; the role of the presidents being to promote ecumenism and to interpret the work of the World Council of Churches, especially in their respective regions.

2. The term of office of a president shall end at the end of the next assembly following his or her election.

3. A president who has been elected by the assembly shall be ineligible for election for a second consecutive term of office.

4. The presidents should be persons whose ecumenical experience and standing is widely recognized among the ecumenical partners of the World Council in their respective regions.

5. The presidents shall be ex officio members of the central committee.

6. Should a vacancy occur in the presidium between assemblies, the central committee may elect a president to fill the unexpired term.

II. Central committee

1. *Membership*

a)   The central committee shall consist of the president or presidents of the World Council of Churches together with not more than 150 members elected by the assembly (see constitution, article V.2.b).

b)   Any member church, not already represented, may send one representative to the meetings of the central committee. Such a representative shall have the right to speak but not to participate in decision-making.

c)   If a regularly elected member of the central committee is unable to attend a meeting, the church to which the absent member belongs shall have the right to send a substitute, provided that the substitute is ordinarily resident in the country where the absent member resides. Such a substitute shall have the right to speak and to participate in decision-making. If a member, or his or her substitute, is absent without excuse for two consecutive meetings, the position shall be declared vacant, and the central committee shall fill the vacancy according to the provisions of article V.2.b.3 of the constitution.

d)   Moderators and vice-moderators of committees, commissions and boards who are not members of the central committee may attend meetings of the central committee and shall have the right to speak but not to participate in decision-making.

e)   Advisers for the central committee may be appointed by the executive committee after consultation with the churches of which they are members. They shall have the right to speak but not to participate in decision-making.

f)   Members of the staff of the World Council appointed by the central committee as specified under rule XII.3. shall have the right to attend the sessions of the central committee unless on any occasion the central committee shall otherwise determine. When present they shall have the right to speak but not to participate in decision-making.

g)   The newly elected central committee shall be convened by the general secretary during or immediately after the meeting of the assembly.

2. *Officers*

a)   The central committee shall elect from among its members a moderator and a vice-moderator or vice-moderators to serve for such periods as it shall determine.

b)   The general secretary of the World Council of Churches shall be ex officio secretary of the central committee.

3. *Meetings*

a)   The central committee shall ordinarily meet once every year. The executive committee may call an extraordinary meeting of the central committee whenever it deems such a meeting desirable and shall do so upon the request in writing of one-third or more of the members of the central committee.

b)   The general secretary shall take all possible steps to ensure that there be adequate representation present from each of the main confessions and from the main geographical areas of the membership of the World Council of Churches and of the major interests of the World Council.

c) The central committee shall determine the date and place of its own meetings and of the meetings of the assembly.

4. *Functions*

In exercising the powers set forth in the constitution the central committee shall have the following specific functions:

a) In the conduct of its business, the central committee shall elect the following committees:

nominations committee;

executive committee;

permanent committee on consensus and collaboration;

programme committee (a standing committee);

finance committee (a standing committee);

reference committee or committees (appointed as needed at each meeting to advise the central committee on any other questions arising which call for special consideration or action by the central committee).

b) It shall adopt the budget of the Council.

c) It shall deal with matters referred to it by member churches.

d) It shall determine the policies to be followed in the work of the World Council of Churches, including the task to initiate and terminate programmes and activities. It shall provide for the organizational structure to carry out the work mentioned herein before and to this end, amongst others, shall elect commissions and boards.

e) It shall report to the assembly the actions it has taken during its period of office and shall not be discharged until its report has been received.

VII. NOMINATIONS COMMITTEE OF THE CENTRAL COMMITTEE

1. In its first meeting during or immediately after the assembly, the central committee shall elect a nominations committee which shall:

a) nominate persons from among the members of the central committee for the offices of moderator and vice-moderator or vice-moderators of the central committee;

b) nominate members of the executive committee of the central committee;

c) nominate a person for the office of president to fill the unexpired term should a vacancy occur in the presidium between assemblies;

d) nominate members of committees, commissions and boards and where appropriate their moderators;

e) make recommendations regarding the election of persons proposed for staff positions under rule XII.3.

In making nominations as provided for by (a) and (b) to (d) above, the nominations committee shall have regard to principles set out in rule IV.4.c and, in applying principles (2), (3) and (4) to the nomination of members of committees, commissions and boards, shall consider the representative character of the combined membership of all such committees. Any member of the central committee may make additional nominations, provided that each such nominee shall be proposed in opposition to a particular nominee of the nominations committee.

2. In between meetings of the central committee, the executive committee shall act as the nominations committee of the central committee.

3. Election shall be by ballot unless the committee shall otherwise determine.

VIII. EXECUTIVE COMMITTEE

1. *Membership*

a)   The executive committee shall consist of the moderator and vice-moderator or vice-moderators of the central committee, the moderators of programme and finance committees of the central committee and 20 other members of the central committee.

b)   If a member of the executive committee is unable to attend, he/she has the right – provided that the moderator agrees – to send a member of the central committee as a substitute. Such a substitute shall – as far as possible – be of the same region and church family, and shall have the right to speak and the responsibility to participate in decision-making.

c)   The moderator of the central committee shall also be the moderator of the executive committee.

d)   The general secretary of the World Council of Churches shall be ex officio the secretary of the executive committee.

e)   The officers may invite other persons to attend a meeting of the executive committee for consultation, always having in mind the need for preserving a due balance of the confessions and of the geographical areas and cultural backgrounds, and of the major interests of the World Council.

2. *Functions*

a)   The executive committee shall be accountable to the central committee, and shall present to the central committee at its next meeting a report of its work for approval. The central committee shall consider such a report and take such action in regard to it as it thinks fit.

b)   The executive committee shall be responsible for monitoring and overseeing the ongoing programmes and activities of the World Council of Churches including the task of determining the allocation of resources. The executive committee's power to make public statements is limited and defined in rule XIII.5.

c)   The central committee may by specific action provide for the election of staff to those positions specified in rule XII.3.a by the executive committee which should report these actions to the next meeting of the central committee.

d)   The executive committee shall supervise the operation of the budget and may, if necessary, impose limitations on expenditures.

3. *Elections*

a)   The central committee shall elect an executive committee at its first meeting during or immediately after the assembly.

b)   Vacancies on the executive committee shall be filled by the next meeting of the central committee.

IX. PERMANENT COMMITTEE ON CONSENSUS AND COLLABORATION

1. At its first full meeting after an assembly, the central committee shall elect from among its members the membership of the permanent committee on consensus and collaboration (the "permanent committee"), consisting of fourteen members, of whom half shall be Orthodox.

2. The Orthodox members of the nominations committee of the central committee, in consultation with all Orthodox members of the central committee, shall nominate the seven Orthodox members, and the other members of the nominations committee of the central committee shall nominate the remaining seven. The central committee as a whole shall elect the permanent committee. For election of the permanent committee, the provisions of rule VII.1. shall not apply: no counter nominations shall be accepted from the floor.

3. Of the overall membership at least half shall be members of the WCC executive committee. Proxies may substitute for absent members. Advisers may be invited from member churches. Observers may be invited from non-member churches, or on occasion from churches in association with the WCC.

4. Two co-moderators shall be elected by the membership of the permanent committee, one by the Orthodox members of the central committee, and one by the other members of the central committee.

5. The term of the members of the outgoing permanent committee shall conclude upon election of replacement members following an assembly. The permanent committee shall be considered a committee of the assembly and shall advise the business committee of the assembly.

6. The permanent committee will have responsibility for:
    a) continuing the authority, mandate, concerns and dynamic of the Special Commission (mandated by the eighth assembly, Harare, Zimbabwe, 1998);
    b) giving advice and making recommendations to governing bodies of the WCC during and between assemblies in order to contribute to the formation of consensus on matters proposed for the agenda of the WCC;
    c) facilitating improved participation of the Orthodox in the entire life and work of the Council;
    d) offering counsel and providing opportunity for action in matters of common interest;
    e) giving attention to matters of ecclesiology.

7. The permanent committee will report to the central committee and to the executive committee.

461

X. PROGRAMME COMMITTEE

1. The programme committee shall consist of up to 40 members including:
    a) a moderator who shall be a member of the executive committee;
    b) not more than 30 central committee members of whom 2 shall also be members of the executive committee;
    c) the moderators of all commissions, boards and advisory groups that relate directly to the programme committee.

2. The programme committee shall normally meet in conjunction with the central committee and shall be required to report to it regularly.

3. Within the guidelines established by the assembly, the programme committee shall have the responsibility to make recommendations to the central committee on all matters regarding the programmes and activities of the World Council of Churches.
In particular, it shall:
    a) ensure that the development of programmes takes account of the major thrusts and policies adopted by the central committee as well as of the available financial resources;
    b) consider in particular the theological inter-relationship of different World Council activities;
    c) recommend to the central committee to initiate and terminate programmes and activities, as well as to make decisions on other basic questions of policy;
    d) provide for and make recommendations for regular evaluation of programmes and activities;
    e) recommend to the central committee the mandate and size of the commissions which are to advise the central committee through the programme committee in areas of constitutional responsibility of the Council;

f) recommend to the central committee the mandate and size of boards, in particular the board of the Ecumenical Institute;

g) appoint other advisory groups for specific areas or constituencies, as required. The size and periodicity of meetings of such advisory groups are to be determined in light of the tasks assigned and the resources available.

XI. FINANCE COMMITTEE OF THE CENTRAL COMMITTEE

1. The finance committee of the central committee shall consist of not less than nine members, including:

a) a moderator, who shall be a member of the executive committee;

b) five members, who shall be members of the central committee, two of whom shall also be members of the executive committee;

c) three members, to be designated by the programme committee from its membership. The programme committee may designate alternates who may attend if the principal member is unable to be present.

2. The committee shall have the following responsibilities and duties:

a) To present to the central committee:

1) in respect of the expired calendar year, an account of income and expenditure of all operations of the World Council of Churches and the balance sheet of the World Council of Churches at the end of that year and its recommendation, based on review of the report of the auditors, regarding approval and granting of discharge in respect of the accounts of the World Council of Churches for the completed period;

2) in respect of the current year, a review of all financial operations;

3) in respect of the succeeding calendar year, a budget covering all activities of the World Council of Churches and its recommendations regarding the approval of that budget in the light of its judgment as to the adequacy of the provisions made for the expenditure involved in the proposed programme of activities and the adequacy of reasonably foreseeable income to finance the budget; and

4) in respect of the year next following the succeeding calendar year a financial forecast together with recommendations thereon as in (3) above.

b) To consider and make recommendations to the central committee on all financial questions concerning the affairs of the World Council of Churches, such as:

1) the appointment of the auditor or auditors who shall be appointed annually by the central committee and shall be eligible for reappointment;

2) accounting procedures;

3) investment policy and procedures;

4) the basis of calculation of contributions from member churches;

5) procedures and methods of raising funds.

XII. STAFF

1. The central committee shall elect or appoint or provide for the election or appointment of persons of special competence to conduct the continuing operations of the World Council of Churches. These persons collectively constitute the staff.

2. The general secretary shall be elected by the central committee. He or she is the chief executive officer of the World Council. As such, he or she is the head of the staff. When the position of general secretary becomes vacant, the executive committee shall appoint an acting general secretary.

3. a)   In addition to the general secretary, the central committee shall itself elect one or more deputy general secretaries, the directors for programme and management, and any other executive director.
b)   The executive committee shall appoint all programme staff and shall report its actions to the central committee.
c)   Specialized, administrative and house staff shall be appointed by the general secretary.

4. The staff leadership group shall consist of the general secretary (moderator), the deputy general secretary or secretaries, the executive secretary in the general secretariat (secretary), and the executive directors. Other staff may be invited for specific items on the agenda.
The staff leadership group is the chief internal management team. Its overall responsibility is to advise the general secretary in his/her role as chief executive officer of the Council. It has the task of ensuring that all activities of the Council are carried out in an integrated and cohesive manner. For this purpose it will:
a)   Implement policies and priorities established by the central and executive committees and facilitate proposals to be submitted to them.
b)   Provide for overall coordination, decide on priorities and the direction of the Council's activities.
c)   Manage and allocate human and financial resources, propose the budget to the finance committees of the executive and central committees and ensure that programme planning is integrated with anticipated resources available.
d)   Assist the general secretary in the appointment of staff and special reference groups.

463

5. There shall be a staff executive group. Its membership shall include ex-officio the members of the staff leadership group, the programme team coordinators, the director of Bossey and the management services managers. It shall meet regularly (normally twice a month); it shall be moderated by a member of the staff leadership group on a rotating basis.
The staff executive group shall advise the general secretary and the staff leadership group. Its purpose is to:
a)   advise on matters of long-range planning, monitoring and evaluation of activities;
b)   consider the preparation of the budget;
c)   assure regular sharing of information and provide for discussion and interpretation of policies and issues affecting the Council as a whole;
d)   facilitate the coordination of the activities of the teams;
e)   appoint ad-hoc or permanent functional staff groups to advise on specific areas of concern;
f)   promote a spirit and style of work to strengthen and promote integration, cooperation and collegiality.

6. The normal terms of appointment for the general secretary and for the deputy general secretary or secretaries shall be five years. Unless some other period is stated in the resolution making the appointment, the first term of office for all other staff appointed by the executive or central committee shall normally be four years from the date of the appointment. All appointments shall be reviewed one year before their expiration.

7. Retirement shall normally be at sixty-five for both men and women and in no case shall it be later than the end of the year in which a staff member reaches the age of sixty-eight.

XIII. PUBLIC STATEMENTS

1. In the performance of its functions, the World Council of Churches through its assembly or through its central committee may issue statements on any situation or concern with which the Council or its constituent churches may be confronted.

2. While such statements may have great significance and influence as the expression of the judgment or concern of so widely representative a Christian body, yet their authority will consist only in the weight which they carry by their own truth and wisdom, and the publishing of such statements shall not be held to imply that the World Council as such has, or can have, any constitutional authority over the constituent churches or right to speak for them.

3. Any commission may recommend statements to the assembly or to the central committee for its consideration and action.

4. When, in the judgment of a commission, a statement should be issued before approval of the assembly or central committee can be obtained, the commission may do so provided the statement relates to matters within its own field of concern and action, has the approval of the moderator of the central committee and the general secretary, and the commission makes clear that neither the World Council of Churches nor any of its member churches is committed by the statement.

5. Between meetings of the central committee, when in their judgment the situation requires, a statement may be issued, provided that such statements are not contrary to the established policy of the Council, by:

    a)   the executive committee when meeting apart from the sessions of the central committee; or
    b)   the moderator and vice-moderator or vice-moderators of the central committee and the general secretary acting together; or
    c)   the moderator of the central committee or the general secretary on his or her own authority respectively.

XIV. ASSOCIATE COUNCILS

1. Any national Christian council, national council of churches or national ecumenical council, established for purposes of ecumenical fellowship and activity, may be recognized by the central committee as an associate council, provided:

    a)   the applicant council, knowing the basis upon which the World Council of Churches is founded, expresses its desire to cooperate with the World Council towards the achievement of one or more of the functions and purposes of this Council; and
    b)   the member churches of the World Council in the area have been consulted prior to the action.

2. Each associate council:

    a)   shall be invited to send a delegated representative to the assembly;
    b)   may, at the discretion of the central committee, be invited to send an adviser to meetings of the central committee; and
    c)   shall be provided with copies of all general communications sent to all member churches of the World Council of Churches.

3. In addition to communicating directly with its member churches, the World Council shall inform each associate council regarding important ecumenical developments and consult it regarding proposed World Council programmes in its country.

4. In consultation with the associate councils, the central committee shall establish and review from time to time guidelines regarding the relationships between the World Council of Churches and national councils of churches.

XV. REGIONAL ECUMENICAL ORGANIZATIONS

1. The World Council of Churches recognizes regional ecumenical organizations as essential partners in the ecumenical enterprise.

2. Such regional ecumenical organizations as may be designated by the central committee:
   a) shall be invited to send a delegated representative to the assembly;
   b) shall be invited to send an adviser to meetings of the central committee; and
   c) shall be provided with copies of all general communications sent to all member churches of the World Council of Churches.

3. In addition to communicating directly with its member churches, the World Council shall inform each of these regional ecumenical organizations regarding important ecumenical developments and consult it regarding proposed World Council programmes in its region.

4. The central committee, together with the regional ecumenical organizations, shall establish and review as appropriate guiding principles for relationships and cooperation between the World Council and regional ecumenical organizations, including the means whereby programmatic responsibilities could be shared among them.

XVI. CHRISTIAN WORLD COMMUNIONS

1. The World Council of Churches recognizes the role of Christian world communions or world confessional bodies in the ecumenical movement.

2. Such Christian world communions as may be designated by the central committee and which express their desire to this effect:
   a) shall be invited to send a delegated representative to the assembly;
   b) shall be invited to send an adviser to meetings of the central committee; and
   c) shall be provided with copies of all general communications sent to all World Council member churches.

3. The central committee shall establish and review as appropriate guidelines for relationships and cooperation with Christian world communions.

XVII. SPECIALIZED MINISTRIES ENGAGED IN ECUMENICAL RELIEF AND DEVELOPMENT

1. Specialized ministries engaged in ecumenical relief and development are those church-based, church-related or ecumenical offices and organizations within the family of WCC member churches, serving the ecumenical movement particularly in the area of world service and development.
Any specialized ministry, committed to ecumenical diaconal services, may be recognized by the central committee as an organization with which the World Council of Churches has working relationships, provided:
   a) the organization, knowing the basis upon which the World Council of Churches is founded, expresses its willingness to relate to and cooperate with it; and
   b) the WCC member church or churches with whom the specialized ministry is related do not formally oppose this form of relationship.

2. Each specialized ministry:
   a) shall be invited to send a delegated representative to the assembly (cf. rule IV.1.b.5);

b) shall be invited to send an adviser to meetings of the central committee; and

c) shall be provided with copies of all general communications sent to all member churches of the World Council of Churches.

3. In addition to communicating directly with its member churches, the World Council may inform each of these specialized ministries regarding important ecumenical developments and consult it regarding proposed World Council programmes in its area of commitment and expertise.

4. In consultation with specialized ministries, the central committee shall establish and review from time to time guidelines regarding the relationships between the World Council of Churches and specialized ministries.

XIII. INTERNATIONAL ECUMENICAL ORGANIZATIONS

1. Ecumenical organizations other than those mentioned under rules XIV, XV, XVI and XVII may be recognized by the central committee as organizations with which the World Council of Churches has working relationships, provided:

a) the organization is international in nature (global, regional or sub-regional) and its objectives are consistent with the functions and purposes of the World Council; and

b) the organization, knowing the basis upon which the World Council of Churches is founded, expresses its desire to relate to and cooperate with it.

2. On the basis of reciprocity, each international ecumenical organization:

a) shall be invited to send a delegated representative to the assembly (cf. rule IV.1.b.5);

b) shall be provided with copies of general communications sent to all World Council member churches.

XIX. LEGAL PROVISIONS

1. The duration of the World Council of Churches is unlimited.

2. The legal headquarters of the Council shall be at Grand-Saconnex, Geneva, Switzerland. It is registered in Geneva as an association according to art. 60ff. of the Swiss civil code. Regional offices may be organized in different parts of the world by decision of the central committee.

3. The World Council of Churches is legally represented by its executive committee or by such persons as may be empowered by the executive committee to represent it.

4. The World Council shall be legally bound by the joint signatures of two of the following persons: the moderator and vice-moderator or vice-moderators of the central committee, the general secretary, the deputy general secretary or secretaries. Any two of the above-named persons shall have power to authorize other persons, chosen by them, to act jointly or singly on behalf of the World Council of Churches in fields circumscribed in the power of attorney.

5. The Council shall obtain the means necessary for the pursuance of its work from the contributions of its member churches and from donations or bequests.

6. The Council shall not pursue commercial functions but it shall have the right to act as an agency of interchurch aid and to publish literature in connection with its aims. It is not entitled to distribute any surplus income by way of profit or bonus among its members.

7. Members of the governing bodies of the Council or of the assembly shall have no personal liability with regard to the obligations or commitments of the Council. The commitments entered upon by the Council are guaranteed solely by its own assets.

XX. CONDUCT OF MEETINGS

1. *General*

   a) These provisions for conduct of meetings shall apply to meetings of the assembly, the central committee, the executive committee and all other bodies of the WCC. During an assembly, the titles "president, moderator and vice-moderators of the central committee" shall refer to the persons holding those offices in the outgoing central committee. During the term of a central committee such titles shall refer to the current presidents and officers of that central committee.

   b) "Delegate" shall mean an official representative of a member church to an assembly with the right to speak and the responsibility to participate in decision-making (rule IV.1.a). For meetings of the central committee, "delegate" shall mean a member of the central committee or that member's substitute (rule VI.1.c), with the right to speak and the responsibility to participate in decision-making.

   c) "Participant" shall include delegates as well as persons invited to the assembly or a meeting of the central committee as persons with the right to speak but not to participate in decision-making (rule IV.1.b).

2. *Categories of sessions*

The assembly shall sit in one of the following categories of sessions: general, hearing or decision. The business committee shall determine the category of session appropriate for different parts of the agenda.

   a) *General session*

   General sessions shall be reserved for ceremonial occasions, public acts of witness and formal addresses. Only matters proposed by the central committee or by the business committee shall be included in general sessions. No decisions shall be made during general sessions.

   b) *Hearing session*

   Hearing sessions shall be designated for plenary presentations, discussion, dialogue, and exchange of ideas as a resource for developing understanding, deepening fellowship among member churches and coming to a common mind on matters on the agenda. A wide range of perspectives shall be encouraged during hearing sessions. No decisions shall be made during hearing sessions, other than to move to a decision session, if deemed necessary or to deal with a point of order or procedural proposals.

   c) *Decision session*

   Decision sessions shall be designated for matters requiring a decision, including:
   1) adoption of the agenda;
   2) proposal for change in the agenda;
   3) appointments and elections;
   4) reception or adoption of reports or recommendations;
   5) actions to be taken on recommendations or proposals of committees or commissions, or arising out of hearing sessions;
   6) adoption of accounts and financial audits; and
   7) amendment of constitution or rules.

3. *Moderating sessions*

a) A moderator for each session of the assembly shall be designated before an assembly by the outgoing central committee, and during an assembly by the business committee, as follows:

    1) in general sessions one of the presidents or the moderator of the central committee shall preside;

    2) in hearing sessions one of the presidents, the moderator or a vice-moderator of the central committee, or a delegate with specific expertise in the subject matter of the hearing, shall preside;

    3) in decision sessions the moderator or a vice-moderator of the central committee or delegate to the assembly who was a member of the outgoing central committee shall preside.

b) The role of session moderators shall be:

    1) to convene the session, including announcing the category of session;

    2) to facilitate and encourage discussion and dialogue, for the exchange and development of ideas, and to assist the meeting to come to a common mind;

    3) during decision sessions, to test any emerging agreement on a particular point and whether the meeting is ready to move to a decision by consensus;

    4) in the event the category of session is to change during a session, to announce the change in category, providing a break in the session to mark the change in category; and

    5) to close the session.

c) The moderator shall consult with the recorder for the session to ensure that the developing consensus is accurately noted and any changed wording promptly made available to the meeting.

d) All moderators shall undertake specific training in conducting meetings based upon the consensus model of decision-making, as described in these rules and the accompanying guidelines.

4. *Moderator of the assembly*

The moderator of the assembly shall announce the opening, suspension and the adjournment of the assembly.

5. *Official minutes, records and reports*

a) The business committee shall appoint recorders from among delegates for each decision session. Their role shall be to follow the discussion of a decision session, to record the language of the emerging consensus, including final language of decisions taken, and to assist the moderator of the session in discerning an emerging consensus. Recorders shall also assist the moderator in ensuring that the final agreed wording of a proposal is translated and available to delegates before a decision is made.

b) The business committee shall appoint rapporteurs for each hearing session and for committee meetings for which official minutes are not maintained, to prepare a report of the meeting including major themes and specific proposals. A rapporteur appointed for a committee meeting shall function as a recorder of that meeting.

c) The business committee shall appoint minute-takers to record the official minutes of general, hearing and decision sessions of an assembly or any meeting for which formal minutes must be kept, and shall include a record of the discussion, motions and decisions. The minutes will normally incorporate by reference any report of the meeting. The minutes shall be signed by the moderator and the minute-taker for the session and shall be sent to the participants of the meeting. For all minutes other than minutes of an assembly, if there is no objection within six months from the sending of the minutes, the minutes shall be considered to be accepted. The first full central committee meeting following an assembly shall confirm the minutes of the assembly.

d) Decision sessions shall produce official minutes, a record and/or report.

e) If, after the close of a meeting, a member church declares that it cannot support a decision of the meeting, the member church may submit its objection in writing and have its position recorded in the minutes or report of a subsequent meeting. The decision itself shall not be rescinded by this action.

6. *Agenda*

a) Matters may be included on the agenda of a meeting according to rule IV.3 and procedures established by the business and programme committees, and any other committee established by central committee for that purpose. Normally, matters included on an agenda will be based upon reports, recommendations or proposals that previously have been fully considered and have the consensus support of the proposing group or committee.

b) The business committee shall ensure that the moderator is advised before each session, and if appropriate during breaks within a session, as to the conduct of the business and the priority of various agenda items.

c) A delegate may propose to the business committee an item of business to be included on, or any change in, the agenda. If after consideration the business committee has not agreed to the proposal, the delegate may appeal the decision to the moderator of the assembly in writing. The moderator shall at a convenient time inform the assembly of the proposal, and a member of the business committee shall explain the reasons for this refusal. The delegate may give reasons for proposing it. The moderator shall then without further debate put the following question: Shall the assembly accept this proposal? If the assembly agrees to accept the proposal, the business committee as soon as possible shall bring proposals for the inclusion of the matter or the change in the agenda.

d) Matters concerning ecclesiological self-understanding: Where a matter being raised is considered by a delegate to go against the ecclesiological self-understanding of his or her church, the delegate may request that it not be submitted for decision. The moderator shall seek the advice of the business committee in consultation with this delegate and other members of the same church or confession present at the session. If agreed that the matter does in fact go against the ecclesiological self-understanding of the delegate's church, the moderator shall announce that the matter will be removed from the agenda of the decision session and may be considered in a hearing session. The materials and minutes of the discussion shall be sent to the member churches for their study and comment.

e) Subject to the provisions of this rule, the agenda shall be proposed, amended and/or adopted in accordance with rule IV.3. and IV.5.

7. *Speaking*

a) In hearing sessions, participants wishing to speak either may submit to the moderator a written request or may queue at the microphones when the moderator so invites, but may speak only when called by the moderator.

b) In decision sessions of the assembly or central committee, only delegates may speak. Delegates wishing to speak either may submit to the moderator a written request or may queue at the microphones when the moderator so invites, but may speak only when called by the moderator.

c) In sessions of committees and advisory bodies where both hearing and decision may take place, participants who are not delegates have the right to speak but not to take part in decision-making.

d) The moderator shall decide who shall speak, ensuring that a fair distribution of opinions is heard, and may take advice on the order of speakers from a small sub-committee of the business committee. If time allows and others are not left unheard, the moderator may permit speakers to intervene more than once.

e) When called by the moderator, a speaker shall speak from a microphone, first stating his or her name, church, country, and role at the meeting, and shall address all remarks to the moderator.

f) Remarks will normally be limited to three minutes; however, the moderator may use discretion in allowing extra time if there is a difficulty in language or interpretation or if the issues being discussed are unusually complex.

g) Procedural proposals – hearing or decision sessions: Provided that a speaker is not interrupted, a delegate may ask for clarification of the pending matter or may raise suggestions about procedure. The moderator immediately shall provide clarification or respond to the suggestion for change of procedure.

h) Points of order – hearing or decision sessions: This provision is available to question whether procedures being followed are in accordance with these rules, to object to offensive language, to make a point of personal explanation, or to request that a meeting move to closed session. Points of order may be raised by a participant at any time, even by interrupting another speaker. A participant gains the attention of the moderator by standing and calling, "point of order!" The moderator shall ask the participant to state the point of order and then (without discussion) shall rule on it immediately.

i) If any delegate disagrees with the moderator's decision on a procedural proposal or point of order, the delegate may appeal against it. In this case the moderator will put this question, without discussion, to the meeting: "Does the meeting concur with the decision of the moderator?" The delegates present shall decide the question according to the decision-making procedures then being employed.

8. *Reaching consensus: seeking the common mind of the meeting*

a) Consensus shall be understood as seeking the common mind of the meeting without resort to a formal vote, in a process of genuine dialogue that is respectful, mutually supportive and empowering, whilst prayerfully seeking to discern God's will.

b) Decisions will normally be by consensus, unless otherwise specified by the rules.

c) A consensus decision on a particular matter shall be recorded when one of the following occurs:

1) all delegates are in agreement (unanimity); or

2) most are in agreement and those who disagree are satisfied that the discussion has been both full and fair and do not object that the proposal expresses the general mind of the meeting.

d) A consensus decision shall mean that there is agreement about the outcome of a discussion. This may mean agreement to accept a proposal or a variation of a proposal; it also may mean agreement about another outcome, including agreement to reject a proposal, to postpone a matter, that no decision can be reached, or that there are various opinions that may be held. When consensus has been reached that various opinions can be held concerning a matter, those various opinions shall be recorded in the final wording of the minutes and the report and the record of the meeting.

9. *Decision-making by consensus*

a) A proposal or recommendation considered in a decision session may be affirmed, modified or rejected. Delegates may suggest modifications, and the moderator may allow discussion on more than one modification at a time. Reaching a common mind may require a series of steps, if there is a variety of opinions being expressed. As discussion proceeds, the moderator may ask the meeting to affirm what is held in common before encouraging discussion on those aspects of a proposal about which more diverse opinions have been voiced.

b) To assist the moderator in discerning the mind of the meeting and to move efficiently towards consensus, the recorder of the session shall maintain a record of the discussion. Delegates may be provided with indicator cards to facilitate participation.

c) A delegate or the moderator may suggest that the matter under discussion be referred for further work to an appropriate group holding a range of points of view. This suggestion itself shall be tested to discern the mind of the meeting. If agreed, the business committee shall schedule consideration of the matter for a later session.

d) When it seems that the meeting is close to agreement on an outcome, the moderator shall ensure that the wording of the proposal (or the proposal as varied during the course of the discussion) is clear to all delegates, and then test whether there is consensus on that outcome. If all are agreed consistent with rule XX.8.c.1, the moderator shall declare that consensus has been reached and the decision made. If the meeting is not unanimous, the moderator shall invite those who hold a minority view to explain their reasons if they wish and to indicate whether they can agree with a decision pursuant to rule XX.8.c.2. If so, consensus shall be declared.

e) If, after every effort has been made to reach consensus, agreement cannot be reached and it is the opinion of an officer or the business committee that a decision must be made before the meeting concludes, the moderator shall ask the business committee to formulate a proposal for how the matter may be considered again in a new form. At the later decision session where this new approach is considered, the meeting itself shall decide whether a decision must be made at this meeting, and, if so, shall proceed on any one of the following courses, which may be followed sequentially:

    1)   to work further towards consensus on the proposal in its new form;

    2)   to work to reach agreement among most delegates with some delegates recording an objection, in which event a meeting shall record acceptance of the proposal, providing that each delegate who does not agree is satisfied with that outcome and has the right to have his or her viewpoint recorded in the minutes, in the report, and in the record of the meeting; or

    3)   to move into voting procedures to decide the matter (rule XX.10).

f) When a meeting discusses by consensus procedures a matter for which decision must be reached at that meeting and there is no ready agreement in accordance with rule XX.9.e.1 or 2, the moderator may offer a procedural proposal: "That the meeting resolve the proposal now by vote". Except for matters described in rule XX.6.d, "matters concerning ecclesiological self-understanding", the moderator shall announce that a vote to decide this change of procedure shall be taken. Delegates shall indicate by voting whether they agree that the matter shall be decided by a vote. If 85 percent of delegates present vote in favour of moving the matter to a voting process, the matter shall so move. If fewer than 85 percent of delegates present vote in favour of moving the matter to a voting process, the matter shall not so move, and the meeting shall decide, again by vote of 85 percent of delegates present, whether discussion should continue to achieve consensus or whether discussion should be discontinued.

10. *Decision-making by vote*

    a)   Some matters require decision by vote, rather than by consensus. These include:

        1)   constitutional changes (two-thirds majority);

        2)   elections (simple majority, with specific procedures in each case);

        3)   adoption of yearly accounts and of the financial audit report (simple majority).

    b)   For matters that have been moved from consensus procedures to decision-making by vote in accordance with rule XX.9.e.3 or rule XX.9.f, and for matters reserved to a voting procedure according to subsection (a) of this section, the following procedures shall be followed:

        1)   All motions must be moved and seconded by a delegate, and the mover has the right to speak first.

        2)   In discussion following the seconding of a motion, no delegate may speak more than once, except that the delegate who moved the motion may answer objections at the end of the discussion.

3) Any delegate may move an amendment, and if a seconder supports it, the amendment shall be considered simultaneously with the original proposal.

4) When discussion is concluded, including the right of the mover to reply (see 2 above), the moderator shall call for the vote and shall put any amendment first. If approved, it will be incorporated in the original proposal, which will then be put to the vote without further discussion.

5) If the mover seeks to withdraw a motion or amendment during the discussion, the moderator will seek the consent of the meeting for the withdrawal.

c) A delegate may move to close the discussion, but in doing so shall not interrupt a speaker. If seconded, the moderator shall call for a vote on this motion immediately without discussion. If two-thirds of the meeting agree, the voting process will then begin. If the motion fails, discussion will proceed, but the same motion to close discussion may be moved again as the discussion continues, but not by the delegate who moved it the first time.

d) Voting shall be by show of hands or indicator cards and the moderator shall ask first for those in favour, then for those against, and finally for those who wish to abstain from voting. The moderator shall announce the result of the vote immediately.

e) If the moderator is in doubt, or for any other reason decides to do so, or if a delegate requests it, a vote on the matter shall be taken immediately by count of a show of hands or indicator cards. The moderator may call tellers to count those voting and abstaining. A delegate may ask that voting be by secret written ballot, and if seconded and if a majority of delegates present and voting agree, a secret written ballot shall be taken. The moderator shall announce the result of any count or secret written ballot.

f) A majority of the delegates present, including those who choose to abstain from voting, shall determine a matter being decided by vote unless a higher proportion is required by the constitution or these rules. If the vote results in a tie, the matter shall be regarded as defeated.

g) If the moderator wishes to participate in the discussion, he or she shall relinquish the position of moderator of the session to another presiding officer until the matter has been resolved.

h) A moderator entitled to vote as a delegate may do so, but may not cast the decisive vote in the event of a tie.

i) Any two delegates who voted with the majority for a previously approved matter may request that the business committee propose reconsideration of the matter. The business committee shall bring the proposal to the next decision session and may express an opinion as to whether the matter should be reconsidered. Reconsideration shall take place only if two-thirds of delegates present agree.

j) Anyone voting with a minority or abstaining from voting may have his or her opinion recorded in the minutes, in the report, and/or the record of the meeting.

11. *Languages*

The working languages in use in the World Council of Churches are English, French, German, Russian and Spanish. The general secretary shall make reasonable effort to provide interpretation for any one of those languages into the others and shall endeavour to provide written translation of the specific wording of proposals. A participant may speak in another language only if he or she provides for interpretation into one of the working languages. The general secretary shall provide all possible assistance to any participant requiring an interpreter.

XXI. AMENDMENTS

Amendments to these rules may be proposed at any session of the assembly or at any session of the central committee by any member and shall be decided according to the procedures in Rule XX.9; if the meeting shifts from consensus to voting, then the procedures in Rule XX.10 will apply. In this case, the proposed change must receive a two-thirds majority of those present to be adopted. No alteration in rules I, VI, VII and XXI shall come into effect until it has been confirmed by the assembly. Notice of a proposal to make any amendment shall be given in writing at least twenty-four hours before the session of the assembly or central committee at which it is to be considered.

APPENDIX VII
ACKNOWLEDGEMENTS

Countless people and organizations helped to make the Porto Alegre Assembly possible – an event which was over three years in the making and which represents the largest and most diverse global gathering of Christians. The World Council of Churches is grateful for the partnership, dedication, hard work and prayerful support of the following:

- the churches of Brazil, the National Council of Christian Churches in Brazil (CONIC) and the Latin American Council of Churches (CLAI) for hosting the first WCC assembly to take place in Latin America and for inspiring the churches world-wide in reflecting together on the transformative power and presence of God's grace in the world;

- the Assembly Planning Committee, under the moderation of Rev. Dr Norman Shanks, for giving the Assembly a vision and a framework to enhance dialogue and understanding among the thousands of people gathered in Porto Alegre;

- the Assembly Worship Planning Committee, under the moderation of H.E. Metropolitan Prof. Dr Gennadios of Sassima, for preparing all that was needed to support the Assembly in prayer and celebration before God;

- the Assembly Office Team in Geneva and in Porto Alegre for their unfailing dedication to ensure that every person and detail was cared for and that the programme and logistics were planned hand-in-hand;

- the Pontifical University and Conference Centre, Fellini Turismo, Raptim Travel and many other service providers for the space and infrastructure to support the Assembly, for catering to participants' needs and for their commitment to ensure a successful event;

- the "Assembly Team" of WCC staff, co-opted staff and stewards who worked tirelessly in Porto Alegre as one team, with many talents, serving the delegates and participants gathered in Brazil;

• the WCC communication teams for producing the Assembly publications, maintaining the Assembly website, serving the journalists present in Porto Alegre and ensuring media coverage throughout the world;

• the WCC language service for translating the Assembly reports and addresses for publication in this report and on the Assembly website at: *http://www.wcc-assembly.info/*; and

• Marie Arnaud Snakkers, Libby Visinand, Douglas Chial and Theo Gill for their work and dedication in preparing this report for publication.

IMPRIMERIE
LUSSAUD
OFFSET&NUMERIQUE

Printed and bound in France
by Imprimerie LUSSAUD
85200 Fontenay-le-Comte

Dépôt légal 3ᵉ trimestre 2007 - n° 4536
N° d'impression : 205456

This printer has a green label guaranteeing
environmentally-friendly printing procedures.